ANNE WITH AN 'E'

≈ 100 Years of ≈

ANNE WITH AN 'E'

THE CENTENNIAL STUDY OF *ANNE OF GREEN GABLES*

EDITED BY HOLLY BLACKFORD

UNIVERSITY OF
CALGARY
PRESS

University of Calgary Press
2500 University Drive NW
Calgary, Alberta
Canada T2N 1N4
www.uofcpress.com

LIBRARY AND ARCHIVES CANADA CATALOGUING IN PUBLICATION

100 years of Anne with an "e" : the centennial study of
Anne of Green Gables / edited by Holly Blackford.

Includes bibliographical references and index.
ISBN 978-1-55238-252-3

1. Montgomery, L. M. (Lucy Maud), 1874-1942. Anne of Green Gables. I. Blackford, Holly Virginia II. Title: One hundred years of Anne with an "e".

PS8526.O55Z82 2009   C813'.52   C2009-900741-X

The University of Calgary Press acknowledges the support of the Alberta Foundation for the Arts for our publications. We acknowledge the financial support of the Government of Canada through the Book Publishing Industry Development Program (BPIDP) for our publishing activities. We acknowledge the financial support of the Canada Council for the Arts for our publishing program.

This book has been published with the help of a grant from the Canadian Federation for the Humanities and Social Sciences, through the Aid to Scholarly Publications Programme, using funds provided by the Social Sciences and Humanities Research Council of Canada.

Printed and bound in Canada by Marquis Printing Inc.
∞ This book is printed on FSC Silva Enviro paper

Cover photo:
British immigrant children from Dr. Barnardo's Homes at landing stage, Saint John, New Brunswick. Photo by Isaac Erb. Courtesy Library and Archives Canada, PA-041785.

Cover design by Melina Cusano
Page design and typesetting by Melina Cusano

to my three girls,
Jade,
Cassie,
and Genevieve,
of spirit
and fire
and dew

TABLE OF CONTENTS

III. Quoting Anne: Intertextuality at Home and Abroad

IV. Maturing Anne: Gender and Empire

Acknowledgments

This book has been published with the help of a grant from the Canadian Federation for the Humanities and Social Sciences, through the Aid to Scholarly Publications Program, using funds provided by the Social Sciences and Humanities Research Council of Canada.

Excerpts from *Anne of Green Gables* are reproduced here with the authorization of the heirs of L. M. Montgomery.

Anne of Green Gables and other indicia of "Anne" are trademarks and Canadian official marks of the Anne of Green Gables Licensing Authority Inc.

L. M. Montgomery is a trademark of Heirs of L. M. Montgomery Inc.

Quotations from *The Selected Journals of L. M. Montgomery*, volumes 1–5, edited by Mary Rubio and Elizabeth Waterston, are reprinted with the permission of Oxford University Press.

INTRODUCTION

Anne with an "e": The Enduring Value of *Anne of Green Gables*

Holly Blackford

All my life it has been my aim to write a book – a "real live" book.... Two years ago in the spring of 1905 I was looking over this notebook in search of some suitable idea for a short serial I wanted to write for a certain Sunday School paper and I found a faded entry, written ten years before: – "Elderly couple apply to orphan asylum for a boy. By mistake a girl was sent them." I thought this would do. I began to block out chapters, devise incidents and "brood up" my heroine. Somehow or other she seemed very real to me and took possession of me to an unusual extent. Her personality appealed to me and I thought it rather a shame to waste her on an ephemeral little serial. Then the thought came, "Write a book about her." ... It was a labor of love. Nothing I have ever written gave me so much pleasure to write. I cast "moral" and "Sunday School" ideals to the winds and made my "Anne" a real human girl.

~ L. M. Montgomery, *Selected Journals* 330–31

Born 30 November 1874, Lucy Maud "spelled 'not with an e'" Montgomery, as she liked to say (Andronik 2), kept journals, notebooks, and scrapbooks throughout her life. As Irene Gammel observes in her introduction to *The Intimate Life of L. M. Montgomery*, "the posthumous publication of the journals had the effect of the proverbial bombshell" (4) on critics and Montgomery enthusiasts. Edited by Mary Rubio and Elizabeth Waterston and now spanning five volumes, the journals reveal a complicated and often troubled woman, battling feelings of depression and unhappiness even during the time she composed *Anne of Green Gables*, generally viewed as an optimistic novel. The recent announcement of Montgomery's granddaughter, that depression may have led to Montgomery's suicide and that the circumstances surrounding her death were kept secret ("L. M. Montgomery"), makes all the more poignant the complex relationship between a writer and her writing, which may conceal as much as reveal. Presumably, Montgomery wrote the above account of the birth of her character Anne after she received notice of the novel's acceptance by L. C. Page – to her, proof of the novel's value after multiple rejections, which she also recounts in the same journal entry of 16 August 1907. As Cecily Devereux argues about Montgomery's remarkable lack of comment during the time she was actually writing *Anne*, "There is nothing [in the journal] of the story that has now become a major part of the Green Gables mythology of Montgomery's putting the manuscript away in a hatbox in a closet after what she indicates in her journal in 1907 were four rejections, and of finding it again the following year" (250). I think we like this "Green Gables mythology" because it mirrors the story of Anne herself – how precarious her position on the margins of acceptance, how close she was to being returned by Marilla, how hard this little gem had to work to win over a harsh publishing world and prove her value.

The public, however, was more than ready to embrace Anne with open arms: "*Anne of Green Gables* went through seven printings within the first six months of its publication in June 1908 and was soon taken up for translation into Swedish, Danish, and Polish" (Reimer 1). No Marillas they, readers around the world were ready to accept the novel's central thesis: the romantic child, a Pan figure reminiscent of J. M. Barrie's 1904 creation of Peter Pan, could with play and imagination cross the threshold of an "infertile" Victorian town and forever transform it. But the above journal entry holds my interest because it also tells a story of Anne's colonization of her own creator's consciousness. The entry traces the development of the child as first a commodity and labourer, briefly reported in objective, journalistic style but "a faded entry," as if marking a fading sense of equating child value with productivity. Secondly, the child is conceived as a site of Sunday School socialization rituals, a target for moralizing and didactic literature, in which the adult narrator would presumably be in charge of teaching a moral. Finally, Anne interests Montgomery because she transforms into a "real human girl," a being of psychological complexity and "real" interiority, with all her consequent imperfections. After taking on this status of full humanity, the child cannot be "wasted" in either economic or didactic frameworks. Anne's full value is called into being by blowing away "Sunday School" ideals with the winds of imagination. Indeed, such winds of change were in the air. Montgomery's retrospective account of Anne, penned after the novel's acceptance and actually paralleling Marilla's gradual embrace of Anne, retells Anne's rather historically contingent story of being assigned one value and gradually altering it to quite another.

Since this transformation of the character's composition parallels changing ideals of childhood during Montgomery's lifespan, Montgomery's passage provides us with the social and shared meaning of Anne, marking for us a gradual acceptance of the twentieth-century approach to childhood. The public, along with Montgomery, was ready to reflect upon a story of how its view of childhood had changed, signifying where it had arrived and how it had developed into the early twentieth century. As T. D. MacLulich points out in a comparison of *Anne* and Kate Wiggin's *Rebecca of Sunnybrook Farm* to Louisa May Alcott's *Little Women*, "Montgomery and Wiggin understand their heroines primarily from a psychological perspective, whereas Alcott understood her characters primarily in moral terms" (11). Anne self-consciously understands her interior multiplicity – "There's such a lot of different Annes in me" (*Anne* 200) – an understanding that we can cross-reference with our sense, from journals, diaries, and letters, of what Gammel calls "the many faces" of Lucy Maud Montgomery. While the influences of romantic poetry and the Victorian bildungsroman are paramount in *Anne*, Anne's modernity stems from her psychological and intertextual depth, often expressed in stream-of-consciousness monologue.

I believe we can understand Anne's popularity by noting the paradoxical way she both symbolizes *the outsider* – the freckled witch bewitching us all – and one who *belongs*. In fact, it seems that she has always belonged to the Island: she is red like the colour of the land, a child in a homestead where no children have ever been or can ever be, a being who takes possession of the landscape and Cuthbert homestead. She is like the brook with "its source away back in the woods ... with dark secrets of pool and cascade" (*Anne* 53). To the broader public, to Montgomery in the above journal entry, and to Cavendish in the novel, Anne is paradoxically alien and intimately familiar, as if she is reflective of a personal and cultural unconscious. Precisely like the dream-work of the unconscious, she serves as a repository for the high and low literature she breathlessly draws upon in speech – "a host of popular (and often inferior) romances and Gothic tales of the kind Henry Fielding parodies with such zest in *Joseph Andrews*" (Epperly 348). She is a sort of walking assortment of fragmented texts, the spawn of a scrapbook as it were, which makes Marilla initially wish to dispatch her "straight-way back to where she came from" (*Anne* 81), whether heaven or hell.

More remarkably, Anne liberates and possesses everyone around her until each, in turn, finds his or her unorthodox desires being expressed. For example, Matthew begins to rebel against Marilla; at first, he is merely smoking in the house and looking increasingly unhappy, but he is soon expressing his opinion on Anne's "bringing up," until he takes an astonishing stand on Anne's right to puffed sleeves. Even more astonishingly, he cleverly enlists the aid of Mrs. Lynde against Marilla, a subtle migration between women who, in my view, compete for ascendancy in the community. But Marilla's inner rebelliousness also emerges; Anne's initial outburst against Mrs. Lynde signifies Marilla's own inner desire to rebel against her controlling neighbour, which she later admits to Anne (283). Anne increasingly brings out repressed memories and feelings in Marilla – feelings about sermons, about her own childhood, about her past love affair, about her distaste for Mrs. Barry. We learn of the tension between the Cuthbert homestead and Lynde's Hollow in the first paragraph of the novel; but the capacity of Anne to bring out an interior, repressed child within Marilla is thoroughly modern in its sensibility. Even as Anne cries before Mrs. Lynde's cruel observations, "An old remembrance suddenly rose up before Marilla. She had been a very small child when she had heard one aunt say of her to another, 'What a pity she is such a dark, homely little thing.' Marilla was every day of fifty before the sting had gone out of that memory" (116). Marilla's response to her community, her desire to laugh and her subsequent indulgences in laughing and weeping, are as much "a surprise to herself" (114) as her initial reprimand of Mrs. Lynde. For Marilla, Anne is the uncanny, who gives expression to the thoughts "deep down" in Marilla, as if Marilla's own "secret, unuttered, critical thoughts had suddenly taken visible and accusing shape and form in the person of this outspoken morsel of neglected humanity" (130). Although the narrator is often aligned with Anne's point of view, we continually glimpse Marilla as a split self whose repressed feelings this Providential child, as if an analyst, can

HOLLY BLACKFORD

bring to the surface. Thus Montgomery teaches us how to read and receive her child as an inner one. Anne *awakens*. As Mrs. Lynde observes of Matthew, "That man is waking up after being asleep for over sixty years" (235).

Despite her Victorian accoutrements and context, Anne signals acceptance of a new twentieth-century lens on the child as a psychological construct interior to the adult who develops from a child. In her book *Strange Dislocations*, Carolyn Steedman argues that ideas of childhood profoundly affected changing ideas of the self, which culminated in the modern period, when childhood became synonymous with the unconscious mind (3–4). Anne typifies the sort of unconscious that pre-Freudian child psychologists were beginning to articulate (see Taylor and Shuttleworth). Developmental psychology, a field in its infancy but beginning to blossom at the end of the nineteenth century, had already overturned John Locke's concept of *tabula rasa* because psychologists' evolutionary and anthropological viewpoint led them to consider the child as atavistic and therefore a carrier of ancestral memory (see Taylor). Over time, those studying the imagination, such as British psychologist James Sully, came to believe that nothing was lost in the child's mind. Even sense memories were stored there to be drawn upon later, as if the child's mind were a deeply closeted collection of decontextualized impressions and perceptions, which could be sorted and recombined at any time. This is a thesis that Henry James explored in 1897 with his modern child character Maisie: "She found in her mind a collection of images and echoes kept for her in the childish dusk, the dim closet, the high drawers, like games she wasn't yet big enough to play.... A wonderful assortment of objects of this kind she was to discover later, all tumbled up too with the things, shuffled into the same receptacle, that her mother had said about her father" (22–23). In light of the twentieth century, in which ideas of childhood would become principally entwined with developmental psychology, let's look anew at Anne, the transient child who arrives at the train station with her carpetbag, which she carries by herself as if it were a harbinger of her rich imagination.

For Anne embodies thresholds in so many ways. She is a child in whom literary and cultural ideas have made their imprint. Montgomery begins the novel not with Anne but with a description of Cavendish women. It is as if the neglected child within always waits on the threshold of consciousness, ready to take possession. After Anne's arrival, Marilla feels that all of Green Gables is bewitched (146), because even her brooch has altered its location on its own accord. Described as one with "brisk mental processes" (67), and subscribing to a theory of spontaneity in speech and play (196), Anne very closely resembles the child being theorized in the child psychology movement sprouting wings at the turn of the century across Europe and North America. Summarizing a new appreciation of the child at play, W. B. Drummond in 1901 writes of the link between theories of play and evolution, perceived as an interactive principle between adapting to and altering environment:

> Play is the means whereby individual powers are acquired; it is the apprenticeship for the work of life; it has permitted the development of individuality; it has given scope for variation and for individual adaptation to different environments; it has favoured the growth of intelligence and thereby permitted man not only to choose, but to some extent to make, his environment and thereby assist in his own evolution. A little child at play is 'at his lessons.' The lesson book is the world. The task is just to learn 'all about everything.' (79)

Anne is "such an interesting little thing" (97), argues Matthew, who cherishes her playful romanticism, rather than "a useful little thing" (97–98), bemoans Marilla, because her approach to life is playful. The child's play had become to psychologists an index of the uniqueness of human consciousness. Study of the child's consciousness through play had been given a new seriousness, as Sully explains in his introduction to *Studies of Childhood* (1896): "Play is the forerunner of developed thought and the product of an assimilative instinct. The child, in his early stage of worldliness, is egoistic and (therefore) anthropomorphic. He confers upon animals and even upon inert matter those psychological properties which he dimly perceives in himself" (Sully xxviii). Mark Twain's praise of Anne, reported by Montgomery in a letter to Ephraim Weber, is that Montgomery created "the dearest, and most lovable child in fiction since the immortal Alice" (*Green Gables Letters* 80), a link Montgomery herself made in the novel by comparing Marilla to the Duchess of Wonderland (*Anne* 107). By extension, of course, Mrs. Lynde is the Queen of Hearts, and Matthew the King who pleads on behalf of the child. Mad tea parties abound; in the most obvious, Diana's drunkenness serves as a ready metaphor for Anne's dizzying narration of a drowned mouse, a narrative spun to the neglect of her friend. Anne even has various looking-glass reflections, imaginary friends who are as real and alive to her as the literary selves she spins in her house of fiction's many windows.

Montgomery adapts the play theory espoused by Lewis Carroll, particularly in the opening pages of *Through the Looking-Glass*, which are mostly monologues by Alice as she spins her looking-glass house. But instead of Wonderland, Anne makes a Neverland out of Everydayland, where the intricate psychology of the child could emerge in such a way as to bewitch a myriad of readers around the world. And while the Carrollian satirical qualities of Anne's adventures are always in the forefront, and were probably a source of delight to Twain, Mary Rubio argues ("Satire"), Montgomery also shared Carroll's bent for the Wordsworthian theme of the inevitability of development (Epperly). Childhood lost to the child appears to be childhood regained for the adult; Marilla weeps at Anne's womanhood, proving that the "saving something about her mouth" (57) is, like Mrs. Darling's kiss, the possibility of keeping open a window into the child's neverland. Montgomery opened that window into her own childhood and into a new cultural ideal, and readers all over the globe were eager to throw Sunday school ideals to the wind and fly with her.

CHANGING IDEAS OF CHILDHOOD

When L. M. Montgomery described in her journal the birth of her character Anne, she gave us a statement of Anne's composition and equated the novel with her own "childhood experiences and dreams" (*Selected Journals* 331), an equation critics largely accept and upon which they expand, demonstrating the parallels between Montgomery and Anne in terms of personality and childhood situation (see Devereux 252). Montgomery lost her mother at an early age and was raised by her maternal grandparents. Her father went west to Saskatchewan as prospects opened on the frontier. She was descended from the first Scottish families who settled Prince Edward Island, a settlement marked with a fascinating political struggle against many landowners who did not live on the island and thus delayed general progress and caused significant political unrest (see Sharpe, Bumsted, Clark). As the contributors explore in *Myth, Migration and the Making of Memory: Scotia and Nova Scotia c. 1700–1990*, edited by Marjory Harper and Michael E. Vance, Scotland as a mythic home had become a romantic origin myth for Prince Edward Island and Nova Scotia, as much as it had in Montgomery's own family. It may also be for Anne, who romanticizes her immigrant parents (Crockett 72), and who recites many poems that "reflect the situations of Scottish immigrants to Canada.... Later in the novel Anne is identified with Mary, Queen of Scots, when she recites the poem of that name by Henry Glassford Bell ... [which reflects how] she does, in a sense, become queen of this island of expatriated Scots" (Doody and Barry 457). Like Alice, then, Anne moves through her panorama of looking-glass selves to become a red Queen.

Montgomery's social world as a child was one that embraced oral storytelling, particularly as practised by her Aunt Mary Lawson, and dramatic poetry, a taste she developed as a young poet and storyteller. My favourite account of Montgomery's early stories, written in a story club she formed with a group of girls, is Catherine Andronik's description of the young Maud's story "My Graves." In it, a travelling minister's wife has a baby, "who always dies" at each place they arrive, thus leaving "an amazing string of infant graves across Canada" (Andronik 25). Like many children of her time, Montgomery encountered diverse poets in her childhood reading. In her autobiography, she recalled early exposure to Henry Longfellow, Alfred, Lord Tennyson, John Whittier, Sir Walter Scott, Lord Byron, John Milton, and Robert Burns (Doody and Barry 457). In the novel, Anne traces her knowledge of poetry to primers. The anthologized way in which children receive various cultural inheritances creates fascinating collages in the child mind, a result Shelby Wolf and Shirley Brice Heath call "the braid of literature" in their study of how children weave together literature and life, a practice literalized in Montgomery and later immortalized in Anne.

Montgomery briefly lived with her father and his new family when she was fifteen, but her stepmother preferred her help with small children to her hopes and dreams of writing. After obtaining her teacher's licence and teaching for a spell, Montgomery briefly attended college classes and began to sell her stories, after which she again taught school. During the composition of *Anne*, however, she was once again living with her grandmother, who was widowed in 1899, helping her to manage the household and the post office that she ran in their kitchen. In 1901–1902, she enjoyed an important literary apprenticeship working for the *Daily Echo* in Halifax, where she received some writing as well as proofreading assignments. But from 1902 until 1911, she lived with her grandmother and experienced her filial duty with some frustration, a fate she similarly inflicts upon her character Anne at the end of the novel.

Montgomery's upbringing and adult sojourn in Prince Edward Island coincide with a shift in thinking about being Canadian. Before Prince Edward Island entered Confederation in 1873 and the completion of the railway, argues Errol Sharpe, "the people of Prince Edward Island had been largely self-sufficient"

HOLLY BLACKFORD

(124), making most necessities and trading with Britain, the United States, the West Indies, Newfoundland, and other Maritime colonies (124):

> Two events, the building of the railway and the introduction of steamships into the waters around the Island, brought drastic changes to the life of the Island communities. With the coming of steam and steel, the Island's shipbuilding industry collapsed, the lumbering industry fell into a decline from which it never recovered, the once busy ports lost their trade and their industry and, most significantly, a new class of comprador middlemen replaced the landlords and the family Compact in controlling the Island's government.... When the railway became the main carrier of Island commerce and the smaller ports fell into decay, the majority of Islanders, who lived on and tilled the land, turned their eyes from the sea to land, from Britain to Canada.... The collapse of the shipbuilding industry, the local financial institutions and the decline of local manufacturing put over 1000 Islanders out of work. (Sharpe 125–30)

Confederation was not a simple gain for the Island, in Sharpe's view, since Prince Edward Island became a place from which to extract natural and agricultural resources, and a market for central Canadian products "sold under the protection of a tariff" (124). Within a context of declining population and perhaps a certain longing to get off the train of modernity, the mythic force of a paradoxically Canadian-born child, yet a marginal outsider who loves the land more than its residents, takes on a certain intensity. But during this period of national transformation, ideas of childhood underwent an even more radical change; the reform of institutions supporting children became part of a national agenda in both Canada and the States.

I find it fascinating to consider that the transformation of the child character from a "faded entry" to a real human girl occurs alongside a discourse of love in Montgomery's journal: "It was a labor of love. Nothing I have ever written gave me so much pleasure to write." A new emotional discourse marked the efforts of child reformers, who spread the doctrine that childrearing and nurturing were to be associated with love and pleasure: "[Most English Canadians of the 1870s and 1880s] would have been baffled by twentieth-century concerns for the emotional life of their own or of the immigrant children" (Sutherland 11). Historical changes laid the groundwork for the birth and reception of *Anne of Green Gables*, for the way in which Anne took possession of her creator and increasingly larger readership territories, for altering the value of the child from labourer to "labor of love." Montgomery's description of her relationship to Anne symbolizes Canadian rhetoric to parents: "In contrast to the general opinion of the 1870s parents now learned that a child was not 'plastic clay … to mold and shape after a human pattern but a seed of divine life' for them 'to nurture and tend.' In this rhetoric one can see the growing influence that a popular and simplistic form of the ideas of Friedrich Froebel were beginning to have in English Canada" (Sutherland 17–18). And yet, as Beverly Crockett has demonstrated in her explication of the callousness with which a newspaper could report "By mistake a girl was sent," the practice of placing children out to service was still thriving in the early twentieth century. This fact signifies an emerging gap between cultural ideals and realities, a gap also nicely symbolized by the way in which Montgomery uses Anne to mark the discrepancy between poetical visions of the child and the very unromantic real world.

Montgomery's theme of Anne's transformation of value, from labourer to "priceless" emotional force, asks us to consider shifting attitudes toward the usefulness of children. In other words, she self-consciously enters a debate about the role of children in the world, one that we should not receive uncritically; she challenges some aspects of childhood and naturalizes others. The gradual removal, in the Victorian and Edwardian periods, of the child from the labour force was one of the most profound alterations of children's lives and of ideologies about childhood. As Viviana Zelizer has recounted, the period "between the 1870s and 1930s" saw a "profound transformation in the economic and sentimental value of children," and the "emergence of this economically 'worthless' but emotionally 'priceless' child has created an essential condition of contemporary childhood" (3). Throughout much of the nineteenth century, it was common practice to indenture dependent children to, particularly, rural homes. But an ideological shift was taking place, which would eventually displace the high demand for teenagers (particularly high in rural Canada) with demands for babies to adopt:

By the 1870s, child welfare workers had begun their campaign against the established instrumental approach to childcare in support of "genuine homes ... where a child would be received ... from the real love of it." ... As William Pryer Letchworth, a member of the New York State Board of Charities, noted in his influential report on pauper and destitute children in 1874, "It is important that the person taking the child should feel an interest in it beyond a purely selfish one.... If this interest is not felt, the child has not found a home in the true sense of the word." (Zelizer 176)

Missionaries in the United States would consistently insist that foster homes not take in a child for merely selfish reasons, something that becomes a point of debate between Matthew and Marilla; the practical woman believes Anne will not be useful, while the more philosophical man claims that the Cuthberts might be some good to Anne. In child savers' rhetoric of the time, the idea that the child will emotionally repay the foster parents became standard, a theme we find in *Anne*. Matthew gives to Anne gifts, receiving back the "priceless" gift of emotional depth and debt, a debt with which Anne is literally confronted toward the end of the novel.

Child reformers always had a tough battle because the idea that work was good for the child was firmly embedded in the public's mind. There was a fine line between the idea of work as exploitation and work as character building. Montgomery's text is a retrospective yet contemporary and thus ambivalent account of this shifting view of the child, who is brought to Cavendish for *his* potential to do farm work and who almost immediately transforms *her* main value, but there are consequences. Matthew's spiritual and emotional "awakening" culminates in his death, a sort of princely sacrifice across the threshold of Green Gables that enables Anne to inherit the kingdom into which she has christened herself. She has, after all, arrived as a pseudo-wife on a day resembling "a bride all in white with a lovely misty veil" (66). Marilla embodies Victorian discomfort with the child's new role, unwilling to relinquish an older sense that the child should be useful. In fact, if we take a suspicious view of Anne's mistakes in the house – "stealing" the brooch, giving Diana drink, flavouring the cake incorrectly – we also note that many of these mistakes are Marilla's fault. Marilla herself has misplaced the brooch, put the cordial in the wrong place, and switched the flavouring with cold medicine. These subtle "tests" of Anne could signify Marilla's desire to disgrace the "priceless" rather than "useful" child.

Ultimately the child and employer strike a middle ground with the new role accorded to the twentieth-century child: that of the schoolchild, seen as more appropriate for the new child. As Lisa Makman recounts about a much earlier novel written against child labour, Charles Kingsley's *The Water-Babies*, school was becoming the appropriate avenue for the child's "work" (122). Marilla feels that her commitment to giving "him a good home and schooling" (59) is a proper exchange for a useful labourer. Although *Anne* challenges this fiercely economic view, there is nevertheless a debt to be paid by the end; as Anne rises in her academic achievements, she also becomes social currency for Marilla. It is symbolically crucial that Marilla, by the end of the novel, faces the loss of Anne and, as a consequence, re-absorption into Mrs. Lynde's household, a symbol of female repression. Montgomery's excursion into discourses of a child's value thus parallels what Makman also states about Diamond in George MacDonald's *At the Back of the North Wind*; the child is removed from the labour force into a realm of play, but the novel paradoxically reifies contemporary discourses about how the real solution is to bring a playful attitude to work and duty. By the end of MacDonald's novel, Diamond is kept as a sort of display object by a family who has offered him a better home (Makman 127–28).

A few fields of labour were much more resistant to child labour law, one being rural farm labour, seen as "good" for children because of an educational and romantic philosophy that associated childhood and nature: "If defending factory work was unusual, farm labour on the other hand was almost blindly and romantically categorized as 'good' work" (Zelizer 77). The romantic association between childhood and nature is a pervasive assumption of *Anne*, participating in a certain vision of the naturalness of sending orphans to rural locations for new opportunities, yet Anne's gender makes the outdoors her playground, the indoors her space of labour.

Anne's love of the histrionic also represents another feature of childhood that the public also thought "natural" and thus exempt from scrutiny: child acting. Defenders of the practice saw child performers, who were in high demand and achieved high visibility in the late Victorian age, as "the emanation of the spirit of childhood" (Zelizer 95), falling within the natural preferences of children to play and perform. Anne's theatricality and tendency toward recitation, particularly in the face she shows adults, are quite in keeping with contemporary discourses of child behaviour, which justified the pleasure adults could glean from watching children.

Montgomery does not hide the power dynamics present when adults such as Mrs. Lynde and Marilla exhort Anne to perform confession or apology, but the spectacle of Anne for readers, as well as Marilla's uncertainty about children performing, provides us with an index to the way in which understandings of child "nature" and adult-child relations were far from settled. In America, child actors such as eight-year-old Elsie Leslie, in 1887, "'took playgoers by storm,' in 'Editha's Burglar' and in her next performance of 'Little Lord Fauntleroy,' which triggered an American 'public craze' with child stars" (Zelizer 86). This child-watching craze is reminiscent of the power dynamics in Carroll's *Alice*, when adult characters are continually demanding that Alice recite for their pleasure. Indeed, a very famous child of fiction parallels Anne; he inhabits a world entirely of imagination, he beckons other children to follow him there, and he symbolizes the pantheism of childhood. His name is Peter Pan, and he was first a creation of the stage, a symbol for the cultural arena of childhood as escape into wonderland. Anne is similarly a Pan figure who beckons others, such as Matthew, across thresholds, a character serving the traditional function of a liminal spirit who beckons others to cross into lands of enchantment. The child *was* perhaps of new use to adults.

Anne more directly addresses the issue of child labour and orphan apprenticeship when Marilla discusses her insistence on a Canadian-born child rather than a Barnardo import:

> Between 1868 and 1925 eighty thousand British boys and girls were sent to Canada to work under indentures as agricultural labourers and domestic servants. All were unaccompanied by parents, although only one-third of them were orphans. Most were not yet fourteen and still too young to leave school for full-time employment in the United Kingdom, although their educational opportunities would be limited in Canada and their work heavy. It seems strange to find such a policy flourishing in the late nineteenth and early twentieth centuries. (Parr 11)

Although the practice of exporting British children to Canada "seems out of step with its time" (11), according to scholar Joy Parr, it was not entirely retrogressive. Indeed, on the one hand, the practice reveals the limited entitlement of a right to childhood. But, on the other hand, those involved in the practice of emigration really seemed to believe that they were giving children of the labouring poor a New World opportunity in a pastoral landscape.

Despite criticisms, advocates of emigration depicted Canada as a wholesome rural environment that would separate children from the unwholesome attachments of immoral family members and the evil influence of cities in Britain:

> British evangelical child-savers' notions about agricultural Canada, like Brace's descriptions of the rural [U.S.] Midwest, were highly idealised, romantic, naturalist and thus easily integrated with popular contemporary analogies between children and young plants. Barnardo called Canada a 'fair garden-like country, yielding abundantly'. Macpherson and Birt liked to refer to emigration as 'spring transplanting'. Their colleague Samuel Smith saw children 'planted in a quiet farm' and saved from the towns by an enlivened interest in animals, flowers and gardens. The sponsors of child emigration claimed that plentiful food and the 'grand Canadian air' made 'slender sickly saplings' thrive and transformed pallid city boys into 'brawny sun-burnt' lads as different from their former selves as 'chalk from cheese'. (Parr 46)

Regardless of the fact that there were instances of abuse and proof that these children could be difficult to integrate into households and to manage, as one can imagine, the spirit of romantic childhood and New World opportunity coalesced in this institutional practice. The transformation of Anne from her sickly, starving initial appearance into a plump young woman, blooming flower-like in the beauty of Prince Edward Island, capitalizes upon this predominant rhetoric. Thus, although Anne is expressly not British, the novel participates in the ideology of a predominant system that equates health with transplanting children to the Canadian countryside. In *Anne*, and in the ideology that permitted "transplanting" of children, who were often teens, we can see the tension between psychologists' paradoxical beliefs in the adaptability of children to new environments and their vision of the child mind as a retainer of impressions and sense memories. It was a tension that troubled educational philosophers such as F. H. Heywood, who in 1904 tried to summarize contributions of the child study movement for educators. In that work, he grappled with the way in which Charles Darwin's ideas of nature had overturned William Wordsworth's. The practice of placing children in the country, however, paradoxically incorporated both visions, even as debates about child nature raged in psychological and educational texts.

Marilla's insistence that she does not want a Barnardo street Arab invokes a deliberate anti-imperial sentiment, which was growing amongst the Canadian public. British rhetoric in support of emigration makes it clear that emigration was seen as an imperial measure, "a way to make 'starving and desperate men into contented and loyal subjects', 'neglected female children' into 'happy, honest mothers of a stalwart' colonial race" (Parr 33). But Canadians, despite their very real need for labour, were experiencing a different point of view. Even earlier, when in 1875 Local Government Board senior inspector investigated Miss Rye, a prominent figure in child emigration, and recommended an overhaul of the apprenticeship system, his suggestions were interpreted as imperial plans "to extend the English workhouse system into Canada" (Parr 51). Subsequently, the plight of British emigrants was used as fuel for anti-imperialist rhetoric (55). Parr references Marilla's prejudice as describing "fears commonplace among Canadians of her time" (99):

> In rural areas an unfavourable impression of the rescue home children coloured the reputations of all British immigrants. The Prince Edward Island convenor of the National Council of Women reported in 1903 that troublesome experience with Middlemore and Barnardo boys and girls, the only immigrants arriving in the province, made Islanders wary of other immigration experiments. (149)

Thus *Anne of Green Gables* arrives on a national scene to express a strong anti-imperial sentiment and a contemplation of the Canadian-born's right to childhood and land:

> A growing number of [Canadians] expressed strong opinions on the matter. In particular, public hearings and subsequent report of Ontario's Royal Commission on the Prison and Reformatory System

acutely aroused public feeling about immigrant children. Echoing what had been said in the House of Commons committee in 1888 and 1889, witnesses before the commission expressed three principal complaints against the youngsters; they flooded the Canadian labour market and drove down wages; 'very many of them' went 'wrong through hereditary taints'; and they corrupted others with whom they associated, putting them up 'to all sorts of evil habits'.... In 1892 the federal inspector of penitentiaries argued that 'these street Arabs' speedily returned 'to their old habits, on arriving in Canada, and, as a consequence, became a burden and an expense upon the taxpayers of the Dominion in our reformatories, gaols, and penitentiaries.' (Sutherland 30)

The national fervour for *Anne* can be understood as part of a context of public feeling that the Canadian child was entitled to the rhetoric of Canada that Britain imperialistically employed. Debates about the quality of British children continued throughout the 1880s and 1890s (see Sutherland 30–36), but those debates took place in the context of a much more profound shift in attitude toward children in English-speaking Canada between the late nineteenth and early twentieth century. As Neil Sutherland argues, it is hard to find evidence of Canadian practices of childrearing in the 1870s and 1880s, largely because they "rarely discussed these subjects" and "were so generally agreed upon what that way [to bring up a child] was that they had no need to talk about it" (4). However, toward the end of the nineteenth century, "reformers began to urge English Canadians to change their methods of bringing up their youngsters" (4). Reformers initiated a broad-scale reform in child health, education, and the penal system. Thus the topic of attitudes toward Canadian youth was part of the environment in which Montgomery conceived, and the Canadian public received, *Anne*.

Commenting on the 1875 Doyle report mentioned above, which occasioned considerable controversy on both sides of the Atlantic, Sutherland says that we can draw several conclusions: "first, English Canadians showed little awareness of children as individual persons; second, they saw nothing of the inner, emotional life of youngsters; third, young people played an important and often central role in rural and in family economies; finally, contemporary English-Canadian child-rearing theory was intimately related to these perceptions and practices"

HOLLY BLACKFORD

(7). What would subsequently be launched from 1880 to 1914 was a crusade for improving the public health of children through schools, to "aim first of all to create a strong and healthy race" (39); the next target for child reform (1895–1920) was better education of mothers in the home; the period 1885–1925 saw a transformation in the treatment of juvenile delinquents, the centrepiece of which was the Juvenile Delinquents Act of 1908; and finally, the period 1890–1920 saw the institutionalization of educational reform, which embodied the combined efforts of various groups but which resulted in a more child-centred curriculum, not unlike the changes occurring in other Western countries. In Canada as elsewhere, Froebelian kindergartens, with their attendant philosophies of active and play-based learning, were growing in influence.

As Sutherland reiterates, "The proponents of Froebelian kindergartens believed, in Hughes' words, in 'reverent love for the child, profound respect for his individuality as the element of divinity in him, and freedom and self-activity as the conditions of most perfect growth physically, intellectually, and spiritually'" (174). In essence a romantic movement inspired by romantic philosophers who conceived of the child as a window into the divinity of nature, which the corrupting influence of man should let well enough alone (*à la* Jean-Jacques Rousseau), the ideas of Froebel and his disciple Johann Pestalozzi became a governing principle of providing a child with a garden in which he or she will thrive. The child will grow and learn on his/her own, if we just stop tampering with his or her transcendental, imaginative powers. Montgomery both depicts this and parodies it, not only with Marilla's frustrations but with Anne's own scrapes, showing us that this model of child development is a beautiful ideal but also, for the inexperienced child, a means to a burst bubble. For example, when Anne plays the Lily Maid, she boards a leaky barge. On the one hand, nature threatens to engulf her, indicative of her child nature – passionate and headstrong. On the other hand, the poem represents the inevitable onset of forces of civilization, which undo the garden of childhood. Elaine is a literary image of womanhood as well as male artistry, socializing and thus drowning the child Anne. The entry of a new kind of teacher, luckily, embodies in *Anne* the extension of the "garden" concept into schools; the arrival of Miss Stacy heralds the infusion of new educational principles that will channel Anne's natural powers. If there was one thing on which developmental psychologists agreed, it was that imagination and play were not frivolous but signs of human intelligence, newly measurable by the work of Alfred Binet in France.

In *Anne* we find interplay between the child mind and her environment, which could have been written only after significant growth of the field of developmental psychology, a field that had become popularized in books for educators, parents, and the general public. In 1901 Drummond looked back upon a fruitful forty years of interest in *The Child, His Nature and Nurture*, demonstrating for educators and parents the "rapid growth of the [child study] movement" and tracing its growth to Darwin and evolutionary theory's "interest in the beginning of things" (14). Darwin's observations of his own infant had been published in 1877, in response to a publication by M. Taine on his child's language acquisition, starting a trend of publishing "baby biographies" and initiating a conversation about the origins of human subjectivity that would blossom over the next twenty years. In 1890, Bernard Perez translated into English Dieterich Tiedemann's *Record of Infant-Life*. The British Child Study Association was founded in 1894 (Monroe 374). The journal *Pedagogical Seminary*, founded by prominent American psychologist G. Stanley Hall, would in 1898 begin to report annually on the progress of the child study movement by summarizing major contributions. William Preyer had published *The Mind of the Child* in 1882. In 1885, Perez published *The First Three Years of Childhood*. In 1893, Frederick Tracy published *The Psychology of Childhood*. James Sully published, among many other works, his *Studies of Childhood* in 1896. In France, investigators such as Binet would pioneer work in intelligence, and M. Gabriel Compayre was by 1898 "so well and so favourably known to American teachers, and the author of an important study of the child" (Monroe 375). In 1894, American psychologist James Baldwin published *Mental Development in the Child and the Race*, a title that demonstrates the correspondence between child development and what was known as race psychology. In 1884, the prolific G. Stanley Hall would be appointed professor of psychology and pedagogy at Johns Hopkins, where he would produce many important works on childhood and adolescence. Hall had studied with William James at Harvard, and James recommended his appointment, claiming that of all the psychologists in the States, only he and Hall were qualified to teach the "new psychology" (White 110). Hall would invite Freud to lecture in 1909 (White 120), and Freud's studies of infant sexuality appeared in 1905.

The international movement of child study both stimulated the composition of, and paved a pathway for the reception of, *Anne* – primarily a psychological study of a developing character who has also experienced trauma. The growth of children's literature during this period is part and parcel of an environment philosophically concerned with studying the child, which had assumed a new importance. Studying the child posed a challenge to traditional methods of psychology; thus researchers relied equally on writers such as William Wordsworth, Robert Louis Stevenson (especially his 1881 essay "Child's Play"), and George Sand, discussed by Sully in his concluding chapter, to give a glimpse of child consciousness. If the autonomy and pretend play espoused in Carroll's work provide one bookend to this period, *Anne of Green Gables* delineates the other, signifying the importance of this period's work on childhood to healing and understanding adults. As I argue elsewhere, the method of composition articulated by Montgomery in her journal entry is very similar to the method described by Henry James in his 1909 preface to *What Maisie Knew*; both reveal a new modernist method of interpreting an interior subjectivity from a child "object" briefly reported in a third-person account. Both authors maintained interest in how the human mind continually composes itself and its world, tracing the journey from the child as adult-defined, passive object to interior subject.

While Montgomery clearly recovered her own childhood self when she birthed Anne, she also faced a Frankenstein paradox because publishers and the public demanded more Anne. On 22 December 1908, she wrote to Ephraim Weber, "I daresay the most of the letter will be about that detestable *Anne*. There doesn't seem to be anything but her in my life just now and I'm so horribly tired of her that I could wish in all truth and candour that I'd never written her" (*Green Gables Letters* 77). Her Marilla-like grumpiness aside, she went on to publish, among other novels, *Anne of Avonlea* in 1909, *Anne of the Island* in 1915, *Anne's House of Dreams* in 1917, *Rainbow Valley* in 1919, *Rilla of Ingleside* in 1920, *Anne of Windy Poplars* in 1936, and *Anne of Ingleside* in 1939. Even at the end of her journal entry of 16 August 1907, Montgomery seemed to realize what she had unleashed with her Anne-girl, and she made a claim for "my" Anne, an impossibility after making Anne into a real human girl. Indeed readers of all nations and times have made their own claims for "their" Anne. There are a great many Annes not only to Anne herself, but also for a great many readers, just as there are, according to James Kincaid, a great many purposes for loving the child. Montgomery's Anne moved from a moral conception to what Montgomery thought a realistic one, but critics seem to each have their notion of whether Anne is indeed a real human girl or a dose of sunshine, romance, sentiment, or local colour (quite literally). Nevertheless Anne has transcended her birth and become real, whatever the definition of reality is, to a great many people. And with the publication of Montgomery's journals, Montgomery herself has become very real.

Academic scholarship on Montgomery's contribution to Canadian and global literature has blossomed with the infusion of women's studies and literature in universities, and will continue to do so with the expansion of childhood studies. This volume covers a broad range of issues for the student, scholar, and fan of *Anne*. The scholars of this collection seek to assess the classic value of *Anne* by placing the novel in its original historical and literary context, as well as by investigating the continuing aesthetic and cultural life of the novel in other times, places, and media. In Part I, "Writing and Placing *Anne*," three scholars explain the composition of *Anne* by exploring Montgomery's sources, her writing strategies of reworking prior material, and her focus on time and place in the novel itself. In Chapter One, "Wildwood Roses and Sunshine Girls: The Making of *Anne of Green Gables* as a Popular Romance," Irene Gammel argues that American and Canadian magazines offered Montgomery models and inspirations for *Anne*. Gammel investigates proto-Annes, such as "Charity Ann" (1892) by the Canadian poet Mary Ann Maitland and "Lucy Ann" (1903) by American author J. L. Harbour, alongside other tidbits that Montgomery would have seen in such venues as *Godey's Lady's Book*. Understanding these sources reveals both the extent to which Montgomery kept her eye on popular formula and liberated herself as a writer beyond those formulae.

Montgomery not only appropriated and revised magazine stories written by others to create *Anne*, but she also recycled and recast her own prior material, argues E. Holly Pike in Chapter Two, "L. M. Montgomery and Literary Professionalism." Pike looks specifically at the composition practices that Montgomery developed as a professional writer. Discussing the stories Montgomery published before *Anne* as well as her period of literary apprenticeship, Pike argues that Montgomery became adept at understanding the complexities of the literary marketplace and revising her material to meet audience demands. Pike's essay also gives us the flavour of what it was like to be an aspiring writer in Montgomery's time and place, providing us with a unique view of how Montgomery calculated her career and market, as well as self-consciously developed disciplined methods of composition.

If the novel, like Anne herself, embodies the practice of innovatively combining and adapting literary sources in a new environment, which perhaps made placing the novel with a publisher challenging, then it makes sense that a novel fondly remembered for its setting is itself concerned with human dependence on time and place as the very fabric of identity. In Chapter Three, "Anne with Two 'G's: Green Gables and Geographical Identity," Joy Alexander analyzes place, space, and time in the novel. In a compelling account of how Anne disembarks from the train of modernity to enter a mythic, isolated region that operates according to pre-industrial rhythms of time, Alexander analyzes the way in which Anne develops context and rootedness in the space-time coordinates of the novel. The recurrent motif of things being out of place, and of Anne renaming places, suggests ways in which identity depends on time and place, along with how a child can transform adult space. The novel's evocation of place is of crucial interest to the Canadian public and to those who journey far and wide to see Prince Edward Island, hoping to find there the flavour appreciated in the novel.

The professional manner by which Montgomery grew into a beloved author could not be more distinct from the romantic way in which "chatterbox" Anne, as Gammel calls her, spontaneously uses literature in dramatic self- and social understanding. However, the character Anne shares with Montgomery a highly self-reflexive style of composition. Montgomery uses Anne's language and romanticism to explore the role of discourse in human development. In Part II, "Romancing Anne: Language and Silence," three scholars press the overt romanticism of *Anne* and foreground the variously defined emotional discourses that circulate in the original novel as well as in the later novels of the series and in the films. They also observe that Anne has to remain silent on certain subjects, and silences become meaningful gaps to interrogate.

In Chapter Four, "Negotiating the Well-Worn Coin: The Shifting Use of Language in L. M. Montgomery's *Anne of Green Gables*," Melissa Mullins traces the romantic, Victorian, and modern theories of poetry and literary criticism that find expression in *Anne*. Mullins draws upon the work of poets and critics in these three periods to distinguish the types of creativity and imagination in Anne's use of language at different points in the novel. Avonlea's shifting attitude toward Anne's use of language, and the shifts that occur in the poetic webs Anne weaves, actually mirror the literary community's shifting attitude toward the role of the poet and critic in society. Mullins's essay acknowledges the influence of various literary movements in *Anne*. While Anne first espouses the theories of poetry espoused by romantics such as William Wordsworth, Percy Bysshe Shelley, and Samuel Taylor Coleridge, she shifts to embrace Victorian poet Alfred, Lord Tennyson, who was appreciated by modernists such as T. S. Eliot. In this shift, she also switches her dominant mode to irony and recitation, signifying a new embrace of the writer-critic over the poet.

In Chapter Five, "'Mute Misery': Speaking the Unspeakable in L. M. Montgomery's *Anne* Books," Hilary Emmett focuses our attention on the things Anne *cannot* say, despite her loquaciousness and spontaneous overflow of poetic feeling. In fact, despite Anne's melodramatic revelling in pretend scenes of grief throughout the 1908 novel, an astounding silence surrounds the traumatic events in Anne's life. By looking at these silences, the grief emergent with the death of Matthew, the frank view of child abuse in the character Mary Vance of *Rainbow Valley*, and the waves of tears, blood, and emotion in subsequent novels such as *Rilla*, Emmett defines the eruption of a female semiotic to express the unspeakable and ineffable. The grief that begins to find expression at the end of *Anne*, as a reaction to trauma, expands in *Rilla* into a cultural and national discourse of mourning over those lost in World War I, just as the narration of Mary Vance fills in the gaps of Anne's child abuse in *Anne of Green Gables*. If Anne has a romantic and "poetical" zest for the larger-than-life, she also is at the centre of a very real romance, Eleanor Nickel reminds us in Chapter Six, "'The World Hasn't Changed Very Much': Romantic Love in Film and Television Versions of *Anne of Green Gables*." Nickel interrogates the tensions introduced by Gilbert in the novel and how they are subsequently explored in the 1934 film and in Kevin Sullivan's 1985 miniseries. She critiques scholars who feel the romance plot of *Anne* embodies compulsory heterosexuality, suggesting that Gilbert and Anne embody audience pleasure in the possibilities of love among equals.

The broad life of romantic and other literature in the novel makes *Anne* uniquely intertextual and indicates Montgomery's intention not only to reflect on her beloved island, but also to transcend time and compose a classic. Montgomery's numerous allusions to other authors cleverly exemplify what T. S. Eliot would subsequently call "Tradition and the Individual Talent" in his essay on writing. In it, Eliot defined writing as a writer's revision of existent literary tradition, and the canon as a relationship between literary objects speaking to one another. When a new writer writes, he/she rewrites existent literary objects and the canon is forever altered. In Part III, "Quoting Anne: Intertextuality at Home and Abroad," three scholars explore the concept of intertextuality in the girls' tradition that defined the original novel, in subsequent Canadian women's fiction, and in Astrid Lindgren's use of *Anne* in her Swedish literature.

In Chapter Seven, "Anne and her Ancestors: Self-Reflexivity from Yonge to Alcott to Montgomery," Laura Robinson draws a genealogy between Charlotte Yonge's *The Daisy Chain* (1856), Louisa May Alcott's *Little Women* (1868–69), and Montgomery's *Anne*. All writers of the emergent genre of girls' coming-of-age fiction, Young, Alcott, and Montgomery depict the process of growing up female as a self-reflexive process of reading and revising literary and cultural tradition. Robinson explicates scenes of reading and writing to argue that growing up female involves an active process of self-construction through transformation of cultural inheritance. Robinson's thesis could also reflect upon the author herself, as discussed in the prior chapters. But what happens to the legacy of Anne when her presence in the psyche of later Canadian women writers becomes "subcutaneous," as Margaret Atwood put it? In Chapter Eight, *"Anne of Green Gables* as Intertext in Post-1960 Canadian Women's Fiction," Theodore Sheckels examines eight motifs constructed by Montgomery, which circulate in the fiction of Marian Engel, Margaret Atwood, Margaret Laurence, Audrey Thomas, and Alice Munro, demonstrating the lasting influence of *Anne* as well as the permeability of Montgomery's motifs in contemporary realism.

The penetration of *Anne* can also be studied in very specific instances of readership in other parts of the world. In Chapter Nine, "Interactions with Poetry: Metapoetic Games with *Anne* in Astrid Lindgren's *Madicken*," Cornelia Rémi examines one extraordinary instance of reception in the work of the Swedish author. Lindgren often reminisced about her childhood enactment of scenes of *Anne*; like the character with whom she was entranced, Lindgren would bring scenes to life by similarly transforming mundane settings to magical ones. Many of the symbols and scenes in *Anne* circulate in Lindgren's fiction – particularly scenes in which Anne bridges reality and fantasy with her poetic mind and games. Rémi compares and contrasts *Anne* and Lindgren's *Madicken*, clearly a novel by a kindred spirit; in *Madicken*, Lindgren appropriates the trope of poetic games and scenes such as walking the ridgepole and enacting the lily maid. The latter are poignant symbols of the balancing acts girls undergo as they enter the threshold between environment and imagination. In many ways, the Swedish translation's de-emphasis of setting and native Canadian plants enabled the novel and character to more easily transcend their birth. Moreover, this transcendence modelled the power of Anne's liminal existence between actual worlds and worlds she creates with her mind and language.

If Anne wove her way into the hearts of readers because of her romantic imagination and revitalizing energies, her development into womanhood and her embeddedness in domesticity remain controversial topics for today's critics. The politics of *Anne* continue to be unresolved but fiercely debated. In Part IV, "Maturing Anne: Gender and Empire," three scholars revisit this issue by focusing on the domestic sphere and colonial context. Does Anne rule her domestic empire or does it rule her? In Chapter Ten, "A Ministry of Plum Puffs: Cooking as Path to Spiritual Maturity in L. M. Montgomery's *Anne* Books," Christiana Salah argues that women's work, such as cooking and tending the home, was a specifically religious duty and therefore Montgomery's experimentation with Anne's cooking mishaps bespeaks her critical perspective on how women become ministering angels in the house. Anne gradually transforms her community's sense of the spiritual, ministering to their souls with a method that undoes a more traditional nineteenth-century conception of Christian womanhood. In Chapter Eleven, "The Ethos of Nurture: Revisiting Domesticity in L. M. Montgomery's *Anne of Green Gables*," Monika Hilder asks that we revisit Montgomery's reification of female domesticity, which has been a point of contention among critics. Hilder argues that Montgomery celebrates an ethos of nurture that transcends gender, particularly through the self-sacrificing heroism of Matthew.

The issue of Anne's modernity and maturity intersects with her embodiment of national hopes and dreams in a post-colonial context. The novel shares roots with novels of other countries that have similar colonial histories. In Chapter Twelve, "Constructing a 'New Girl': Gender and National Identity in *Anne of Green Gables* and *Seven Little Australians*," Sharyn Pearce examines the similarities between Montgomery's novel of 1908 and Ethel Turner's Australian novel of 1894. Both emergent from a colonial context, the two novels represent "new girls" to articulate future hopes for nations that can break from their more traditional parents and forge independent cultural identities, given their imperial contexts.

If there is one thing Anne has achieved, it is independence. Just as Anne herself is "placed out" and finds a home, the novel has a Canadian home yet has been "placed out" in the broader world. *Anne* embodies the complexities of classic literature in every possible way. It is really Anne's ability to compose and re-compose herself and her world that invites others into her landscape and gives them permission to rewrite her meaning. In her journal, Montgomery equated her novel's value with Anne: "There is plenty of incident in it but after all it must stand or fall by 'Anne.' *She* is the book" (*Selected Journals* 331). Montgomery's sense that her novel stands by Anne, and her thematic emphasis on Anne winning over larger and larger communities, encoded the reception of *Anne* into various reading communities. As a particular cultural ideal of the child, of the rejuvenating and healing possibilities of our fragmented pasts, Anne has written her way into the homes of many readers in many places and times. As her own muse, Anne declines and becomes quiet at the end of the original novel, which is no surprise, and may not matter since the spirit of Anne lives on no matter what age she becomes. Whether she embodies the romance of place, women's dreams, literariness, imagination, spirituality, national sentiment, or other fantasies of societies organized around the young, she will enchant and bewitch readers for years to come. In doing so, she can never really grow old.

When Montgomery wrote a story of a girl's otherworldly propensity to possess others, she cleverly gave readers a model for receiving Anne into the innermost recesses of the mind, heart, and soul. Anne offers the promise of settlement to so many, perhaps including female scholars who seek to make a place for themselves in worlds expecting boys. All kinds of marginalized groups find themselves in and through Anne. For example, Zenia, a thoroughly multicultural character in Margaret Atwood's *The Robber Bride*, is an inverse Anne upon whom native-born Canadians project their desires, explaining why her aura is "deep red" (57). Like blood, certain characters seize cultural imaginations by tapping into unconscious fears, hopes, desires, and dreams. Anne has now taken possession of others, as she did her author, for one hundred years. And although she grows into a woman throughout a well-loved series, it is the child Mark Twain called "the most lovable child since the immortal Alice" who earned *Anne* immortality.

WORKS CITED

Andronik, Catherine M. *Kindred Spirit: A Biography of L. M. Montgomery, Creator of* Anne of Green Gables. New York: Atheneum, 1993.

Atwood, Margaret. *The Robber Bride*. New York: Random, 1993.

Baldwin, James Mark. *Mental Development in the Child and the Race*. 1894. New York: Augustus M. Kelley, 1969.

Barrie, J. M. *Peter Pan and Other Plays*. Ed. Peter Hollindale. New York: Oxford UP, 1999.

Blackford, Holly. "Apertures into the House of Fiction: Novel Methods and Child Study, 1870–1910." *Children's Literature Association Quarterly* 32.4 (2007): 368–89.

Bumsted, J. M. *Land, Settlement, and Politics on Eighteenth-Century Prince Edward Island*. Montreal: McGill-Queen's UP, 1987.

Carroll, Lewis. *Alice in Wonderland: Authoritative Texts of* Alice's Adventures in Wonderland, Through the Looking-Glass, The Hunting of the Snark, *Backgrounds, Essays in Criticism*. 2nd ed. Ed. Donald J. Gray. New York: W.W. Norton, 1992.

Clark, Andrew Hill. *Three Centuries and the Island: A Historical Geography of Settlement and Agriculture in Prince Edward Island, Canada*. Toronto: U of Toronto P, 1959.

Crockett, Beverly. "Outlaws, Outcasts, and Orphans: The Historical Imagination and *Anne of Green Gables*." *Imagining Adoption: Essays on Literature and Culture*. Ed. Marianne Novy. Ann Arbor: U of Michigan P, 2001. 57–82.

Darwin, Charles. "A Biographical Sketch of an Infant." 1877. *Classics in the History of Psychology*. Ed. Christopher D. Green. Toronto: York University. 7 July 2006. <http://psychclassics.yorku.ca/Darwin/infant.htm>.

Devereux, Cecily. "'See My Journal for the Full Story': Fictions of Truth in *Anne of Green Gables* and L. M. Montgomery's Journals." *The Intimate Life of L. M. Montgomery*. Ed. Irene Gammel. Toronto: U of Toronto P, 2005. 241–57.

Doody, Margaret Anne and Wendy E. Barry. "Literary Allusion and Quotation in *Anne of Green Gables*." *The Annotated Anne of Green Gables*. Ed. Wendy E. Barry, Margaret Anne Doody, and Mary E. Doody Jones. New York: Oxford UP, 1997. 457–62.

Drummond, W. B. *The Child, His Nature and Nurture*. London: J. M. Dent, 1901.

Epperly, Elizabeth. "Romancing the Voice: *Anne of Green Gables*." *Anne of Green Gables*. Norton Critical Ed. New York: W.W. Norton, 2007. 343–58.

Gammel, Irene. "Introduction: Life Writing as Masquerade: The Many Faces of L. M. Montgomery." *The Intimate Life of L. M. Montgomery*. Toronto: U of Toronto P, 2005. 3–15.

Harper, Marjory and Michael E. Vance, ed. *Myth, Migration and the Making of Memory: Scotia and Nova Scotia c. 1700–1990*. Halifax: Fernwood, 1999.

James, Henry. *What Maisie Knew*. New York: Meridian, 1984.

Kincaid, James. *Child-Loving: The Erotic Child and Victorian Culture*. New York: Routledge, 1992.

"L. M. Montgomery suicide revealed." *CBC News* 22 September 2008. 14 November 2008. http://www.cbc.ca/canada/.

MacLulich, T. D. "L. M. Montgomery and the Literary Heroine: Jo, Rebecca, Anne and Emily." *Canadian Children's Literature* 37 (1985): 5–17.

Makman, Lisa Hermine. "Child's Work is Child's Play: The Value of George MacDonald's Diamond." *Children's Literature Association Quarterly* 24.3 (Fall 1999): 119–29.

Monroe, Will S. "Status of Child Study in Europe." *Pedagogical Seminary* 6 (1898/1899): 372–81.

Montgomery, L. M. *Anne of Green Gables*. Ed. Cecily Devereux. Peterborough: Broadview, 2004.

———. *The Green Gables Letters: From L. M. Montgomery to Ephraim Weber, 1905–1909*. Ed. Wilfrid Eggleston. Toronto: Ryerson, 1960.

———. *The Selected Journals of L. M. Montgomery*. Vol. 1. Ed. Mary Rubio and Elizabeth Waterston. Toronto: Oxford UP, 1985.

Parr, Joy. *Labouring Children: British Immigrant Apprentices to Canada, 1869–1924*. Montreal: McGill-Queen's UP, 1980.

Perez, Bernard. *The First Three Years of Childhood*. NY: E. L. Kellogg, 1894.

Preyer, William. *The Mind of the Child: Parts I and II*. NY: Arno, 1973.

Reimer, Mavis. "Introduction: The Anne-Girl and the Anne Book." *Such a Simple Little Tale: Critical Responses to L. M. Montgomery's* Anne of Green Gables. Ed. Mavis Reimer. Metuchen, NJ: Children's Literature Association and Scarecrow, 1992. 1–10.

Rubio, Mary. "Satire, Realism, and Imagination in *Anne of Green Gables*." *L. M. Montgomery: An Assessment*. Ed. John Sorfleet. Guelph, ON: Canadian Children's P, 1976. 27–36.

Sharpe, Errol. *A People's History of Prince Edward Island*. Toronto: Steel Rail, 1976.

Stairs, Michele. "Matthews and Marillas: Bachelors and Spinsters in Prince Edward Island in 1881." *Mapping the Margins: The Family and Social Discipline in Canada, 1700–1975*. Ed. Nancy Christie and Michael Gauvreau. Montreal: McGill-Queen's UP, 2004. 247–70.

Steedman, Carolyn. *Strange Dislocations: Childhood and the Idea of Human Interiority 1780–1930*. Cambridge: Harvard UP, 1995.

Stevenson, Robert Louis. "Child's Play." *Virginibus Puerisque*. 1881. 16 October 2008. <http://www.gutenberg.org/dirs/etext96/virpr10.txt>

Sully, James. *Studies of Childhood. Significant Contributions to the History of Psychology 1750–1920*. Ed. Daniel Robinson. Washington DC: University Publications of America, 1977.

Sutherland, Neil. *Children in English-Canadian Society: Framing the Twentieth-Century Consensus*. Toronto: U of Toronto P, 1976.

Taine, M. "On the Acquisition of Language by Children." *Mind* 2 (1877): 252–59.

Taylor, Jenny Bourne. "Between Atavism and Altruism: the Child on the Threshold in Victorian Psychology and Edwardian Children's Fiction." *Children in Culture: Approaches to Childhood*. Ed. Karin Lesnik-Oberstein. New York: Routledge, 1998. 89–121.

Taylor, Jenny Bourne and Sally Shuttleworth. *Embodied Selves: An Anthology of Psychological Texts 1830–1890*. New York: Oxford UP, 1998.

Tiedemann, Dieterich. *Record of Infant-Life*, Trans. Bernard Perez. Syracuse, NY: C. W. Bardeen, 1890.

Tracy, Frederick. *The Psychology of Childhood*. Boston: Heath, 1909.

White, Sheldon. "G. Stanley Hall: From Philosophy to Developmental Psychology." *A Century of Developmental Psychology*. Ed. Ross D. Parke, Peter A. Ornstein, John J. Rieser, and Carolyn Zahn-Waxler. Washington: APA, 1994. 103–26.

Wolf, Shelby and Shirley Brice Heath. *The Braid of Literature: Children's Worlds of Reading*. Cambridge: Harvard UP, 1995.

Zelizer, Viviana. *Pricing the Priceless Child: The Changing Social Value of Children*. Princeton: Princeton UP, 1985.

I

WRITING AND PLACING *ANNE*

CHAPTER ONE

Wildwood Roses and Sunshine Girls: The Making of *Anne of Green Gables* as a Popular Romance[1*]

Irene Gammel

"When I am asked if *Anne* herself is a 'real person' I always answer 'no' with an odd reluctance and an uncomfortable feeling of not telling the truth," Lucy Maud Montgomery noted in her journal on 27 January 1911. "For she is and always has been, from the moment I first thought of her, so real to me that I feel I am doing violence to something when I deny her an existence anywhere save in Dreamland" (*Selected Journals* 2, 39–40). Montgomery's sense that she may not have been "telling the truth" about *Anne* is an intriguing choice of words – all the more as there is not a single reference to *Anne* in the author's journals or correspondence during the time when she was writing what would become a world-renowned literary classic. She kept her novel a secret.

Moreover, her retrospective remarks about *Anne of Green Gables* are cryptic and even, occasionally, misleading. On 16 August 1907, months after the novel had been accepted for publication, Montgomery first wrote in her journal that the plot of *Anne of Green Gables* was inspired by the real-life story of a little orphan girl whose adopters requested a boy (*Selected Journals* 1, 330).[2] She later identified this girl as a relative, Ellen Macneill (*Selected Journals* 2, 40), who arrived in Cavendish in 1892. But Ellen was too quiet and well-behaved to serve as the effervescent heroine of our story. "Anne," the celebrity writer wrote a full decade later in her 1917 autobiography, using a dramatic Anne-style tone, "flashed into my fancy already christened, even to the all important 'e'" (*Alpine Path* 72).

"I have used real places in my books and real incidents," she added. "But hitherto I have depended wholly on the creative power of my own imagination for my characters" (*Alpine Path* 73). My chapter, however, will tell a different story, taking us on a journey into the popular magazine culture of the era to uncover some of the inspirations for, and influences on the shape of, *Anne*. Like Anne's first jaunt from Bright River Station to Avonlea, ours is a ride of surprises and discoveries, although our journey begins with a more mundane observation.

The young L. M. Montgomery, like her famous chatterbox creation Anne, loved to use cliché and imagery drawn from contemporary formula fiction and poetry. For instance, sixteen-year-old Maud gushed in a love poem to her girlfriend Penzie Macneill: "And there she blooms my own sweet wildwood rose / Her sweetness and her beauty but for few / And all the lovelier that her blushing grace / In Nature's freshness and concealment grew" ("My Friend's Home" 99). Years later, Montgomery would dismiss her poetic effusions to Penzie – "I certainly gilded the violet with a lavish pen" (20 Oct. 1936, *Selected Journals* 5, 106) – but the mature author's irony cannot mask the fact that she was profoundly influenced by formula literature. Since there has been to date little scholarly analysis of her use of such material,[3] readers may be surprised to learn that, contrary to Montgomery's own statements, *Anne of Green Gables* was not born in a flash. Its plot was not based entirely on Montgomery's personal experiences and observations, nor was it solely the product of her imagination. Rather, the novel took years to develop and is deeply steeped in the popular culture of the Victorian and Edwardian periods. In fact, Montgomery's apprenticeship was the product of the global cultural context that shaped the writing practices of the era.

FORMULA FICTION

In her study of "middlebrow" reading in the Victorian and Edwardian era, Janice Radway has explained the distinction made, at the time, between a literary and popular book. The literary book was bound in high-quality paper and hard covers. The elaborate material package indicated its status as a distinctive commodity of enduring value; in fact, such a book was an investment, to be displayed in the parlour or preserved in the family library. The popular book, in contrast, was often cheaply packaged. Books of this type, calculated to entertain a great number of readers, were more interchangeable than literary books. Typically, the name of the author functioned as a brand-name for a series featuring a recurring character. The popular book relied on "an endless process of circulation or cultural recycling, as a reformulation and ever-widening distribution of previously existing material" (135).

Although literary scholars have tended to dismiss popular literature as derivative and escapist, fiction and poetry of this sort actually play an important social and cultural role. In his classic study, *Adventure, Mystery, and Romance: Formula Stories as Art and Popular Culture*, John Cawelti explains, "Formula stories may well be one important way in which the individuals in a culture act out unconscious or repressed needs, or express latent motives that they must give expression to but cannot face openly" (26). Cawelti also contends that at least some formula fiction has literary merit: "A successful formulaic work is unique when, in addition to the pleasure inherent in the conventional structure, it brings a new element into the formula, or embodies the personal vision of the creator. If such new elements also became widely popular, they may in turn become widely imitated stereotypes and the basis of a new version of the formula or even of a new formula altogether" (12). Such was indeed the case with Montgomery's *Anne*.

Before she made her name as a novelist, magazine stories were Montgomery's bread and butter. She unapologetically wrote for money, bragging in a 1904 letter to her pen friend and struggling writer Ephraim Weber, "I made *nearly* $600 last year – $591.85 to be exact. Shan't be content until I reach the thousand mark though" (*Green Gables Letters* 27). She studied the market and the genre, tailoring her stories to the demands of editors and magazines. A shrewd businesswoman who marketed her work in a global publishing economy, the scribbler from small-town Cavendish played hardball in the world of assembly-line writing. Still, her first novel, *A Golden Carol*, written around 1899 or 1900, failed to find a publisher precisely because its heroine never moved beyond one-dimensional formula (16 July 1925, *Selected Journals* 3, 240). Montgomery's failure to find a publisher for the manuscript, which she consequently destroyed, was a salutary experience. She constantly worked to innovate, to improve her style, and to place her stories with the very best American magazines: "Had a lot of acceptances lately," she boasted to Weber in May 1905, just as she was beginning the writing of *Anne of Green Gables*; "'The Schoolmaster's Love Letters' ... is something of a new departure in style for me" (*Green Gables Letters* 31).

When Montgomery began "brooding up" *Anne of Green Gables* in the early months of 1905, she meant to write an ephemeral story for a Sunday school newspaper (*Selected Journal* 1, 330). At some point, Montgomery undoubtedly began to hope and then believe that her story would transcend the category of the popular, to be regarded as a literary work. That she peppered her narrative with allusions to such undoubtedly literary figures as Alfred, Lord Tennyson, Henry Wadsworth Longfellow, Robert Browning, and William Shakespeare indicates an effort, on her part, to situate the novel within a more prestigious literary tradition (Epperly, *Fragrance passim*; Wilmshurst 15–45). Yet she owed an equally strong debt to the popular fiction of the era. In the novel, chatterbox Anne quotes, paraphrases, and dramatizes the clichés and formulas of popular romance literature. Perhaps Montgomery is using the character of Anne to make the same point as Cawelti: that individuals use the conventions of formula fiction to convey their own thoughts, needs, and motives. By demonstrating her authorial understanding of these conventions, Montgomery may also be signalling to the reader that this particular novel is self-consciously acknowledging, but also transcending, the genre of popular romance. Is Montgomery perhaps poking fun at herself for her own past mimicry of generic conventions in her effort to write potboilers? She did routinely recycle episodes, characters, and names in a variety of the stories she submitted to editors, assuming that at least some of these stories were destined to be as ephemeral as the cheap newspaper on which they were printed. Yet she had enormous literary ambitions and considered the writing she did for periodicals to be an important apprenticeship. Since childhood, her fondest dream was to write the novel that would make her famous.

As she was blossoming into a literary writer, Montgomery was defining herself *against* the formula roots, but as we shall see, traces of formula fiction are still readily discernible in *Anne of Green Gables*, although they may have become obscured for the twenty-first-century reader. Our journey into the ephemeral formulaic magazine culture of the past – relegated long ago to the vaults of archives and largely forgotten today – takes us into the heart of the mystery of how *Anne* came about. In particular, I discuss two stories of orphan girls, discovered in the course of my archival research, whose evident influence on Montgomery's novel has not yet been recognized: "Charity Ann," by the Canadian poet Mary Ann Maitland, and "Lucy Ann," by American author J. L. Harbour. Each story is fewer than fifteen hundred words, yet profound in its impact on the novel. Explicating these proto-Annes may shed light on which aspects of *Anne of Green Gables* are shared with popular magazine traditions of the time, and which elements comprise Anne's "e" – her distinctiveness, her lasting charm, and her unique blend of chatterbox cliché and literary innovation. By clearly discriminating the formula parts of her story, after more than a century, we are finally able to see why *Anne* became a literary superstar, and why the formula stories that went into making it have sadly become lost and obscured – relegated today to the darkness of archival storage rooms. Our journey takes us into the past, first into the year 1892, a year of leisure, during which Maud, a flirtatious teen, was in a kind of limbo, having just come back from her year-long visit to Prince Albert, Saskatchewan, before returning to the Cavendish school in August to study for her entrance examination at Prince of Wales College.

"Charity Ann" (1892)

The year 1892 started out mild and sunny. In early January, seventeen-year-old Maud read some Emerson and went gum-picking with her cousin Lu. On 9 January, she writes, "Around us lay the moist, golden fields sleeping in the sunshine and sloping from where we stood in a gentle decline down to where the sea lay soft and hazy and blue" (Unpublished Journals 148). She does not mention the arrival, in the Cavendish Post Office, of the January 1892 issue of *Godey's Lady's Book*, a Philadelphia magazine that included a story by Mary Ann Maitland entitled "Charity Ann. Founded on Facts." And yet, when I discovered this story in 2004, in the New York Public Library, I realized that "Charity Ann" – who drifted into Cavendish the same year as the real-life orphan Ellen Macneill – must be considered one of the earliest models for *Anne of Green Gables*.

In Maitland's story, an eight-year-old orphan runaway named Ann arrives just before midnight, on a New Year's Eve in the early 1870s, at the home of an old Scottish couple, Donald and Christy McKay. The McKays are simple farming folks living in an unnamed locale; they are sitting by the kitchen fire when they hear the late-night knock on the door. Ann, desperate to escape the abusive poorhouse, is determined to find a home and earn her keep as a servant with the MacKays: "I can wash dishes, and scrape pots, and peel tawties, and mind the babies, and everything" (70). Like Montgomery's Anne, in the eyes of Avonlea, Charity "Ann was not a pretty child": her tawny hair is dull and straggling, and her gray eyes "were too large and lustrous to mate with that forlorn and hungry look" (71).[4] Also like Anne Shirley, who dislikes her first name, Ann is reluctant to give her name: "Did you niver hear your ither ane?" asks Cristy; "Oh, aye! But I dinna like it," replies "Charity Ann," who does not know her father's name (71). Like Anne Shirley, she has raised several sets of twins: "The babies?

How many had she? Twins I suppose," Donald asks, and Charity Ann retorts, "Yes lots o' twins; nine o' them" (71). Compare with Anne's prior predicament: "Mrs. Hammond had eight children. She had twins three times. I like twins in moderation but twins three times in succession is *too much*" (*Anne of Green Gables* 90).[5] Despite the humour of Maitland's dialect story, the McKays are horrified to learn that Charity Ann has been physically abused. The purple bruises on her arms and blisters on the feet provide a point of graphic realism that will be softened in *Green Gables*.

Soon a treasured member of the family, Ann becomes a diligent household helper for Christy, who is plagued by rheumatism. Donald showers her with affection and gifts, such as sweets and a little ribbon, just as Matthew spoils Anne with chocolates and puffed sleeves. Ann eventually blossoms into a rosy, plump girl. The happy ending seems contrived: a long-lost McKay relative turns up to discover that Ann is his daughter, and she finds herself "transplanted from the chilly airs of orphanhood into such an atmosphere of almost tropical affection" (73). The story's saccharine last line, "*Charity Ann* no more, but *Love Ann*" (73), belies the social realism of the story's first part. Montgomery wrote similarly contrived endings for several of her orphan stories, but not for *Green Gables*, in which the transformation of the local landscape would replace this rather Dickensian *deus ex machina*.

Mary Ann Maitland (1839–1919) was a native of Elgin, Scotland, and immigrated to Canada with her parents when she was eighteen. She married George Maitland and lived in the Niagara region, where George, a photographer, owned studios specializing in tinted photographs and cameo pictures. The couple had four girls and a son (George junior would later join the *Toronto Star* editorial staff). A devout Baptist, Maitland published secular and religious poetry, stories in Canadian and American magazines, and two books of poetry, *Autumn Leaves* (1907) and *God Speed the Truth* (1919). Like Montgomery, she enjoyed a nostalgic backward glance, expressed in her *Autumn Leaves*: "Oh, the pleasant haunts of childhood! / What fond memories ebb and flow" ("Looking Backward" 1). Perhaps it is ironically appropriate that the earliest traces of Anne can be found in the writing of a forgotten Canadian woman poet, a country-woman silenced by the ephemeral quality of formula orphan fiction.

How did Montgomery come by the story? For several years, Grandma Lucy Macneill took a subscription to *Godey's Lady's Book* and, as Montgomery recalled on 10 January 1914, "its monthly advents were 'epochs in my life'" (*Selected Journals* 2, 141). In those days of bangs, bustles, and puffed sleeves,

Maud would open the pages of *Godey's* to survey gorgeous hand-tinted fashion plates, complete with sewing instructions. The fashion pages were followed by the literary treats – short stories and serials, which the young Maud devoured, and sheet music, equally useful to her since she was learning to play the organ. Popular fiction in these magazines thus permeated the everyday world of female fashion and accomplishments. However, *Godey's* was also Montgomery's window into the global world of writing; she remembered some of the stories years and decades later. This popular and expensive magazine, published in Philadelphia from 1830 to 1898, featured such pre-eminent American writers as Edgar Allan Poe, Henry Wadsworth Longfellow, and Ralph Waldo Emerson. It was from *Godey's* that Montgomery clipped "The Fringed Gentian" when she was just nine years old; this poem, which she pasted in her writing portfolio, gave her more inspiration than "all Milton's starry splendor" (22 Nov. 1926, *Selected Journals* 3, 316). She'd forgotten the author's name but never forgot the message: "climb / The Alpine path" and "write upon its shining scroll / A woman's humble name." These lines became the motto of her career; she would use the metaphor of the "Alpine path" as the title of her autobiography.[6] The magazine was undeniably a formative influence as well as a prototype for structural and emotional elements of *Anne of Green Gables*.

Montgomery was also culling tidbits from *Godey's* advice columns, advertisements, caricatures, jester's pages, fashion pages, and poetry, just as she collected in her scrapbooks personal mementos such as cards, invitations, clippings, ribbons, fashion plates, fabrics (including a piece of her yellow garter), and even hair. Notebook and scrapbook were the tools of her trade: "When I come across an idea for story or poem – or rather when an idea for such comes across me, which seems the better way to put it – I at once jot it down in my notebook," she explained to Ephraim Weber. "Weeks, months, even *years* after, when I want an idea to work up I go to the notebook and select one that suits my mood or magazine" (28 June 1905, *Green Gables Letters* 35–36).[7] She rarely bothered to identify the context or the name of the magazine from which she'd drawn an idea. Yet a careful reading of the issues of *Godey's* published in 1892 and 1893 indicates that the periodical provided a treasure trove of plot ideas and images to be used in writing *Anne of Green Gables*.

Perusing *Godey's* February health column, for instance, Montgomery would have read: "Among the most frightful diseases, and one which attacks young children without a moment's notice, is croup." The column constituted a how-to manual for the mother as heroic saviour of her ill child: "Then it is that a mother, while waiting for a physician, may be able to save the life even of her little one" (Phillips 177). *Voilà*! A perfect scenario for Anne, who saves the life of Diana's little sister by administering ipecac. Anne recalls the instructions, "Give syrup of ipecac in small doses, every five minutes, until vomiting is induced" (Phillips 178), while she orders Mary Joe to heat up hot water: "Cloths wrung out in hot water and applied to the chest will give great relief"(178). The magazine thus became intertwined with the notebook composition of *Anne*.

Providing a precedent for Matthew's death, Marian Reeves's story "Eve of St. John: A Midsummer Day's Dream," which appeared in the June 1892 issue, describes the sudden death of the heroine's father during a transatlantic journey. The story dwells on the heroine's sense that the death can be attributed to her father's discovery of a bank failure: "But Madge knew he had gotten his death-blow from the latest American paper, … a paper lightly opened, and which contained the latest particulars of the great bank failure, sweeping clean away the fortune he had meant to leave his child" (503). This economic theme anticipates the manner of Matthew Cuthbert's demise in *Green Gables*. Matthew has a heart attack when he reads of the failure of the Abbey Bank in the newspaper, an event that also echoed the collapse of the Bank of Prince Edward Island in 1883. These ideas for possible plots were likely recorded in Montgomery's notebook in 1892, presumably alongside the reference she jotted down in her notebook that year concerning the orphan girl Ellen Macneill.

Like the interlacing strands of Anne's flaming braid, Montgomery's personal memories were also intertwined with her reading. "Made Austin awfully mad in school to-day," the eighteen-year-old noted in her journal in February 1893. She'd written the ditty "The Boy With the Auburn Hair," mocking her red-topped schoolmate Austin Laird (1876–1962), who'd made her scream in class when he punched her in the side. For weeks the two foes ignored each other, and when he was anxious to make up ("This little girl and I are old friends," he said), she treated him with lofty disdain, refusing to sit with him in school (17 Feb. and 25 April 1893, *Selected Journals* 1, 88, 89). This real-life tempest in the school teapot, which lasted from February to late April, inspired the episode of Anne's feud with Gilbert Blythe, which begins when Gilbert refers to the redheaded heroine as "carrots."

Coincidentally, just a few months after her tussle with "Cavendish Carrots," as Maud had nicknamed her favourite enemy, Austin, a silly mock rhyme on the theme of a red-haired woman was published on *Godey's* jester's page. The piece bore the intriguing and prescient title "To Anne":

They said

Her hair was red.

To me it was pure gold,

A-blush, because it did enfold

A face and neck so fair...

And yet they* said

Her hair was red.

* The Women

(Lampton, "To Anne" 450)

Although her notebooks are no longer extant, there is evidence to suggest that Montgomery had clipped this ironic ode "To Anne" into her notebook, presumably in proximity to "The Boy with the Auburn Hair," her own barbed ode to "Cavendish Carrots." Was it, perhaps, the disjunction between the flowery perspective of the speaker and the refrain "Her hair was red" that caused her to conceive Anne, a romantic with a mundane head of hair? It seems too much of a coincidence that on the same jester's page, there appeared a joke, concerning a quarrelling couple, in which the woman refuses to reconcile with her husband by saying, "No; my feelings have been injured beyond repair" (Lampton, "No Time for a Joke" 450). The remark, and the situation, recall Anne's melodramatic refusal to heal the breach after Gilbert pokes fun at her carroty hair, and her delight in indulging clichéd feeling: "Gilbert Blythe has hurt my feelings *excruciatingly*, Diana" (157).

There was a decade-long hiatus during which less material appears to have been added to the treasure chest of Montgomery's notebooks. During those years, she was busy teaching school, attending college, and working as a newspaper woman,[8] experiences that would be worked into the *Anne* sequels but were less important for *Anne of Green Gables*. In 1903, however, several important new elements were added to the mix that would eventually result in *Anne of Green Gables*.

"Lucy Ann" (1903)

In July 1903, the mailman Mr. Crewe, whose long white beard and kind eyes are reminiscent of Matthew's in the novel, delivered to the Cavendish Post Office the current issue of *Zion's Herald*, a Boston Methodist magazine to which Montgomery was a regular contributor of short stories. It contained her own short story "The Little Three-Cornered Lot," as well as a story that would have made her pause, given that its title was the name of her own grandmother: J. L. Harbour's "Lucy Ann."[9] Like "Charity Ann," the story "Lucy Ann," although not mentioned in Montgomery's journals, served as yet another formula model for *Anne of Green Gables*, this time energizing the growth of a unique character. In particular, the relationship between Lucy Ann and her adoptive mother, Miss Calista May, anticipates the emotional complexity of the mother-daughter bond that slowly develops between Anne Shirley and Marilla Cuthbert, which contributed a persistent means for narrative tension and resolution in *Anne*.

Meet Lucy Ann Joyce: red-haired and freckled, the twelve-year-old "a-goin' on to thirteen" is on holidays from the workhouse in the city. Like Anne Shirley, this protagonist, alert and lively and different, animates the plot. Like *Anne of Green Gables*, this orphan's story begins with a memorable buggy ride: Miss Calista May, a "very prim-looking maiden lady" like Marilla, "narrow" and "rigid" in the beginning of the novel, picks her up at the country train station. On the way home, the city girl who's never been to the country begins to rejoice at the rural sights: "Oh, just see them lovely flowers in that fence corner! Ain't they *sweet*" (956); she rejoices at the sight of the corn and even ordinary apples. Like Anne, who thrills at the vision of white apple blossoms and the purple twilight of the sunset on her first ride with Matthew, Lucy Ann speaks in emphatic italics: "Oh, do see that *beau*-tee-ful bird" (956). Lucy Ann is poor: her straw hat is cheap, its blue ribbon faded, as is her dress, but she holds a Japanese fan as a proud talisman. "She's a humly little thing, with that red hair and all them freckles," Miss Calista muses to a neighbour, and yet admits that there was "something kind o' likeable about her" (957). "I guess I can stand it for three weeks even if she does keep the house in a good deal of a muss. Of course, I can't expect a child to keep things just so, speshly a half-heather" (957). Again like Anne, Lucy Ann is "a born lover of nature," who gathers wildflowers and enjoys wading in the brook at the foot of the orchard (957). And just as Marilla warms toward Anne, so "Miss Calista's not very tender heart warmed toward the forlorn little orphan" (957). Her "unwonted gentleness" signals her own growth as a person (957). When Lucy Ann saves the life of her benefactress, Miss May, in a manner similar to the way in which Anne saves the life of Minnie May, the story ends with Miss May's happy decision to adopt her. The final sentence captures the triumphant resolution: "Lucy Ann said nothing, but she ran and hid her face on Miss Calista's pillow, and they kissed each other for the first time" (957). The author, Jefferson Lee Harbour (1857–1931) of Dorchester, Massachusetts, was a writer of short stories and was on the staff of the *Youth's Companion*, a magazine to which Montgomery contributed stories. Many years later Montgomery recalled having read his stories.[10] Today, like Mary Maitland, he has dropped into oblivion, except for a few of his stories that are anthologized by an evangelical Christian organization.

In Maitland's "Charity Ann," the formula consisted of reconstituting a home for the orphan through the sudden and implausible re-emergence of a long-lost relative. The lonely orphan recovers a place in the biological family, a popular fantasy Montgomery used in several short stories prior to *Green Gables*.[11] In "Lucy Ann," however, Montgomery found a more intriguing resolution in which the orphan finds an adoptive parent who is unrelated but benefits from the match, a resolution Montgomery deployed in short stories as well as in *Green Gables*.[12] In her book *Little Strangers: Portrayals of Adoption and Foster Care in America, 1850–1929*, Claudia Nelson notes that post-Victorian orphan stories undergo a shift in emphasis. In stories of the Victorian period, the benefit for the adopting family is usually economic; for example, the orphan works as a hired hand or performs household tasks. In later stories, the benefit is more likely to be emotional (5). In both Maitland's and Harbour's stories the orphan girl has to earn the adoption by providing a service, whereas *Anne of Green Gables* announces the shift noted by Nelson: clumsy at household tasks, Anne actually talks herself into staying at Green Gables, bewitching Matthew (and Marilla) and awakening their emotions.

Orphan stories were as plentiful in the mass media magazines as the whitewashed shells on the Cavendish beach, but is there a text of origin, an *ur-text*, for these Ann magazine stories? One likely candidate is James Whitcomb Riley's *Little Orphant Annie* (1885), a popular nursery rhyme poem:

Little Orphant Annie's come to our house to stay,

An' wash the cups an' saucers up, an' brush the crumbs away, ...

An' make the fire, an' bake the bread, an' earn her board-an'-keep.

(1169)[13]

The Hoosier dialect poem was based on the life of Mary Alice (Allie) Smith (1850–1924), a girl orphaned at age ten during the American Civil War. Smith found a home as a servant in the Riley household in Greenfield, Indiana, in the winter of 1862. She told the children tales of elves, witches, and goblins. Somehow her name, Allie (from Alice) morphed to Annie during typesetting, but Allie Smith was seventy years old before finding out that she was little orphan Annie, the model for the famous poem! Given that the popular poem spawned numerous spin-offs, it is possible that it sparked several "Ann" orphan stories, such as "Charity Ann" and "Lucy Ann." No doubt the poet Maitland would have been familiar with Riley's poem. Of course, the name Ann, with or without an "e," was (and remains) extremely popular: Montgomery's own grandmother and stepmother had "Ann" for a middle name. Anne's insistence on the "e," however, demands her distinction from the more common name. Just as Montgomery's close friend Nora Lefurgey called Maud by the nickname "Maude" with an "e" (Montgomery and Lefurgey 20), so the "e" in Anne's name is like a personal code, reflecting the vision of L. M. Montgomery that transcends formula writing.

The omnipresence of these formula adoption stories in the late Victorian era and the proliferation of "Ann" magazine stories, in particular, undermine the arguments of those scholars who see *Anne of Green Gables* as too narrowly influenced by one novel: the best-selling *Rebecca of Sunnybrook Farm*. Published in September 1903 by Philadelphia-born author Kate Douglas Wiggin, also known as Mrs. Riggs, this children's classic was made into a silent movie starring Mary Pickford in 1917. With her pink parasol in hand, her black hair and glowing eyes, Rebecca Rowena Randall is poised to win over her Aunt Miranda, a thin, spare New England spinster living in Riverboro, Maine. Although the similarities are striking, a good many of them can, in fact, be traced to earlier sources and formula genres from which both writers obviously drew.[14] Moreover, the same cultural and historical environment accounts for a number of parallels (Careless 143–74). Period laundry techniques (such as boiling of fabrics in harsh soaps which faded dyes and shrank clothing) explain the stock wording (faded, ugly, worn). Wincey (the fabric worn by Anne and by Tommy in J. M. Barrie's novel *Tommy and Grizel*) was cheap material used in clothing for the poor. The fashion in hairstyles dictated long hair for girls with either one or two braids.

Had Montgomery read Wiggin's novel? Though she did refer to Wiggin's other fiction in a letter to G. B. Macmillan on 7 April 1904 (Careless 157–58), she never mentioned *Rebecca of Sunnybrook Farm*, nor was the book in her personal library. Yet it's safe to assume that she was aware of the novel: the opening of *Rebecca* (Wiggin, "Rebecca and the Stage-Driver" 1566–67) was excerpted in *Zion's Herald* (Dec. 1903), in which Montgomery's work regularly appeared;[15] a rave review and a summary of Wiggin's novel appeared in the issue of the *Delineator* (Feb. 1904) that also contained Montgomery's story "The Promise of Lucy Ellen." According to the *Delineator*, "Rebecca with her quaint ways and vivid imagination, should find life almost unbearable when transplanted into a household of commonplace people. The story is told in Mrs. Riggs's happiest vein" (Starr 307). Since Montgomery joined the Cavendish Literary Society Book Committee at about this time, she may well have placed a purchase order for the novel for the library, although *Rebecca* was just one of many juvenile books being positively reviewed by the magazines she read.

In comparing the two novels, the Canadian literary critic T. D. MacLulich perhaps put it best: "Montgomery has done more than imitate Wiggin's successful formula. She has improved on her model" (11).[16] What struck me when I read *Rebecca* was not the formulaic parallels but the differences. Rebecca, a budding author who is forever writing poetry, is in many ways closer to that other Montgomery heroine, Emily, than she is to Anne. Moreover, Rebecca is a model housekeeper whose story is laden with morals. Consider a typical scene, in which she leads Church congregation in prayer: "As 'dove that to its window flies', her spirit soared towards the great light, dimly discovered at first, but brighter as she came closer to it. … this is surely the most beautiful way for the child to find God" (Wiggin, *Rebecca of Sunnybrook Farm* 177). Pious passages such as this one became increasingly less popular in the course of the twentieth century. Ironically, *Anne of Green Gables*, though written by a Sunday School teacher and future minister's wife, is a much more secular and subversive text. In fact, the comparison of *Anne* with *Rebecca* puts in relief Montgomery's literary innovations. The "e" in Anne's name stands for the heroine's exuberant irreverence that dares to confront the powerful Mrs. Rachel Lynde in a standoff: "You are a rude, impolite, unfeeling woman" (*Anne of Green Gables* 112). The "e" stands for emotion and energy: the heroine's amazing capacity for love and life that changes people, communities, and readers. The "e" also stands for Eros, the pagan nature worship and sensuous romantic friendships that animate the novel. And finally, the "e" stands for her élan in transforming the prosaic into poetry, the formulaic into art, the fashionable into personal style – a creative gift the heroine shares with her creator. All of these seem to account for the novel's popularity across a remarkable time span and diversity of cultures.

Anne of Green Gables, in turn, would help shape the shared structure of early twentieth-century orphan novels, such as Jean Webster's *Daddy-Long-Legs* (1912) and Eleanor Porter's *Pollyanna* (1913), a structure that American writer Claudia Mills has identified in her study "Children in Search of a Family: Orphan Novels through the Century" as "the effervescent, bubbly orphan rushing pell-mell into her new home, compelling cold hostile spinsters to love her in spite of themselves" (Mills 231).[17] Of course, the effervescent orphan is a close relative of the many orphans in nineteenth-century fiction cast in the tradition of the innocent, romantic child. Charles Dickens's David Copperfield and Oliver Twist survive in a corrupt world with their moral integrity intact. Mark Twain's Huckleberry Finn and Tom Sawyer became the symbol for the orphan's unfettered freedom and a powerful vehicle for social satire in America's Gilded Age. The early literature on orphan girls was steeped in moral correctness: Goody Two-Shoes (1766), for example, is a lover of books who becomes a schoolteacher. By the mid-nineteenth century, there were many best-selling novels featuring religious orphans, for example, Ellen in Susan Warner's *The Wide Wide World* (1850), and Gertie in Maria Cummins's *The Lamplighter* (1854). The orphan girl is unlikely to be conventionally pretty, but she has strength of character. Charlotte Brontë's Jane Eyre (1847), plain but passionate, defies vicious relatives and institutional authorities; Alice Hegan Rice's rebellious Lovey Mary (1903) is far from amiable but takes responsibility for a little boy. No matter that Maud may not have read all of these texts; she had imbibed the literary and popular orphan literature of the era and was able to both mimic and transform it.[18] At the same time, *Anne of Green Gables* is also a deeply personal text.

From Sunshine Girl to "Real-Life" Character

"Oh, if mother had only lived," thirty-year-old Maud Montgomery sobbed to herself on 2 January 1905, just a few months before writing *Anne of Green Gables* (*Selected Journals* 1, 300). In part, the story of the little orphan girl Anne was born out of her own sense of being orphaned, having lost her mother at barely twenty-two months of age, and having been deserted by her father, who lived in western Canada with his new family. By the time Montgomery wrote the novel, she had been an orphan and a "charity child" for virtually all her life. Montgomery idealized her parents, in particular her father, and dedicated *Anne of Green Gables* to their memory. In the same January of 1905, when Montgomery was going through a period of belated and acute mourning for her childhood loss, *The Sunday School Advocate* – a New York newspaper that published Montgomery's stories – tried to cheer its readers by serializing Louise Baker's "The Major's Sunshine." It was the heartwarming illustrated story of a little girl who loses her parents but whose happy disposition and glorious crown of yellow hair win her an adoptive father and her name – Sunshine. Going on four at the start of the serial, she develops over a period of eleven years into a young lady, the Major's pride and joy. "The Major's Sunshine" reads like a blueprint for the serial Montgomery was planning to write that spring. She had a way of healing herself through dreaming up and writing "sunshine stories," and after a hard and long winter during which she had suffered from the blues – feeling hopeless, lonely, restless, and depressed; trapped in the kitchen with the homestead buried under mountains of snow – she was in need of a pick-me-up. Perhaps prompted by "The Major's Sunshine," she returned to her notebooks in the spring. There she found not only the kernel for the original plot idea for *Anne* – that is, the note regarding the arrival of a girl who was supposed to have been a boy – but also the recipes for the Ann magazine stories, "Charity Ann" and "Lucy Ann." Eureka! Deeply indebted to the formula fiction she had read from girlhood on, the novel was the product of an intriguing variety of Canadian and American and British sources. But the inspired novel also allowed Montgomery to make Anne a "real-life" girl by inserting herself, her own locale, and psychological complexity into the narrative.

With the Macneill orchard suddenly bursting into life that May, bringing intense joy and exuberance after a hard winter, Montgomery made the novel a glorification of spring. In *Anne*, she pictured her own renewed sense of optimism and hope. Steeped in the ordinary world of Avonlea, the novel was a wish-fulfill-ment dream for the author. She tapped the memories of old days, injecting into the novel her own nostalgia and sweet pain: her love of nature and love of home, her intimate "bosom friendships," and her experience as a "charity child." She knew the pins and pricks of small-town society inside and out – she had fought her own battles with her favourite school enemies, had observed Grandfather Macneill tossing barbs around the kitchen table, and had recorded the debates in the Literary Society. In her fiction she combined her keen observations with the oral storytelling tradition of her Scottish and Maritime heritage to craft witty repartees, finely nuanced dramatic irony, and brilliant barbs excoriating traditional authority. Her dialogues crackle with the snappy wit of a keen in-telligence. They have the ring of truth. And it comes as no surprise that her trajectory as a literary portrait painter of small-town life would lead straight to Margaret Atwood, Alice Munro, Margaret Laurence, Kat Lawson, and Kit Pearson, to name but a few of the renowned Canadian women writers and social satirists who were influenced by Montgomery.

What was innovative and what made Anne a lively character was precisely her lack of piety, her pagan pleasure seeking, her sorcery in transforming her community, and her rousing passion as a flame bearer of optimism and hope. It was a novel to chase away the blues – with a vengeance. Indeed, with its non-traditional family set-up – a brother-and-sister couple adopting a child – the novel also presented a way of repairing and reconstructing, in new ways, the family and community that was increasingly under siege during the Edwardian era, when images of cars, motorboats, and phonographs were first beginning to intrude and then to dominate the global advertisement culture. In comparison with the earlier magazine Anns, this particular novel about a redheaded girl orphan transcended its formulaic antecedents to become iconic. This transcen-dence happened because Montgomery was a consummate literary writer with a powerful sense of style and humour, as her journals also testify; she had reached the apex of a long apprenticeship.

Finally, Montgomery created a microcosm, in *Anne*, of her composition struggles – her relentless mining of popular material for a sense of dramatic and romantic situation, along with a comic view of her own ambitions for a grander literary stature. By making the formula her own, in fact, by transforming it from the inside out, Montgomery came into her own. The story of how *Anne of Green Gables* came about is really the story of Montgomery's own liberation as a writer, as the novel embodied what Cawelti calls "the personal vision of the creator" in more ways than one. She had dared to stray from the rutted road of formula success and brought herself into the story with her emotions, dreams, and ambitions. After receiving her acceptance letter from her publisher L. C. Page in Boston, she noted in her journal on 16 August 1907: "The dream dreamed years ago in that old brown desk in school has come true at last after years of toil and struggle. And the realization is sweet – almost as sweet as a dream!" (*Selected Journals* 1, 331). It was a dream that would be shared by millions of readers the world over, making the story of A-n-n-e spelled with an "e" an unprecedented twentieth-century classic.

WORKS CITED

Baker, Louise R. "The Major's Sunshine." Drawings by W. B. Davis. *The Sunday School Advocate* 7 Jan. 1905: 1–3.

Bolger, Francis W. P. *The Years Before 'Anne': The Early Career of Lucy Maud Montgomery, Author of 'Anne of Green Gables.'* Halifax: Nimbus, 1991.

Careless, Virginia A. S. "L. M. Montgomery and Everybody Else: A Look at the Books." *Windows and Words: A Look at Canadian Children's Literature in English.* Ed. Aïda Hudson and Susan-Ann Cooper. Ottawa: U of Ottawa P, 2003. 143–74.

Cawelti, John G. *Adventure, Mystery, and Romance: Formula Stories as Art and Popular Culture.* Chicago and London: U of Chicago P, 1976.

Classen, Constance. "Is *Anne of Green Gables* an American Import?" *Canadian Children's Literature* 55 (1989): 42–50.

Dawson, Janis. "Literary Relations: Anne Shirley and Her American Cousins." *Children's Literature in Education* 33.1 (March 2002): 29–51.

Epperly, Elizabeth R. *The Fragrance of Sweet-Grass: L. M. Montgomery's Heroines and the Pursuit of Romance.* Toronto: U of Toronto P, 1992.

———. "Visual Drama: Capturing Life in L. M. Montgomery's Scrapbooks." *The Intimate Life of L.M. Montgomery.* Ed. Irene Gammel, Toronto: U of Toronto P, 2005. 189–209.

Gammel, Irene, ed. *The Intimate Life of L.M. Montgomery.* Toronto: U of Toronto P, 2005.

Harbour, J. L. "Lucy Ann." *Zion's Herald* 29 July 1903: 956–57.

Hardy, Albert H. "Godey's Past and Present." *Godey's Lady's Book* 125 (1892): 363–68.

Lampton, W. J. "No Time for a Joke." *Godey's Lady's Book* 127 (Oct. 1893): 450.

———. "To Anne." *Godey's Lady's Book* 127 (Oct. 1893): 450.

MacLulich, T. D. "L. M. Montgomery and the Literary Heroine: Jo, Rebecca, Anne, and Emily." *Canadian Children's Literature* 37 (1985): 5–17.

Maitland, Mary Ann. *Autumn Leaves.* Toronto: W. Briggs, 1907.

———. "Looking Backward." *The St. Mary's Journal* 6 Mar. 1919: 1. Archives of Ontario, Toronto.

———. "Charity Ann. Founded on Facts." *Godey's Lady's Book* 124 (Jan. 1892): 70–73.

———. *God Speed the Truth: A Little Volume of Cheerful Canadian Verse.* Toronto: Hunter Rose, 1919.

Mills, Claudia. "Children in Search of a Family: Orphan Novels through the Century." *Children's Literature in Education* 18.4 (1987): 227–39.

Montgomery, L. M. *The Alpine Path: The Story of My Career.* 1917. Markham: Fitzhenry and Whiteside, 1997.

———. *Anne of Green Gables.* 1908. Ed. Cecily Devereux. Peterborough: Broadview, 2004.

———. *The Annotated Anne of Green Gables.* Ed. Wendy E. Barry, Margaret Anne Doody, and Mary E. Doody Jones. New York: Oxford UP, 1997.

———. *Emily of New Moon.* 1923. Toronto: McClelland and Stewart, 1989.

———. "The Girl in the Red Scarf." *The Sunday School Advocate* July 1905. L. M. Montgomery Magazine Clippings. Confederation Centre of the Arts, PEI.

———. *The Green Gables Letters: From L. M. Montgomery to Ephraim Weber, 1905–1909.* Ed. Wilfrid Eggleston. Ottawa: Borealis, 2001.

———. *Akin to Anne: Tales of Other Orphans.* Ed. Rea Wilmshurst. Toronto: McClelland and Stewart, 1992.

———. "My Friend's Home." Bolger 98–101.

———. Letter to Penzie Macneill dated 3 Nov. 1890. Bolger 96–97.

———. "The Little Three-Cornered Lot." *Zion's Herald* 29 July 1903: 954–55.

———. "The Osbornes' Christmas." *Zion's Herald* 16 Dec. 1903: 1604–05.

———. *The Selected Journals of L.M. Montgomery.* 5 vols. Ed. Mary Rubio and Elizabeth Waterston. Toronto: Oxford UP, 1985–2004.

———. Unpublished Journals. Handwritten. L. M. Montgomery Collection, University of Guelph Archives.

Montgomery, L. M. and Nora Lefurgey. *The Diary of L. M. Montgomery and Nora Lefurgey.* *The Intimate Life of L. M. Montgomery.* Ed. Irene Gammel. 18–87.

Nelson, Claudia. *Little Strangers: Portrayals of Adoption and Foster Care in America, 1850–1929.* Bloomington and Indianapolis: Indiana UP, 2003.

Nodelman, Perry. "Progressive Utopia, Or, How to Grow Up Without Growing Up." *Such a Simple Little Tale: Critical Responses to L. M. Montgomery's "Anne of Green Gables."* Ed. Mavis Reimer. Metuchen, NJ: Scarecrow, 1992. 29–38.

Phillips, Olivia E. "Advice from Everywhere, II. Care of Children." *Godey's Lady's Book* 124 (Feb. 1892): 177–78.

Radway, Janice A. *A Feeling for Books: The Book-of-the-Month Club, Literary Taste, and Middle-Class Desire.* Chapel Hill: U North Carolina P, 1997.

Reeves, Marian C. L. "Eve of St. John: A Midsummer Day's Dream." *Godey's Lady's Book* 124 (June 1892): 503–505.

Riley, James Whitcomb. "Little Orphant Annie." 1885. *The Complete Works of James Whitcomb Riley.* Indianapolis: Bobbs-Merrill, 1916. 1169–72.

Starr, Laura B. "Among the Newest Books." *The Delineator* Feb. 1904: 305–08.

Swift, Lindsay. *Literary Landmarks of Boston.* Boston: Houghton Mifflin, 1922.

Wiggin, Kate Douglas. *Rebecca of Sunnybrook Farm.* 1903. New York: Puffin, 1994.

———. "Rebecca and the Stage-Driver." *Zion's Herald* 9 Dec. 1903: 1566–67.

Willoughby, John H. *Ellen.* Charlottetown, PEI: n.p., 1995.

Wilmshurst, Rea. "L. M. Montgomery's Use of Quotations and Allusions in the *Anne* Books." *Canadian Children's Literature* 56 (1989): 15–45.

NOTES

1   This chapter is based on research conducted for my book, *Looking for Anne of
Green Gables: The Story of L.M. Montgomery and Her Literary Classic* (Toronto: Key
Porter, 2008).

2   Montgomery identifies the girl's name
on 27 January 1911, *Selected Journals* 2,
40. See also Willoughby's *Ellen* for a
biographical study of Ellen Macneill.

3   There has been an intensive preoccupation
with the literary influences on *Anne* (e.g.,
Careless 143–74, Dawson 29–51, Classen 42–50, Epperly, *Fragrance passim*,
MacLulich 5–17, Wilmshurst 15–45),
but the formula writing has remained
unexplored.

4   Compare with the description of Montgomery's Anne Shirley: "Mrs. Thomas
said I was the homeliest baby she ever
saw, I was so scrawny and tiny and nothing but eyes" (89); see also the description
of Rebecca in Kate Douglas Wiggin's
Rebecca of Sunnybrook Farm: "She ain't no
beauty – her face is all eyes" (33). Obviously, both authors drew on the same
formula of the starved waif.

5   Wiggin's Rebecca claims, "Hannah and
I haven't done anything but put babies
to bed at night" (8), just as twins and
triplets are discussed in the novel (10).
It is significant that fans later expected
Montgomery to be the mother of twins;
it was obviously a formula in this type of
literature, symbolizing the unfair work-
load of the apprenticed orphan.

6   She cites and discusses this poem on several occasions: see *Alpine Path* 10, 95, and
Emily of New Moon 305. *Godey's Lady's
Book* was founded in 1830 by Louis A.
Godey (1804–1878) of Philadelphia, and
edited by Mrs. Sarah J. Hale (1788–1879),
who boosted its literary contributions;
for more detail see, for instance, Hardy,
"Godey's Past and Present," 363–68.

7   See also Epperly, "Visual Drama"
189–209, for a detailed discussion of
Montgomery's scrapbooking practices.

8   When she didn't live in Cavendish, she
taught in Bideford (1894–95), Belmont
(1896–97), and Lower Bedeque (1897–
98), all regions of Prince Edward Island,
with two brief stints in Halifax, where
she attended Dalhousie College (1895–
96), as well as working for six months
as a newspaperwoman at the *Daily Echo*
(1901–1902).

9   Montgomery's "The Little Three-Cornered Lot" is the story of the Swift children who, with the help of Jim, transform
an infertile piece of land into a beautiful
garden; since she owned a copy of this issue, it is safe to assume that Montgomery
would have read Harbour's story.

10 For a brief notation on Harbour, see
Swift 30; see also Montgomery, 29 Nov.
1910, *Selected Journals* 2, 29; see also editors' note, *Selected Journals* 2, 409.

11 Several of Montgomery's orphan stories
– including "Why Not Ask Miss Price"
(1904), 89–91; "Millicent's Double"
(1905), 143–53; "The Fraser Scholarship" (1905), 177–85; "Her Own People"
(1905), 187–97; and "Penelope's Party
Waist" (1904), 155–64 – end with the
happy reunion of separated family members; these stories are collected in *Akin to
Anne: Tales of Other Orphans*.

12 See, for instance, Montgomery's "Charlotte's Ladies" (1911), in *Akin to Anne:
Tales of Other Orphans* 237–50. Like
Anne, Charlotte has difficulty being adopted because she is freckled.

13 Riley's *Little Orphant Annie* (1885) in-
spired Harold Gray's 1924 comic strip
Little Orphan Annie, as well as the 1918
Raggedy Ann Doll (a combination of
Little Orphant Annie and Riley's *Raggedy
Man*); Gray's *Little Orphan Annie* became
the Broadway musical *Annie* in 1977.

14 See, for instance, Classen 42–50 and
   Dawson 29–51, who present similar arguments and marshal much of the same
   evidence, yet without considering the
   possibility that earlier formula sources
   influenced both writers. See also MacLulich 5–17 and Careless 143–74 for more
   discerning comparative approaches. See
   Epperly, *Fragrance* 251, for a discussion of
   an intriguing textual overlap: in quoting
   Emerson to her friend G. B. Macmillan
   on 3 December 1905, Montgomery misquoted him in the same way *Rebecca* had
   misquoted Emerson two years earlier.
   Either Montgomery had copied the mis-
   quotation from *Rebecca* or both authors
   misquoted from a third source, such as
   a popular magazine (which routinely
   quoted poetry).

15 "Rebecca and the Stage-Driver,"
   1566–67, reproduces the conversation in
   which Rebecca and Mr. Cobb discuss the
   number of children in her family (seven),
   as well the housework and responsibility
   for the babies. A week later, Montgomery
   published "The Osbornes' Christmas" in
   Zion's Herald, 1604–05.

16 In its review of *Anne of Green Gables*, the
   American *Outlook* 89 (22 August 1908)
   described Montgomery's novel as "a sort
   of Canadian 'Rebecca of Sunnybrook
   Farm' ... But the book is by no means an
   imitation; it has plenty of originality and
   character" (in *The Annotated Anne of Green
   Gables* 487).

17 See also Nodelman 29–38, who echoes
   Mills's taxonomy, adding that there is
   no suspense or conflict as the novels
   progress; rather, each episode repeats and
   amplifies the preceding episodes (31).

18 In a 20 May 1905 journal entry, Montgomery notes that she has been rereading Dickens's *Pickwick Papers* and *David
   Copperfield* (*Selected Journals* 1, 306).
   Her unpublished journals of April 1904
   indicate that she had reread the Scottish
   novelist James Matthew Barrie's *Tommy
   and Grizel* (1900), a novel in which she
   delighted; Barrie redeveloped some of
   the same themes in his immensely popular *Peter Pan* (1904).

CHAPTER TWO

L. M. Montgomery and Literary Professionalism

E. Holly Pike

In *The Labor of Words*, Christopher P. Wilson argues that in "the three decades following 1885," American writers developed a particular notion of literary professionalism (xi). This notion was, in fact, refined from Victorian ideas of the writer's craft, and was defined as "a later stage within which prose writers ... came to see their craft predominantly as a product of technical expertise rather than inspiration, viewed the market as the primary arbiter of literary value, and were guided principally by an internalized sense of responsibility to their public" (204). Writing at this time became a true profession, "cut loose from its Romantic, aristocratic, or part-time moorings," for "writers and editors now spoke not of an author's 'inner muse' or 'vocation,' but of the value of ritualized routines, careful sounding of the market, and hard work" (3). Wilson quotes George Lorimer, editor of the *Saturday Evening Post* at the turn of the century, who stated that "a man must prepare himself for writing as he would for any profession, by study and practice.... I know of [no profession] that involves more drudgery and hard work during the years of preparation, or that requires more continuous effort to maintain a once-won place with the public" (60).

Of course, market conditions gave impetus to the rise of professionalism. Nelson Lichtenstein points out that "the 1890s produced a score of cheap magazines" (42); Samuel S. McClure, and other syndicators who began distribution at this time, "dramatically expanded the demand for the short story and short essay." Furthermore, the syndication of stories to newspapers across the country forced the price of short fiction "to double what it had been before 1885" (40).

These market changes helped make freelance journalism and fiction writing a remunerative career for professionals able to meet the demands of the market.

These changes had positive and negative effects, and they provide us with a framework for understanding L. M. Montgomery's career, responsiveness to the market, and literary ambitions. Considering the negative effects of this new professional market, Lichtenstein acknowledges that the price of success in this career was that "Professional writers shaped their material for a specific market or a particular editor" (46). Quite often, authors had to write to an editor's specifications (42). Like Wilson, Lichtenstein argues that at this time, "literary professionalism emphasized the skills needed for market success rather than the values traditionally associated with literary endeavor" (47), a tradition in which "a gentleman amateur ... exhibited his talent to his social equals but did not depend upon it for a living" (35). While Montgomery did not necessarily view the market as the primary arbiter of literary value, she certainly prided herself on her technical expertise and compositional discipline. She developed a sense of responsibility to the public, partly fuelled by financial need, which shaped her career once *Anne of Green Gables* had been accepted for publication. At that point, she was clearly a professional in the terms Wilson applies to the period.

However, even before the publication of *Anne of Green Gables*, Montgomery's career in writing romantic and juvenile fiction was equally shaped by the market she could find for her literary wares, and she worked conscientiously at improving and developing as a writer to meet the demands of that market. While she claimed that *Anne of Green Gables* was written "for love, not money" (*Selected Journals* 1, 331), she could not have written such a commercially and critically successful book without her apprenticeship as a freelancer. We can assess the influence of this apprenticeship by analyzing how she initiated and planned her composition, integrated and revised previously used material, and sought a publisher, all practices developed and honed during her career as a freelancer for Canadian and American magazines. Montgomery's achievement in *Anne* is all the more apparent when we view the professional techniques with which she developed the novel and character whose one-hundredth birthday we celebrate with this volume.

The Freelance Career

In both her letters and autobiography, *The Alpine Path*, Montgomery discusses some of her composition practices, all of which rely on organization and regularity. As noted above, the climate of literary professionalism emphasized hard work, study and practice, ritualized writing routines, and the ability to sound the market as well as write to an editor's or magazine's order. Montgomery's development of such professional techniques and composition strategies enabled her success as a writer. Montgomery's organization was exemplified in her use of a notebook, a practice she described to Ephraim Weber, also an aspiring writer, in a letter of 28 June 1905: "When I come across an idea for story or poem – or rather when an idea for such comes across me, which seems the better way to put it – I at once jot it down in my notebook. Weeks, months, often *years* after, when I want an idea to work up I go to the notebook and select one that suits my mood or magazine" (*Green Gables Letters* 35–36). In the same letter, she identified an entry in "an old Halifax notebook" as the source of one of her recently published stories (36), indicating that she had kept notebooks at least since the period of her most recent 1901–02 sojourn in Halifax. The notebook thus embodies an ideal of research as an ongoing activity and illustrates how Montgomery thought about writing as deeply intertwined with the practice of research. When it was time for her to write, she looked in her notebooks for ideas. Because she treated writing as her job, Montgomery developed a routine for it; she set aside a time for writing every day, and continued this practice throughout her career (*Green Gables Letters* 26). By 1901 she was using a typewriter, which she believed "has paid me…. Editors used to growl over my handwriting" (*My Dear* 3). The technology of her composition was clearly important to her.

Since Montgomery also believed that study was an important part of preparation for the profession of writing, when she decided to go to Halifax to attend Dalhousie University for a year, she stated that her attendance would better prepare her for her profession: "I am anxious to spend a year at a real college as I think it would help me along in my ambition to be a writer" (*Selected Journals* 1, 136). Montgomery stressed what those around her might not understand, the importance of "intellectual training" for both her ambitions and hoped-for achievements. We see this lack of understanding when she described the reactions of friends and neighbours to her decision to attend college (*Selected Journals* 1, 143). Her dedication to study went further than formal education, for in her journal entry for 31 December 1898 she stated that "Nearly everything I think or do or say is subordinated to a desire to improve in my work. I study people and events for that, I think and speculate and read for that" (*Selected Journals* 1, 228). This firm belief in study and improvement became the basis of her development of technique.

Montgomery's desire to improve was based on her understanding that her earning potential as a writer was linked to her reputation, which in turn depended on the quality of her work. As early as 21 March 1901, after *Munsey's* acceptance of a poem, she noted with pleasure that "several new magazines have taken my work." In her view, this meant that her work was improving: "I *know* that I am improving in regard to my verses. I suppose it would be odd if I did not, considering how hard I work and study" (*Selected Journals* 1, 258). Continual improvement would enable her to achieve her ambition to have "a recognized place among good workers in my chosen profession" (*Selected Journals* 1, 258), thus ensuring her ability to earn a living. Improvement was thus directly tied to study and financial success. Even earlier in her freelance career, Montgomery explicitly equated her professional reputation with her ability to support herself. In March 1901 she recorded in her journal that she had been cited in an article on poets of Prince Edward Island. This citation in the *Daily Patriot* marked her as "the foremost of the younger school of writers" (*Selected Journals* 1, 257). With this comment, she was noting a significant achievement in a market in which a well-known name increased the saleability of one's work. Recognition as a poet was important because Montgomery wrote and sold verse as prolifically as fiction. By 3 December 1903, she noted the importance of her name and reputation as commodities: "Editors often *ask* me for stories now; my name has been listed in several periodicals as one of the 'well-known and popular' contributors for the coming year, and the Editor of the Pres.[*sic*] Board of Publication in Philadelphia wrote recently to ask for my autographed photo" (*Selected Journals* 1, 290). She said, "I *am* beginning to realize my dreams," and knew that her success as a writer was secure enough to silence those who "sneered at" her ambitions (*Selected Journals* 1, 290). The development of such a reputation and demand for her work placed Montgomery firmly within the professional ranks in her field, something she expressly cultivated.

The clearest indication of Montgomery's success as a freelance writer is the fact that for several years before writing *Anne of Green Gables* she was making a much better living as a writer than she had as a teacher with an annual salary of $180 (*Selected Journals* 1, 143). For instance, in May 1900 Montgomery recorded that in the previous year she had made only $96.88 from her writing (*Selected*

Journals 1, 249), but by December 1900 she claimed that "I'm beginning to make a livable income for myself by my pen" (*Selected Journals* 1, 255), though she did not specify an amount. Her journal recorded some of the amounts she was paid for individual stories and poems during this period. Her letters to Ephraim Weber and G. B. MacMillan also discuss her earnings and achievements. What they reveal is that she was conscious of having a career path to follow, with landmarks along the way, such as getting into certain publications, or reaching a certain level of remuneration: in December 1903 she stated that she made $500 that year. At the end of 1905 she told Weber that she made "*nearly* $600 last year – $591.85 to be exact" (*Green Gables Letters* 27), more than three times her earnings as a teacher ten years earlier.

Montgomery's statement to Weber, that she selected incidents from her notebook to suit her magazine (*Green Gables Letters* 35–36), reveals how fully she had adapted to the demands of the marketplace. She assumed that knowledge of the intended market for her work was just as reasonable a starting point for her daily stint of writing as was her mood or inspiration. Montgomery's process for finding the appropriate market for her verse and fiction, as outlined in her letters, also shows a high level of organization and knowledge. In a letter to MacMillan dated 29 December 1903, she said she had a list of "about 70 different periodicals" to which she sent work. Like a colleague, she offered to share the information with him, "a few in each letter until I have gone through the list" (*My Dear* 3).[1] At the end of the letter she began that process by describing the payment rates, style, and needs of some of the periodicals: "The Congregationalist Boston, Mass. is a religious weekly which pays *very fair* prices for work.... It accepts or rejects promptly and sends a complimentary copy" (4). Montgomery indicated that she received $5 each for two poems published in the *Congregationalist* and $7 each for two thousand-word juvenile stories (4), revealing a market sense of genre value. She revealed similar details about *The Messenger of the Sacred Heart*, *The Youths' Companion* ("the foremost paper of its class in America"), and *The Farm and Fireside* (4–5), showing her carefully researched knowledge of publisher specialization, as well as her pragmatic approach to the process of composition.

Montgomery's breadth of ability as a writer, and skill at adapting to different markets, are evident in the geographic and demographic range of periodicals in which she published. In 1906, she published forty-four stories in twenty-seven magazines, indicating a considerable range of styles and a consistent effort at writing and sending out material. The periodicals in which Montgomery published fiction at this time include Sunday school papers, children's papers, newspapers, religious periodicals, women's magazines, and agricultural papers. For instance, the *Ladies' Journal*, in which she published "A Baking of Gingersnaps" in July 1895,[2] was a Canadian publication aimed primarily at women, containing fiction and verse; household, health, and family advice; patterns for fancy work; and columns aimed at boys and girls. The *Family Herald*, printed in Montreal, in which Montgomery began publishing stories in 1898, was an agricultural paper containing news, fiction and verse, general interest columns, special columns for girls and boys, music, a checkers column, advice, and instructions on crafts. Montgomery published both children's stories, such as "Jen's Device" (15 November 1898), and adult fiction, such as "A Home-Sick Heart" (28 November 1900), in the *Family Herald*. The periodical in which Montgomery published the greatest number of stories was a newspaper, the *Springfield Republican* of Massachusetts, in which she published both romantic fiction (e.g., "A Long Delayed Wedding," 30 March 1902; "The Story of a Camping-Out," 20 July 1902) and more moralistic stories (e.g., "Of Miss Calista's Peppermint," 11 November 1900; "The Girls' Impromptu Party," 12 September 1906).

The type of publication deeply influenced Montgomery's choice of subject, style, and point of view, especially when she wrote for several children's periodicals, such as *East and West* of Toronto and *Golden Days for Boys and Girls* of Philadelphia. *East and West* was published by the Presbyterian Church in Canada. It featured moral tales, serials, Bible lessons, temperance stories, and other material aimed at moral instruction for a young audience. Montgomery's works for *East and West* were mostly very brief stories that contained explicit lessons for the reader, though the paper also published her serial "By Way of the Brick Oven." Although Montgomery published at least nineteen stories in *East and West*, she told Weber that they "only pay $5 per story so I just send them second-rates" (*Green Gables Letters* 46), a statement that illustrates her ability to assess both her own work and the requirements of the publication. More varied in content than *East and West*, each number of *Golden Days* contained several stories, the lead one being illustrated with a lithograph, at least one serial, a cycling column, jokes and puzzles, instructions for various crafts and activities, and, in the Golden Days Club, requests for information and correspondents. The overall tendency of the magazine was instructional, in both the fiction and the nonfiction. Montgomery's stories were published in it between 1896 and 1899. In them, young readers were supposed to learn the importance of being honest, trustworthy, and forthright. Some well-known names of the time were represented in the fiction published, including Horatio Alger, Jr., Sydney Dayre, and Frank H. Converse, so Montgomery's publications in this periodical indicated a certain professional stature. The range of periodicals in which she published reveals her skill at meeting both the needs of editors in different regions and the target audience for different genres.

During her stay in Halifax, in 1901, Montgomery further developed as a professional by undertaking a variety of tasks for the *Daily Echo*, a newspaper for which she was nominally hired as proofreader. She completed quite a variety of assignments for the paper. She had to write up pieces on the wares available at various Halifax merchants for Christmas, to "fake up" society letters from around the province, to complete a serial when the final chapters were misplaced, and to expurgate the ending of another serial, "Under the Shadow," that was running too long.[3] Such a variety of tasks suggests not only a high level of skill, but also a recognition of her professional status by the editor of the paper. As well, it was while working at the *Echo* that Montgomery learned to write under less than ideal conditions, a necessary skill in a professional writer. While she had previously learned to rise early in a cold room and write before teaching school for the day while living in Belmont (*Selected Journals* 1, 168), until living in Halifax she had assumed that "undisturbed solitude was necessary that the fire of genius might burn" (*Selected Journals* 1, 270). However, because she knew that she could not subsist on what the newspaper paid her, she forced herself to write in the office, despite the noise, bustle, and demands on her time. These composing conditions, however, did not affect the quality of what she produced, as shown by the magazines from which she indicated she was receiving acceptances at this point: *The Delineator*; *Smart Set*, which published the poem "To My Enemy" in January 1902 (*Selected Journals* 1, 92); and *Ainslee's*, which also published the poem "Harbor Sunset" in January of that year (490).[4]

Most significantly, through producing the weekly column "Around the Table," consisting of observations on human behaviour and the activities of a fictional household consisting of Theodosia, Aunt Janet, Ted, Polly, and Cynthia (the writer of the column), Montgomery learned to find sufficient material and maintain a consistent voice for sustained production. Sometimes the column contained useful information, as in the column on photography, sometimes fashion tips, and sometimes funny anecdotes. Perhaps because she was under pressure to produce a set amount of material every week, Montgomery began reusing material that she had already used in her magazine fiction.[5] This is significant, if we look forward to *Anne of Green Gables*. In the "Around the Table" column for Monday, 5 May 1902, Montgomery recounted three baking disaster stories that she had recently used in fiction. Ted bakes the mustard-flavoured gingerbread that is the central incident of "Uncle Chatterton's Gingerbread"; Polly is responsible for the saleratus-flavoured icing that is the centre of "Patty's Mistake" (and is later used again in "The Cake That Prissy Made"); and a Methodist parson's wife, Gwennie, is responsible for the liniment cake of "A New-Fashioned Flavoring." While the phrasing was not repeated, the central incidents of the last story, as printed in "Around the Table," remain very similar to the version previously published. The housewife is merely hurrying rather than having a cold, but "her husband had broken the liniment bottle and had poured what remained of its contents into an old empty vanilla bottle. It was just the same color as vanilla" (*Echo* 5 May 1902, 8). The one guest who does eat the cake is assumed to have "thought it was merely some new-fangled flavoring," a slightly slangier version of the title of the story. However, Montgomery did later use some of the same phrasing in *The Alpine Path* when she told the source of the liniment cake story in her own experience. There, she repeated the phrase "its charming mistress" (74) from the "Around the Table" version, as well as the statement that the visiting minister "ate every crumb of his piece of cake. Possibly he imagined it was simply some new-fangled flavouring" (75). Montgomery kept a scrapbook, now in the provincial archives in Charlottetown, Prince Edward Island, which contained all the "Around the Table" columns. It is possible that she mined them, just as she mined her journals, when the request for the story of her career was made (*Selected Journals* 2, 201). The multiple use of the incident, adapted to various stories, shows her willingness and ability to recast material for a variety of purposes.

Montgomery also learned to deal as a professional with the inevitable rejections and the necessary drudgery of her job. Her first rejections pained her: "I flinched, as from a slap in the face." But from them she "learned the first, last, and middle lesson 'Never Give Up'" (*Selected Journals* 1, 261). When she commented on Cavendish envy of her "bits of success" in 1896, very early in her career, she had already accepted rejection as part of the process and wrote that people "do not realize how many disappointments come to one success" (*Selected Journals* 1, 162). Accordingly, she was frank with Weber about the frequency with which stories were rejected and expressed her delight when a twice-rejected story was accepted with a payment in advance of $100 (*Green Gables Letters* 49). Her assumption at this point seems to be that rejection meant only that she had not approached the appropriate market.

Montgomery's understanding of the market, while ensuring her success, led to a rather relentless writing routine that created a sense of drudgery. Her pattern of writing every day, working the way a professional in any field would ("I peg away a couple of hours every day" (*Green Gables Letters* 26)), sometimes became tedious, as Montgomery expressed in her journal entry of 21 March 1901, in which she described herself as having "toiled away industriously this summer and ground out stories and verses." Despite these images of hard labour, she continued, "But oh, I love my work! I love spinning stories and I love to sit by the window of my den and shape some airy fancy into verse" (*Selected Journals* 1, 263). In part, the drudgery seemed to stem from the way in which writing juvenile fiction required a certain mechanical stance:

> I write a lot of juvenile yarns. I like doing these but would like it better if I didn't have to lug a moral into most of them. They won't sell without it. The kind of juvenile story I like to write – and read, too, for the matter of that – is a rattling good jolly one – "art for art's sake" – or rather "fun for fun's sake" – with no insidious moral hidden away in it like a spoonful of jam. But the editors who cater to the "young person" take themselves too seriously for that and so in the moral must go, broad or narrow, as suits the fibre of the particular journal in view. (*Selected Journals* 1, 263)

Expressing a similar feeling in 1906, she wrote to MacMillan that she was completing "a very sensational yarn, written to suit the taste of the journal that ordered it and I don't care much for writing such but they give a good price for it" (*My Dear* 23). These passages reflect Montgomery's sense of the market and need to meet the requirements of a genre and editor rather than write to suit herself. To some extent she saw her job more as supplying a commodity than as expressing herself.

From the composition process itself, Montgomery gleaned a good sense of which works were merely commodities and which were more than that. She claimed to see a difference between potboilers and writing that gave her pleasure. The simple moralistic stories that she wrote for juvenile publications did not give her the same pleasure as the writing of *Anne of Green Gables*, of which she says, "Nothing I have ever written gave me so much pleasure to write.... I wrote it for love, not money – but very often such books are the most successful" (*Selected Journals* 1, 331). The major difference, Montgomery felt, between *Anne* and works she had previously composed was that the heroine "appealed to me, and I thought it rather a shame to waste her on an ephemeral little serial" (72). Her assessment that writing for pleasure was the best road to success echoed W. D. Howells's *Literature and Life*, in which he said, "The best that you can do is to write the book that it gives you the most pleasure to write, to put as much heart and soul as you have about you into it" (20). Since Howells had also experienced the world of journalism, he must have been speaking from personal experience of the frustration of writing to order. Writing for pleasure was a risk, however. Montgomery's claim that she "wrote most of [*Anne of Green Gables*] in the evenings after my regular work was done" reveals an understanding that love may not pay: "I could not afford to take time from my regular work to write it" (*Selected Journals* 1, 330–31).[6] Montgomery did not see how much her literary apprenticeship prepared her for the discipline of writing a great novel, in teaching her both hard work and what sells, and in suggesting to her the elements that distinguish a potboiler from a literary work. Ironically, once Montgomery achieved success with the book she wrote "for love, not money," she was back in the trap of writing to order, because her publisher immediately requested a sequel and her contract committed her to his company for some time to come (*Selected Journals* 1, 331).

ANNE OF GREEN GABLES

For readers accustomed to thinking of *Anne of Green Gables* as a seamless whole, a novel written to delineate the experiences of a particular character, it may not be clear how many incidents in the novel, points of characterization, or even phrases had been used by Montgomery in previous literary and journalistic work. Her skill at adapting the material to its new context was the result of having spent the previous ten years trying to meet the requirements of a variety of editors and audiences. Montgomery accounted for the composition of *Anne* in *The Alpine Path*. There, she recorded *Anne*'s genesis as a planned serial for a Sunday school paper. After looking through her notebook for an idea and choosing "a faded entry, written many years before, … I began to block out the chapters, devise, and select incidents and 'brood up' my heroine" (72). That is, she was following her usual method of composition for magazine fiction. In selecting incidents for the novel, Montgomery chose at least two plot devices originating in her own life – the liniment-flavoured cake that Mrs. Estey made (also used in "Around the Table") and her father jumping on a visitor in the spare room (*Selected Journals* 1, 43). Both earlier appeared as stories in *Golden Days*. She reshaped the stories to make them work as part of a longer single narrative. These reshapings also symbolize the way in which Montgomery adapted her prior composition practices to the task before her.

Chapter 21 of *Anne of Green Gables*, "A New Departure in Flavourings," reworks "A New-Fashioned Flavoring," a typical story of the sort Montgomery wrote for *Golden Days*. By reworking the incident and placing it in a different context, Montgomery changed both the targeted audience and the significance of the incident itself. In the original, the young people of the family, left alone for the day, are forced to entertain the miserly and unsympathetic uncle who could provide them with all the good things they are missing in their relative poverty. Unlike Anne, fifteeen-year-old Ivy is a responsible and competent young woman, but sixteen-year-old brother Edmund is unreliable and a practical joker. The story is clearly structured for a young reader, with primarily short, simple or compound sentences, easy diction, and plenty of dialogue. But in general outline, it is not much different from the liniment cake incident in *Anne of Green Gables*. The young woman makes a layer cake on an occasion when she particularly wants to impress the guest and has a bad cold. The vanilla bottle snatched in a hurry is filled with anodyne liniment, which the baker is unable to smell and therefore accidentally uses for flavouring. While the plot of the story, as it appears in *Golden Days*, is more complex, bringing in the siblings, the family history, and the benefits to be gained by reconciliation, the key incident remains the flavouring accident. Furthermore, some phrases carry over from this version to the *Anne of Green Gables* version. In the *Golden Days* version, "she clapped the layers together with ruby jelly" (352), while in *Anne of Green Gables*, she "clapped it together with layers of ruby jelly" (211). Edmund "helped himself to a generous slice" (352) and Mrs. Allan helped herself "to a plump triangle" (212). Both cakes are fed to the pigs (354, 215). Unlike Anne, however, who regards the event as a tragedy, Ivy snickers at the end of her explanation to Uncle Eugene.

The *Golden Days* story is intended for a juvenile audience and contains an explicit message about the virtue of doing your duty and being honest about your mistakes. Edmund and Ivy are rewarded for having treated their uncle respectfully and for having reacted with good humour to the disaster. There is no such lesson implied in the related chapter of *Anne of Green Gables*. In one sense, it is simply another of the mistakes that distinguish Anne from other girls, mistakes that are rendered comically and left without narrative judgment; in another sense, the scene embodies a learning experience for Anne, since Mrs. Allan tells her not to take things so seriously, but it is not explicitly a lesson for the reader. Rather, it reveals Mrs. Allan to the reader as a kindred spirit. As well, *Anne of Green Gables* is clearly aimed at an older, more sophisticated reader than is *Golden Days*, so the intended "moral" of the incident need not be made explicit, yet Montgomery is successful in creating and selling both versions. This adapted material becomes a pattern for many of Anne's errors, suggesting Montgomery's shift away from a moral tone and toward an interest in internal character development.

Another revision of a previously used incident makes even more explicit the change in Montgomery's treatment of the juvenile market. The other *Golden Days* story based on Montgomery's personal history that is reused in *Anne of Green Gables* is "Our Uncle Wheeler." In this story, two teenage brothers and a friend make a running jump into the spare room bed, landing on their unsuspecting, crusty old uncle. The same incident is reworked for Chapter 19 of *Anne of Green Gables*, "A Concert, a Catastrophe, and a Confession," with Miss Josephine Barry, Diana's crusty old aunt, as the victim. Again, in *Golden Days* the story is explicitly about the requirement that boys be honest and forthright and not harm others. Because the brothers have allowed their uncle to believe that the Winsloe boys, who were also at the house, were the ones who jumped on him, he has threatened to withhold deserved help from Mr. Winsloe. The brothers have not confessed their part in the escapade because they do not want to lose Uncle Wheeler's financial support for college. However, when they reveal their guilt in order to spare Mr. Winsloe, Uncle Wheeler rewards them with an extra gift of cash as well as the expected financial support for their education. Thus the moral is perfectly clear to the young reader.

Some of these details carry over into *Anne of Green Gables*, when Anne honourably refuses to let Diana take the blame for their jump; though she fears the confrontation, she does not want Diana to suffer the loss of music lessons and so confesses to Miss Barry, who becomes a good friend. Like the revised material mentioned above, the narrative places primary importance on the accident as a way of discovering another kindred spirit, allowing a relationship to emerge in the text. The reward is not tangible and immediate as in the *Golden Days* story, but Anne does learn that there are plenty of "kindred spirits" around, even if they are not recognizable at first sight. Again, as in the cake episode, in the context of the novel the lesson is for the character, not for the reader, and if the reader is to take a lesson from the incident, there is no explicit indication that this is so. Thus the incident forms a natural, believable part of a more or less realistic novel instead of forming a contrived, moralistic work of its own, demonstrating Montgomery's skill at adapting material to appeal to different audiences; she used the incident to develop the central character and to show the complexity of social encounters rather than to condescend to teach the reader.

Montgomery's adaptation of other material for *Anne of Green Gables* is equally seamless and effective in the context of the novel. She reworked the plot of "The Gold-Link Bracelet," published in the *Philadelphia Times* in September 1897, in which a girl borrows her aunt's bracelet and loses it only to have it turn up safely later, to form the basis of the amethyst brooch incident in *Anne of Green Gables*. This scene functions to provide a lesson for both Anne and Marilla, promoting their understanding of each other. Adapting them for character enhancement, Montgomery also reused favourite names and character associations, including the names Anne and Gilbert, which she had previously used as the pair of lovers in "Aunt Susanna's Birthday Celebration" (*New Idea Woman's Magazine*, February 1905). She had also previously used the name Josie Pye in "Ida's New Year Cake" (*Days of Youth*, 31 December 1905). The characterization of Mrs. Rachel Lynde reworks material from the story "Lavender's Room," published 11 February 1905 in *East and West*. In the story, "Mrs. Lynde was one of those people who pride themselves on saying just what they think, and who always seem to be thinking unpleasant things" (41). In *Anne of Green Gables*, "Mrs. Rachel prided herself on always speaking her mind" (59), and "was one of those delightful and popular people who pride themselves on speaking their mind without fear or favour" (112). The less attractive trait of "thinking unpleasant things" is dropped to allow Mrs. Lynde to develop into a more sympathetic character in the novel, where extended characterization is required. The conjunction of name and character trait, and the character names mentioned above, may have arisen unconsciously in Montgomery's mind when she was writing *Anne of Green Gables*, or she may have made a conscious decision to reuse these details. The publication of these stories overlapped the writing of *Anne of Green Gables* according to her journal account of the novel's composition, which has her starting in the spring of 1905 (*Selected Journals* 1, 330), though *The Alpine Path* gives spring 1904 (72).

Just as she used material developed for fiction in "Around the Table," Montgomery also adapted for the novel material from her journalistic writing. A version of the comical statement attributed to Anne after her fall from the

Barry roof, "No, Diana, I am not killed, but I think I am rendered unconscious" (222), is attributed to Cynthia in "Around the Table" of 2 January 1902. After a fall, Cynthia thinks, "no, I am not dead, but I am unconscious," and describes the thought ironically as "brilliant" (8). As well, the narrator's comment that "Marilla was as fond of morals as the Duchess in Wonderland" (107) repeats Cynthia's comment about herself in the column of 23 December 1901 (12). Anne's statement in regard to continuing her studies while teaching, "As 'Josiah Allen's wife' says, I shall be 'mejum'" (328), closely repeats Cynthia's advice of 2 November 1901, "As Josiah Allen's wife says, 'Be mejum'" (1). These may well be phrasings that Montgomery used commonly in everyday life, and therefore it would be natural for her to use them in her writing. However, her repeated use of them in the context of both journalism and novel writing shows her awareness of the malleability of content. Montgomery's recycling of these incidents does not indicate a lack of imagination or an undue haste in composition, but an ability to revise and recast material so as to make it serve more than one function – a facility, carefully honed, for making the most of available material. Just as a teacher may approach a subject from various points of view for various levels of students, or a lawyer apply contract law in a variety of instances, the professional writer sees incidents, characters, or descriptions not as peculiar to a certain combination of effects, but capable of being used in new combinations to create new effects.

When Montgomery had finally written her novel, she had to move from the periodical market with which she was familiar into a new field. Her attempts to find a publisher were not initially successful, although she did have rationales for sending the manuscript to the various publishers she tried. The first, Bobbs-Merrill of Indianapolis, she described as a "new firm" who had some recent "best-sellers" (*Selected Journals* 1, 331). Bobbs-Merrill was indeed an innovator in the publishing world of the time, having inaugurated "Pocket Books" in 1905, books "as tall as the ordinary book, narrow enough for the pocket" (Tebbel 510). Bobbs-Merrill's ability to spot a bestseller was demonstrated by its acceptance of Mary Roberts Rinehart's *The Circular Staircase* after five other publishers had rejected it (Tebbel 4). Montgomery's assessment of the firm's strengths was accurate. After her disappointment with the "new firm," Montgomery tried "an old established firm" (*Selected Journals* 1, 331), Macmillan, which in 1893 was building its New York branch, one of the earliest British publishers to set up an American branch (Tebbel 354). Montgomery described Lothrop, Lee and Shepard of Boston, to whom she next sent the manuscript, as a "betwixt and between" firm (*Selected Journals* 1, 331). The predecessor company, Lee and Shepard, had made "standard juvenile literature a specialty" and the merger with Lothrop joined "the two oldest publishers of children's books in America" (Tebbel 274). The company had branched into adult literature early in the twentieth century and had a significant bestseller in Irving Bachellor's *Eben Holden*. Thus Montgomery's assessment fairly described a publisher straddling the worlds of bestsellers and children's books, a position that makes sense for a potential publisher of *Anne of Green Gables*. The Henry Holt Company was a less obvious choice as a publisher of a children's book, but was probably known to Montgomery as the publisher of Anthony Hope's *The Prisoner of Zenda*, an enormous bestseller (Tebbel 313–14).

Ironically, of the Page Company, to which she later sent her manuscript, Montgomery says she knew "absolutely nothing" (*Selected Journals* 1, 331). The company had been formed in 1897 by L. C. Page, who had begun his career in the publishing house of his stepfather, Dana Estes, and like Estes's firm, L. C. Page was "more inclined to popular trade books than literary works" (Tebbel 402). Since Montgomery claimed to know nothing of the Page Company, it is difficult to guess why she chose to send her manuscript to them, unless she had seen other works published by them that seemed to her to appeal to the market she was trying to reach. Carole Gerson identifies Page's "recent publication of books by Charles G. D. Roberts and Bliss Carman" as a factor (52), though their work would be aimed at a different audience. When Montgomery received an offer from L. C. Page, she commented in her journal, "They have given me a royalty of ten percent on the *wholesale* price, which is not generous even for a new writer" (*Selected Journals* 1, 331), an opinion supported by W. D. Howells's statement in *Literature and Life* that a usual royalty would be ten percent of the retail price (13). Although Montgomery's professional knowledge of publishing would not secure her a great contract and would, in fact, land her back in the self-perpetuating cycle of market expectations, Montgomery's adaptation of her prior material signifies both her use of and departure from her freelance writing self.

CONCLUSION

Success had a price. Once *Anne of Green Gables* had been accepted, Montgomery found herself back in the position of having to write to satisfy others, as first the publisher and later the public demanded sequels; in these circumstances her professional methods of composition did not change. When she started work on "the sequel to 'Anne,'" she wrote in her journal, "I have been busy all summer collecting material for it, blocking out chapters, devising incidents and fitting them into each other, and 'brooding up' the characters" (*Selected Journals* 1, 332), the same process by which she approached the intended serial which became *Anne of Green Gables*. Once she had become proficient at the process of writing short fiction, Montgomery realized that with a central idea and character in mind, "[a]ll you have to do is to spread it out over enough chapters to amount to a book" (*Selected Journals* 1, 330). Montgomery's career as a freelance writer of verse and fiction for periodicals forced her to develop the discipline of daily writing, to collect material for later use, to think about the demands of genre and audience, to recast material for multiple purposes, and to match the material to the publisher. Through years of producing both romantic and juvenile fiction for the periodical market, she developed a thorough knowledge of public and editorial taste, as well as a rigorous composition process that allowed her to draw on "plots, incidents, characters and descriptions" that she had collected and sometimes used before (*Selected Journals* 1, 330). Because she had developed such a wealth of material and experience on which to draw, in *Anne of Green Gables* Montgomery was able to create a character and novel that were immediate successes and that testify to the efficacy of her composition process, which she deployed for the rest of her career. Yet *Anne of Green Gables* remains unique in its conceptualization and composition, its ability to please a market and yet transcend time. Drawing on both Montgomery's professionalism and her love for the character, the novel is like the liniment cake. It surprised its baker and consumers, producing unexpected results and revealing a network of kindred spirits all over the globe.

WORKS CITED

Gerson, Carole. "'Dragged at Anne's Chariot Wheels': The Triangle of Author, Publisher, and Fictional Character." *L. M. Montgomery and Canadian Culture*. Ed. Irene Gammel and Elizabeth Epperly. Toronto: U of Toronto, 1999. 49–63.

Howells, W.D. *Literature and Life*. 1902. Port Washington, NY: Kennicat, 1968.

Lichtenstein, Nelson. "Authorial Professionalism and the Literary Marketplace." *American Studies* 19.1 (Spring 1978): 35–53.

Montgomery, L. M. "A New-Fashioned Flavoring." *Anne of Green Gables*. 1908. Ed. Cecily Devereux. Peterborough, ON: Broadview, 2004. 344–56.

———. *Anne of Green Gables*. 1908. Ed. Cecily Devereux. Peterborough, ON: Broadview, 2004.

———. "Aunt Susanna's Birthday Celebration." *New Idea Woman's Magazine* Feb. 1905: 30–31. Rpt. in *Across the Miles: Tales of Correspondence*. Ed. Rea Wilmshurst. Toronto: McClelland and Stewart, 1995. 155–62.

———. "The Cake that Prissy Made." *Congregationalist* 11 July 1903: 59.

———. *The Green Gables Letters from L. M. Montgomery to Ephraim Weber, 1905–1909*. Ed. Wilfrid Eggleston. Toronto: Ryerson, 1960.

———. "The Gold-Link Bracelet." *Philadelphia Times* 26 September 1897: 30.

———. "Ida's New Year Cake." *Christmas with Anne and Other Holiday Stories*. Ed Rea Wilmshurst. Toronto: McClelland and Stewart, 1995. 189–98.

———. "Lavender's Room." *East and West: A Paper for Young Canadians* 3.6 (11 Feb. 1905): 41–42.

———. *My Dear Mr. M.: Letters to G. B. MacMillan from L. M. Montgomery*. Ed. Francis W. P. Bolger and Elizabeth R. Epperly. Toronto: Oxford UP, 1992.

———. "Our Uncle Wheeler." *Anne of Green Gables*. 1908. Ed. Cecily Devereux. Peterborough: Broadview, 2004. 335–44.

———. "Patty's Mistake." *Zion's Herald* 16 April 1902: 494.

———. *Selected Journals*. 5 vols. Ed. Mary Rubio and Elizabeth Waterston. Toronto: Oxford UP, 1985–2004.

———. "Uncle Chatterton's Gingerbread." *What to Eat* January 1902: 26–27. Russell, R.W., D.W. Russell, and Rea Wilmshurst. *Lucy Maud Montgomery: A Preliminary Bibliography*. Waterloo, ON: U of Waterloo Library, 1986.

Tebbel, John. *A History of Book Publishing in the United States, Vol. II: The Expansion of an Industry 1865–1919*. New York: R.R. Bowker, 1975.

Terhune, Albert Payson. *To the Best of My Memory*. New York: Harper and Brothers, 1930.

Wilson, Christopher P. *The Labor of Words: Literary Professionalism in the Progressive Era*. Athens, GA: U of Georgia P, 1985.

Notes

1 This practice is reflected in Montgomery's "The Adventures of a Story," published in the *Philadelphia Times* in September 1897. In it, a young woman who aspires to a career as a writer has an alphabetical list of juvenile publications to which she successively submits her story without success. When the young woman has given up, her friend enters the story in a baking powder contest and wins enough money for the two to take a vacation, and the writer wisely abandons her ambitions, since it is clear that, despite her list, she is not skilled enough to meet the demands of the fiction market.

2 Information on the original publication of Montgomery's short stories and poems is given in R. W. Russell, D. W. Russell, and Rea Wilmshurst, *Lucy Maud Montgomery: A Preliminary Bibliography*.

3 Since there is a discrepancy between the dates that Montgomery recorded in her journal and the publication dates of the story in the newspaper, it is very difficult to say at just what point she began cutting the story. She recorded in her journal entry on 20 May 1902 the comment made by Miss Russell, "That story *Under the Shadow* is the strangest one I ever read. It wandered on, chapter after chapter, for week and never seemed to get anywhere; and then it just finished up in eight chapters, *licketty split*" (*Selected Journals* 1, 281), but the serial did not actually conclude in the *Echo* until 29 May 1902. It was on 4 May 1902 that Montgomery recorded being asked to cut the remainder of the novel, removing about two-thirds by her account (*Selected Journals* 1, 280–81). If we consider her acquaintance's assertion, that the difference is apparent in the last eight chapters, then the publication of Montgomery's expurgated conclusion must have begun on 9 May 1902.

4 Albert Payson Terhune, a contemporary of Montgomery's who was best known for his dog stories and as a reporter for the New York *Evening World*, also claimed to have done freelance work while at his day job in order to make enough money (Terhune 178).

5 Terhune reported having made even more extensive re-use of material in his career than Montgomery did. In *To the Best of My Memory*, he stated that he used "a sketch of Jean Jacques Rousseau" in the series "Fifty Failures Who Made Good," "Fifty Blackguards of History," and "Fifty 'Ifs' That Changed History," with only minor changes from one use to another (106–7). He also recounted repeating plots in his serials (168) and being able to "rewrite old articles and revamp the notes, giving the stuff a slightly different slant" (177).

6 Interestingly, Howells also expressed the opinion that "the fresh thing, the original things, were apt to come from [remote and obscure] places" (69), so that as an editor he was more apt to look closely at such contributions, a factor that might also have influenced other editors and account for Montgomery's success writing from remote Prince Edward Island.

CHAPTER THREE

Anne with Two "G"s: Green Gables and Geographical Identity

Joy Alexander

The history of Prince Edward Island is inextricably bound up with the story of its railroad (see Stevens, Legget). The main line across the Island was completed by 1875, with numerous branch lines gradually added to it. Since initially construction of the railway line was paid for by the mile, contractors built a meandering track. The principal reason why Prince Edward Island entered the Canadian Confederation in 1873 was that entry provided a means of dealing with the crippling debt that resulted, rescuing the independent colony from bankruptcy.

L. M. Montgomery herself had memorable familiarity with the railroad, since a very significant journey in her early life was the three-thousand-mile train journey across Canada she made in 1890, to stay with her father. Aged fifteen, she travelled with her grandfather from Kensington to Summerside to get the ferry: "I never was on a train before but I enjoyed this, my first ride, very much" (*Selected Journals* 1, 26). When they reached the mainland, their onward rail journey took them to Saint John, then to Montreal, and on through Winnipeg to Regina, finally reaching their destination of Prince Albert, Saskatchewan, eight days after leaving Prince Edward Island. She noted in Montreal that the "thronged streets were brilliantly lighted by electricity" (*Selected Journals* 1, 27), as new an experience for her as the train ride, since at that time on the Island only Charlottetown had electricity. This journey was Maud's introduction to the modern world, simultaneous with her coming-of-age.

It is also by train that eleven-year-old Anne Shirley makes her entrance in *Anne of Green Gables* and comes to Avonlea. But her journey is antithetical to Maud's journey toward modernity. It is her first time on the Island and may well have been her first train journey. Even though she was a native of Nova Scotia, which as Marilla said was "right close," leading her to expect that their orphan "can't be much different from ourselves" (60), Anne must have felt, as she sat waiting on a pile of shingles at Bright River station, that she had gone back in time to a more primitive time and place.

Although the train was a momentous force in Prince Edward Island's regional history, in Montgomery's personal life, and in the experience of her character Anne, its impact on nineteenth-century society was greater still. Historically, the cultural landscape was entirely reconfigured both spatially and temporally by the train. The train in history and in literature is "a speeding symbol of the experience of modernity itself" (Thacker 153). With its conquest of space, the train altered the sense of distance, as lines of rails linked an ever-expanding network of places. It was to facilitate the railway system that standard time was instituted in the United States and Canada in 1883. Organized by timetables, the clock and the train served each other. The railway network facilitated industry and commerce. In fact, the commencement of railroad construction on Prince Edward Island in 1871 was strongly contested, regarded by many residents as a threat to the way of life on the Island: "Train schedules changed the entire schedule of rural life" (Murray 1).

The threat that the train represented to a slower, traditional way of life is perhaps symbolized by the fact that Anne's stay with the Thomases, who took her in when her parents died, is terminated when Mr. Thomas is "killed falling under a train" (90), possibly when drunk. The railroad in this instance brings danger and change, associated as it is with irresponsible men who shirk their duties to family. On Prince Edward Island, as elsewhere, the advance of the railroad brought many benefits, but the societal change it instituted was as equivocal as it was irrevocable. Daily life was no longer regulated by the sun but by the clock, while the shrinking of space altered the mental and actual geographies of everyday existence so that the world was no longer the parish. This cultural shift is reflected in the literature of the time, most appositely by Henry David Thoreau, for whom the peace of Walden Pond was interrupted by the locomotive's whistle:

They go and come with such regularity and precision, and their whistle can be heard so far, that the farmers set their clocks by them, and thus one well-conducted institution regulates a whole country. Have not men improved somewhat in punctuality since the railroad was invented? Do they not talk and think faster in the depot than they did in the stage-office? There is something electrifying in the atmosphere of the former place.... To do things "railroad fashion" is now the byword.... We have constructed a fate, an *Atropos*, that never turns aside. (83–84)

In Thoreau's view, the train altered the thoughts and contours of the human mind itself.

The image of farmers resetting clocks by trains centres on the opposition between human consciousness as defined by chronological or historical time versus other coordinates for identity, such as space, the agrarian cycle, or the family. Maria Nikolajeva has investigated the principle of time in children's narrative fiction, which develops from "nonlinear time, typical of archaic or mythical thought, towards linearity" (1). In her view, this movement corresponds to the process of individuation and maturation in the protagonist, which simultaneously in *Anne of Green Gables* corresponds to the journey of the land toward modernity. Anne herself eventually adapts from the temporal framework of a traditional, archaic culture to the regulated timetables which govern more modern patterns of living, such as the ordered sequence of classes at Queen's. But the first novel of the series starts with the converse movement of Anne finding herself in mythic space. Anne leaves the train and enters a world benignly governed by space, place, and nature.

In *Anne of Green Gables*, Montgomery depicts a culture on the cusp of a new modern era. Avonlea's rural, pre-industrial manner of living is about to be irretrievably lost, with the encroaching train as the symbolic agent of change. Any work of fiction is defined by its coordinates in space and time. The spatial and temporal referents of Green Gables itself belong to that older world, with geographical inscriptions on character and personality influencing and shaping Anne. Montgomery posits a dynamic relationship between individuals and their environment, one centred in a pre-modern relationship to place.

Montgomery was, of course, the most place-conscious of writers. In *Anne of Green Gables* we find, virtually, a cult of place as the author imaginatively appropriates Prince Edward Island, with its iconography of red roads and pointed firs, and superimposes on the landscape that was so familiar to her a carefully delineated map whose perimeters roughly encompass the fictional settings of Avonlea, Carmody, Bright River, White Sands, and Newbridge. It is a world which is spatially defined, with the contours and topography of its specific locales described in considerable detail. However, it is a mistake to suppose that this is merely a matter of Montgomery's power to evoke local colour. Anne's attachment to place is a crucial aspect of her psyche, deriving from her orphan status. The spatial dimensions of the book are not merely descriptive but active determinants of the lives they frame. The landscape exerts an influence on characters, principally Anne, rather than vice-versa. As will be seen, the worst part of being an orphan, to Anne's way of thinking, is to be rendered "place-less." "I've never belonged to anybody – not really" (65), she declares plaintively to Matthew when she first meets him. She is inordinately sensitive to trees because they are the most stable and enduring feature of her environment, rooted in time and space as she so longs to be. The overriding theme of the book is Anne's transition from not belonging to belonging. This transition is mostly a matter of quite literally finding one's place.

THE TRAIN RECONFIGURES SPACE AND TIME

The appearances of the train in *Anne of Green Gables* "fix" the story according to space-time coordinates. The extension of the branch railroad to Carmody makes it possible for the students at Queen's to get home on weekends from Charlotte-town, which is all of thirty miles distant. Thus the railway is the precursor of a shrinking world. But prior to its advent, the perimeters of Anne's world are necessarily limited. Anne describes the eight miles from Bright River to Avonlea as "a long piece" (65). The space she inhabits may have the limitation of being confined and parochial, but it has the benefit of being intimately known. Trains also mean timetabled time. Anne arrives in Chapter 2 on the five-thirty train but finds no one to meet her. There are two possibilities here. Perhaps Matthew arrives late, though "he thought he was too early" (62). Almost certainly, he observes local time and not standard time. Mrs. Lynde notes that he drove through Lynde's Hollow at half-past three (54), which should have allowed him ample time to travel the eight miles to the station. It seems unlikely that he would not be in good time for such a significant event in the Cuthbert household, but in any case, it is evident that he does not have a watch. The other possibility is that the train had been half-an-hour early, which, though it may seem an odd happening to a modern commuter, may have occurred in the early days of the railroad. The significance of this seemingly minor detail is that the Avonlea world is apparently not tyrannized by time and pays scant regard to clock-rule. There is an obvious disjunction between train time, Anne time, and Green Gables time, the mythic place of Anne's destiny.

A further incidental detail relating to the train is worthy of remark. Mrs. Alexander Spencer deposits Anne at Bright River and then, according to Marilla, "she goes on to White Sands station herself" (59). It seems strange that Anne is left at a point eight miles from Avonlea when, if she remained with Mrs. Spencer on the train until White Sands, Matthew would only have to go five miles (88) to collect her; indeed Marilla makes this very journey with Anne the following day to sort out the mistake about the orphan's gender with Mrs. Spencer. Here Montgomery is respecting the logic of storytelling rather than the logic of real life; there are no distractions from the quiet but memorable drama of Matthew and Anne's first meeting, where they have the stage, or rather the Bright River platform, to themselves. It also means that Anne spends a night at Green Gables before her fate is decided, and the place captivates her even more than the people who live there. When Mrs. Blewett's severity causes Marilla to determine to keep her, Anne's immediate reaction is to refer to this already valued place: "Oh, Miss Cuthbert, did you really say that perhaps you would let me stay at Green Gables?" (96).

Pre-industrialized, pre-train Avonlea existence takes place in a contained and isolated rural district in which time is measured by natural rhythms. The inhabitants follow the dictates of an agricultural and domestic way of life. It is a world away from the more modern Charlottetown, where Anne spends her first night at Queen's: "Outside of her window was a hard street, with a network of telephone wires shutting out the sky, the tramp of alien feet, and a thousand lights gleaming on stranger faces" (307). This is powerful writing, economically creating the impression of forbidding and alienating modernity, inhumane and denatured. The street, the telephone, and electricity represent industrialization and urbanization, which the advance of the railroad helped to facilitate. The network stands opposed to the solitary island, actually shutting out the sky and thus the integrity of the self in nature.

Clocks scarcely feature in *Anne of Green Gables*, and the story does not go by "clock time." Despite the general accuracy of detail in the illustrations by

M. A. and W. A. J. Claus in the first edition, they surely give the clock undue prominence in their first picture of Anne's arrival at Green Gables (75), though there was a "clock shelf" (180) in the kitchen. Days are marked by the movement from sunrise to midday to sunset. Four years of Anne's life are recounted and the passage of the months is faithfully detailed, but their progression is related to nature (weather, plant-life) and to the agricultural calendar. The imprecision with regard to time is more than compensated for by the precise location in space, which, prior to train timetables and a shrinking world, takes precedence. The first pages of the novel are concerned with very precisely positioning the "old Cuthbert place." Before she even reaches Green Gables, on her drive with Matthew from the station, Anne re-visions the new locale in which she finds herself and begins to construct her world: the Avenue becomes the White Way of Delight and Barry's Pond becomes the Lake of Shining Waters. The characteristics of her environment are those of an oral culture. Whereas the modern world is hyper-conscious of time, for pre-industrial societies place was of much greater importance. History and memory, instead of being recorded, were inscribed on the landscape. Place names, such as Bright River, Avonlea, White Sands, and Spencervale, are derived from natural features; person and place are closely linked: Mr. William Bell's birch grove, Mr. Harmon Andrews' field, Mr. Andrew Bell's big woods. Houses – Lynde's Hollow, Orchard Slope, Beechwood – are named by their location. "Green Gables" is an interesting exception. "Green" connotes the natural world but "Gables" implies the farmhouse; both the house and its setting are therefore together centrally significant in the novel. Identity inheres strongly in place, in a move symptomatic of suspicion of modernity and its principles.

The Geographies of *Anne of Green Gables*

If *Anne of Green Gables* were to be mapped on its own terms, the result would look very different from conventional representations of space, and not at all like Prince Edward Island. Green Gables would be in the centre, the topography radiating from it, with detail decreasing with distance and distance reckoned in miles from Avonlea. The chronology of the book would be measured by months and seasons. The geographies within the story can be mapped in a variety of ways. Within a house – pre-eminently Green Gables – there is a geography of defined areas and unspoken boundaries – bedroom, spare room, kitchen, cellar, upstairs, downstairs. Significant as this is for the story, Montgomery is much more a writer of the outdoor pastoral landscape than of interiors. The first fact we know about Anne before we even meet her is the station-master's statement that "she preferred to stay outside" (62) rather than go into the ladies' waiting-room (in itself an interesting culturally determined space). Much as she likes her east gable bedroom, she sees it within its wider environs: homesick at Queen's, she thinks of "her own white room at Green Gables, where she would have the pleasant consciousness of a great, green, still outdoors" (307). Anne is an effect of Green Gables.

The immediate vicinity of Green Gables is described in detail so that the contours of the area bounded by the road in one direction, and by Barry's land in another, become intimately familiar to the reader. The rural setting is small-scale and confined, perhaps because it is on an island; there are brooks and streams rather than rivers, and groves and woods rather than forests. This is nature close-up and intimate rather than sublime and awe-inspiring. Notable by its absence – oddly, for an island – is the sea, except as an occasional and rather unreal poetic backdrop. It is a reminder that, from the Avonlea perspective, White Sands and the Shore Road just five miles away, with the Gulf and sea beyond, are remote. With place so heavily imprinted in the imagination, it is not surprising that geography easily merges into metaphor: "where the brook and river meet," "the bend in the road," life as a path.

People and place are closely linked. The relationship between people and their environment is best seen in Matthew, who is almost always depicted in the barn, the back yard, or the hay field. The narrator carefully elaborates the farmstead acreage, which is designated by position – the brook field – or by use – the horse pasture. This is also gendered space; it is the expected place for Matthew or Jerry Buote to be found, but for Anne to be in the hay field, helping to make the hay, would presumably be a breach of protocol either beyond even her imagination or beyond what her author was prepared to sanction. There is a clear demarcation between public and private spaces; if Matthew crosses boundaries, it is for momentous reasons, as when he attempts to buy a dress in Samuel Lawson's store or when he goes upstairs into Anne's bedroom, not having been upstairs for the previous four years (118). It is neither his innate reticence nor his resolve not to interfere that determines Matthew's place (literally) in the book. He is a liminal figure, belonging on the land or at the boundaries of domestic space. He even dies "in the porch doorway," falling "across the threshold" (319). Anne's abiding memory is of their parting "at the gate" (321) the previous evening. His coffin is carried "over his homestead threshold and away from the fields he had tilled and the orchards he had loved and the trees he had planted" (322). Such boundary-crossing, liminal characters are commonly found in the fairy stories, ghost stories, and folk tales that were a pleasurable part of the oral culture of Montgomery's youth, as she notes in her autobiography: "There were many traditions and tales on both sides of the family, to which, as a child, I listened with delight while my elders talked them over around winter firesides" (*Alpine Path* 12). Often liminal figures have a power that comes from their ambiguous border position. Matthew stands on the margin of the modern world, but his values and identity tie him to the older way of life that is quickly disappearing and that serves to signify the childhood domain that Anne must leave behind.

Montgomery voices some intriguing reflections on Matthew in *The Alpine Path*:

> Many people have told me that they regretted Matthew's death in *Green Gables*. I regret it myself. If I had the book to write over again I would spare Matthew for several years. But when I wrote it I thought he must die, that there might be a necessity for self-sacrifice on Anne's part. (75)

I believe that the author's original instincts were correct and that Matthew's death is a necessary element in the book's wider meaning. Anne has her own thresholds to cross, both in time and space, a rite of passage from childhood to adulthood, from scholar to teacher, from Avonlea to Charlottetown, from traditional to contemporary lifestyles. Matthew symbolizes what she must leave behind, the interface she must cross (always a death to self), while at the same time representing the source of greatest strength in her inner being. For Matthew is Green Gables too.

Within the fundamental values of the story, Anne's great feeling for Matthew is based not solely on deep affection, but also on his identity with the land on which Green Gables is built and with the fact that he is a planter of trees (the significance of which I discuss later). Although it is not a point that is strongly highlighted, it is nevertheless important to remember that Matthew and Marilla's parents were the original settlers on the site. Their father cleared the land and founded the farmstead (55). The timber that built Green Gables would have been from the trees that he cut down. Their mother had originally emigrated from Scotland and planted flowers "in the homestead garden in her bridal days" (320). They have a birthright stake in Green Gables. One essential requirement, for Marilla, in any orphan that they take in, is that he must be "a born Canadian" (59). Therefore Anne, as Matthew and Marilla's surrogate daughter by adoption, lays claim, not just to a house, but to a home, a heritage, and a country. It seems that Matthew's father built a first farmstead, probably a log cabin, and then a more substantial "big, rambling, orchard-embowered house" (55) was constructed when Matthew and Marilla were already grown (60–61). This detail means that Anne is the only child who has ever resided at Green Gables, which gives her a kind of moral claim to inherit it. For her, as for the pioneering homesteaders, it is a site of self-formation and self-actualization. Anne stands for the myth of a rooted nation.

It is by naming that Anne creates and "fixes" her world, making it her own – Dryad's Bubble, Idlewild, Willowmere, Violet Vale, the Birch Path, Lover's Lane, Haunted Wood. Personification humanizes her environment and provides her with companions – Bonny (a geranium), Snow Queen (the cherry tree outside her bedroom window); she might have been expected to find in farm animals and local wildlife such friends, but like the sea, those things are curiously absent. For an orphan, nothing is more important than rootedness and a sense of belonging to a specific place, where identity literally resides. These are the factors that explain the centrality of geographies to the story.

One of the strongest motifs in the storyline is of things or people being misplaced, not in their rightful place, or out of their intuitive place. We have already noted how Matthew breaches his usual spatial limits; the seating arrangements in the school and their various rearrangements feature several times in the plot, as do the misplacings of Marilla's brooch, raspberry cordial/currant wine, and vanilla/liniment. At school Anne's place is the "little brown desk beside Diana" (226); Marilla's brooch belongs in the pincushion on her bureau; the raspberry cordial should be found on "the second shelf of the sitting-room closet" (165). Trouble comes when things are not where they should be. There are variations on this theme of being out-of-place, such as when Anne invades Aunt Josephine's bed in Barrys' spare room, or when she climbs up to the ridge-pole of their kitchen roof.

A proverbial expression that may have been known to Montgomery could aptly be applied to her fictional world: "a place for everything and everything in its place." Examples of this orderliness abound in *Anne of Green Gables*. Marilla deliberates about where to put Anne on her first night in Green Gables. Not on a couch in the kitchen chamber, which would have been appropriate for an orphan boy. Not in the spare room, which is "out of the question for such a stray waif" (78). So she is designated the east gable room, thus cementing her literal association with, and residence within, the Gables. The demarcation of space, whether on the basis of gender or class, is endemic in Avonlea society. Mrs. Lynde says to Marilla: "Take this chair, Marilla; it's easier than the one you've got; I just keep that for the hired boy to sit on" (121). In church, families have their own pew. Places are assigned to particular people, so that Marilla tells Anne, "You shouldn't have gone into my room" (70–71), and in school Mrs. Lynde doesn't "believe in making the girls sit with the boys for punishment. It isn't modest" (161). Each space has its appropriate activity or behaviour; for example, "bedrooms were made to sleep in" (163), as Marilla reminds Anne when she wants to decorate her room with maple boughs. Although Anne transgresses spatial norms, she is not really a rebel, since she generally finds ways to adapt to, rather than to overturn, the prescribed *mores*. Often her imagination comes to her aid, permitting her to imagine her situation differently while in reality conforming to what is required of her. In Avonlea everyone, to use a time-honoured phrase, "knows his or her place," and Marilla and Mrs. Lynde serve as the guardians of social order and induct Anne into it: "you don't go to school to criticize the master" (151). Biological or developmental time as well as space is governed by notions of correctness. Ruby Gillis believes that the right time to have a beau is at the age of fifteen; Diana thinks that she ought not to wear her hair up until she is seventeen.

Because of its mythic evocation of pre-industrial space, the novel's perspective is deeply conservative. It is not primarily so in a political sense, though it is indicative of a colonial mindset and of the strength of feeling of pioneers who wanted to preserve their hard-earned place and way of life. Avonlea's controlling ethos is that of a "highly ritualized society, supported on the twin pillars of church and work.... Propriety and conformity, a regard for 'decency and decorum,' prevail" (Whitaker 12). The conservatism that underlies *Anne of Green Gables* is driven by an antipathy to change. Montgomery freezes Avonlea, as it were, in space and in time. The pathological dislike of change is doubly reinforced, representing first of all Anne's reaction against her unsettled childhood, which saw her shunted through four homes and left her with a strong feeling of being unwanted, but expressive also of Montgomery's own childhood history. The preservation of the status quo and its corollary, resistance to change, extend from the broad features of Prince Edward Island society, such as its social strata, down to its smallest details, like Marilla's rosebud tea-set, which is never used "except for the minister or the Aids" (164). For Marilla, it is even "a wicked thing" (250) to dye and therefore alter hair colour.

ANNE'S ATTRACTION TO TREES

Directly related to the conservatism that runs throughout the story is Anne's passion for trees. An appreciative review published in March 1909 in the London *Spectator* – "the most influential of contemporary reviews" (Waterston 19) – praised the Prince Edward Island scenery and the "admirable descriptions of its sylvan glories which lend decorative relief to the narrative" (qtd. in Devereux 395). While the reference to the wooded pastoral terrain is accurate, the trees in the book are more than decorative and are, in fact, integral to the narrative. It is strange that, although Green Gables is a working farm, there are only fleeting references to its cows and hens. Even more puzzling is the total lack of cats and dogs, especially since Montgomery often writes in her journal about the succession of cats she kept as pets. It would seem more natural for Anne to befriend a kitten rather than a geranium or a cherry tree, but in *Anne of Green Gables* it is the actual landscape, and not the creatures that inhabit it, that is foregrounded. Surely the feature of trees that commends them to Anne is their rootedness and the fact that they belong forever to their place. Mortal animals move about and age, whereas trees remain anchored and stable throughout a person's lifetime. I would suggest that the sea, just visible from Green Gables (82), is never more than a faraway backdrop – odd since the story takes place on an island and at five miles' distance from the shore – because the sea is emblematic of restless movement, the opposite of all that Anne instinctively craves. The island/sea relationship is ambiguous because "the undifferentiated space of the sea poses a threat to the order of the land, while paradoxically providing its security" (Smethurst 375).

Green Gables is closely associated with trees. Matthew and Marilla's father had built his farmstead "as far away as he possibly could from his fellow men without actually retreating into the woods" (55). The first thing Anne learns about Green Gables from Mrs. Alexander Spencer is that "there were trees all around it" (68), which prompts her to affirm, "I just love trees." The house is described as "peering through its network of trees" (247), so different from the "network of telephone wires" outside her lodgings in Charlottetown. Mrs. Lynde disdains Green Gables as a residence because "trees aren't much company" (55), one of many of her opinions that Anne does not share. Anne would happily live in a tree. If Matthew had failed to collect her at Bright River station she would have climbed up into a "big wild cherry-tree" and slept in it (64). Green Gables satisfies her yearning to live among trees; for her, trees are living presences and unchanging companions. They are also projective spaces for her imagination, whereas animals might have some personality. The inadequacy of the other homes she has known is revealed by their relation to trees. The Hammonds' house was "among the stumps" (90), the trees having presumably been cleared to supply Mr. Hammond's saw-mill, but the stumps are symbolic of harshness, inhospitableness, and industrial exploitation. Similarly the trees at the orphanage, in the ironically named Hopetown, represent its confinement and lack of human nurture:

> "There weren't any [trees] at all about the asylum, only a few poor weeny-teeny things out in front with little whitewashed cagey things about them. They just looked like orphans themselves, those trees did." (68)

Trees function for Anne almost as proxy parents; they symbolize the stability and permanence of a home where she can put down roots and belong.

Anne's development can be tracked from Idlewild to the Unfortunate Lily Maid episode in Chapter 28, resulting in her recognition of Green Gables as her true home. Idlewild – "a little ring of white birch trees" (137) – serves Diana and Anne as an imagined house with pretend chairs and shelves and dishes (138). Inevitably she grows out of this childish play, though when Mr. Bell cut down the grove of trees she "sat among the stumps and wept, not without an eye to the romance of it" (254). The latter phrase is a fine example of the author's amused yet astute irony as she achieves some distance from her heroine, an astringent objectivity that deflects her from the romanticizing to which she was disposed. (It is the most Austen-esque moment in the book.) Immediately after abandoning "such childish amusements as play-houses," Anne transfers her attention to

Barry's Pond, envisioned as Camelot. The Lily Maid plays at death; the Grim Reaper enters the story in reality nine chapters later. Once again Anne's inscriptions upon the romanticized landscape are not sustained, and once again it is stumps that signify the destruction of her dreams. In this case she ends up shipwrecked on one of the bridge piles, which are "just old tree trunks" with "lots of knots and old branch stubs on them" (257). As she herself admits, "it was a very unromantic position." Anne learns not to impose fancifully on the landscape; her true home is Green Gables, as it is, real and not ideal, surrounded by living trees, "a really truly home" (71).

Anne of Green Gables is a bildungsroman tracing Anne's development from childhood to adulthood. Although I have argued that the story is situated in a pre-modern world at the point when it is moving into a new, industrialized century, Montgomery does not indulge in nostalgia. It is inevitable that horsepower will give way to the steam engine. Matthew draws his strength from the old ways and does not cross the threshold toward the future, but that is not a realistic option for Anne, as Marilla the pragmatist understands. If life experience had not taught Montgomery to accept this, she would have encountered it in some literature that she knew well. *Rob Roy* was one of only three novels in Maud's childhood home (*Alpine Path* 49). Sir Walter Scott depicts in all of his Scottish novels the necessary advance of civilization from the colourful Highland clans to a more progressive though perhaps more mundane social order. William Wordsworth in his ode on "Intimations of Immortality" portrays the splendid visions of childhood – "the glory and the dream" quoted by Montgomery when referring to her own childhood (*Alpine Path* 47) and the title of Chapter 36 of *Anne of Green Gables* – which gradually, as adulthood approaches, "fade into the light of common day." Anne develops from the child's sense of "mythic time" (Nikolajeva) to conformity to linear time. She has no choice but to leave Matthew behind, as it were. She undergoes a process of adaptation as she moves with the times, undertakes domestic responsibilities, and participates fully in contemporary society. However, the fact that she can do so confidently and with discernment is due to her rootedness in a place to which she belongs.

BEGINNINGS AND ENDINGS

That the themes discussed above lie at the very heart of *Anne of Green Gables* is evident from the fact that they are announced in its opening paragraphs and dominate its closing pages. The correspondence between place and character is introduced at the start of Chapter 1, which invites the reader to imagine human relationships as a map of intersecting topographies. The first paragraph of the book, one sentence long, repays careful consideration. Contained within it are many motifs which are repeated or developed in later chapters:

> Mrs. Rachel Lynde lived just where the Avonlea main road dipped down into a little hollow, fringed with alders and ladies' eardrops and traversed by a brook that had its source away back in the woods of the old Cuthbert place; it was reputed to be an intricate, headlong brook in its earlier course through those woods, with dark secrets of pool and cascade; but by the time it reached Lynde's Hollow it was a quiet, well-conducted little stream, for not even a brook could run past Mrs. Rachel Lynde's door without due regard for decency and decorum; it probably was conscious that Mrs. Rachel was sitting at her window, keeping a sharp eye on everything that passed, from brooks and children up, and that if she noticed anything odd or out of place she would never rest until she had ferreted out the whys and wherefores thereof. (53)

In this passage, the reader's imagination is immediately drawn into a mapping exercise. The first presentation to the mind's eye is a place; the initial statement establishes the centrality of where someone lives. Green Gables is obliquely referred to as "the old Cuthbert place," associated with the woods and the "intricate, headlong brook" with its "dark secrets." The almost primordial image of the Cuthbert terrain in the mysterious wood evokes the rootedness of the original Cuthbert farmstead rather than the house Green Gables itself. The Cuthbert "wood" is in sharp contrast to the "quiet, well-conducted little stream" next to "Mrs. Rachel Lynde's door." Her "door" is a synecdoche for her house, and surnames, given surprising emphasis, belong as much to places as to people – Cuthbert place, Lynde's Hollow.

Mrs. Rachel Lynde is defined in relation to a place; she is "sitting at her window," emblematic of her character and curiosity, for she likes to watch the world go by. The dominant feature of this rural scene is trees – the alders along the road and the woods beyond. The brook is personified; it has secrets, it conducts itself well, it is conscious of being watched by Mrs. Lynde. Nature is a living presence with human depth and psychology. I believe that the footnote in *The Annotated Anne of Green Gables* (39–40) is correct in identifying this description as a reference to Alfred, Lord Tennyson's poem "The Brook." But the tone in *Anne* is not so much literary as notable for its whimsical humour, and for the leisurely mode of storytelling that allows the single sentence to meander through the paragraph as intricately as the brook meanders through the land. Elizabeth Epperly provides a somewhat different reading of this sentence, focusing on its "comic tension . . . between vigilance and rebellion" (Epperly 20), but demonstrating just how richly the passage permits interpretation. Mrs. Lynde looks for stories where anything is "out of place"; in this, as we have seen, she is like Montgomery. The movement of the opening is from place to person; only when the first paragraph has established geographical positioning does the second paragraph continue with description of Mrs. Lynde's personality, which then becomes an effect of her placement. The movement is also from space to time. The third paragraph tells us that it is an afternoon in early June, a detail self-evident and indeed superfluous given the fact that the orchard is in bloom and that the "meek little man," not "Mr. Rachel Lynde" but an archetype of meekness before nature and matriarchy, is "sowing his late turnip seed." Matthew Cuthbert should be doing likewise, but in the first crucial displacement in the novel, Matthew is not in his expected place. He is instead on his way to the railway station and to the event which launches the plot of the story. The theme of displaced persons conjures the apparition of Anne herself.

As for the culmination of that plot, Montgomery offers the potential of a fitting climax, affirming Green Gables – both house and farmstead – as a central character, when she introduces into the plot the necessity for Marilla to sell Green Gables. This situation prompts Anne to protest: "Nothing could be worse than giving up Green Gables – nothing could hurt me more. We must keep the dear old place.... I'm heart glad over the very thought of staying at dear Green Gables. Nobody could love it as you and I do – so we must keep it" (328). Unfortunately, the problem is resolved almost as soon as it is encountered. Mr. Barry rents the farm, and this particular bend in the road is straightened out before there is time for it to impinge on the plot. I believe it would have been more satisfying to allow this element of the plot to take precedence over the reconciliation with Gilbert. The Gilbert affair needs to be sorted out, but there would have been a rightness in ending the book by confirming and consolidating, a little less tritely, Anne's claim to be Anne of Green Gables.

In her introduction to *The Annotated Anne of Green Gables*, Margaret Anne Doody points out how much of herself Montgomery invested in this part of the story. When her grandfather died, he "left nothing to Maud, and to his wife bequeathed only the farmhouse for her lifetime" (Doody 15). In the introduction to the Broadview edition of *Anne of Green Gables*, Cecily Devereux details the reasons for supposing that the book was written between June and October 1905 (Devereux 13). In a journal entry on 1 October 1905, Montgomery writes:

> I am half sick now with anxiety and worry and have been so for the past two months. Uncle John and Prescott have been using grandmother shamefully all summer. Prescott, forsooth, wants to get married and get this house to live in! ... Grandmother told them she would *not* leave the home where she had lived and worked for sixty years. (*Selected Journals* 1, 310)

Montgomery's resentment at her uncle's behaviour and its consequences is reflected in the storyline of *Anne of Green Gables*, as argued by Doody:

> [O]ne must be 'of' a house and grounds in the Montgomery world. The need to be so grounded arose within the author's imagination once she knew she had lost her place and become but a pilgrim and sojourner. (20)

Similarly, Catherine Sheldrick Ross delineates in detail how Montgomery's life is entwined with Anne's at this point:

> Montgomery has made sure that her fictional character could stay on 'at dear Green Gables' at a time when she herself was increasingly worried about losing the house at Cavendish. (25)

Ross finds the ending convincing because "the emotional weight of the whole book" (25) lies behind Anne's fear of losing the farmstead – the understandable fear of a "solitary orphan who transforms the hostile world into a place of belonging" (27).

Montgomery settles for romance to round off her story, "a conventional, audience-pleasing end" (Epperly 38), but she does not neglect geographical appropriateness. Marilla observes Gilbert and Anne talking for half-an-hour "at the gate" (332), exactly where Anne had spoken to Matthew the evening before he died. This tacit link suggests that Gilbert may in some respects step into Matthew's place in relation to Anne. The last paragraphs set Anne at her bedroom window within the gable, with the wind in the cherry boughs outside. This placement brings the story full circle. When she woke up on her first morning at Green Gables, she spent time at the sunlit window, imagining that she would stay there as she drank in her first view of the homestead, since it had been "already quite dark" (73) when she had arrived with Matthew the previous evening. In the novel's final scene, she might do well not to be too reliant on "her birthright of fancy," "her ideal world of dreams" (334), and Browning's blissful belief that "all's right with the world," especially when experience has led her to appreciate a more solid birthright and the real world. However, it is entirely appropriate that her literal locale gives way to a more honestly realized metaphorical place, with a near horizon toward which leads a path edged modestly with "flowers of quiet happiness" (332). A bend in the road will gradually reveal both blessings and sorrows:

> "I don't know what lies around the bend, but I'm going to believe that the best does.... I wonder how the road beyond it goes – what there is of green glory and soft, checkered light and shadows – what new landscapes – what new beauties – what curves and hills and valleys further on." (328)

Anne has a strongly affective response to place. By naming her world she makes it hers. Most importantly, she names herself, having temporarily tried out "Cordelia" (76) and later the nom de plume "Rosamond Montmorency" (245). To Mrs. Lynde she is "child"; Miss Barry calls her "that Anne-girl"; the cause of her rift with Gilbert Blythe is because he calls her "carrots." She repays him with an even worse punishment by rendering him un-named: "I can't tell you the person's name because I have vowed never to let it cross my lips" (200). When they are finally reconciled in the last chapter, the first word Anne says to him is his name, Gilbert (331). She is herself, in fact, nameless in a sense until she arrives in Green Gables because Matthew forgets to ask her name. It is she who names herself "Anne of Green Gables," saying to the looking-glass: "You're only Anne of Green Gables.... But it's a million times nicer to be Anne of Green Gables than Anne of nowhere in particular" (109). Significantly, this self-naming occurs in the chapter in which she learns that she is to stay at Green Gables. Her attachment to the name grows along with her attachment to the place: "I'd rather be Anne of Green Gables sewing patchwork than Anne of any other place with nothing to do but play" (137). Later when Miss Barry asks her, "Who are you?" her reply is, "I'm Anne of Green Gables" (197). Her achievement in the course of the story is to find contentment in being who she nominates herself to be: "I don't want to be anyone but myself.... I'm quite content to be Anne of Green Gables" (303). Here her self-identification is complete; in the novel's inextricable linkage of person and place she has found her preferred state of being. Susan Drain's comment is pertinent here: "It is only with the independence made possible by the security of belonging that the fullest meaning of belonging can truly be realized" (Drain 120). Green Gables is a resonant and valorized space because it is Anne's space of belonging.

Anne's achieved maturity is confirmed a few weeks later, when Marilla regrets that Anne has grown up. Anne replies:

> "I'm not a bit changed – not really. I'm only just pruned down and branched out. The real *me* – back here – is just the same. It won't make a bit of difference where I go or how much I change outwardly; at heart I shall always be your little Anne, who will love you and Matthew and dear Green Gables more and better every day of her life." (304)

These are, in fact, the last words she is reported as saying before she leaves Avonlea to go to college. She speaks of herself as of a tree. She says that at a deep level she is unchanging. She connects Marilla, Matthew, and Green Gables, seeing herself as equally the child of them all. The "great patriarchal willows" (56) bordering the backyard are both her and the Cuthberts' heritage. The horror for her as an orphan, of having no place and belonging only to a group, is harshly voiced by Mrs. Lynde when she describes orphans as "brought from goodness knows where" (114). In the very first description of Green Gables, Mrs. Lynde states her opinion that "she did not call living in such a place *living* at all. 'It's just *staying*, that's what'" (55). Anne holds the exact opposite point of view. An orphan ceases to be an orphan when she has a home: "It's lovely to be going home and know it's home. I love Green Gables already and I never loved any place before. No place ever seemed like home" (123). After her stay with Miss Barry in Charlotte-town, upon her return to Green Gables, the house greets her like a parent: "The kitchen light of Green Gables winked her a friendly welcome back" (269). Anne claims, "The best of it all was the coming home." A common motif in children's literature is for children to subvert or manipulate adult constructions of space, but Anne goes further and creates her identity by forming and possessing her own context. "Anne *with-an-e*" individualizes her, but her identity inheres much more deeply in "Anne *of Green Gables*." It signifies her belonging to, and rooted-ness in, a known and valued place, which Anne rearranges to make room for herself. The timeless achievement of Anne's adoption of space is something that no train, no modernity, can ever really change.

WORKS CITED

Devereux, Cecily, ed. *Anne of Green Gables*. By L. M. Montgomery. Peterborough, ON: Broadview, 2004.

Doody, Margaret Anne. "Introduction." *The Annotated Anne of Green Gables: L. M. Montgomery*. Ed. Wendy E. Barry, Margaret A. Doody, and Mary E. Doody Jones. New York: Oxford UP, 1997.

Drain, Susan. "Community and the Individual in *Anne of Green Gables*." *Such a Simple Little Tale: Critical Responses to L.M. Montgomery's* Anne of Green Gables. Ed. Mavis Reimer. Metuchen, NJ and London: Children's Literature Association and Scare-crow, 1992. 119–30.

Epperly, Elizabeth R. *The Fragrance of Sweet-Grass: L. M. Montgomery's Heroines and the Pur-suit of Romance*. Toronto, Buffalo, London: U of Toronto P, 1992.

Legget, Robert F. *Railroads of Canada*. Vancouver: Douglas, David and Charles, 1973.

Montgomery, L. M. *The Alpine Path: The Story of My Career.* 1917. Markham, ON: Fitzhenry, 1997.

———. *Anne of Green Gables.* Ed. Cecily Devereux. Peterborough, ON: Broadview, 2004.

———. *The Annotated Anne of Green Gables: by L. M. Montgomery.* Ed. Wendy E. Barry, Margaret A. Doody, and Mary E. Doody Jones. New York: Oxford UP, 1997.

———. *The Selected Journals of L. M. Montgomery.* 5 vols. Ed. Mary Rubio and Elizabeth Waterston. Don Mills, ON: Oxford UP, 1985–2004.

Murray, D. *Confederation Trail Paper #1.* 2001. 21 August 2006 <http://www.gov.pe.ca/photos/original/tou_railhistory.pdf>.

Nikolajeva, Maria. *From Mythic to Linear: Time in Children's Literature.* Lanham, MD, and London: Children's Literature Association and Scarecrow, 2000.

Rev. of *Anne of Green Gables,* by L. M. Montgomery. *The Spectator* 13 March 1909. *Anne of Green Gables: by L. M. Montgomery.* Ed. Cecily Devereux. Peterborough, ON: Broadview, 2004. 395–96.

Ross, Catherine S. "Readers Reading L. M. Montgomery." *Harvesting Thistles: The Textual Garden of L. M. Montgomery.* Ed. Mary Henley Rubio. Guelph, ON: Canadian Children's P, 1994. 23–35.

Smethurst, Paul. "There Is No Place Like Home: Belonging and Placelessness in the Postmodern Novel." *Space and Place: The Geographies of Literature.* Ed. G. Norquay and G. Smyth. Liverpool: John Moores UP, 1997. 373–84.

Stevens, George Roy. *History of the Canadian National Railways.* New York: Macmillan, 1973.

Thacker, Andrew. *Moving through Modernity: Space and Geography in Modernism.* Manchester: Manchester UP, 2003.

Thoreau, Henry David. *Walden.* 1854. New York: Signet, 1960.

Waterston, Elizabeth. *Kindling Spirit: L. M. Montgomery's Anne of Green Gables.* Toronto: ECW, 1993.

Whitaker, Muriel A. "'Queer Children': L. M. Montgomery's Heroines." *Such a Simple Little Tale: Critical Responses to L. M. Montgomery's Anne of Green Gables.* Ed. Mavis Reimer. Metuchen, NJ and London: The Children's Literature Association and Scarecrow, 1992. 11–22.

Wordsworth, William. "Ode: Intimations of Immortality from Recollections of Early Childhood." *Key Poets: Classic Poetry for National Curriculum Key Stages 3 and 4.* Ed. Jenny Green. London: Penguin, 1995. 257–63.

II

ROMANCING ANNE:
LANGUAGE AND SILENCE

Chapter Four

Negotiating the Well-Worn Coin: The Shifting Use of Language in L. M. Montgomery's *Anne of Green Gables*

Melissa Mullins

When Anne Shirley arrives in Avonlea, or quite properly, Bright River, the reader is thrust into an understanding of both her unique, language-driven character and the effect of it on the community she enters. At this moment of arrival, the Anne-that-had-been is already changing, yet we are given a few narrative flashbacks to her pre-Avonlea character to guide us in our comprehension of this considerable transformation. Worthy critical attention has been given to Anne's possession, and subsequent loss, of the imaginative faculty.[1] Yet there is space still to explore how Montgomery constructs Anne's use of language as an imaginative and creative tool, and how this seemingly small detail changes as Anne continues on in Avonlea. Anne's use of language, as a means of both renaming/reforming her environment and conforming to it, specifically mirrors a historical shift in the broader turn-of-the-century literary-critical environment: namely, the literary community's shifting attitude toward the role of the poet within society. We can best view this shift by calling upon key treatises from the Romantic, Victorian, and Modern periods,[2] such as William Wordsworth's preface to *Lyrical Ballads* (1800), Matthew Arnold's "The Function of Criticism at the Present Time" (1864), Friedrich Nietzsche's "Truth and Falsity in an Ultramoral Sense" (1873), and finally, T. S. Eliot's "Tradition and the Individual

Talent" (1917). While also using the critical work on *Anne* as a touchstone, this chapter will illuminate how Montgomery transitions poet-figure Anne in a negotiation between Romantic ideals and Modernist methods.

In arguing that Anne's use of language mirrors a shift in literary attitudes about the role of the poet and poetry within society, this chapter seeks only to broach the very tip of definitions of the literary movements in question – fields of overlap or spaces of some agreement within the broad nature of what it actually means to be "Romantic," "Victorian," or "Modernist." Within the broad range of time and talent produced by the Romantic age, for example, several recurrent themes can be traced. Primarily in reaction to the development of more scientifically or objectively centred lenses of making sense of the world, and in the midst of massive social and political upheaval, the poets whom we now associate with Romanticism were faced with the daunting challenge of establishing their worth and function within society, just as Anne is faced with establishing her worth to Marilla and a community with a different theory of language.

Ironically, Romantic poets defined the poet's value by according him/her a space outside of quotidian society, and yet it was still a space absolutely integral in the human relationship to nature. Because imagination was seen as vital in this job, the role of the critic, was, in contrast, devalued. The critic created little; he/she was merely a parasite in comparison with the poetic genius of originality. As Romanticism started to give way to the Victorian period, and subsequently the Modern period, a handful of poets, including Arnold and Eliot, began to recognize and reclaim the value of the critic. In his poetry, Eliot specifically unfolds a sort of Modern viewpoint that heavily utilizes intertextuality. While these qualities – the emphasis on the emerging worth of the literary critic and the use of explicit intertextuality as a building block of poetic form – do not, by any means, fully represent theories of Modernism, it is this slice of a definition that helps us understand Anne's own shift from Romantic poet of her own imagination to one who quotes, recites, and conveys fractured texts written by others. Thus in arguing that Anne moves from Romantic ideals toward Modernist methods, I am merely arguing that concepts of imagination-fuelled production give way to an emphasis on intertextual forms and the critical eye. Anne is both intertextual as poet and, increasingly, as critic, dovetailing with the newly valued role of writer-critic, who similarly synthesizes and transforms texts.

The general shift that this chapter examines – focusing specifically on Anne's use of language and its relationship to literary movements – has been observed through other lenses by several critics of the *Anne of Green Gables* series.

However, critics tend to see the shift as a process of conformity. Looking at the first book and beyond, Gillian Thomas argues in "The Decline of Anne: Matron vs. Child" for the "progressively unsatisfactory nature of the five Anne sequels" because of their lack of what the first book has in abundance (23). She argues that Anne transforms from an individual to a conformist, an "unwilling victim of social convention" (Thomas 25). She further states that, while Anne's childhood role "is to transform Green Gables and its surroundings by the exercise of her 'imagination,'" the series shows her sinking into the role of "social engineer, bringing about the unions and reunions on which popular literature is so dependent" (27). In "Community and the Individual in *Anne of Green Gables*: The Meaning of Belonging," Susan Drain also acknowledges that *Anne of Green Gables* and books of this type, including *Pollyanna*, *The Wide, Wide World*, and *Elsie Dinsmore*, demand some level of conformity from their characters, whether it's the child protagonist "subdued to the pattern of the adults" or the other way around, where the "child manages by the sweetness of her character and the power of her example to transform the narrow and bitter adults around her" (119). Unlike Thomas's, Drain's idea of conformity is inextricably linked with the idea of belonging, and thus takes on a positive implication. Ultimately, belonging through conformity means a rejection of isolation, but also a construction of individuality; that is, Drain argues, individuality and conformity to the community are not mutually exclusive. She concludes, "Individuality, then, is established not in contrast to a community, but by a commitment to it, and the individual's freedom is not in the isolation of independence, but in the complexity of connection" (Drain 129). Anne's role as the poet who separates from the social environment to create something anew is replaced with the sense that creation and individuality can occur within that social environment and may even depend on it.

The child Anne is the distillation of the Romantic in a post-Romantic world. Perry Nodelman, in "Progressive Utopia: Or, How to Grow Up Without Growing Up," acknowledges the common structure of the "traditional novel for girls," placing *Anne* with others of its ilk, including *Pollyanna*, *Rebecca of Sunnybrook Farm*, and *The Secret Garden* (29). He argues that the structure of these novels – which inevitably include some variation of a solitary girl arriving in a place, effecting a transformation through her innocent magical abilities, and subsequently learning to lose that innocence – fills a lack which was formed when the Romantics, Wordsworth particularly, perceived (and in doing so, created) a "divorce of childhood from maturity" (Nodelman 37). He concludes that this divorce "makes childhood, which inevitably passes, agonizingly enticing to us," and that we are capable through the "wish-fulfillment world of the novels of progressive utopia" to attain it again in small part (37). Nodelman, then, is less interested in whether Anne's (or any girl's from such stories) transformation of self and community is positive so much as he is concerned about the reasons that we find childhood so attractive and the transition from childhood to adulthood so compelling. Aligning Nodelman's emphasis on the frustrating loss of child-hood with Anne's development away from a Romantic persona gives us the sense that the way we feel about leaving behind childhood mirrors how we feel about our post-Romanticism, specifically as a means of understanding artistic produc-tion: it happened, we cannot forget it, it permeates, still, the way we see art, but, as post-Romantics, we can never again fully embrace that "poetical" point of view. As Anne arrives in Avonlea, it is already slipping away, as is her very childhood. But her childhood is replaced by a new sensitivity to what language does, and how it operates.

When Anne arrives at the Bright River train station and is collected by an as-tonished and speechless Matthew, there is little pause before she launches into what the reader will soon recognize as her characteristic descant. This first epi-sode is particularly significant, however, in that it gives Anne the opportunity to observe her new surroundings, and begin renaming and refiguring them. She re-envisions two trees immediately, one as an appropriate and desirable bed for her to spend the night and one as a "bride, of course – a bride all in white with a lovely misty veil" (Montgomery 53). Nodelman observes that the archetypal girl protagonist in progressive utopian stories often falls within the Romantic model of the child; that is, "childhood innocence is automatically sympathetic with the healing beauties of nature, which are themselves divine, and which we become blind to in maturity" (Nodelman 34–45). Anne's speech continues to reflect Romantic sensibilities when she admits to Matthew, "I've always heard Prince Edward Island is the prettiest place in the world, and I used to imagine I was living here.… It's delightful when your imaginations come true, isn't it?" (Montgomery 55). She proves her imagination is in some part capable of what Samuel Taylor Coleridge terms the primary imagination, or "the living power and prime agent of all human perception, and as a repetition of the finite mind of the eternal act of creation in the infinite *I am*" (Coleridge 478). Her imagination has literally managed to create a physical existence. This creative conjuring act of the imagination is reified by Matthew's impression of Anne as a "freckled witch" (Montgomery 55) – a description used repeatedly throughout the first part of the narrative.

As Anne and Matthew pass a couple of natural landmarks, the "Avenue" and "Barry's Pond," on the way to Green Gables, Anne interrupts her own monologue to gasp and yelp in wonder as she inquires after them. Her ecstatic encounter with the "Avenue" leaves her temporarily speechless, "Its beauty seemed to strike the child dumb. She leaned back in the buggy, her thin hands clasped before her, her face lifted rapturously to the white splendour above" (58). Matthew mistakes this reaction for physical concerns, thinking she's tired and hungry, when, actually, this incident is our first and most documented glimpse of Anne the Romantic poet figure, specifically the Wordsworthian poet figure. Matthew's words break the silence, and Anne comes "out of her reverie with a deep sigh" and looks at him "with the dreamy gaze of a soul that had been wandering afar, star-fed," declaring, "It's the first thing I ever saw that couldn't be improved upon by imagination" (59). But, indeed, Anne does insist on improving it by renaming it "the White Way of Delight." This is only the first of many such incidents throughout the book (and series) in which Anne renames a location with such authority that it is never again referred to by its original name. This experience with the "Avenue" – Anne's exuberant exclamation, "Mr. Cuthbert! Oh, Mr. Cuthbert!! Oh, Mr. Cuthbert!!!" followed by her distant silence and subsequent naming – recalls Wordsworth's thoughts on the creation of poetry, which should be:

[T]he spontaneous overflow of powerful feelings; it takes its origin from emotion recollected in tranquility: the emotion is contemplated till, by a species of reaction, the tranquility gradually disappears, and an emotion, kindred to that which was before the subject of contemplation, is gradually produced, and does itself actually exist in the mind. In this mood successful composition generally begins. (Wordsworth 444)

It is this ability, according to the Romantics, that allows the poet a special position between nature and his/her audience. Percy Bysshe Shelley later expands on this sentiment when, in "A Defense of Poetry," he refers to poets as "the hierophants of an unapprehended inspiration ... the unacknowledged legislators of the world" (Shelley 529). This definition presumes that most people are not fit to be considered poets, that poets are a special lot, outside of the normal, but utterly necessary to those who cannot do the job themselves. Anne establishes this very role for herself as she renames the "Avenue," and, later in the trip to Green Gables, "Barry's Pond." Nodelman refers to the common thread of the "heroine's magic ability to awaken dormant joyousness ... her magical qualities seem to triumph over every bad circumstance," and these "wonderful qualities she starts with and never loses have remarkable effects on other people, who change miraculously" (Nodelman 30–31). Nodelman's argument is delightfully playful here, but he points to a very integral part of the narrative. The hyperbolic tone of transformation, which he observes in *Anne of Green Gables* (as well as the other novels for girls he groups into one master narrative), is akin to the seriousness with which the Romantic poets circumscribed their role in society.

Anne, therefore, can be seen as the Romantic ideal of the poet sent in to legislate the poetry of Avonlea to its unenlightened residents, first feeling the impressions of the landscape and the people (she is often referred to as a "sensitive" child) and then reforming them in the tranquility of recollection. The sense of Anne as Romantic poet is even further heightened by the fact that she is hyper-conscious of her own imaginativeness. After she names the "Avenue" the "White Way of Delight," she immediately inquires of Matthew, "Isn't that a nice imaginative name? When I don't like the name of a place or a person I always imagine a new one and always think of them so" (Montgomery 59). This self-consciousness mirrors the wholly new attitude present in the circle of thinkers who contributed to the Romantic movement. Harry Garvin argues, "The Romantics were the first in the contemporary world to give a sense of having become aware of the problem of defining themselves both as individuals in their own right and as phenomena of and in a world that was clearly different from that of preceding ages" (Garvin 16). Just as they were conscious of defining a literary movement, so too is Anne, on some level, conscious of her place within that community of thinkers – so much so that she has created her own term, "kindred spirit," to refer to what we might call her discourse community.

However, Anne's migration away from Romantic poet begins, in a small way, as soon as the Cuthberts allow her to remain in the small community at

Green Gables, but Montgomery allows us to see more of Anne the Romantic poet through references to her former residences and experiences. While talking with Marilla, after being allowed to stay on at Green Gables, she admits to two situations in which she created imaginary friends. The first was born of the single remaining pane of a bookcase brutalized by Mr. Thomas, her drunken guardian. Anne states, "I used to pretend that my reflection in it was another little girl who lived in it. I called her Katie Maurice and we were very intimate" (Montgomery 106). To Anne she is clearly very real. She admits, "When I went to live with Mrs. Hammond it just broke my heart to leave Katie Maurice. She felt it dreadfully, too, I know she did, for she was crying when she kissed me good-bye through the bookcase door" (107). Bereft of Katie Maurice, Anne creates another imaginary friend at the Hammonds'. She explains that "just up the river a little way from the house there was a long green valley, and the loveliest echo lived there. It echoed back every word you said, even if you didn't talk a bit loud. So I imagined that it was a little girl called Violetta and we were great friends and I loved her almost as well as I loved Katie Maurice" (107). Again, Violetta is very real to Anne and their goodbye echoes that of Katie Maurice: "The night before I went to the asylum I said good-bye to Violetta and oh, her goodbye came back to me in such sad, sad tones. I had become so attached to her that I hadn't the heart to imagine a bosom friend at the asylum, even if there had been any scope for imagination" (107). Anne's imaginary creations are essentially pieces of herself, a reflection and echo, and her creative output is based on some kind of identification of the poetic self as the key to self-creation, as opposed to some outside force like God or the Muses. This theory of creativity is particularly relevant if we consider her place within the Romantic ideal of the poet, which emphasized the poet and the art of creation over the production of poetry itself.

As we've seen above with Shelley and with Wordsworth, the poet is the most important figure in the relationship between nature, audience, poet, and poem, for the poet is able to lessen the psychical distance between audience and nature. Coleridge, too, argues for the centrality of the poet in the imaginative act:

> The poet, described in *ideal* perfection, brings the whole soul of
> man into activity, with the subordination of its faculties to each other
> according to their relative worth and dignity. He diffuses a tone and
> spirit of unity, that blends, and (as it were) *fuses*, each into each, by

that synthetic and magical power, to which we have exclusively appropriated the name imagination. (480)

Anne's choice to create imaginary characters, which are essentially looking-glass selves, betrays the importance she places on her poetic agency in the self-creation process. She gives her imaginary agents the tone and spirit – her sadness, her voice – of the Romantic poet.

Although she continues to name objects and places after she is welcomed into the community at Green Gables and Avonlea, subtle changes in her use of language and significant/traumatic incidents signal a shift away from the Romantic ideal of the poet. Marilla is one of the first catalysts in this process, as she, unlike Matthew, curtails Anne's imaginative outpourings. When Marilla asks Anne to relate her history, she is uninterested in the imagined narrative Anne would like to offer. Anne hopes for an audience who will allow her to be the self-aggrandizing and vital poetic figure she would like to be, and pleads, "Oh, what I *know* about myself isn't really worth telling.... If you'll only let me tell you what I *imagine* about myself you'll think it ever so much more interesting" (Montgomery 85).

Marilla, however, is not the ideal audience for the Romantic poet figure, insisting that she "stick to the bald facts. Begin at the beginning. Where were you born and how old are you?" (85). A Victorian enforcer of the bildungsroman, Marilla exacts a David Copperfield account of Anne's birth, chronology, and parentage. Marilla does not merely limit Anne's control over her narrative production; she takes control herself, dictating the narrative frame (one which must begin at the beginning) and the information that is relevant to self-creation (birth location and age). When Anne attempts to regain control and assert the Romantic poet's claim in the power of the relationship between name and object, Marilla seizes it back, insisting that "it doesn't matter what a person's name is as long as he behaves himself" (85). Marilla's retort indicates that the poet Anne cannot get at the essence of something simply in her ability to name it imaginatively. Marilla's position on imagination is reified when Anne attempts to call her "Aunt Marilla." She insists, "I'm not your aunt and I don't believe in calling people names that don't belong to them" (103). When Anne suggests that they could imagine her as Anne's aunt, Marilla insists that she's incapable of this, that she never imagines things "different from what they really are" (103). Similarly, when Anne talks to Marilla about Katie Maurice and Violetta, Marilla works as the opposing force to this imaginative venture, insisting, "It will be well for you to have a real, live friend to put such nonsense out of your head" (107). She goes on to compare this creative act to lying or the more archaic phrase "telling stories" (107). In this way, Marilla begins to shuttle Anne away from her Romantic inclinations; she is, in a sense, the Victorian environment, as she insists on order (which we might compare to the Victorian cataloguing impulse) and a strict adherence to facts based on objective observation (which corresponds to the flourishing scientific method). She also serves as critic to Anne's narrative (which, as we will see, corresponds to changing attitudes about the value of literary criticism).

Marilla asserts herself as the force that attempts to curb and tailor Anne's creative imagination, but Anne's involvement in community, provided first by Green Gables and then by Avonlea as a whole, induces her consciously to transform herself. We see this transformation begin immediately after her official acceptance into the Green Gables household. Going to bed, she imagines an elaborate décor for her east gable room, and attempts to top it off with an imaginative alteration of self. She declares, "My name is Lady Cordelia Fitzgerald," but no sooner has she attempted to conjure herself into Lady Cordelia than she amends, "No, it isn't – I can't make *that* seem real.... You're only Anne of Green Gables.... But it's a million times nicer to be Anne of Green Gables than Anne of nowhere in particular, isn't it?" (109) Although she does continue to use her imaginative powers, Anne's entry into the community of Avonlea sets into motion a series of events that affect the way in which she uses her imagination. Montgomery establishes a narrative pattern in this renovating force: first, Anne uses her imagination; then, she is either worried that her imagination has brought something terrible into reality, or it actually *has* brought something terrible into reality; subsequently, the situation is topped off with a dose of ridiculous humour, meant to shame Anne for allowing her imagination to get her into the situation to begin with.

We see this pattern emerge first with Anne and Diana's tea party. Having created a story about Diana's falling ill with smallpox and Anne's sacrificing her own life to save her, Anne misinterprets Diana's sudden illness as the result of her story: "Oh, Diana, do you suppose that it's possible you're really taking the smallpox?" (185). Convinced, seemingly, that the power of her fiction has caused her friend to fall deathly ill, Anne is ultimately chastised and her fears made a little absurd by the realization that Diana's sickness is drunkenness, not a dramatic, romantic, life-threatening condition. Anne's invention of the "Haunted

Wood" works similarly. She observes, with Diana, that the places around Green Gables "are so – so – *commonplace*" and, once again, exhibits her imaginative power to make these places more "romantic" (230). She uses her naming magic to conjure the ghost of a "white lady [who] walks along the brook just about this time of the night and wrings her hands and utters wailing cries," "the ghost of a little murdered child … [which] creeps up behind you and lays cold fingers on your hand," a headless man, and glowering skeletons, making the creations so real that she refuses to traverse the distance to Diana's house at night alone (230). Again, Marilla steps in as Anne's un-ideal audience, forcing Anne to confront her creation in an attempt to dispel it. The experience is so traumatizing that Anne is once more forced to acknowledge the pitfalls of the R/romantic imagination.

These two experiences seem merely practice runs for Anne's humiliating assumption of the lily maid character, the final incident that seems to seal Anne's metamorphosis away from full-fledged Romantic poet. When Anne, Diana, Ruby, and Jane decide to re-enact the tragic death scene of Alfred, Lord Tennyson's "Lancelot and Elaine," they turn to real physical objects to carry out their imaginative work. No longer content to burden words with the task of calling a thing into existence, they must substitute a real flat for a barge, and a real black shawl to represent the "blackest samite" (295). True, there is call for transformative imagination in this task, but the need for literal props betrays Anne's growing inability or unwillingness to create with her imagination. She is also dubious about her ability to assume fully the role of the lily maid and pleads her red hair as the imaginative obstacle. We've seen Anne's difficulty with imagining her red hair away before, of course, but the use of it here clarifies a recognition of the other perceived obstacles. Anne's re-enactment, however, seems at first a very promising venture, as she manages to resign herself to the hair obstacle. She has a few minutes in which she "enjoyed the romance of her situation to the full," and then the tide changes, as it were, and "something happened not at all romantic. The flat began to leak" (296). Rather than being able to carry the romantic imagining to its fruition, solidifying her creative achievement, she is caught in an alarmingly real situation of dealing with a boat filling with water. The new situation has all of the potential of lending itself to the romantic, especially as she escapes the boat, clings to the bridge piles, and is eventually rescued by Gilbert. But Anne, turned startlingly aware of the real at this point, finds a situation in which her imagination is defunct. She tells Mrs. Allen, "It was a very unromantic position, but I didn't think about that at the time. You don't think about romance when you have just escaped a watery grave" (297).

Montgomery makes an interesting narrative choice at this point. She shifts back and forth between a straight third-person narrative of Anne's catastrophe and Anne's reflective account, post-incident, to Mrs. Allen. In the reflective account, she is able to regain some of her old romanticizing characteristics – she is able to declare something "romantic" or "unromantic" and label her potential death in the flowery phrase "watery grave." But Montgomery's insistence that this reflective account be juxtaposed with a first-hand account of the situation betrays Anne's inevitable transition out of the fully Romantic poet figure, showing her very real lack of creative control over the situation. The absurdity with which the re-enactment episode ends (and all other previously mentioned Romantic gestures) has a distinctly Modernist flare. As Alan Sinfield argues, the common mode of Modernist poetry tends toward "tentative irony which eschews large statements" (Sinfield 250). That Anne is ultimately unable to assume authentically the role of Elaine and carry it out to its fruition, and that she faces very real, violent death rather than a quiet, idealized mock death, betrays the ultimate irony of Montgomery's construction of this scene.

The choice of Tennyson for this key scene of transformation seems particularly relevant. In "The Visual Imagination of L. M. Montgomery," Elizabeth Epperly argues that "Montgomery's way of seeing was thoroughly Romantic" (85). She goes on to state that Montgomery lived with and was transported by nature, "like the Romantic-inspired writers she loved most," including Tennyson (85). It's true, of course, that Tennyson was inspired by the Romantics, but as a Victorian poet, he also has one foot creeping toward Modernism. In "*In Memoriam* and the Language of Modern Poetry," Sinfield argues that Tennyson is a difficult poet to place because it is "hard to disconnect him completely from our modern sensibility" (Sinfield 258). While reminding the reader constantly of the differences posed by Tennyson's poetry, Sinfield makes a case of comparison with Eliot, Hulme, Symbolism, and Imagism. Although Tennyson tends to approach his material from a different perspective than the Modernists, Sinfield argues that they are often "tackling the same problem – the status of the creative imagination in a scientific age" (254). Anne, faced with Marilla and Cavendish, is tackling the same issue and conversing in the same ironic mode. Far from being irreconcilable with Imagist theory, "In his general outlook, his attitude to form, and his syntax Tennyson either anticipates or is recognizably a predecessor of Hulme" (255).

Unlike his attitude toward the Romantics,[3] Eliot's attitude to Tennyson's work was one of admiration. In an essay on *In Memoriam*, Eliot declares Tennyson a "great poet for reasons that are perfectly clear. He has three qualities which are seldom found together except in the greatest poets: abundance, variety, and complete competence" (Eliot 174). It is not simply that Tennyson's poetry encompasses the concerns of Romanticism, while anticipating elements of Modernism. Montgomery's choice is also compelling because of the way in which she employs that intertext. Although the story of Elaine the lily maid and the Lady of Shalott share similar plots (so much so that Sullivan's 1985 adaptation of *Anne*, presumably because it would be more popularly known, chose to utilize "The Lady of Shalott"), it seems significant that Montgomery specifically chose "Lancelot and Elaine" for the girls to re-enact. Both poems can be potentially read as a metaphor for the female artist and the consequences of female artistic venture. The Lady of Shalott is under an ambiguously assigned curse, compelling her to weave the images of the outside world (that she perceives in a mirror) into a tapestry. One of these scenes, that of Lancelot passing by on his way to Camelot, compels her to look directly at the outside world; this glance breaks the mirror and her weaving, and the curse comes upon her, forcing her to float down the river in a barge to her eventual death. Elaine is under no such curse, but she too weaves a casing for Lancelot's shield, which is the exact replica of the scenes worked into the armour. Unlike the Lady of Shalott, however, Elaine not only creates the shield casing, but she also attempts to interpret the stories worked into the shield itself. Tennyson describes her as having "read the naked shield, / Now guessed a hidden meaning in his arms, / Now made a pretty history to herself" (Tennyson lines 16–18). As such, she is both the creator of new stories – the writer figure – and that force which interprets what is already in the text (the shield) – the literary critic.

Montgomery connects Anne with Elaine rather than with the Lady of Shalott, allowing us to understand more fully Anne's transition away from the fully Romantic poet figure to something which bridges the gap between the two conflicting ideologies of Romantic and Modern poetry. One of the hallmarks of the Modernist period, which began to take hold in the work of Victorian poets like Matthew Arnold, was the importance of the literary critic in the relationship between work, poet, and audience. Arnold is critical of the Romantics' notion that the most important work to be done in the world is poetry and that, in turn, poetry is something only a few privileged individuals can do. Arnold argues that "free creative activity" is important, but can be achieved in more than the production of "great works of literature or art" (Arnold 593). He writes, "if it were not so, all but a very few men would be shut out from the true happiness of all men. They may have it in well-doing, they may have it in learning, they may have it even in criticizing" (593). Arnold also reforms the notion of what constitutes "creative literary genius." For him, it "does not principally show itself in discovering new ideas, that is rather the business of the philosopher" (593). He writes, "The grand work of literary genius is a work of synthesis and exposition ... of dealing divinely with these ideas, presenting them in the most effective and attractive combinations, – making beautiful works with them, in short" (593). The critic, for Arnold, contributes a priceless service toward creating an atmosphere in which this synthesis can occur. In choosing to re-enact *Elaine*, Anne is working as both artist and literary critic of sorts. She's synthesizing Tennyson's text into her own life to create something new, but she's also making executive decisions about what is important to the success of the re-enactment, just as a critic decides which material is important for scrutiny and interpretation. The very nature of adaptation is critical in that it is an interpretation of what the adapter finds most relevant in a work of art.

Traces of Arnold's work can be found in Eliot's "Tradition and the Individual Talent," and so, too, does Anne reflect Eliot's reformation of Arnold's work. Eliot solidifies the idea that the focus should be directed away from poet as "personality" and, rather, placed on the idea that the poet is a "finely perfected medium in which special, or very varied feelings are at liberty to enter into new combinations" (Eliot 763). He argues that "the progress of an artist is a continual self-sacrifice, a continual extinction of personality" (Eliot 762). Through Eliot's perception of the poet, we can perhaps recast the way in which Anne changes throughout the course of the book (and the series). Rather than merely seeing her transformation, as Thomas suggests, as a sinking into conformity where imagination is replaced with social engineering, we may see her conformity as the Modernist's extinction of personality, operating less as a fountain of new ideas and more as a conduit for the reformation of already existing material. Her work, as such, becomes highly intertextual, just as Eliot's poetry explicitly calls on intertextual gestures and Anne-like fragments[4] to form his poetry and call attention to a cultural heritage in which high- and low-brow literature exist in equal fragments.

Sinfield argues that this type of literary allusion is a response to the "absence of an agreed system of images whose connotations would be relied on" (Sinfield 256). As the series progresses, and Anne becomes enmeshed in a systematic approach to education and the community that education creates, her creative activities centre less on naming locations and developing fantastical stories and more on finding the right quotation to express her feelings during a social situation. Looking at *Green Gables* alone, we see the beginning of this tendency in the last line of the novel, when Anne quotes Browning: "'God's in his heaven, all's right with the world'" (396). Sometimes cliché-bound and sometimes illuminating, Anne crystallizes the modern condition of fragmented and thereby freshly woven texts.

Anne's tendency toward intertextuality in *Green Gables* is perhaps best exemplified by her growing participation in recitations. The recitation, by nature, is a curious creative act, which, like the process of the intertextual gesture, compels the speaker to take the work of another artist and reinterpret it through her choice of voice, diction, and hand gestures. Anne becomes a master of this act, beginning in Miss Stacy's small circle and eventually establishing herself at the White Sands Concert, which is a high-society cultural event mixing the "countrified" folks of Avonlea with the Charlottetown Symphony Club. Ultimately, Anne's experience at the White Sands recitation somewhat reflects the Modernist sensibility of the "fragmentation of society" and the kind of alienation which follows the "process of depersonalization" (Sinfield 246, Eliot 762). She is initially out of place at the event, falling into the group to which the "tall scornful-looking girl in a white lace dress" allots "the country bumpkins and rustic belles" (Montgomery 352). She nearly loses herself to stage fright, and even after she has delivered a riveting performance, she is uncomfortable with the gathering, declaring to Jane and Diana on the ride home, "You wouldn't change into any of those women if you could. Would you want to be that white-lace girl and wear a sour look all your life, as if you'd been born turning up your nose at the world?" (356). Recitation extinguishes the Poet's personality.

For all the gestures toward Modernist thought that we see develop throughout the course of the narrative, ultimately Anne represents a kind of Nietzschian middle ground between Romanticism and Modernism. Nietzsche argues in "Truth and Falsity in the Ultramoral Sense" that language (which we link to truth and knowledge) is nothing more than a bunch of metaphors that we've forgotten are metaphors – "worn out metaphors which have become powerless to affect the senses; coins which have their obverse effaced and now are no longer of account as coins but merely as metal" (636). He is suspicious of language for this reason, and so, too is Anne, in her way. Marilla notices in "Where the Brook and River Meet" that Anne has become much quieter. She notes, "You don't chatter half as much as you used to, Anne, nor use half as many big words. What has come over you?" (Montgomery 332). Anne explains that her reservations about talking and using big words are connected both to how her language is construed and critiqued by other people and to her newfound belief, through Miss Stacy, that "the short [words] are much stronger and better" (332). The flowery diction of the young is no longer considered appropriate. In spite of her changing position on language, Anne still personifies Nietzsche's idea of Art, both as the little girl who continues to name locations and partake in the creation of fantastical stories and the woman who relies on different manifestations of the intertextual gesture to express herself. Nietzsche writes, "This impulse [of Art] constantly confuses the rubrics and cells of the ideas by putting up new figures of speech, metaphors, metonymies; it constantly shows its passionate longing for shaping the existing world of waking man as motley, irregular, inconsequently incoherent, attractive, and eternally new as the world of dreams is" (638). When Anne arrives in Avonlea, the community has become disconnected from the metaphors that it uses to designate itself. Anne is able to use her language as a transformative force, altering the surroundings and the people of Avonlea. Once she has used the power of the Romantic poet figure to transform others through language, and once she has, in turn, been accepted into the community of Avonlea (although she is forever a somewhat liminal figure), her work becomes more intertextual. Like the Lady of Shalott and Elaine, she weaves her creations out of the fabric of the community and her existence within it. But unlike them, she lives on, her broad tapestry of readers now spanning one hundred years.

Although I think it would be a stretch to propose that Montgomery fits particularly well within the context of Modernism as such, her creation of Anne as figure which both embraces Romanticism and critiques it suggests that she is conscious of her relationship to Modernist thought. In Anne's transition from isolated entity to member of the community, from childhood to young adulthood, and specifically in the way the shift in her use of language marks these epochs in her life, Anne reflects the literary community's growth and change. Her transition can be described as from initially establishing the poet as central figure to subsequently de-emphasizing the poet's personality. The loss with which many readers regard Anne may ultimately be the loss that marks the passing of a very attractive theory of poetry, one that marked and theorized the poetic capacity of the outsider. The orphan, at home in nature, becomes part of a text of Victorian bildungsroman, and a loss occurs in that shift. But ultimately, Anne's silence, recitation, and fractured or even ironic intertextuality may only speak to our broader dissatisfaction with a Modern sense of what words can do and mean. In a post-Romantic world, shaped irreversibly by Romanticism, perhaps we long for the idealized Romantic poet, who, somewhere along the way, was rendered synonymous with the child who inevitably grows up.

Just as we have collectively been compelled to do through the philosophical writing of the nineteenth and twentieth centuries, Anne moves from complete faith in the creative power of language to a distrust of the relationship between signifier and signified. Anne's place, then, and Montgomery's too, is the space of overlap – the realm of commonality found in every ideological movement that is compelled to define itself through what it is not, and in doing so, inevitably carries a piece of that movement with it. Just as Anne is the glue that binds together the Avonlea community, while operating simultaneously outside it, she is the symbol of what all literary movements share no matter how irreconcilable they may seem.

WORKS CITED

Anne of Green Gables. Dir. Kevin Sullivan. Sullivan Films, 1985.

Arnold, Matthew. "The Function of Criticism at the Present Time." 1864. *Critical Theory Since Plato*. Ed. Hazard Adams. New York: Harcourt Brace Jovanovich, 1971. 592–603.

Coleridge, Samuel Taylor. "Biographia Literaria." 1817. *Critical Theory Since Plato*. Ed. Hazard Adams. New York: Harcourt Brace Jovanovich, 1971. 476–81.

Drain, Susan. "Community and the Individual in *Anne of Green Gables*: The Meaning Of Belonging." *Such a Simple Little Tale: Critical Responses to L. M. Montgomery's* Anne of Green Gables. Ed. Mavis Reimer. Metuchen, NJ: Scarecrow, 1992. 119–30.

Eliot, T.S. "*In Memoriam*." In Memoriam. Ed. Robert H. Ross. New York: Norton, 1973.

———. "Tradition and the Individual Talent." 1917. *Critical Theory Since Plato*. Ed. Hazard Adams. New York: Harcourt Brace Jovanovich, 1971. 761–64.

Epperly, Elizabeth. "The Visual Imagination of L. M. Montgomery." *Making Avonlea: L.M. Montgomery and Popular Culture*. Toronto: U of Toronto P, 2002. 84–98.

Garvin, Harry, ed. *Romanticism, Modernism, Postmodernism*. Lewisburg, PA: Bucknell UP, 1980.

Montgomery, L. M. *The Annotated Anne of Green Gables*. Ed. Wendy Barry, Mary D. Jones and Margaret Anne Doody. New York: Oxford UP, 1997.

Nietzsche, Freidrich. "Truth and Falsity in an Ultramoral Sense." 1873. *Critical Theory Since Plato*. Ed. Hazard Adams. New York: Harcourt Brace Jovanovich, 1971. 634–40.

Nodelman, Perry. "Progressive Utopia: Or, How To Grow Up Without Growing Up." *Such a Simple Little Tale: Critical Responses to* Anne of Green Gables. Ed. Mavis Reimer. Metuchen, NJ: Scarecrow, 1992. 29–38.

Shelley, Percy Bysshe. "A Defense of Poetry." 1840. *Critical Theory Since Plato*. Ed. Hazard Adams. New York: Harcourt Brace Jovanovich, 1971. 516–30.

Sinfield, Alan. "*In Memoriam* and the Language of Modern Poetry. *In Memoriam*. Ed. Robert H. Ross. New York: W. W. Norton, 1973. 245–58.

Tennyson, Alfred Lord. "Lancelot and Elaine." 1859. 6 November 2005. <http://www.lib.rochester.edu/camelot/idyl-l&e.htm>

Thomas, Gillian. "The Decline of Anne: Matron vs. Child." *Such a Simple Little Tale: Critical Responses to L. M. Montgomery's* Anne of Green Gables. Ed. Mavis Reimer. Metuchen, NJ: Scarecrow, 1992. 23–28.

Wordsworth, William. "Preface to the Second Edition of *Lyrical Ballads*." 1800. *Critical Theory Since Plato*. Ed. Hazard Adams. New York: Harcourt Brace Jovanovich, 1971. 437–47.

NOTES

1   See Gillian Thomas's "The Decline of Anne: Matron vs. Child" and Susan Drain's "Community and the Individual in *Anne of Green Gables*: The Meaning of Belonging."

2   Western Romanticism is generally thought to extend to the early part of the nineteenth century. The Victorian period, which begins officially with Victoria's taking the throne in 1837, but flourishes artistically in the last third of the century, began shifting into the Modern period in the early part of the twentieth century. This timeline, of course, is not without shifting and unclear boundaries, as there are writers in all periods of literary production who seem to anticipate subsequent periods.

3   Elements of Romantic poetry, nevertheless, find their way into Modernist poetry simply by virtue of being the force against which the Modernists most violently reacted.

4   Holly Blackford, in a personal communication, has suggested that, in this sense, Anne is like the walking embodiment of the River Thames in "The Waste Land."

CHAPTER FIVE

"Mute Misery":
Speaking the Unspeakable in
L. M. Montgomery's *Anne* Books

Hilary Emmett

"Anne, you have talked even on for ten minutes by the clock,"
said Marilla. "Now, just for curiosity's sake, see if you can hold your
tongue for the same length of time."
~ *Anne of Green Gables* (93)

"I was often very hungry before I came to Green Gables – at the
orphanage ... and before. I've never cared to talk of those days."
~ Anne from *Anne of Ingleside* (245)

The very first thing we learn about our orphan heroine is that she has, in the
words of the Bright River stationmaster, "a tongue of her own, that's for certain"
(11). In fact, Anne's interaction with every new person she meets is characterized
by her ceaseless chatter, her comical employment of all sorts of "big words" to
express her even bigger ideas (15). Yet while Lucy Maud Montgomery's series
of *Anne* novels continually draws attention to her heroine's prodigious gifts of
verbal and written expression, there are some notable scores on which Anne
remains if not precisely *silent*, then, at the very least, tongue-tied. In this chapter,

I explore that which is repressed by the irrepressible Anne; in doing so, I illustrate that despite attempts at repression, ideas and events deemed unspeakable by Anne and her intimates nevertheless insinuate their way into their discourse and eventually find textual enunciation.

Traumatic events in the *Anne* novels present particular obstacles to free expression. Much is left unsaid in Montgomery's rendering of such circumstances as Anne's miserable childhood before she came to Green Gables, and her responses to the deaths that frame the series: that of her beloved father-figure Matthew in the first novel, and that of her son, Walter, in the series' final instalment, *Rilla of Ingleside*. Montgomery's treatment of grief and loss undergoes a profound shift between her 1915 *Anne of the Island* and her 1917 *Anne's House of Dreams*; this shift was wrought by her own direct experience of loss on both a personal and national scale. The devastating still-birth of her second son, Hugh, who was born and died in the same week that war was declared in Europe in August 1914, had a marked effect on the representation of mourning in her later novels. Maternal mourning and the carnage of war were thus intimately linked for Montgomery; their intersection ensures that loss is depicted in ways that surpass what might otherwise have been understood as a more generalized grief at the senseless loss of a generation of young Canadian men.

Additionally, the quandary of how to mourn those young men who gave their lives for the great and glorious good of the Empire re-invokes Montgomery's private grief for Herman Leard – a man presented by her journals as utterly unmarriageable, but nevertheless the love of her life. Just as Anne, Rilla, and Gertrude in *Rilla of Ingleside* cannot adequately mourn their dead, because of the patriotic demands made upon them by nation and Empire, Montgomery herself was denied the right to mourn the man who was "neither husband nor son" (*Rilla* 184). Whereas in the earlier books death is met with forbearance and a quiet acceptance of the superiority of everlasting life, the very language of *Rilla of Ingleside*, the last in the Anne series, draws into the world of the text a viscerally felt grief that is simultaneously personal and communal. In reading *Anne of Green Gables* alongside its series of sequels and Montgomery's own journals, I track the ways in which her narrative concerns and strategies developed over the course of twenty years so as to give voice not only to such unspeakable topics as child abuse and domestic violence, but also to incorporate into her novels her own increasingly nuanced – because increasingly personal – conception of the nature of grief.

From very early on in her writing career, Montgomery evinced an interest in the relationship between speech and trauma. Her journal describes her third novel, *Kilmeny of the Orchard* (1910), as "a love story with a psychological interest," yet the young author seems entirely unaware of exactly how topical her "psychological" concerns would prove to be (*Selected Journals* 1, 362). *Kilmeny* tells the story of a young woman who is mysteriously rendered mute from birth as a result of her mother's unforgivable sin. Her ability to speak miraculously returns when she is shocked into speech by the imminent murder of her beloved. In linking speech, trauma, and inexorable, hereditary guilt, Montgomery evinces interest in a set of concerns remarkably similar to those preoccupying Sigmund Freud, who, with his *Dora* in 1905, just three years before the publication of *Anne of Green Gables*, published his own landmark narrative of an adolescent girl's search for validation by her family and peers. While there is conclusive evidence that Montgomery was familiar with Freudian theories of family dynamics by the time she wrote *Anne of Ingleside* in 1939, there is nothing in her early journal entries to suggest that she had encountered his thought at the time of writing either *Green Gables* or *Kilmeny*.[1]

Nevertheless Montgomery not only recognized the intimate relation between shame, guilt, pain, and non-speech, but she also advocated her own version of a "talking cure." Due to the long stretches the author spent without ready access to her most kindred of spirits – dearly beloved relatives such as her father, or friends such as Frederica (Frede) Campbell – her desire for a talking cure was very early on adapted into what we might call a "writing cure." This writing cure was not simply the sense of relief and release that she undoubtedly felt after unburdening her secrets into her journal; rather, writing became the occasion for "self-analysis," for "putting her real thoughts and feelings into words" (*Selected Journals* 2, 1). Writing was very much a therapeutic process for Montgomery, both in the way that her journal played the part of a confidant and in the more "psychoanalytic" sense that setting her thoughts and experiences down in writing allowed for advances in self-knowledge.

Yet before such a writing cure could be put into effect, certain barriers to free expression had to be negotiated. In both her public and private writing, Montgomery faced obstructions caused by the burdens of grief and pain, the demands of patriotic discourse, and even the fear of unseemliness. In addition to these barriers, she was well aware that writing, like speaking, can be a cathartic process, yet can also cause the writer or speaker to relive the events described to the point of reproducing not only mental anguish, but also bodily sensation. In telling the story of her shameful entanglement with Herman Leard, for example, she ploughs on through her account, though each successive detail recorded in her journal is "still more racking" to her harrowed nerves than the one that came before (*Selected Journals* 1, 208).[2] A less melodramatic example is her record of the death of her son, Hugh. Still-born as a result of a knot in his umbilical cord, Hugh's death was an experience of unprecedented agony, which presented Montgomery with a new set of obstacles to both speech and writing. As a mother, the trauma of putting her grief into words proved insurmountable, as evinced by her refusal to record her first visit to her son's grave (*Selected Journals* 2, 155). More than any other experience recorded in her early journals, the untimely death of her child called into question the goodness of God; but as a minister's wife, her very ability to mourn was constrained by the social pressures incumbent upon her.

Montgomery shared the experience of losing a child with another best-selling novelist and clergyman's wife: Harriet Beecher Stowe. In commenting on Stowe's loss and its resonance in *Uncle Tom's Cabin*, Marianne Noble has situated the separation of mother and child, more usually through the death of the mother, as the "emotional core" of almost all of the significant sentimental fictions of the nineteenth century (65–66). Sentimentalism, she argues (along with most theorists of the topic), is characterized by the desire for unity, the reparation of sundered domestic relationships. Such texts work upon their readers, she suggests, by achieving a state of union through the depiction of suffering; that is, they offer us a "visceral and intuitive understanding of the other's fear and anguish" (65).[3] But if readers would agree that *Anne of Green Gables* has the most sentimental of plots – a mistreated orphan girl is adopted by a middle-aged spinster and her brother, all three of whom come to experience the redemptive power of familial love and the sacrifices made in the name of that love – then why are paradigmatic scenes of loss and suffering so rapidly passed over by Montgomery's narration?

This chapter is structured by the significant occlusion of suffering in the *Anne* books – in particular, the suffering associated with the death of those close to Anne. I begin with Matthew's death in *Anne of Green Gables*, then consider the death of little Joy in *Anne's House of Dreams*, and finally discuss *Rilla of Ingleside*, in which sorrow, rage, and pain erupt through the tissue of patriotic stoicism with which all Montgomery's female characters are imbued. By moving through these losses, I trace the development of the author's own narrative strategies for dealing with events that are both unspeakable and ineffable: unspeakable because socially unacceptable and ineffable because imbued with emotion too intense for linguistic representation. Insofar as grief and mourning are represented as experiences beyond individual characters' capacities for expression, Montgomery nevertheless supplies her readers with scenes of reading and writing, within the novels themselves, which instruct them how to recognize true feeling. That is, in pillorying the "silly sentiment" and sensationalism that characterized certain well-known exemplars of sentimental fiction,[4] Montgomery's earlier novels teach readers that authentic suffering is located not in voluble displays of emotion, but in between the lines of otherwise exemplarily decorous discourse. Through the strategic use of silence, understatement, humour, and displacement, Montgomery embeds in these novels traumatic stories of bodies and minds in pain.

Yet, given that a parallel purpose of sentimental literature is to instruct its readers in the uncomplaining forbearance of earthly trials, it is easy to read the silences of Montgomery's characters as capitulations to the demands of sentimental stoicism. However, her novels also demonstrate that the most deeply felt suffering is not encapsulated by the symbolic register of language alone, but is also written on, and betrayed by, the body. At key moments throughout the series, it is not what characters say, so much as the way in which they say it, that telegraphs their feelings of grief, shame, or rage to readers. Montgomery thus figures the manifestation of these feelings as eruptions from the register of language that Julia Kristeva has termed the semiotic *chora*. In her theory of communication and desire, Kristeva uses the term "semiotic" to describe a realm of meaning that is non-verbal, comprising gesture, intonation, and sounds that are non-sensical, such as cries or moans. These seemingly involuntary eruptions underscore the disciplinary force of the symbolic register (as in the case of hand gestures, for example), which is the register of words: their commonly understood meanings and their arrangement into syntactic, logical order. However, these involuntary eruptions also, in many ways, *undermine* the disciplinary structure of the symbolic because tone and bodily contortion can affect the meaning of what is said. I conclude that Montgomery's sympathetic demonstration of semiotic mourning, most vividly glimpsed in *Rilla of Ingleside*, represents a rebellion against prevailing contemporary models of sentimental stoicism. In directing us to read her novels in ways that draw attention to these moments of rebellion, Montgomery reveals to us a grief that is neither resolved nor accepted.

"Reading Between the Lines"

Those familiar with the unfortunate fates of Ladies Cordelia Montmorency and Geraldine Seymore will be well aware that sudden and tragic deaths figure largely in young Anne's literary productions. Indeed all the stories produced by the members of the story club – Anne, Diana Barry, Jane Andrews, and Ruby Gillis – "are very pathetic and almost everybody died" (211). If readers are not tipped off already by Anne's hyperbolic descriptions of Cordelia's "duskily flashing" and Geraldine's "velvety purple eyes," they know to take their cue from the hilarity these stories provoke in the Reverend and Mrs. Allan, and Miss Josephine Barry (208). While these three are clearly not Anne's ideal readers, for "they laughed in all the wrong places and [she] like[d] it better when people cry," they are clearly Montgomery's (211). The Allans, in particular, are characters whom Montgomery has set up to be the most sympathetic to both her heroine and to the author's reading public. Anne's intense desire for Mrs. Allan's approval leads younger and adult readers alike to align themselves with the minister's wife in her warmly amused, but always infinitely understanding, responses to Anne's undertakings. Anne's beloved teacher, Miss Stacy, is also such a character. The novel's strongest statement against "silly sentiment" comes in the form of the teacher's sharp criticism of any writing that does not stem from Anne's everyday experiences in Avonlea (283, 255). The most effective prose, she teaches, is the simplest and the shortest.

As though the author has followed Miss Stacy's instructions, death, when it eventually comes to Green Gables, is, in fact, given scarcely more textual space than the heart-rending tale of "The Jealous Rival; or, In Death not Divided." While the occasional Anne-like descriptor escapes into the narrative – Matthew has been "crowned" by "the white majesty of death" (294) – the sparse record of Matthew's death gestures to an experience up to this point completely alien to Anne: the inability to put her thoughts and feelings into words. The words and the tears that have come so easily to Anne, in times of both joy and sorrow throughout the novel, fail her at this moment, leaving only the "horrible dull ache of misery" (295).[5] This shift in narrative register serves an obvious structural purpose in setting aside the episode of Matthew's death, and its attendant very real trauma, from the melodramatic episodes that have elicited such tempestuous and deeply felt responses from Anne in the past – her abject mourning for the loss of her hair comes to mind here! Yet in presenting Anne's response to Matthew's death as an instantiation of the inadequacy of language itself, Montgomery also introduces readers to what will become her ongoing concern with the ineffability of grief, a concern that will extend into questions of how to articulate trauma on a broader scale.

The most important distinction to draw here is the difference between those experiences that are simply too painful to articulate and those that are constrained by social taboos. Both of these dilemmas are presented in a variety of ways throughout the *Anne* series, and both kinds of experiences will ultimately find modes of expression, even if they seem far removed from the original pain. With respect to the question of what *may* be talked about in polite society, we can clearly see the development of Montgomery's narrative strategy if we set in relief Anne's story before she came to Green Gables and the biography of Mary Vance, as it is told in *Rainbow Valley*. Immediately obvious to readers of both novels is the almost total absence of Anne's back story in *Anne of Green Gables*. We know that she is the daughter of respectable people, and that over the course of her eleven years she has been shunted from one disreputable family to the next, before ending up in the ironically named Hopeton asylum. The one detail Anne shares of this experience is her exasperation with the three sets of twins to whose care she has had to dedicate a large portion of her short life.

The comic relief offered by the vision of three sets of twins masks the drudgery to which Anne has been subjected, while her passing acknowledgment of Mrs. Thomas's "drunken husband," coupled with the breakneck pace of her narrative, allows readers to gloss over the potential for violence encoded in that short phrase (39–40). Given that we know that Anne does not enjoy "talking about her experiences in a world that had not wanted her," her bowdlerizing of her past may certainly be understood, in part, as a defence mechanism (40). In reciting her story as though it is a lesson she has learned by heart, Anne keeps at bay any of the disturbing memories that may manifest themselves somatically as she fills Marilla in on her personal history. Indeed, without delving too deeply into an analysis of Anne's immense capacity for imaginative dissociation, and what this might tell us about the violence she has suffered in her past, it is sufficient to note here that when Marilla presses her for more information, Anne responds with physical discomfort. Tellingly, her reaction is an inarticulate expression of shame and embarrassment: "'O-o-o-h,' faltered Anne. Her sensitive little face suddenly flushed scarlet and embarrassment sat on her brow" (41).[6] Up to this point, the rapidity of her delivery and her matter-of-fact tone have resisted our pity, and, it seems, Marilla's. It is not until Marilla takes note of the language of Anne's body that her sympathy for this "sensitive, 'highstrung' child" is stirred (46). It is not an elaborately worded entreaty, but enough is telegraphed by Anne's posture of rigid anxiety and her "look of mute misery" that Marilla is able "to read between the lines and divine the truth" of Anne's experience (41, 46).

Anne's inability to speak in the scenes leading up to her lucky escape from Mrs. Blewett – a woman memorably described as "exactly like a gimlet" – throws into sharp relief the two sources of silence in the *Anne* series (47). Anne does not reveal the details of her unhappy childhood both because she cannot and because she must not. The fact that words themselves are often incommensurable with traumatic experiences plays a part in her silence, as in the case of Matthew's death, but just as significantly, there are certain social niceties that must be observed, even by a narrator gifted with the power of free indirect discourse. The veil drawn over Anne's past by the novel's very narrative structure suggests the author's unwillingness to present her heroine as damaged in any way. Anne does finally share her entire story with the sympathetic Mrs. Allan, who is, more than coincidentally, the minister's wife and whose ears are therefore more suitable receptacles for confessions than Diana's, or even the maiden Marilla's. But readers are not privy to this particular conversation. Instead, it is not until "The Advent of Mary Vance" in Montgomery's 1919 *Rainbow Valley* that the details of what it must have been like for Anne to be "an unloved little drudge" (*Rainbow* 81) finally come to light.

As Perry Nodelman has noted in the Fall 2008 special issue of *Canadian Children's Literature*, Montgomery's *Anne* stories are characterized by her tendency to revisit and transform ideas and images from her earlier works. Anne admits to seeing something of herself in imaginative, outspoken Mary Vance, and while this resemblance is immediately quashed by Miss Cornelia's refusal to consider the obviously déclassé Mary as in any way similar to her beloved Anne (to whom Miss Cornelia feels herself to be both socially and spiritually kindred), Anne's empathy for Mary's position allows us to read their stories as parallel. A further link is forged between the two by Faith Meredith's identification of the Hopeton asylum as "the same place Mrs Blythe came from" (33). In hearing Anne's name invoked so shortly after Mary's tales of "lickings," "larrupings," neglect, and near starvation, readers who may not have made the connection between the two "homeless little orphans" are reminded of the circumstances of Anne's life before she came to Green Gables (62). Mary's account of her life is vouchsafed by the bruises and starvation so plainly displayed on and by her "scrawny arms and thin hands" (31). Such emphasis on her malnourished frame, and "the old plaid dress, much too tight and short for her," causes us to wonder what kinds of scars and what evidence of abuse and neglect that other "very short, very tight, very ugly dress of yellow-ish grey wincey" may have hidden all those years ago (*Rainbow* 30, *Green Gables* 11).[7]

But in openly confessing and displaying the gruesome details of her personal history – those same kinds of details that Anne's natural delicacy excised from her account – Mary Vance shows us that she does not "come from the same place" as "Mrs Dr" Blythe, née Anne Shirley. Anne is somehow essentially different from Mary because of her inherited refinement of sensibility. Unlike the discourse of the "ladylike" Anne, which entails, as Marilla approvingly notes, "nothing rude or slangy" and thus reveals her connections to "nice folks" (*Green Gables* 41), Mary Vance's speech is peppered with profanities and slang terms. Far from being "nice folks," her parents were violent, alcoholic suicides, driven to their deaths by "booze" (*Rainbow* 33). Mary's unabashed account of the violence she suffered at their hands and the hands of the unpleasantly named Mrs. Wiley, from whom she has escaped, illustrates that social class plays a key role in what may and may not be spoken by particular characters in Montgomery's novels.

The introduction of Mary Vance into the last two books of the series finally makes public the plight of abused, overworked, and neglected children. But it does so in a way that distances Mary from Anne even as similarities are identified between them. Mary's traumatic history can be laid relatively bare without fear that young readers will identify with her to the extent that they are somehow traumatized in turn. By manipulating the strategies of sentimental narrative in ways that had earlier been employed by survivors of slavery, such as Harriet Jacobs, Montgomery manages to expose the abuses of child domestic labour without compromising the innocence of her readers. Both these writers make use of the structure of the sentimental novel in order to garner the understanding of her readers; the familiar domestic space of such narratives "seduces" them into sympathy with characters who might otherwise have scandalized their sensibilities.[8]

Yet like Jacobs's text, both *Rainbow Valley* and *Anne of Green Gables* introduce the trope of domestic spaces that are not always safe. All three of these narratives employ sentimental discourse only to subtly overturn it in ways that expose what Toni Morrison has famously referred to as those "unspeakable things, unspoken" (199) – the physical (and even more unspeakably, sexual) violence meted out upon slaves, and in Mary Vance's and Anne's cases, on children "employed" as domestic servants.[9] Jacobs was well aware of the fine line between "chaste civility" and the authentic recitation of her experiences. She therefore insisted on the publication of *Incidents in the Life of a Slave Girl* in manuscript form before she herself testified publicly to her experience. Using the mediating structure built into novels in general, and domestic fiction in particular, Jacobs was able to maintain the alliance with her readers that would have been destabilized by her embodied, racialized presence. A sentimentalized, textual body stands in for the actual, abused body with the result that sympathy is converted into support for abolition and radical political action. In a similar yet not necessarily identical move, Mary Vance's body stands in for Anne's, displacing the realities of child abuse onto the working-class child. Montgomery's deeply personal concern with the mistreatment of children thus manifests itself without sabotaging the purity of her heroine.

On hearing of the phenomenal success of *Anne of Green Gables* in 1908, Montgomery wrote in her journal that she was glad she had kept "the shadows of [her] life out of [her] work" (*Selected Journals* 1, 339). However, Mary's appearance in Rainbow Valley suggests that a significant development in Montgomery's thinking and writing about childhood took place between 1908 and 1919 – one which encourages us to look again at the supposedly shadow-free narrative of *Green Gables*. Unlike in the narrative of the first *Anne* book, in which abuse, violence, and neglect are obscured, such things are now explicitly acknowledged as presences in the "rainbow valley" of childhood, just as the brutal truth that young boys grow up to be soldiers underlies *Rainbow Valley*'s poignant concluding vignette of the Blythe and Meredith children meeting together in the valley for the last time:

> The lads who were to fight, and perhaps fall, on the fields of France and Flanders, Gallipoli and Palestine, were still roguish schoolboys with a fair life in prospect before them: the girls whose hearts were to be wrung were yet fair little maidens a-star with hopes and dreams. (224)

HILARY EMMETT

"What a Terrible Thing It Is To Be a Mother"

Montgomery's own difficult marriage, the still-birth of her second son, Hugh, and the outbreak of World War I undoubtedly challenged her resolve to be only a "messenger of optimism and sunshine" (*Selected Journals* 1, 339). *Anne's House of Dreams*, the first book of the four that describe Anne's life as a wife and mother, is a veritable catalogue of male violence, feminine manipulations, and the suffering of innocents (Robinson 28). Significantly, the steady litany of complaints about abusive husbands is placed in the mouth of the comical, "man-hating" Miss Cornelia Bryant. We, as readers, are presumably supposed to assume that her accounts are exaggerated or somehow unfounded – and to simply dismiss them as a harmless form of gossip. Yet as Jenny Rubio has shown, it is precisely through gossip that women are able to express support for one another and articulate certain feelings that the demands of "decorum" might otherwise force them to internalize. Projecting one's own experiences of rage or jealousy onto absent others provides an outlet for socially unacceptable feelings of "anger and frustration" (Rubio 173).

Furthermore, in making Miss Cornelia a source of amusement, Montgomery once again manages to represent an unpalatable social reality while providing her readers with distance from the unfortunate women and children whose male protectors regularly starve, strike, and browbeat them. Several of Miss Cornelia's tales, in fact, have a basis in reality. The unfortunate Henry Hammond, who sustains brain damage after his father "threw a stump at him when he was small" (*House* 50), has a historical counterpart in Dan Fraser, the brother of Simon Fraser, with whom Montgomery boarded while teaching school in Belmont (*Selected Journals* 1, 165). Moreover, in several key instances, Miss Cornelia's stories of domestic abuse are confirmed or subtly endorsed by other, more "reliable" characters. Even Gilbert, the impartial man of science, and the magnanimous Captain Jim are forced to acknowledge that Billy Booth has a dangerously jealous streak (*House* 112), and that Lewis Taylor starves his family and works his wife into the ground (94).

The "demonic marriage" of Leslie Moore forms the gruesome centrepiece of this series of tableaux of domestic discord.[10] Captain Jim and Miss Cornelia come to one of their rare moments of agreement when they acknowledge the series of "tragedies" that have befallen Leslie throughout her life, tragedies that culminate in her forced marriage to the boorish, drunken despoiler of women,

Dick Moore. However, as Irene Gammel has noted, the details of this union are tellingly absent from Montgomery's novel ("My Secret Garden" 55). Anne enjoins Leslie not to speak of the agonies she endured upon her brother's death, as well as upon her discovery that her husband not only "drank," but was also responsible for the unfortunate fate of "the girl down at the fishing cove" (*House* 127). The ordinarily outspoken Miss Cornelia also stops short of recounting what is presumably a tale of seduction and abandonment, simply labelling the story a "nasty" one (73). But whereas Gammel directs readers to Montgomery's account of her own marital difficulties in her journals, in order to fill in the gaps left in the fictional narrative, my intention here is to emphasize the narrative strategies Montgomery employed *in* the novels to represent the seemingly unrepresentable violence of thought and deed. Through a form of negation – the explicit refusal to speak, or the denial of speech – such events and feelings obtain a glaring textual presence by means of their very absence.

Injunctions against speaking immediately point toward what is left unsaid and what must not be heard. Even wordless injunctions, like the cotton wool Susan Baker stuffs in her ears to drown out the sounds of Anne's long and difficult labour, direct our attention to yet another silence in Montgomery's novels – the unmentionables, except in coy euphemisms, of pregnancy and childbirth (*House* 114). Given the very real possibilities of infant and maternal mortality, in addition to Montgomery's actual experience of the death of her son through complications during birth, it is unsurprising that pregnancy and childbirth should be referred to only obliquely. The refusal to name Anne's condition during either of her pregnancies in *House of Dreams*, and again in *Anne of Ingleside*, may be understood as a form of superstition, an unwillingness to "jinx" the safe passage of both mother and baby through pregnancy and labour. Yet in Montgomery's writing motherhood brings with it a whole host of other necessary silences – fears that must remain unspoken, and resentments and rages that run contrary to the demands made on mothers by both church and state. For example, in her later novel, Anne and her daughter, Rilla, will force themselves to wave their boys off to war with smiles that reflect their patriotic support for the war effort (*Rilla* 138). Similarly, Anne is rebuked for voicing her contention that her baby's death was the work of the devil, which God failed to avert.

Anne's labour pains may have been muffled by Susan's judicious use of cotton wool, but her raw anguish on learning of the death of her baby, little Joy, is harder to silence. Refusing to countenance the idea that little Joy's death is evidence of God's benign will, Anne declares that it may just as easily be the

HILARY EMMETT

result of "a thwarting of his purpose by the Power of Evil" (*House* 118). She is immediately hushed by a scandalized Marilla, but not before Anne's outburst and Marilla's reaction have done their work. This brief scene, made all the more poignant by the transmigration of Montgomery's own pain, illustrates the limits imposed upon maternal mourning by the Christian creed voiced here by Miss Cornelia: "the Lord [giveth] and the Lord [taketh] away" (*House* 116). In being cut off by well-meaning and morally upstanding characters like Marilla and Miss Cornelia, Anne's rebellious exclamations can be permitted to remain in the text. A blasphemy that Montgomery, as a minister's wife, could never have uttered openly is given safe expression by her fictional character. Anne is gently taken to task for it, but our readerly sympathies for her are so engaged by this point that her words remain with us despite Marilla's attempt at silencing.

Despite the tragic loss of little Joy, the greatest test of Anne's maternal endurance will ultimately come with the outbreak of war in *Rilla of Ingleside*. As Montgomery confided on more than one occasion in her journal, mother-love, "exquisite as it is, is full of anguish too" (*Selected Journals* 2, 101). She tormented herself with the prospect that she might die in childbirth, leaving her child to experience the suffering of a motherless existence (*Selected Journals* 2, 97), while the very thought of her own child being "neglected or ill-used" elicited from her cries of abject horror (*Selected Journals* 2, 102). To be a mother is to sacrifice forever the unequivocal pleasures of imagination. Once a well-spring of comfort, escape, and autonomy, the imagination becomes the source of unspeakable agonies. For mothers, imagination is no longer a refuge from the world's reality, but rather an extension of it.

If to be a mother is already to imagine all the most terrifying things that may befall a child, then how much more agonizing must it be to be the mother of soldiers? Throughout the preceding *Anne* books, the imagination has consistently been invoked as a means of escape. As an abused and neglected domestic drudge, Anne maintained an original and autonomous subjectivity through the power of her imagination. Throughout the series, therefore, there is no situation that cannot be improved upon or escaped from by the power of imagination. But the outbreak of war and the initial enlistment of her eldest son, Jem, finally defeat the diversionary power of her legendary imagination. After Jem leaves for the Front, she declares:

"I hate going to bed now. All my life I've liked going to bed, to have a gay, mad, splendid half hour of imagining things before sleeping. Now I imagine them still. But much different things." (*Rilla* 99)

Anne's voice trails off, leaving readers to contemplate the different ways in which a mother might imagine the unnatural horror that the violent and premature death of a son signifies.

In industrialized warfare lies a rather grim irony. Families of soldiers fighting in World War I had more access to the particulars of the battlefield than civilians had had during any prior conflict, yet the most crucial knowledge – the whereabouts and safety of one's loved ones – remained unavailable.[11] In *Rilla of Ingleside*, the cruel promise of this information overload is dramatized by the contrast between Montgomery's comic rendering of Susan Baker's exponential learning curve and the agony of "not knowing" in the chapters of Jem's disappearance:

The gallant Anzacs withdrew from Gallipoli and Susan approved the step, with reservations. The siege of Kut-El-Amara began and Susan pored over maps of Mesopotamia and abused the Turks.... Sir John French was superseded by Sir Douglas Haig and Susan dubiously opined that it was poor policy to swap horses crossing a stream.... "There was a time," she said sorrowfully, "when I did not care what happened outside of P.E. Island, and now a king cannot have a toothache ... but it worries me. It may be broadening to the mind as the doctor said, but it is very painful to the feelings." (*Rilla* 160)

Yet all this access to reports, newsreels, radio broadcasts, and postcards cannot yield the information that the Blythe family desires when Jem is reported "wounded and missing." Rilla agonizes:

"Must we go for weeks and months – not knowing whether Jem is alive or dead? ... I think this is even worse than the news of his death would have been.... Perhaps we will never know. I – I *cannot* bear it – I *cannot*. Walter and now Jem. This will kill mother – look at her face ... and you will see that." (*Rilla* 264)

In such lacunae within the official war record, a dangerous, uncontrollable form of imagination resides. In the absence of information, images leap unbidden to the mind's eye, such as when Rilla stands to recite at a Red Cross fundraiser in the Glen. She sees before her not a sea of her friends' and neighbours' faces, but only the face of her brother, Walter, who has just enlisted. Yet it is not his presence in the audience that she "sees." Rather, she envisions all the possible ways in which he might meet his death:

> . . . one face only – that of the handsome, dark-haired lad . . . she saw it in the trenches, saw it lying cold and dead under the stars – saw it pining in prison – saw the light of his eyes blotted out – saw a hundred horrible things as she stood there on the beflagged platform of the Glen hall with her own face whiter than the milky crab blossoms in her hair. (*Rilla* 128)

In *Rilla of Ingleside*, imagination is transformed from a delightful escapist tool into a source of prophetic truth.

Rilla seems to have been blessed (or cursed) here with a little of what we might call the "clairvoyant" or "mystic" imaginations of Walter Blythe and Gertrude Oliver. At the lighthouse dance, the night before the outbreak of war is declared to the youth of Glen St. Mary, Miss Oliver dreams that a tidal wave of blood washes over the Glen, obliterating life as the Prince Edward Islanders know it. Gertrude recounts a variation of a dream that Montgomery herself recorded in her journal (*Selected Journals* 2, 177). Gertrude explains,

> "The Glen was being swallowed up. I thought, 'Surely the waves will not come near Ingleside' – but they came nearer and nearer ...

and everything was gone – there was nothing but a waste of stormy water where the Glen had been. I tried to draw back – and I saw that the edge of my dress was wet, *with blood.*" (*Rilla* 20)

Similarly, after war has been declared, Walter has a vision:

"Before this war is over," he said – or something said through his lips – "every man and woman in Canada will feel it – you Mary, will feel it to your heart's core. You will weep tears of blood over it. The piper has come – and he will pipe until every corner of the world has heard his awful, irresistible music." (36)

Ostensibly, this blood is the blood of the men (including fifty thousand Canadians) who gave their lives during World War I. The blood that flows is that of slaughtered sacrificial victims – an explicit theme in *Rilla*. Walter departs for the war, "not radiantly, as to a high adventure, like Jem … but in a *white flame of sacrifice*" (*Rilla* 226; my emphasis); and in the letter home, which he knows to be his last, he writes that he fights, and will die, for the fate of all humanity. But even more than signifiers of sacrifice, the tears and torrents of blood that ebb and flow throughout *Rilla* function as a semiotics of a specifically feminine mourning, a particular grief that has no verbal expression in the novel, but nevertheless betrays itself on the level of Montgomery's very language.

Although, as Donna Coates has argued, the mourning of wives, mothers, and sisters was "socially sanctioned" (76), characters evince very little tolerance for public outpourings of grief in *Rilla of Ingleside*. Both Rilla and Anne are frequently exhorted to "keep a stiff upper lip." The rousing lines "When our women fail in courage, / Shall our men be fearless still?" are quoted more than once in the novel (*Rilla* 43, 127). Anne sees Jem off with a wave and a smile and even Shirley is given a stoic blessing to go to the Front, despite Walter's recent death. However, it is my contention that the voice of mourning erupts through the veneer of stalwart patriotism encasing Montgomery's narrative. Her patriotic edifice is assailed first in the waves of blood, which are so like the blood and water that attend both birth and death, and secondly in the metaphor of rending that recurs throughout the text, most notably in reference to the utterances of

HILARY EMMETT

Gertrude Oliver. Behind the patriotic and empowering depiction of Anne and Rilla at their war work, there lurks an abiding and deeply disturbing current of grief that operates directly at odds with the representation of women as guardians of the Home Front. The public sphere, represented by "the Call greater and more insistent than the call of [familial or erotic] love," is everywhere assailed by feminine affects that will not stay private (*Rilla* 131). Rilla "passionately" responds to her mother's description of this call: "our boys give only *themselves*. *We* give them" (131). That is, there are bonds of familial love and loyalty that men may be prepared to break, but such commitments will be upheld by women in defiance of any priority the state claims to have over the family.[12]

Rilla's most significant contribution to the war effort is her adoption of the war baby, "James Kitchener Anderson," who awakens her nascent maternal urges and provides the occasion for Rilla's transition from girlhood to womanhood, when she will become a fitting wife for the dashing Kenneth Ford. On his last night of leave, Ken visits Ingleside in order to reveal his feelings for Rilla. In a scene that is both hilarious and cringe-inducing, "Little Kitchener" begins to cry at the top of his voice and Rilla is forced to spend her last evening with Kenneth with her war baby and Susan as chaperones. In a tableau that speaks directly to the burden of suffering placed on the women who gave their men to defend the Empire, we see Rilla pictured as the Madonna cradling the infant Christ:

> Jims ... cuddled down against her just where a gleam of light from the lamp in the living-room struck across his hair and turned it into a halo of gold against her breast. Kenneth sat very still and silent, looking at Rilla ... he thought she looked exactly like the Madonna that hung over his mother's desk at home. (*Rilla* 146)

This image of the Madonna and child is made all the more poignant in this context via the way that this representation of maternal love always already contains within it the pietà of Mary cradling the dead body of her son cut down from the cross.

In her treatment of the pietà figure in "Stabat Mater," Julia Kristeva argues that the milk and tears of Marian iconography are part of "a semiotics that linguistic expression does not account for" (174). The milk that nurtures the body of the child, the tears that prefigure its death, and, I would add, the blood that flows in the event of both birth and death are powerful metaphors of "non-speech." That is, they are symbolic of what Montgomery herself saw as the ineffable "agony and tragedy of motherhood" (*Selected Journals* 2, 162). Whereas Kristeva quotes Simeon's words to Mary from the Gospel of Luke ("and a sword will pierce your own soul too"), Montgomery puts similar words of prophecy in the mouth of Walter Blythe. Walter's words to Mary Vance – "you Mary, will feel it to your heart's core and you will weep tears of blood over it" – echo the Biblical prophecy, and, even more significantly, foreshadow the piercing, stabbing, and rending of flesh that accompany the rare expressions of grief by women in the novel.

The first such moment occurs when Jem announces his intention to enlist alongside his childhood friend, Jerry Meredith, who is also the sweetheart of Nan, Anne's oldest daughter and her namesake: "Jem turned to the phone again. 'I must ring the manse. Jerry will want to go too.' At this Nan cried out 'Oh!' as if a knife had been thrust into her, and rushed from the room" (*Rilla* 45). Again and again the women in the novel express their grief through "cries," "exclamations," and "moans." Their grief is involuntary and inarticulate. It wells up from the Kristevan semiotic – that modality of significance erupting into the symbolic and bearing a surplus relationship to it. For Kristeva, the semiotic is associated with the maternal body and the pre-linguistic domain of rhythm, intonation, and gesture, while the symbolic is the modality of language and meaning – the public sphere of the *Non/Nom du Père*, the name and the law of the father (Kristeva, *Revolution* 26, 29). The cries and exclamations of Nan, Rilla, and Gertrude Oliver articulate a sorrow that cannot be bound by the social injunction against the public display of mourning. They express a very real, almost physical, agony that erupts into their otherwise carefully scripted performances of patriotism.

It is Miss Oliver, the type of clever and charming – though occasionally mocking and cynical – schoolteacher so familiar to readers of Montgomery's novels and journals, who is most prone to these eruptions of grief. To her the whole world is a "shriek of anguish" (*Rilla* 114). On hearing of her fiancé's supposed death (he is subsequently found to be only wounded), she first laughs "such a dreadful little laugh just as one might laugh in the face of death" (184). Later that night, Rilla hears emanating from the other woman's room "a dreadful, sudden little cry as if she had been stabbed" (185). The visceral nature of Gertrude's articulations of grief is significant because in the eyes of many of the other characters in the novel, there is something indecorous and even politically suspect about her eruptions. "It isn't ladylike to talk like that" is Cousin Sophia's reaction to Miss Oliver's diatribe against those who will not recognize her right to mourn:

> "It's true I haven't lost a husband, I have only lost the man who would have been my husband. I have lost no son – only the sons and daughters who might have been born to me – who will never be born to me now." (184)

It is not only unpatriotic, but also unladylike to evince any kind of strong re-action to the "*dulce et decorous*" death of men in the service of their country. Furthermore, the possibility of public action, either political (the recognition of a right to vote) or social (the community's recognition of a right to mourn), is denied to both these young women. Since it is neither Miss Oliver's husband nor her son who is enlisted to fight, she cannot vote in the elections of 1917. Only those women with an immediate relative at the Front could participate. Rilla, too, is denied a vote, despite the loss of one brother and the active service of two more, because she is not yet of age (246). As a result, private onslaughts of tears, dreams of waves of blood erupting from the unconscious, and immediately censured (and censored) outbursts are the only ways in which grief, rage, and frustration can be enacted.

CONCLUSION: "IN DEATH NOT DIVIDED"

We might hear in such outbursts the haunting echoes of Antigone's famously denied claim. Like Sophocles' heroine, who is denied both the right to mourn her brother publicly and to bury his body, those in Montgomery's novel whose claims are unrecognized by state or society cannot perform the tasks required adequately to mourn the dead and commit them to memory. While Rilla is the character placed most immediately in Antigone's position – she has, after all, lost her brother – both Gertrude Oliver and Una Meredith inhabit this role in perhaps even more significant ways; their losses are utterly denied and de-valued. Una's case is particularly heartbreaking in the way that her love goes unacknowledged by even the beloved himself (*Rilla* 135). The hardest grief to bear, this novel seems to argue, is grief that dares not speak its name because it is socially illegitimate. Maternal mourning may be ineffable in its fundamentally visceral quality, but the grief for those men who are neither sons nor husbands is unspeakable because the structures of respectability require it to be so. By once again staging a scene of writing that directs our reading practice, Montgomery finds a way to speak such grief. "I rage and cry," Rilla tells us, "but I do it all in private and blow off steam in this diary" (76).

In what is by now a familiar strategy, Montgomery makes the private public by giving open expression to socially unacceptable subjects and feelings through the incorporation of a private narrative (the journal) into the publicly circulating narrative of her novel. Yet as latter-day readers of *Rilla of Ingleside*, we are able to give her technique one further turn of the interpretive screw that her contemporary readers could not. We can read into this reference the acknowledgment that Montgomery's own journals were sites of explosive anger and passionate sorrow. Given that the most autobiographical character in *Rilla of Ingleside*, Gertrude Oliver, is the character who calls repeatedly for recognition of the grief belonging to those who have no legal or socially sanctioned claim to such sorrow, it is not unreasonable to turn to Montgomery's diaries for illumination. It is in these pages that we learn of Montgomery's secret but enduring love for Herman Leard – a man to whom she could not bear to unite herself in life, but whose premature demise ensured that he should be "mine, *all* mine in death" (*Selected Journals* 1, 240). As Gammel has noted, the possessiveness of this thought intimates Montgomery's determination to inter Leard in "the mausoleum of her memory, snatching him from the clutches of [his widow] Ettie Schurman," who frequently and publicly mourned at his graveside (Gammel, "I loved" 148).

The "death" and resurrection of Gertrude's fiancé, along with the authorial directive to seek expressions of pain and grief in the pages of a journal, suggest that the grief Montgomery undoubtedly felt for the generation of young men sacrificed in World War I coalesced around a very particular figure who was neither son nor husband, and who died fifteen years before war was even declared. Thus, in the last of the *Anne* novels (in terms of their action, if not their production), we see Montgomery's complex interplay of repression and revelation in its most virtuosic of instantiations. Not only does she make palpable the mourning of Canadian women and the challenge such sorrow mounted against a public sphere that saw the death of young men as the right and proper response to the irresistible "Call" of patriotic duty, but she also harnesses the power of this communal grief to simultaneously mask and disclose her own secret suffering.

Montgomery's contemporaries would not know to read Gertrude Oliver's grief as her own for Herman Leard, but we, the recipients of both her fiction and journals, can unravel her textual clues to see them "in death not divided."

Ultimately, the significance of Montgomery's extraordinary gift for incorporating into her narratives this heady mix of coyness and disclosure lies in the possibilities for reading that her texts invite. The truly unspoken and unheard of idea behind the *Anne* books, at the time of their writing and publication, was that these tales written for children, by a woman living at one of the most remote outposts of Empire, might one day be a valid object of literary study. The complexity of Montgomery's deployment of speech and silence, public and private discourses, bodily affects and voluble chatter, and the careful reading that this technique demands, is precisely what enables volumes such as this to come into being. More importantly, it ensures that pleasures, sorrows, and conversations inspired by *Anne of Green Gables* will continue well into its second century.

WORKS CITED

Coates, Donna. "The Best Soldiers of All: Unsung Heroines in Canadian Women's Great War Fiction." *Canadian Literature* 151 (1996): 66–99.

Freud, Sigmund. *Dora: A Fragment of an Analysis of a Case of Hysteria*. Ed. Philip Rieff. New York: Touchstone, 1997.

Gammel, Irene. "'I loved Herman Leard madly': L. M. Montgomery's Confession of Desire." Ed. Irene Gammel. *The Intimate Life of L. M. Montgomery*. Toronto: U of Toronto P, 2005. 143–53.

———. "'My Secret Garden': Dis/Pleasure in L. M. Montgomery and F. P. Grove." *English Studies in Canada* 25 (1999): 39–65.

Goldsby, Jacqueline. "'I Disguised my Hand': Writing Versions of the Truth in Harriet Jacobs' *Incidents in the Life of a Slave Girl* and John Jacob's 'A True Tale.'" Ed. Deborah Garfield and Rafia Zafar. *Harriet Jacobs and* Incidents in the Life of a Slave Girl: New Critical Essays. New York & Cambridge: Cambridge UP, 1996. 11–43.

Griffin, Farah Jasmin. "Introduction." *Incidents in the Life of a Slave Girl*. By Harriet Jacobs. 1861. Ed. Farah Jasmine Griffin. New York: Barnes and Noble, 2005. xiii–xxvi.

Hegel, G. W. F. *The Phenomenology of Spirit*. Trans. A. V. Miller. Oxford: Oxford UP, 1977.

Herman, Judith. *Trauma and Recovery: The Aftermath of Violence – From Domestic Abuse to Political Terror*. New York: Basic, 1997.

Hynes, Samuel. "Introduction." *The Return of the Soldier.* By Rebecca West. New York: Penguin, 1998. vii–xvi.

Jacobs, Harriet. *Incidents in the Life of a Slave Girl.* 1861. Ed. Farah Jasmine Griffin. New York: Barnes and Noble, 2005.

Kristeva, Julia. *Revolution in Poetic Language.* Trans. Margaret Waller. New York: Columbia UP, 1984.

———. "Stabat Mater." *The Kristeva Reader.* Ed. Toril Moi. New York: Columbia UP, 1986. 160–86.

Montgomery, L. M. *Anne of Green Gables.* 1908. Toronto: Bantam, 1998.

———. *Anne of Ingleside.* 1939. Toronto: Bantam, 1981.

———. *Anne's House of Dreams.* 1917. Toronto: Seal, 1996.

———. *Emily of New Moon.* 1923. New York: Dell and Laurel, 1993.

———. *Kilmeny of the Orchard.* 1910. New York: Starfire, 1989.

———. *Rainbow Valley.* 1919. Toronto: Bantam, 1998.

———. *Rilla of Ingleside.* 1921. London: Angus and Robertson: 1987.

———. *Selected Journals of L. M. Montgomery.* Vol. 1: 1889–1910. Ed. Mary Rubio and Elizabeth Waterson. Toronto: Oxford UP, 1985.

———. *Selected Journals of L. M. Montgomery.* Vol. 2: 1910–1921. Ed. Mary Rubio and Elizabeth Waterson. Toronto: Oxford UP, 1985.

Morrison, Toni. *Beloved.* London: Picador, 1988.

Noble, Marianne. *The Masochistic Pleasures of Sentimental Literature.* Princeton: Princeton UP, 2000.

Nodelman, Perry. "Rereading *Anne of Green Gables* in *Anne of Ingleside*: L. M. Montgomery's Variations." *Canadian Children's Literature/Litterature canadienne pour la jeunesse* 34.2 (Fall 2008): 75–97.

Robinson, Laura. "Bosom Friends: Lesbian Desire in L. M. Montgomery's *Anne* Books." *Canadian Literature* 180 (Spring 2004): 12–29.

Rubio, Jenny. "'Strewn with Dead Bodies': Women and Gossip in *Anne of Ingleside. Harvesting Thistles: The Textual Garden of L. M. Montgomery.* Ed. Mary Henley Rubio. Guelph: Canadian Children's P, 1994. 166–77.

Warner, Susan. *The Wide, Wide World,* 1850. New York: Feminist, 1987.

NOTES

1 See, for example, Anne's dismissal of the writings of Dr. V. Z. Tomachowsky, who admonishes, "'You must never kiss your little son lest you set up a Jocasta complex.' She had laughed over it at the time and been a little angry as well. Now she only felt pity for the writer of it. Poor, poor man! For of course V. Z. Tomachowsky was a man. No woman would ever write anything so silly and wicked" (*Ingleside* 114). Montgomery's inversion of the Oedipus complex here suggests knowledge of Freud's ubiquitous theory, while Anne's skepticism leaves us in little doubt of what Montgomery's thoughts were on the subject.

2 See also her account of the death of her first pet, Pussywillow, the rendering of which entails the "sickening" re-experiencing of "that unforgettable and unforgotten pain" (*Selected Journals* 1, 379).

3 Noble references Elizabeth Barnes, David Denby, and Nina Baym as theorists who emphasize the centrality of unity and community to both Anglo-American and Continental sentimental literatures.

4 It is my speculation that L. M. Montgomery felt a certain ambivalent kinship with *Ellen* Montgomery, the orphaned heroine of Susan Warner's phenomenally successful, and paradigmatically sentimental, 1850 novel, *The Wide Wide World*. Certain scenes in Montgomery's semi-autobiographical *Emily of New Moon* read as though they are rewritings of key moments in Warner's novel, with Emily cast as a far less long-suffering, less accepting version of Ellen. Compare, for example, Emily's first meeting with the volatile yet compelling Ilse Burnley with Ellen's encounter with the harum-scarum Nancy (*Emily* 112–15; *Wide, Wide World* 123), or her immortally haughty rebuff to Cousin Oliver, "I don't *sell* my kisses," with Ellen's indignation at the kindly Mr. Van Brunt's offer to rig her up a swing in exchange for a kiss (*Emily* 26, *Wide, Wide World* 116).

5 Although she would later claim that Matthew's death was simply a plot device to ensure "the necessity for self-sacrifice on Anne's part" (*Selected Journals* 2, 44), Anne's response to Matthew's death closely mirrors Montgomery's own wordless and despairing reaction to her father's death. See *Selected Journals* 1, 248–49.

6 We might see Anne's feelings of shame, and her immediate provision of justification for Mrs. Thomas's and Mrs. Hammond's cruelty, as evidence of what Judith Herman calls "the double self." Herman writes, "When it is impossible to avoid the reality of the abuse, the child must construct some system of meaning which justifies it" (103).

7 We can also add the parallel episodes of children dying of croup to this catalogue of similarities: Mary Vance saves Jims in *Rilla of Ingleside* (218–22), just as Anne saves Minnie May Barry in *Anne of Green Gables* (141–43).

8 On Jacobs's manipulation of the conventions of the sentimental novel, see Farah Jasmine Griffin (xx–xxi). See also Jacqueline Goldsby's analysis of the ways in which Jacobs managed to tell the truth of her tale, despite those elements that tested the limits of "chaste civility" (16–19).

9 Morrison took this phrase as the title of her 1988 Tanner lecture on "Human Values," but it appeared first in her 1987 novel *Beloved* as a description of the aphasia that the traumatic history of slavery had imposed upon the "60 million and more" (dedication) "black and angry dead" (198) to whom the novel is dedicated.

10 The phrase "demonic marriage" is Irene Gammel's ("My Secret Garden" 55); I use it here for its power to evoke the effective "sale" of Leslie's body and soul by her manipulative mother.

11 Samuel Hynes details the unprecedented access that families on the Home Front had to newsreels, photographs, news-

paper reports, and letters during World War I, describing it as "the first war a woman *could* imagine, and the first a woman could write into a novel" (viii–ix). Hynes does not take into account, however, the horrifying consequences of such knowledge: namely, that while women did not know the precise whereabouts of their loved ones, they knew in excruciating detail exactly what kind of fate may have befallen them.

12   G. W. F. Hegel terms this conflict, "the eternal irony of the community" – an irony embodied by "womankind." The commitment of women to the natural ethics of "Divine Law" is a necessary precondition for the male citizen's adoption of the "known law and prevailing custom" that is the Human Law of the community – a community from which women themselves are excluded. For Hegel, Antigone is the exemplar of womankind *par excellence* because her performance of burial rites for her dead brother reveals the Divine Law in its purest form. "The feminine, in the form of the sister, has the highest *intuitive* awareness of what is ethical." Women – as epitomized by Antigone – are the "everlasting irony" or utter negativity of the community because although they are necessary to its reproduction, they will always privilege family over citizenship. This contestation continually brings the community to crisis, but for Hegel the resolution is always the affirmation of the state: an affirmation that is dialectically settled, but nevertheless necessarily ongoing (274–75, 288).

CHAPTER SIX

"The World Hasn't Changed Very Much": Romantic Love in Film and Television Versions of *Anne of Green Gables*

Eleanor Hersey Nickel

In the 1934 film version of *Anne of Green Gables*, Anne tells Matthew the plot of *Romeo and Juliet* in a sly attempt to get information about Marilla's rivalry with the Blythe family. She asks with exaggerated innocence, "You don't think people act that way today, do you?" Matthew, who is mending a fence with characteristic stoicism, replies, "When you get as old as I am, you'll know the world hasn't changed very much." This comment reflects the continuity between Anne's romance with Gilbert in L. M. Montgomery's novel and its film and television adaptations. In the century since Anne first broke her slate over Gilbert's head, scholars have generally avoided discussing romance in the novel, have devoted few articles to the romance-heavy 1934 Hollywood film, and have criticized the love story in Kevin Sullivan's 1985 miniseries. Yet perhaps "the world hasn't changed very much" after all. Anne's relationship with Gilbert in the novel contains many classic elements of romance fiction, which the 1930s film and the 1980s miniseries extend in ways that reflect our ongoing interest in love between intellectual, moral, and emotional equals.

Gilbert's role in the novel – as intellectual rival, kindred spirit, and future husband – provides many tensions and pleasures that have been overlooked or denied by scholars throughout the 1980s and 1990s (see Hersey 50). This pattern continues in the twenty-first century. Marah Gubar's article, "'Where Is the Boy?': The Pleasures of Postponement in the *Anne of Green Gables* Series" (2001), represents the recent trend of explicitly labelling Anne's relationship with Gilbert as "heterosexual," opening up the possibility for alternative forms of romance, but ironically leading to the presumption that male-female relationships are inherently insincere, coercive, or oppressive. Gubar argues that the series consistently postpones marriages for the sake of "passionate relationships between women that prove far more romantic" (47). While Anne immediately bonds with Diana, her refusal to forgive Gilbert until the end of the first novel links their love "to the cessation of the pleasures of narrative" (60). Benjamin Lefebvre agrees in "Stand by Your Man: Adapting L. M. Montgomery's *Anne of Green Gables*" (2002):

> Montgomery's novels focus on the emotional and artistic development of her female characters, delaying the "inevitable" romantic ending as much as possible even while appearing to remain within the confines of the domestic novel; as part of this strategy, many of her tacked-on romantic dénouements appear underdeveloped and contrived. (151)

Neither critic acknowledges that virtually all romantic fictions – from William Shakespeare to Jane Austen to contemporary Hollywood films – postpone romantic reconciliation until the end. Nor is it surprising that Anne's relationship with Gilbert is "the hard-won product of an extremely painful process" (Gubar 60), since her romance with him demands considerably more maturity and wisdom than her friendship with Diana.

Several articles in Irene Gammel's collection *Making Avonlea: L.M. Montgomery and Popular Culture* (2002) criticize the heterosexual nature of the romance plot, as in Brenda R. Weber's claim that "I find the relentless heterosexual logic about the possibilities for women rather depressing in both [novel and miniseries] versions of Anne" (53). Speaking for the generation of women that first read the books in the 1960s, Margaret Steffler focuses on the liberating experience of reading Montgomery's journals in the 1980s and 1990s, expressing a common second-wave feminist cynicism about romance, which leads her to celebrate independence and subversion:

It is no mistake that we remember the slate over Gilbert's head more vividly than the conversation between Anne and Gilbert at the conclusion of *Anne of Green Gables*. We respond to the tension that precedes the conventional love relationship and are bothered by the unrealistic dissipation of that tension when love and marriage are applied. Even as young readers, we knew we were questioning and subverting the successful love relationships that compromised Anne and Emily for us. (77)

Even "successful" love relationships are seen as compromising the heroines, and Steffler suggests that Montgomery would have struggled with depression and suicidal thoughts no matter whom she had married.

Gammel finds an alternative to heterosexuality in the novel's "erotic land-scapes," arguing that "Montgomery's girls are profoundly modern in that they do not wait for pleasures to materialize in heterosexual romance. Montgomery empowers her girls to be agents in their erotic universe" ("Safe Pleasures" 118). Not surprisingly in this context, K. L. Poe criticizes Sullivan's miniseries for its supposed departure from the author's intentions: "Had Montgomery wanted to have the romance be the focus of her series, she most likely would have called it *Anne and Gilbert*, not *Anne of Green Gables*, *Anne of Avonlea*, and so on" (149). Poe joins other critics in the collection by asserting that "it is not the heterosexual unions in the Anne series that form the basis of the narrative" (149).

This idea finds a more thorough expression in Laura Robinson's "Bosom Friends: Lesbian Desire in L. M. Montgomery's *Anne* Books" (2004). Robinson clarifies Montgomery's highly conflicted feelings about female friendships, lesbianism, and marriage, complicating the idea that she simply "tacked on" a formulaic ending to a novel that is really about Anne's love for Diana:

The single life, while an option, is simply not appealing. Marilla is a dry old maid. Wealthy Miss Barry laments her loneliness when Diana and Anne leave.... By, on the one hand, affirming the power and fulfillment derived from women's love for each other, and then, on the other, emphasizing the inevitability of marriage, Montgomery's novels underscore the fact that, at the turn of the twentieth century, heterosexuality was indeed compulsory. (20)

Although Robinson's initial conference presentation of this argument provoked an international scandal, her reading is very balanced in its recognition that Montgomery declared, "'I am not a Lesbian'" and was "disturbed yet fascinated" by another woman's interest in her (12). Surely a total rejection of heterosexuality would be inadequate to describe Montgomery's views, the novels' plots, or the pleasures that generations of straight female readers have taken in the novels and films.

For myself and many other third-wave feminists who first read the novels and watched the films in the 1980s, Anne's relationship with Gilbert seemed less like a reiteration of compulsory heterosexuality than a welcome antidote to the bitterness and instability of the American divorce culture. The assumption that heterosexual romance is inevitably oppressive and patriarchal raises important questions about the response of third-wave feminism to marriage and to men: must we continually smash our slate (representing our writing) over the boy's head (ironically destroying our ability to write), or can we take a cue from the final chapter and reconcile with him in order to get some studying done? Perhaps he serves to stimulate healthy competition. Whatever our contemporary attitudes toward male-female relationships, Montgomery's novel assumes that they are the core of most women's lives and that an intelligent girl will learn to distinguish between good and bad forms of courtship, men, and marriages. Montgomery did not craft Gilbert's character merely as a representative of "relentless heterosexual logic about the possibilities for women" but as a particular kind of man – handsome, politically liberal, intelligent, ambitious, witty, competitive, and deeply loyal – that will make Anne an ideal marriage partner.

"HER FRIEND THE ENEMY": GILBERT IN 1908

When Montgomery created the character of Gilbert Blythe, she seems to have been looking back to her adolescent friendship with Nathan Lockhart, whom she introduces in the first pages of her *Selected Journals*: "He is crazy about books and so am I. We exchange those we've got and talk about them. And the other scholars don't like it because we talk of things they don't understand" (1–2).

Nate romantically pursues the fourteen- and fifteen-year-old Maud, but she is unsure of her own feelings. While she is excited and gratified by his attentions, she keeps him at a distance, eventually complaining that he has spoiled their friendship by being "absurdly sentimental" (1, 24). Their strained relationship effectively ends when Nate leaves for college, and she expresses her shock when she learns in 1906 that he is married, practising law, and growing gray: "Nate *gray*!!! What an idea! Why, wasn't it only the other day that he was a curly-headed schoolboy? What business has he to be getting gray? Nate! *Gray?*" (1, 318). Her many exclamation and question marks suggest that this was still a conflicted relationship for her during the time that she was working on *Anne of Green Gables*. By having Anne reconcile with Gilbert at the end of her novel, Montgomery was not simply employing a formula but revising her own history, reconsidering her Anne-like behaviour from a critical distance and seeing both its humour and long-term consequences.

Gilbert's first day back at Avonlea School in Chapter 15 leads to the famous slate-breaking scene, a variation on the time-honoured theme of future lovers starting out as "'good enemies'" (332), which links Anne and Gilbert to literary predecessors including Elizabeth Bennett and Fitzwilliam Darcy (Austen, *Pride and Prejudice*), Emma Woodhouse and George Knightley (Austen, *Emma*), and Jane Eyre and Edward Rochester (Charlotte Brontë, *Jane Eyre*). Diana tells Anne about Gilbert as they walk to school, emphasizing his romantic desirability:

"He's *aw'fly* handsome, Anne. And he teases the girls something terrible. He just torments our lives out."

Diana's voice indicated that she rather liked having her life tormented out than not. (152)

Besides being a handsome flirt, Gilbert is quickly identified as an intellectual rival. When Diana says that Anne "won't find it so easy to keep head after this," Anne immediately responds: "I'm glad ... I couldn't really feel proud of keeping head of little boys and girls of just nine or ten" (153). While Gilbert appeals to Diana as a way to gratify her beauty, he appeals to Anne as the first man in her life who will both challenge *and* love her, setting him apart from the drunken and dangerous Mr. Hammond, the ineffectual Mr. Phillips, and the overly tolerant Matthew.

Montgomery's focus on eyes and gazes, throughout Anne's first interactions with Gilbert, suggests that he sees her more accurately than anyone else in the novel. When Matthew first meets Anne, he "was not looking at her and would not have seen what she was really like if he had been" (63). Similarly, when Marilla's "eyes fell on the odd little figure in the stiff, ugly dress, with the long braids of red hair and the eager, luminous eyes, she stopped short in amazement" and asked about the expected boy (74). Mrs. Blewett and Rachel Lynde see only a "wiry" potential labourer (96) who is "terrible skinny and homely" (112). We don't learn much about Diana's first impressions as the girls are "gazing bashfully at one another" (132). In contrast, Gilbert's immediate attraction to Anne focuses on her eyes: "She *should* look at him, that red-haired Shirley girl with the little pointed chin and the big eyes that weren't like the eyes of any other girl in Avonlea school" (154). His act of calling her "Carrots" has short-term results when "Anne looked at him with a vengeance" (154), but robs him of her friendship for the next few years as she vows that "she would not even look at him. She would *never* look at him again!" (156). Anne's actions simultaneously signify her childishness and her Marilla-like toughness. Anne cracking her slate over his head symbolizes the rivalry to come: she will attack him forcefully with her best intellectual efforts, even when the attack becomes increasingly stubborn and unfair.

Anne spends the majority of the novel snubbing Gilbert, but constant allusions to him (twelve extended scenes and twenty brief references) point to a repressed desire that is key to her intellectual and emotional development. Any seasoned reader of romance fiction would clearly see the irony in the moments that Anne forgets her vow never to speak his name. In fact, she inadvertently nicknames him by constantly starting to say "Gil – " and then censoring herself. Anne is glad to be Conservative, she says, "because Gil – because some of the boys in school are Grits" (181), although her recent discussion of women's suffrage suggests that she may have more in common with Gilbert's politics than she realizes. Anne worries about missing school "for Gil – some of the others will get head of the class" (185), even though her act of saving Minnie May Barry's life emphasizes her intellectual connection to the talents and ambitions of this future doctor. She sobs about the anodyne liniment cake fiasco because "Gil – the boys in school will never get over laughing at it" (213), even though Gilbert would be the last person to laugh at her mistakes. Finally, she worries about failing her entrance examinations to Queen's "especially if Gil – if the others passed" (286), even though none of us are surprised when she ties with him for first place.

Montgomery also created several public concerts in which Anne and Gilbert "stage" their ongoing conflicts and desires. At Anne's first Avonlea Debating Club concert, she pointedly reads a library book while Gilbert recites "Bingen on the Rhine," and then sits "rigidly stiff and motionless while Diana clapped her hands until they tingled" (193). Diana chastises her afterwards, pointing out that he looked right down at Anne when he recited the line "There's another, *not a sister*" (194). Anne's response indicates that she has not yet progressed beyond her passionate love for Diana, which the novel represents as immature and even laughable: "Diana … you are my bosom friend, but I cannot allow even you to speak to me of that person. Are you ready for bed?" (194). When the girls jump into bed with Josephine Barry, another cranky and lonely old maid who alludes to a possible future for the maiden, Montgomery reinforces the point that Anne will never truly be satisfied until she recognizes her love for Gilbert. Yet the Avonlea School Christmas concert affords another opportunity for Diana to deplore Anne's behaviour:

> "I do think it's awful mean the way you treat Gil. Wait till I tell you. When you ran off the platform after the fairy dialogue one of your roses fell out of your hair. I saw Gil pick it up and put it in his breast-pocket. There now. You're so romantic that I'm sure you ought to be pleased at that."

> "It's nothing to me what that person does," said Anne loftily. "I simply never waste a thought on him, Diana." (239)

The reader knows that Anne really can't stop thinking or talking about Gilbert, and the pleasurable suspense continues to grow – what will he finally do to win her over?

This question begins to be answered when Gilbert rescues Anne from her thwarted attempt to dramatize "Lancelot and Elaine," a turning point in her attitude toward Gilbert and her capacity to feel romantic love. When Gilbert asks her to be friends, she hesitates: "She had an odd, newly awakened consciousness under all her outraged dignity that the half-shy, half-eager expression in Gilbert's hazel eyes was something that was very good to see. Her heart gave a quick, queer little beat" (258–60). Even though she snubs him once again, Montgomery's language indicates that this desire is fully natural, something that is being "awakened" rather than a mere product of cultural expectations. Soon after this incident, Anne secretly realizes that "the old resentment she had cherished against him was gone" (277). The power of their rivalry returns at the White Sands Hotel concert, where her misrecognition of Gilbert's "taunting" expression empowers her to give a great recitation (301), but surpassing him no longer sustains her in the same way.

By the time they are at Queen's, she finds herself jealous of Gilbert's attachment to Ruby Gillis and "could not help thinking, too, that it would be very pleasant to have such a friend as Gilbert to jest and chatter with and exchange ideas about books and studies and ambitions" (310). When she finds out that Gilbert will not be attending Redmond with her, "Anne felt a queer little sensation of dismayed surprise.... What would she do without their inspiring rivalry? Would not work, even at a co-educational college with a real degree in prospect, be rather flat without her friend the enemy?" (316). Montgomery has set the stage for the novel's dénouement, in which Anne overcomes her childish pride and demonstrates her mature ability to humble herself and ask forgiveness.

Anne's decision to befriend Gilbert after he sacrifices the Avonlea School for her forms the novel's climax, not surprising given the dozens of hints leading up to it. Although the relationship remains a friendship, the last pages of the novel tell us a lot about Gilbert's moral and emotional assets. Rachel tells Anne about Gilbert's decision, pointing out that "it was real kind and thoughtful in him, that's what. Real self-sacrificing, too" (330). When Anne finally confesses to Gilbert that she is sorry for their long emotional separation, he declares the inevitability of this union: "We were born to be good friends, Anne. You've thwarted destiny long enough" (332). Contemporary feminist scholars might be uncomfortable with this ending because Anne's sacrifice of her education is so closely linked to her relationship with Gilbert, but the two are hardly mutually exclusive. Anne postpones her college career for Marilla, not Gilbert, and their friendship will not prevent her from completing it later. The constant suppressed references to "Gil – " prove that from the perspective of this narrative, Gilbert *is* Anne's destiny, a romantic partner who recognizes and appreciates more of her unique qualities than any other character and who is willing to sacrifice *his* educational opportunities for *her* domestic responsibilities.

"I Want You To Be My Girl": Gilbert in 1934

The 1934 film directed by George Nichols, Jr. has attracted very little scholarship; Gammel's *Making Avonlea: L.M. Montgomery and Popular Culture* contains no discussion of this film, which does not even appear in the "Works Cited." Yet this film provides a missing link between the novel, which its early scenes follow closely, and the Sullivan miniseries, which copies much of its dialogue and shots: Matthew peeking around the corner to see Anne at the train station, Marilla pausing outside Anne's room after her first bedtime prayer, Anne adding an "e" to her name on the blackboard, Marilla's declaration of her love for Anne when she leaves for Queen's, and many others. Nichols's emphasis on a trial period, in which Anne proves herself to the Cuthberts, and a love story, in which Marilla disapproves of Gilbert based on her history with his father, also provide the basis for the miniseries' structure. While this film is certainly outdated and clichéd, it has much to tell us about the way that Depression-era filmmakers perceived Gilbert as a romantic hero, as well as much to tell us about our need for Gilbert as Anne's complement today.

Gilbert (played by Tom Brown) initially appears in this film on Anne's first day of school – one of many condensing strategies that were replicated by the later miniseries. The first shot of Gilbert shows his amused appreciation as Anne rattles off her entire family history to Mr. Phillips. Once Anne sits down, Gilbert tries to get her attention by looking and winking, then by showing her a caricature that he has drawn of the teacher. When she refuses to take her attention away from the geography lesson, he becomes disgusted and calls her "Carrots." After she breaks the slate over his head, a humorous close-up of a stunned Gilbert with the slate frame around his neck demonstrates the film's emphasis on his boyish, mischievous qualities. In keeping with Montgomery's physical description of him as "a tall boy, with curly brown hair, roguish hazel eyes and a mouth twisted into a teasing smile" (153), this version of Gilbert is decidedly non-intellectual. He admires Anne initially for her use of words, but he tends to respond to her conversation with mystified facial expressions that finally lead to his declaration later in the film: "I think you read too much!" Rather than an intellectual equal or rival, this Gilbert is valuable largely as a supporter of Anne's ambitions and a source of the romantic love she craves, balancing out her intellectual tendencies much as Matthew does in all three versions.

After Gilbert's attempt to apologize, the script takes a new direction loosely based on Marilla's confession about her thwarted affair with John Blythe at the end of the book: "'I always felt – rather sorry. I've always kind of wished I'd forgiven him when I had the chance'" (325). This film replaces the intellectual rivalry between Anne and Gilbert – in which the main forces keeping them apart are Anne's pride and stubbornness – with a family rivalry in which the Cuthberts refuse to associate with the Blythes because John stole Matthew's fiancée many years ago. Anne is surprised when Marilla does not seem upset about the slate-breaking and seeks out the history from Diana (both scenes that reappear in the miniseries). Diana claims: "Matthew was never the same after that. Marilla didn't get married either because she thought it was her duty to take care of Matthew." By drawing attention to Marilla's and Matthew's unmarried status, the film develops a latent tension that the novel leaves largely unexamined, except for Marilla's brief cautionary tale: how can an old maid and a bachelor adequately prepare Anne for married life, which was the primary goal of most women at this time? How can Anne learn the skills of courtship from such shy and stubborn people as the Cuthberts admit themselves to be? The "Romeo and Juliet" scenario created by the film is all too familiar, but it does highlight the urgency of Anne's need to have a relationship with Gilbert that is unlike Marilla's relationships with either John Blythe or Matthew.

The family rivalry is set aside during the middle section of the film, which focuses on Anne's determination to assert her power over Gilbert by getting him to show romantic interest in public. These scenes dramatize Anne's conflicted psychological state, in which she alternately desires and scorns Gilbert. Anne boasts to Diana, "All I have to do is wave my little finger at Gilbert Blythe, and he'll come a-begging." Unfortunately, Gilbert overhears this and gets revenge by ignoring her completely and making a big fuss over Diana (another scene borrowed for the later miniseries). Anne retaliates by pretending that she is courting Herbert Root, a former Avonlea pupil, and then is humiliated when Herbert shows up for a visit. This feud finally ends with the "Lancelot and Elaine" sequence, in which Gilbert's act of rescue is laden with exaggerated romantic conventions: Gilbert sees her boat sink from the shore and runs to save her, calls "Don't be afraid!" and pulls Anne into his arms. The couple is finally reconciled when Gilbert tells her that he only made fun of her hair "because I just couldn't keep my eyes off it. It was kinda nice looking at it." The ending to the courtship battle is marked by a series of scenes in which Anne and Gilbert appear with different clothes and hairstyles to show the passage of time.

This rivalry over, the couple still faces the inevitable discovery of their love by the feuding families. From this point on, the film departs from the novel's plot in a manner that would be legitimately frustrating to Montgomery and her contemporary scholars, but remains interesting from a cultural and historical perspective. In a series of scenes that will reappear with slight variations in the miniseries, Marilla finds out from a friend that Anne and Gilbert are courting, tries to convince Matthew that it's a problem, confronts Anne and then Gilbert about the fact that Anne "has ambitions to make something of herself," and inspires the couple to break up. Anne goes off to Queen's, and here the Nichols film engages a unique plot device in which Matthew is very sick, but cannot afford the best doctor because the Cuthberts are spending all their money on Anne's schooling. Anne finds out and rushes home to be with Matthew, sacrificing her education by failing to sit for her final exams. Fortunately, she discovers that Gilbert knows the doctor, Matthew's life is saved, and Marilla finally relents and offers her support of the couple.

The film ends with Anne gazing lovingly at Matthew while Marilla declares her intention to "get Gilbert Blythe and bring him right back here." In the novel, Matthew's death and the family's economic crisis become the catalysts for Anne's reconciliation with Gilbert, which takes place when she finally matures to the point of being honest, humble, and his equal in self-sacrifice. In Depression-era filmmaking, the heroine's development clearly takes a back seat to a simple and satisfying plot with a clear resolution and a pointed reference to the fact that family ties are more important than financial stability.

"THIS CHILDISHNESS HAS GONE ON LONG ENOUGH": GILBERT IN 1985

Kevin Sullivan's 1985 miniseries inherits the connection between Marilla and Mr. Blythe and the tension and resolution of Anne's love for Gilbert, expanding both of these plots with a feminist emphasis on the need for men to appreciate women's intellects and career choices. The length of the miniseries allows the filmmakers to add more original scenes, including Anne's first meeting with Gilbert (played by Jonathan Crombie) when she and Diana enter a three-legged race at a picnic. Diana anxiously observes that "there aren't any other girls in it," but Anne challenges gender conventions: "You're a sturdy-looking girl, and I'm fast. I know we'd stand a good chance." The miniseries' first shot of Gilbert shows him tying his leg to Moody's while he looks with amused interest at this new girl who has broken into his male competition. When Anne and Diana win the race, Gilbert gives her an impressed look and a wink, demonstrating his admiration for her boldness with a gesture that she finds "awfully bold" herself. While the following conversation with Diana provides the basic background information about Gilbert, this three-legged race symbolizes the race for intellectual and emotional prizes that will preoccupy them for the rest of their early adolescent lives.

The slate-breaking scene also contains its unique twists despite generally following the plot of the novel. When the camera focuses on Anne telling her history to Mr. Phillips, Gilbert appears in the bottom right corner of the frame, watching her with a smile of interest and approval. He is the only classmate to appear consistently in this shot, facing the camera and the viewer to signify his privileged status as Anne's observer, who mirrors our pleasure in looking at and listening to her. This composition continues when Anne sits down and attempts to concentrate on her lesson, with Gilbert appearing over her shoulder trying to get her attention by winking, flicking paper at her, and finally calling her "Carrots." In this version, the outraged Anne actually smashes *his* slate over his head in a more vengeful and pointed act of violence than in the novel or the previous film. The sequence occurs very rapidly, signalling Anne's impetuousness.

The rest of the miniseries exploits all of the sources of suspense about Anne's relationship with Gilbert that appeared in earlier versions, bringing back the novel's focus on intellectual rivalry while borrowing the earlier film's emphasis on family tensions. The scene in which Diana tells Anne about Marilla's "tragic romance" exemplifies the miniseries' seamless interweaving of information from Nichols's film (Diana overheard her mother talking to Mrs. Blair) and the novel (Marilla is the one who was thwarted by a Blythe): "Mother said you have a disposition just like Marilla's. She said something about Marilla having been betrothed once, many years ago, but because of a quarrel, she never married, and she's had to live with her brother ever since." John Blythe is not identified as the betrothed here, allowing that news to come as a surprise at the end, when Marilla confesses. But the phrase "she's had to live with her brother" reinforces the sense that this is a fate that Anne must avoid, especially since she has no biological family to support her.

The miniseries also develops Nichols's innovation of a sequence of events in which Anne vows to assert her power over Gilbert by getting him to make a romantic gesture, this time at a Christmas Ball based on the Debating Club concert from the novel and the hayride from the film. Gilbert looks longingly at Anne from the dance floor while she boasts to Diana, "If I wanted him to ask me, which I don't, he certainly would. Gilbert Blythe would stand on his head for me if I asked him to." Gilbert is smart enough to see through the dare and ignores her, yet secretly steals her dance card in a romantic gesture inspired by his stealing of a rose from her hair in the novel.

Gilbert maintains the upper hand in their rivalry until the "Lancelot and Elaine" sequence, which once again marks the turning point in their friendship. The miniseries uniquely combines the news about the Queen's Pass List with Gilbert's aid to the humiliated Elaine, allowing the scene to focus on their equality rather than his role as "rescuer." The scene redeems Anne's foolishness by reasserting her intellectual prowess. Once Anne and Gilbert reach the shore of the lake, he tells her that they have tied for first place, and both openly admit their mutual admiration: Gilbert says, "I figured you'd have it for sure," and Anne responds, "I never expected to beat you." This airing of their competitive history opens up the possibility of relationship:

> Gilbert: Can't we be friends? This childishness has gone on long enough, don't you think?
>
> Anne: The fact that you rescued me unnecessarily hardly wipes out past wrongs.
>
> Gilbert: Look, I'm sorry I ever said anything about your hair. You've no idea how sorry. But it was so long ago. Aren't you ever going to forgive me?
>
> Anne: You hurt my feelings *excruciatingly*.
>
> Gilbert: I only said it because I wanted to meet you so much.

Gilbert correctly identifies Anne's behaviour as "childishness," and when he repeats "Can we be friends now?" she responds with another immature retort: "Why don't you figure it out, if you're so clever?"

The miniseries then follows the lead of the 1934 film in shifting attention to Marilla's disapproval of Anne's budding relationship with Gilbert, creating suspense through the well-worn plot device of the disapproving parent but also mirroring the potential concerns of a second-wave feminist audience. Marilla meets Gilbert on the road and reminds him that "she has the talent to make something of herself, but she's still very young," chastising him for his supposed interest in distracting her from her career goals (which Gilbert never does in any version). Marilla's suspicions are heightened when Rachel sees Anne and Gilbert together, leading to another 1934-inspired sequence in which Marilla reminds Anne that she shouldn't make any ties in Avonlea that she will regret. Anne turns down Gilbert's offer to accompany her to a concert, creating another thread of tension that lasts throughout their time at Queen's and finally breaks with Marilla's confession about her regret that she did not marry John Blythe. While Montgomery places this dialogue *before* Anne decides to give up her college education, suggesting that it might have played a role in her decision, the miniseries places it *after* Anne has already announced her decision to stay home, reassuring viewers that she is not sacrificing her education for Gilbert.

The last scene in the miniseries begins with Gilbert riding in on a horse, one of the more obvious but forgivable romantic clichés, and telling Anne about his decision to give up the school for her. Hearing this information directly from him rather than from Rachel condenses the story while enhancing the release of tension when Anne proves that she has finally matured, through acknowledging her gratitude at his sacrifice. Her words are from the novel: "Thank you for giving up the school for me, Gilbert. It was very good of you. I want you to know that I really appreciate it." However, the miniseries invents the closing lines, which precede the final shot of Gilbert walking toward Green Gables with his arm around Anne:

> Gilbert: I figure you can give me a hand with my work and we'll call it a fair exchange.
>
> Anne: Aren't you worried? I'm liable to break another slate over your head.
>
> Gilbert: I'm more worried I might break one over yours, Carrots.

Anne's joking reference to their first fight proves that she can finally laugh at the "excruciating" incident and acknowledge her own bad behaviour. Gilbert's words seem more nonsensical, in keeping with the fact that he whispers them tenderly while caressing her face. As the final words in the film, however, they seem to demand interpretation. Is Gilbert's mock threat a subtle indication of the anger and desire that he has been fighting all this time, while his use of the nickname "Carrots" shows his power by proving that he can now get away with it? This line does predict the miniseries' 1987 sequel, in which Gilbert and Anne will continue fighting and bickering until their final romantic reconciliation at the end of the series. In other words, their relationship is by no means resolved in the *Anne of Green Gables* adaptation. But the line expresses the film's sense that Gilbert has been consistently kind to Anne and has not really had a chance to retaliate. The line bodes, slightly, of a future darkness, or at least a little cynicism.

The Sullivan team departs from the novel and the earlier film by placing Gilbert at the very end of the text, demonstrating their firm belief in Gilbert's role as the one who resolves Anne's needs for both education and love. In a letter to me in September 2000, series co-writer Joe Wiesenfeld responded to critics of the romance plot: "The romantic complications were deliberate, and in my view, necessary. It is not a question of 'appealing' more to viewers, but one of confronting a major element of the story, rather than ignoring it." Kevin Sullivan pondered Gilbert's appeal in an interview later that year, claiming that "I see Gilbert as being a very honorable, steadfast character," and that audience feedback through forums, letters, and emails shows that "they really see Gilbert as the kind of perfect romantic hero." Gilbert remains a key element of the pleasure of the text not simply because he fills a stock role in a formulaic genre, but because Montgomery created him in such a compelling way that he stands out among other characters like him. For a girl as flighty as Anne Shirley, such an "honorable, steadfast" hero is especially desirable.

CONCLUSION: PICTURING GILBERT

It is tempting to believe the stereotype that popular literature performs complex challenges to patriarchal values while popular film and television go for the cheap thrill of romantic love. A glance through the illustrations by M. A. and W. A. J. Claus for the first edition of the novel (reproduced in Devereux's Broadview edition) proves that Gilbert was highly significant back in 1908. Gilbert appears three times in these illustrations, while Marilla appears twice and Matthew, Rachel, and Diana once. The illustrations provide an overview of Anne's relationship with Gilbert, starting from the slate-breaking scene in which he cowers beneath Anne with his back to the viewer, reaching out his hand to protect himself as she raises the slate over her head. While the first joke is on Gilbert, the roles have been reversed in the "Lancelot and Elaine" illustration, as he reaches out to help a soggy and miserable Anne. Although Gilbert is turned toward Anne, we can see his concerned facial expression, and her closed eyes influence us to identify more with him. In the final illustration, Gilbert walks beside Anne with their faces turned toward each another, representing their new status as equals, no longer trying to dominate one another. In each drawing, Gilbert points the reader toward Anne, but reminds us of his own significance. What would *Anne of Green Gables* be like without Gilbert Blythe? The first century of the novel's reception has shown his consistent appeal as a romantic hero, which will certainly continue to influence scholarship and popular adaptations in the next hundred years.

WORKS CITED

Anne of Green Gables. Dir. George Nichols, Jr. RKO, 1934.

Anne of Green Gables. Dir. Kevin Sullivan. Sullivan Films, 1985.

Gammel, Irene, ed. *Making Avonlea: L. M. Montgomery and Popular Culture.* Toronto: U of Toronto P, 2002.

———. "Safe Pleasures for Girls: L. M. Montgomery's Erotic Landscapes." Gammel 114–27.

Gubar, Marah. "'Where Is the Boy?': The Pleasures of Postponement in the *Anne of Green Gables* Series." *The Lion and the Unicorn* 25.1 (2001): 47–69.

Hersey, Eleanor. "'Tennyson Would Never Approve': Reading and Performance in Kevin Sullivan's *Anne of Green Gables.*" *Canadian Children's Literature* 105–06 (2002): 48–67.

Lefebvre, Benjamin. "Stand by Your Man: Adapting L. M. Montgomery's *Anne of Green Gables.*" *Essays on Canadian Writing* 76 (2002): 149–69.

Montgomery, L. M. *Anne of Green Gables.* Ed. Cecily Devereux. Peterborough, ON: Broadview, 2004.

————. *The Selected Journals of L. M. Montgomery.* Vol. 1. Ed. Mary Rubio and Elizabeth Waterston. Toronto: Oxford UP, 1985.

Poe, K. L. "Who's Got the Power?: Montgomery, Sullivan, and the Unsuspecting Viewer." Gammel 145–59.

Robinson, Laura. "Bosom Friends: Lesbian Desire in L.M. Montgomery's *Anne* Books." *Canadian Literature* 180 (2004): 12–28.

Steffler, Margaret. "'This has been a day in hell': Montgomery, Popular Literature, Life Writing." Gammel 72–83.

Sullivan, Kevin. Telephone interview. 23 Nov. 2000.

Weber, Brenda R. "Confessions of a Kindred Spirit with an Academic Bent." Gammel 43–57.

Wiesenfeld, Joe. Letter to the author. 15 Sept. 2000.

III

Quoting Anne:
Intertextuality at Home
and Abroad

CHAPTER SEVEN

Anne and Her Ancestors: Self-Reflexivity from Yonge to Alcott to Montgomery

Laura M. Robinson

"[I]t sounds so nice and romantic, just as if I were a heroine in a book, you know." ~ Anne from *Anne of Green Gables* (88)

Not only an extremely popular storybook heroine herself, Anne is first and foremost a reader, actively interpreting her world and experience through the literature she reads. The convention of a heroine measuring herself against "storybook heroines" is an old one, one mocked by Jane Austen in *Northanger Abbey*, in which an avid reader of Gothic novels constructs an imaginary Gothic out of a perfectly ordinary manor. Active reading substitutes for the very limited experience of the young, and particularly of young women, but in novels of female bildungsroman it is more than substitution in a circumscribed universe. It is, in fact, the way in which girls self-reflexively construct their particular feminine subjectivity, both as a performing agent and an inevitably parodic lens. *Anne* with an "e," as distinctive as this novel and its heroine are, self-consciously reflects upon the novels that pioneered the girl's story tradition and the construction of the storybook girl.

In *Secret Gardens*, Humphrey Carpenter traces a particular connection among Briton Charlotte Yonge's *The Daisy Chain* (1856), American Louisa May

Alcott's *Little Women* (1868–69), and Canadian L. M. Montgomery's *Anne of Green Gables* (1908). With a contempt that characterizes some approaches to women's writing and girl culture, he links Alcott to Montgomery to lament the fact that *Little Women* gave rise to several similar but "inferior" girls' books, such as Montgomery's, whose heroines had an "aggressive femininity" and "unbearable cheerfulness" (98). His indictment of the post-Alcott novels aside, Carpenter's connection of these three writers leads us to consideration of a specifically emerging tradition of girls' stories. Not only are these three writers working from traditional forms of literature in order to tell a new story primarily about and for girls, but their novels also comment upon and transform one another. Through self-reflexive commentary on various literary traditions, each novel emphasizes how texts influence people and other texts. Moreover, the novels also draw attention to where they deviate from tradition, thus demonstrating that ideology, literary conventions, and tradition, while necessarily lifted from previous scripts, are not reconstituted unchanged. In being self-reflexive, in calling attention to its own construction, each novel necessarily, if inadvertently, reveals the degree to which the girls' story, and thus the girl, is an ever-changing ideology and not an essential, fixed being. Ultimately, the self-reflexivity of each novel highlights the agency of, first, its girl hero and, then, by extension, its girl readers, by revealing the degree to which the reading heroine is actively engaged in self-construction and transformation of her cultural inheritance.

UNDERSTANDING GIRLHOOD: THEORIZING PERFORMATIVITY AND AGENCY

In a telling scene of intertextuality and literary interpretation, the characters in *Little Women* play a game in which they tell stories; the game, however, is only to begin a story and allow another to take up the story where it has been left off. The characters' game embodies and crystallizes the novel's self-conscious playfulness as it shows a host of available genres that model subjectivity for the characters. Each character, in fact, alters the genre and thus alters the model of subjectivity, overturning expectations of the prior player by picking up the story with a new genre. The genre each character selects and deploys is significant. Amy, for example, chooses to invoke a fairy tale about a goose girl, who is, of course, herself as she is often called goose by the other girls (Alcott 3–4). The tutor, Mr. Brooke, relates a traditional romance, exposing how he, as a knight in fantasy, would like to rescue the princesses, particularly "one sweet face" (128), which the reader understands is Meg. Turning Brooke's tale into a Gothic romance, interestingly, Meg rewrites Brooke's princesses, turning them into one evil spectre. She is possibly not ready for his advances. Laurie's tale tells of how impossible it actually is for the knight to break into the domain of princesses, something he must feel deeply as an outsider in the March girls' lives. Through this parlour game, albeit played outdoors, Alcott's novel exposes how individuals necessarily and inevitably rewrite the stories they inherit; while they locate their identity through the stories they tell, in doing so they rewrite the possibilities of the story and thus of subjectivity. Who they are is a product of the stories they read and write.

Similarly, girls' stories necessarily revise, alter, and trouble the works that influence them. I would like to invoke Judith Butler's arguments in *Gender Trouble* to understand the tradition of girlhood that emerges in nineteenth-century literature. In her conclusion, entitled "From Parody to Politics," Butler tackles the issue of agency in light of her argument that identity and subjectivity are actively constructed.[1] A pre-existing subject does not choose various identities for herself, Butler asserts; rather, the subject is constituted by the identity that articulates it in any given moment. The subject establishes an effect of coherence with repeated articulations, but these articulations are never self-identical. Butler convincingly asserts, "Construction is not opposed to agency; it is the necessary scene of agency, the very terms in which agency becomes culturally intelligible" (147). For Butler, and I agree, the subject's need to repeat itself in order to be culturally intelligible is the site of agency. She writes:

> The critical task is ... to locate strategies of subversive repetition enabled by those constructions, to affirm the local possibilities of intervention through participating in precisely those practices of repetition that constitute identity and, therefore, present the immanent possibility of contesting them. (147)

The repetitions will inevitably yield an articulation that is troublesome, different, unintelligible, which underscores the subject's agency; the subject is always more than one single identity or articulation can capture. The various ways in which girls in literature compare themselves to, and realize their difference from, fictional heroines reveal the necessity of employing previous scripts in order to articulate the self. Significantly, this repetition potentially subverts as much as it sustains.

The girls within the literature I discuss actively articulate themselves through various identities and relate to literary heroines, often with comic results because of the unlikely effect. This self-consciousness reveals how agency operates, in Butler's eyes. The "practices of parody," the attempt to repeat one's identity that always results in failure, exposes the performative nature of identity. In attempting to define, write, and explore the identities of girl and girlhood, these books necessarily turn to existing inscriptions (and prescriptions) of this identity. While the parodic effect is inescapable for any iteration in Butler's arguments, it is perhaps more obvious in girls' stories as the heroines juggle with and sift through the traditions before them. Through these troublesome and self-conscious explorations of the ever-changing girlhood traditions, the novels highlight the degree to which girlhood is an ideology and pinpoint the agency inherent in subject formation, which is to perform and thereby sift through various textual locations.

PERFORMING GIRLHOOD: REPETITION AND REVISION

Several literary and cultural studies scholars explore the emerging tradition of girls' stories and the culture of girlhood.[2] Shirley Foster and Judy Simons tackle a chronological analysis of novels for girls in *What Katy Read*, which itself follows in the tradition of books such as Mary Cadogan and Patricia Craig's *You're a Brick, Angela!* Girlhood ideology and culture blossomed, because of, in part, the many nineteenth- and early twentieth-century writers sculpting girls within their fictions. Sarah A. Wadsworth argues that "Alcott ... was instrumental in defining, shaping, reinforcing, and revising" the qualities, interests, and aspirations of the girls who comprised the market" (19). Arguably, the same can be said for Yonge, who preceded her. In addition to Carpenter's genealogy, which depicts Montgomery's novel as an indirect offspring of Yonge's, many critics have excavated the various traditions that influenced each of these three writers. While Yonge has not received the same type of critical attention that Alcott and

Montgomery have, critics are quick to point to the influence of Tractarianism and, particularly, of the intellectual John Keble.[3] Others identify specific traditions of children's writing and genres that infuse her novels. Cornelia Meigs, Anne Thaxter Eaton, Elizabeth Nesbitt, and Ruth Hill Viguers report that Yonge pays tribute to late eighteenth-century stories for children (155). Showing two of Yonge's influences, Barbara Dennis suggests that Yonge Christianizes the genre of romance and romanticizes a Christian narrative, while June Sturrock argues that, in her sequel to *The Daisy Chain* at least, Yonge drew upon the popular literature of the time, particularly the new sensation novels ("Sequels" 104). Foster and Simons assert that Yonge revisits John Bunyan's *The Pilgrim's Progress* and writings by such authors as Margaret Oliphant and Susan Warner (66–67).

Similarly, Alcott scholars determine a wide array of influences at work upon her. Alcott was clearly affected by Transcendentalism; her father, Bronson Alcott, was a keen, if often misguided, proponent of Transcendentalist beliefs and practices. Of this intellectual circle, Louisa Alcott was particularly smitten with Ralph Waldo Emerson. Moreover, Elaine Showalter cites German writer Johann Wolfgang von Goethe as an inspiration to Alcott, who received one of Goethe's novels from Emerson (Showalter 47). In addition to Alcott's intellectual milieu, shadows and traces of various literary traditions pervade her writings. Several critics explore Alcott's reworking of Bunyan's *The Pilgrim's Progress* (see Armstrong, Walters, Blackford), a work overtly alluded to in *Little Women*'s preface. Donna M. Campbell argues that Alcott also uses and revises Susan Warner's *The Wide, Wide World*, a best-selling novel in the decade prior to the publication of *Little Women*. Michelle Ann Abate draws a clear line from Harriet Beecher Stowe's *Uncle Tom's Cabin* to *Little Women*. John Seelye claims that Charlotte Brontë's *Jane Eyre* underwrites Alcott's famous girls' story (see also Doyle), while Karen Sands-O'Connor suggests that Alcott is recursively rewriting Charlotte Yonge's *The Heir of Redclyffe*. Moreover, as Carpenter does, critics tend to concur about Alcott's widespread influence on later writers: for example, Harbour Winn suggests that *Little Women* gives rise to Kate Chopin's delightful girl hero in "Charlie," and Beverly Lyon Clark details the widespread readership and impact of Alcott's March girls.

As I mentioned, however, Carpenter laments Alcott's popularity because her novel generated a spate of what he considers lesser girls' stories, such as *Anne of Green Gables*. John Seelye feels quite the contrary in his book *Jane Eyre's American Daughters*. Seelye similarly regards *Anne* as following in this emerging girls' story tradition, but unlike Carpenter, he finds Montgomery's novel to be the most hopeful American [sic] version of *Jane Eyre*,[4] more empowering for young women than *Little Women*. As Carpenter and Seelye do, many critics link *Anne* with *Little Women*.[5] Moreover, Montgomery's critics are keenly aware of the author's extensive reworkings of her literary inheritance; citing intertexts as diverse as Alfred, Lord Tennyson's *Idylls of the King* and Robert Browning's "Pippa Passes," scholars explore Montgomery's use of literary allusion and particularly her parodies (see Ross, Yeast, and Epperly for a few examples; see also Irene Gammel's essay in this collection). Constance Classen asserts that Montgomery patterned *Anne* after Kate Douglas Wiggin's *Rebecca of Sunnybrook Farm*. Montgomery critics also cite the author's widespread influence: Calvin Trillin discusses the Japanese love for the feisty redhead, and the many critics who treat the film adaptations, products, television shows, and stage performances can testify to Montgomery's lasting impact on girlhood culture.[6]

THROUGH THE LOOKING-GLASS: GENERIC SELF-REFLEXIVITY

As all these critics recognize, what is striking is the extent to which the three novels self-consciously address their literary and cultural heritage in order to sketch a portrait of girlhood,[7] interrogating and often dismissing various genres and identities in order to establish their own heroine's identity. Through the focus on reading, all three novels insist that literature shapes the reader's understanding of him- or herself; the texts thus self-consciously acknowledge their own didactic potential. Specifically, Yonge, Alcott, and Montgomery each offer a rewriting of traditional genres and conventions. A family chronicle, *The Daisy Chain* employs such genres as the mission story, the traditional romance, and the story of accomplishment in order to indicate how this novel differs from other stories. A mission story emerges in the novel as the wealthy neighbour, Meta Rivers, longs to be a missionary herself and tells Ethel that she feels like Lucilla in *Faithful Little Girl*, a Sunday school book (Yonge 252). Lucilla wished to be a boy so she could be a missionary. In *The Daisy Chain*, Meta becomes a missionary after all, moving to New Zealand with her husband, Norman May. Unlike Lucilla in the story, Meta wishes for mission work not because she is "cross at home" but because she wants to be useful and purposeful. And, while she must marry one, she also does not need to be a boy.

The Daisy Chain emphasizes its revision of genres when the characters engage in "the story play": each participant tells a story, incorporating a common word that one person has to guess – in this case, "glory." Yonge's plot rewrites the characters' traditional stories with its own version, stressing by this "playfulness" where the novel alters tradition. For example, the ambitious sister Flora tells a story of female accomplishment: a young woman climbs Mont Blanc and achieves fame. Yonge's novel argues that this sense of glory for glory's sake is an empty victory by having Flora pay dearly with the life of her child, for attempting a similar, if more everyday, accomplishment: achieving fame and glory through her husband's work. Similarly, in Ethel's romance, several kings battle to prove themselves worthy of a beautiful damsel, Gloria. One good king refuses to fight the others and instead performs good works and lives patiently. When another king fights him, the good king does not have the strength or skill to retaliate, and dies, but not before Gloria declares him the winner. He too realizes his victory as he is on his way to God. Flora notes that Ethel has lifted the story from an old French book and altered the ending. The king represents Ethel, as she is named after a king. Ethel sacrifices herself to family duty at the end of *The Daisy Chain* and tries to rest content by turning to the glory of God, like the slain king. In her story, then, Ethel does what Charlotte Yonge does in *The Daisy Chain* and alters the ending of a traditional romance.

Alcott's novel also rewrites old stories and employs self-reflexive writing to emphasize the conventions it uses. Carpenter argues convincingly that *The Daisy Chain* was a source for Alcott's *Little Women* (Carpenter 94). Certainly, Alcott uses the same style and devices in her family chronicle as Yonge, and Jo weeps over *The Heir of Redclyffe*, Yonge's most popular novel. Both Yonge and Alcott present a family struggling through a difficult time with a parent missing. Religious beliefs and acts of charity are a central focus in each. The families are named after the months May and March. The name "Daisy" refers to the youngest May child, in addition to being their father's pet name for them all, and also makes its way into *Little Women* as Meg's nickname and her daughter's name. The heroines, Ethel and Jo, are similar ages and share physical characteristics. Finally, Ethel and Jo are convinced that their duty is to their families, particularly after their sisters' deaths. The similarities are numerous and intriguing, but most fascinating is how Alcott rewrites Yonge's tale. Not only is Jo more clearly the main character in *Little Women*, but she finds a partner and begins her own family circle instead of remaining devoted to her father and siblings, as Ethel does. It may not be a perfect solution to the dilemma of growing up female, but at least Jo moves on from girlhood.

However, Alcott also uses conventions gleaned from Bunyan's *The Pilgrim's Progress*. Many of her chapter titles are taken from Bunyan's allegory. The narrative often focuses on the girls' attempts to be like Christian and plod on through life in order to reach the "desired country." Linda K. Kerber suggests that the use of Bunyan in *Little Women* is oppressive to the girls (166). Bunyan's text may convey a message of submission to one's circumstance; however, Alcott's use of it has an ironic twinkle. Rather than show the serious and steady Christian overcoming obstacles, Alcott's novel presents four very imperfect, human girls whose attempts to overcome similar obstacles – Vanity Fair, the Valley of Humiliation, the Slough of Despond – are sources of gentle humour. Their attempts to conquer their perceived flaws are often failures, yet Alcott deals gently with them, allowing Amy to learn at home after she's been punished at school, for example, and not punishing Meg for giving in to frivolity at her Vanity Fair – a weekend party at a wealthy friend's house. Alcott diverges from Bunyan's conventions by making each of Christian's situations very ordinary and by having the girls succumb to the temptations. In doing so, the novel recognizes both the impossibility of the religious model and the need to alter the script.

Montgomery's bildungsroman carries on the girls' story tradition established by *The Daisy Chain* and *Little Women*. Anne despairs when her hair is cut off, for example, comparing herself to story heroines: "This is such an unromantic affliction. The girls in books lose their hair in fevers or sell it to get money for some good deed" (Montgomery 252). This reference is clearly to Jo, who cuts her hair to finance her mother's trip to their sick father. Montgomery also echoes Alcott when Anne, like Amy, is punished at school. Amy is discovered with forbidden pickled limes in her desk. As punishment, she is struck by a ruler and must stand on a platform in front of the school. She refuses to take this punishment lightly and leaves the school, never to return. On the other hand, Anne breaks her slate over Gilbert's head in a fit of temper and must stand on the platform before the class. Unlike Amy, she bears this punishment. Like Amy, Anne feels she suffers an overruling physical affliction, her hair colour comparable to Amy's nose. However, when Anne must sit with the boys as punishment for being late, she endures the day, but leaves school with no intention of returning. "I'll learn my lessons at home," she announces to Marilla (Montgomery 160). Montgomery refers back to *Little Women*, but significantly alters what motivates Anne's refusal to attend school – not only a humiliating punishment, but a transgression of clear gender roles. Montgomery also rewrites the tradition by stripping Anne of the family that characterized the novels of her predecessors, thus tapping into the orphan tale rather than the family chronicle.[8]

Montgomery's novel abounds with other literary allusions, revealing the traditions that have influenced it and where it deviates from them. The novel presents a humorous twist on Tennyson's "Lancelot and Elaine" from *Idylls of the King*, for example. A victim of unrequited love and Lancelot's callous disregard, Tennyson's Elaine dies on a barge journeying to Camelot. Although described as "wilful," Elaine has relatively little power or agency in this idyll, except for her effect on the jealous queen and in her dramatic death. Montgomery's retelling of the legend creates irony by having the vibrant, inherently imperfect, but lovable Anne play the role of the good, faithful Elaine who loves the imperfect, sinful Lancelot. Moreover, in the novel's version, after Anne reclines in the "barge" to float down the river, "something happened not at all romantic," and the "barge" springs a leak (Montgomery 256). Anne is left gripping on to a bridge pile, praying for rescue. Unlike Elaine, she lacks the desire to die for romance. Also unlike Elaine, Anne is rescued. Gilbert happens by in his father's dory and hauls her into his boat. She thanks him curtly but refuses to befriend him, despite his overtures of friendliness. The other girls are not blind to the romance of being rescued by Gilbert (Montgomery 261), but Anne, more like Lancelot than Elaine, refuses to see the potential for love and romance. However, Montgomery's novel clearly shows where it overturns traditional romance and invests its heroine with more agency. The romance collapses in the mundane world of leaky boats and outspoken boys.

THE HEROINE'S SELF-REFLEXIVITY

The heroines of all three novels, each active readers, understand themselves through their reading. Their references to themselves as storybook heroines are not only ironic – they *are* – but these moments of self-reflexivity also comment on how the novels overturn convention even while employing it. One example of self-reflexive writing occurs when Margaret and Alan Ernescliffe try to determine whether they should be engaged: "Ethel had a happy conviction that this was only the second volume of the novel" (Yonge 271). However, their story instead turns tragic because of Margaret's death. Through Ethel's focus on fantasies gleaned from romance novels, Yonge's novel blurs the line between reader and heroine. After her reading, for example, "Ethel had to go down to breakfast with a mind floating between romance, sorrow, and high aspirations, very unlike the actual world she had to live in" (Yonge 57). The last statement smacks of irony as Ethel is the heroine of a novel containing heterosexual romance, sorrow, and high aspirations. The subtitle of *The Daisy Chain* is *Aspirations*, for example.[9]

The March girls frequently understand themselves through reference to the novels they read. Alcott's novel again demonstrates where it diverges from the traditions that preceded it by showing the girls' confusion over the difference between their life and fiction. In trying to determine whether Meg loves Brooke, for example, Jo reveals that her understanding of love comes from novels: "In novels, the girls show it by starting and blushing, fainting away, growing thin, and acting like fools" (Alcott 302). Healthy Meg has none of these symptoms. Amy also describes her relationships as if she were a character in a novel. During her flirtation with Fred in Europe, Amy writes home: "I felt as if I'd got into a romance, ... waiting for my lover – like a real story-book girl" (Alcott 319). When she begins her serious love relationship with Laurie, Amy does not use fictional metaphors to describe it. Laurie imagines his proposal to her in fictional terms, however: "He had rather imagined that the denouement would take place in the chateau garden by moonlight, and in the most graceful and decorous manner" (Alcott 430). This preferred setting is the stuff of romance novels, overtly contrasted with the muddy lanes upon which Jo's romance occurs. Moreover, Alcott asserts that she is not giving her readers a romance novel by having the proposal settled "on the lake, at noonday, in a few blunt words" (Alcott 430). This disruption of domestic romance is shaken back into conventionality when Jo puts the letter announcing their engagement down after reading it, "as one might shut the covers of a lovely romance" (Alcott 438). Even meek Beth is compared to a novel character. When she dies after her long illness, the narrator writes, "Seldom, except in books, do the dying utter memorable words, see visions, or depart with beatified countenances" (Alcott 419). Through irony – all the girls are, after all, characters in a book – Alcott's novel links the heroines with the reader, who similarly becomes painfully aware of the discrepancy between fiction and life.

Like Yonge's and Alcott's, Montgomery's self-reflexivity emphasizes Anne's inevitable agency: traditions are never reproduced unchanged. Elizabeth Epperly states that Anne has been "indoctrinated by literary romances" (27) and is never unaware of the potential romance of her situation. When she and Diana have to suspend their friendship, Anne feels "not a little consoled for the time being by this romantic parting" (Montgomery 174). Similarly, when she is off with Diana to save Minnie May from the croup, Anne is "far from being insensible to the romance of the situation" (Montgomery 183). Most frequently, Anne inadvertently undermines the content of the romances she reads, again demonstrating where Montgomery's novel diverges from the literary traditions that inform it. On the way to Green Gables, Anne explains to Matthew that her red hair is her lifelong sorrow: "I read of a girl once in a novel who had a lifelong sorrow, but it wasn't red hair. Her hair was pure gold rippling back from her alabaster brow. What is an alabaster brow?" (Montgomery 69). That Anne knows the lines by heart yet does not understand them exposes the phrases as fictional conceits that only leave her with a sense of inadequacy. Even Shakespeare is not spared Anne's inadvertent criticism, a criticism that comically renders the playwright's grand phrases banal by pairing them with the ordinary. She tells Marilla, "I read in a book once that a rose by any other name would smell as sweet, but I've never been able to believe it. I don't believe a rose *would* be as nice if it was called a thistle or a skunk cabbage" (Montgomery 89). Montgomery's novel also indicates how real life might never live up to the expectations gleaned from reading. She tells Marilla, "Long ago, before I had ever seen a diamond, I read about them and I tried to imagine what they would be like. I thought they would be lovely glimmering purple stones. When I saw a real diamond in a lady's ring one day I was so disappointed I cried" (Montgomery 140). Not only are the girls engendered by the textual ideals they absorb through their readings, but they always feel inadequate and lesser than those ideals. While at first glance they may appear to be presenting a poor imitation of a previous text, in their failure to conform to the previous script, they inscribe their own particular, and lovable, identity.

Anne literally rewrites her world through her daily imaginings and naming of things motivated by her excessive reading. For example, Anne explains to Marilla why she burnt a pie. She had imagined she "was an enchanted princess shut up in a lonely tower with a handsome knight riding to my rescue on a coal-black steed" (Montgomery 201–02), an imaginary moment antithetical to the real world of female labour. Montgomery creates irony here. Anne is a skinny little girl in a rural Canadian kitchen, very unlike an enchanted princess. Anne's choice of story, though, lets readers understand the sense of loneliness and captivity she may feel. Similarly, Anne renames many of the ordinary places in Avonlea with grandiose names certainly culled from romance novels, transforming the world around her rather than merely reflecting on self. The Avenue becomes the "White Way of Delight." Barry's pond becomes the "Lake of Shining Waters." In naming a path through the woods "Lover's Lane," Anne reveals that the idea did come from a book: "Diana and I are reading a perfectly magnificent book and there's a Lover's Lane in it. So we wanted to have one, too" (Montgomery 149). In each novel, the heroine's comparison of herself and her environment to books is a sign of her affinity to the real reader, for whom the active reading process is modelled.

THE HEROINE, THE READER, THE WRITER

Like a hall of mirrors, each novel insists not only that the heroine is a reader, but that any reader is also a writer, actively rescripting her traditions and her world. Yonge's Ethel wants to write fiction because she reads of girls writing fiction. Ethel's desire to write is not for the sake of fame or fortune for herself, but for the greater purpose of establishing a church in the poor community of Cocksmoor. What Ethel would choose to write is a domestic romance for a Christian purpose, very much like Yonge's project. Ethel obviously has quite a store of romance fantasies to work from: "To earn money by writing was her favourite plan, and she called her various romances in turn before her memory, to judge which might be brought down to sober pen and ink" (Yonge 55). This conflation of heroine and writer exposes the inherent theory of composition entailed when a girl interprets literature as a reader.

The narrator's often intrusive comments in *Little Women* similarly blur the lines between writer and heroine. After the narrator's tangential lecture on spinsters, she returns to the novel's action: "Jo must have fallen asleep," she writes and adds a parenthetical apology, "(as I dare say my reader has during this little homily)" (Alcott 441). Similarly, after presenting the girls' Pickwick Paper in its entirety, the narrator adds in parentheses: "(I beg leave to assure my readers [that this paper] is a *bona fide* copy of one written by *bona fide* girls once upon a time)" (Alcott 104). Alcott's narrator intrudes again when Jo is negotiating with an editor, Mr. Dashwood. First, Dashwood says, "We'll take this," and the narrator adds in parentheses "(editors never say 'I')" (Alcott 347); adding the narrator's voice here establishes a link between Jo and the narrator and encourages the reader to consider the narrator's writing process. This parenthetical aside takes the reader outside the boundaries of the fiction to the problems the writer must face. Alcott's narrator intrudes again a few paragraphs later. Jo's "moral reflections" have been excised from her story by Dashwood, and she is bewildered because she believes morals are important. Dashwood replies, "'morals don't sell nowadays;'" and the narrator adds, "which was not quite a correct statement, by the way" (347). The appearance of Alcott's narrator in a discussion about writing becomes ironic, and critical of certain publication venues. The narrator, like the author, writing a gently moral text for young women, knows that morals do indeed sell, evident by the widespread popularity of the first volume of *Little Women*.

These delightfully self-conscious moments have the effect of conflating the author and the narrator. But the novel goes even further. The most intriguing element of self-reflexivity in Alcott's novel is Jo's writing, which a number of critics explore (see Bernstein, Keyser, and Bassil, for example). Veronica Bassil points out that Jo learns to write for her family; in so doing, Jo finds her subject in the March family's domestic life: "Here Alcott's novel turns back on itself, for Jo is both the subject and the author of *Little Women*" (195). In depicting Jo as a writer whose niche is discovered to be the domestic product the reader holds in her hands, the text becomes metafictional, writing about the process of writing. This metafictional quality to *Little Women* not only highlights the inevitable transformation of literary traditions, but also demonstrates how the girls might profit from their attempts to rescript familiar stories.

Like Ethel, who wishes to write, and Jo, who does, Anne also boasts artistic ambitions. Anne's writing, like Jo's, creates textual self-consciousness. While Montgomery does not create a metafiction as Alcott does, she uses Anne's stories to expose romance traditions and to suggest where she changes the story (or to suggest their inadequacies in real life). In doing so, her novel links the heroine and the writer, both stuck in real worlds that are in dire need of romance. Anne explains to Diana the plot of one story she wrote. Two young women, very beautiful, are the best of friends until Bertram DeVere arrives in town. Anne interrupts her retelling of the story to explain how she researched the proposal scene. She asked Ruby Gillis, who has older, married sisters, how proposals are conducted. Ruby relays how she eavesdropped on one sister's proposal: "Malcolm told Susan that his dad had given him the farm in his own name and then said, 'What do you say, darling pet, if we get hitched this fall?' And Susan said, 'Yes – no – I don't know – let me see,' – and there they were, engaged as quick as that" (Montgomery 243). Anne does not find this real life example romantic or compelling. She makes her fictional proposal "very flowery and poetical and Bertram went down on his knees, although Ruby Gillis says it isn't done nowadays" (Montgomery 244). Montgomery's novel, like Yonge and Alcott's before it, highlights agency by showing that girls make choices among the traditions they inherit, and by choosing and rewriting, the tradition of coming-of-age female will be ever-dynamic and flexible.

TRANSFORMING GIRLS: THE READER AS WRITER

Each novel clearly emphasizes how it strays from the tradition it necessarily works within. In doing so, the three writers establish a new tradition of girls' stories that link the heroine with the writer in her active rescripting of her world. Because the novels also highlight the heroine's reading and how that reading influences her, they send a strong message to their own readers: revising traditions and reinventing identity are not only possible, but, as Butler would argue, inevitable to the construction of subjectivity itself. Anne acknowledges her inability to conform to gender roles when she laments to Marilla: "It's at times like this I'm sorry I'm not a model little girl; and I always resolve that I will be in the future" (237). Anne's statement highlights her desperate desire to conform to the ideals of storybook heroines, and yet the novel's comedy rests upon her certain failures. And, that is precisely why readers love her. The girls produced by Yonge's, Alcott's, and Montgomery's novels are notably unable to conform to the notion of model girlhood endorsed by their communities and their reading. While girls' stories focus anxiously on this lamentable lack of conformity, they ultimately celebrate it. Anne is indeed a model little girl, but not for the reasons she might wish. What she models for her readers is a failure that allows for her ultimate triumph: the creation of a distinctive subjectivity.

WORKS CITED

Abate, Michelle Ann. "Topsy and Topsy-Turvy Jo: Harriet Beecher Stowe's *Uncle Tom's Cabin* and/in Louisa May Alcott's *Little Women*." *Children's Literature* 34 (2006): 59–82.

Alcott, Louisa May. *Little Women*. 1868–69. New York: Penguin, 1989.

Armstrong, Frances. "'Here Little, and Hereafter Bliss': *Little Women* and the Deferral of Greatness." *American Literature* 64.3 (September 1992): 453–74.

Bassil, Veronica. "The Artist at Home: The Domestication of Louisa May Alcott." *Studies in American Fiction* 15.2 (Autumn 1987): 187–97.

Berg, Temma F. "Sisterhood Is Fearful: Female Friendship in Montgomery." *Harvesting Thistles: The Textual Garden of L. M. Montgomery.* Ed. Mary Henley Rubio. Guelph, ON: Canadian Children's P, 1994. 36–49.

Bernstein, Susan Naomi. "Writing and *Little Women*: Alcott's Rhetoric of Subversion." *American Transcendental Quarterly* 7.1 (March 1993): 25–43.

Blackford, Holly. "Vital Signs at Play: Objects as Vessels of Mother-Daughter Discourse in Louisa May Alcott's *Little Women*." *Children's Literature* 34 (2006): 1–36.

Butler, Judith. *Gender Trouble: Feminism and the Subversion of Identity.* New York: Routledge, 1990.

———. *Undoing Gender.* New York: Routledge, 2004.

Cadogan, Mary, and Patricia Craig. *You're a Brick, Angela! A New Look at Girls' Fiction from 1839–1975.* London: Victor Gollancz, 1976.

Campbell, Donna M. "Sentimental Conventions and Self-Protection: *Little Women* and *The Wide, Wide World*." *Legacy* 11.2 (1994): 118–29.

Carpenter, Humphrey. *Secret Gardens: A Study of the Golden Age of Children's Literature.* London: George Allen and Unwin, 1985.

Clark, Beverly Lyon. *Kiddie Lit: The Cultural Construction of Children's Literature in America.* Baltimore: Johns Hopkins UP, 2003.

Classen, Constance. "Is *Anne of Green Gables* an American Import?" *Canadian Children's Literature* 55 (1989): 42–50.

Dennis, Barbara. "The Two Voices of Charlotte Yonge." *Durham University Journal* 34 (March 1973): 181–88.

Doyle, Christine. *Louisa May Alcott and Charlotte Brontë: Transatlantic Translations.* Knoxville: U of Tennessee P, 2000.

Epperly, Elizabeth Rollins. *The Fragrance of Sweet-Grass: L. M. Montgomery's Heroines and the Pursuit of Romance.* Toronto: U of Toronto P, 1992.

Foster, Shirley, and Judy Simons. *What Katy Read: Feminist Re-Readings of 'Classic' Stories for Girls.* Iowa City: U of Iowa P, 1995.

Gammel, Irene, ed. *Making Avonlea: L. M. Montgomery and Popular Culture.* Toronto: U Toronto P, 2002.

Inness, Sherrie A. *Delinquents and Debutantes: Twentieth-Century American Girls' Culture.* New York: New York UP, 1998.

Kaplan, Ann. Rev. of *Gender Trouble: Feminism and the Subversion of Identity*, by Judith Butler. *Signs* 17.4 (Summer 1992): 843–47.

Kerber, Linda K. "Can a Woman Be an Individual? The Limits of Puritan Tradition in the Early Republic." *Texas Studies in Literature and Language* 25.1 (Spring 1983): 165–78.

Keyser, Elizabeth Lennox. *Whispers in the Dark: The Fiction of Louisa May Alcott*. Knoxville: U of Tennessee P, 1993.

Meigs, Cornelia, Anne Thaxter Eaton, Elizabeth Nesbitt, and Ruth Hill Viguers. *A Critical History of Children's Literature*. Revised Ed. London: MacMillan, 1969.

Montgomery, L. M. *Anne of Green Gables*. 1908. Ed. Cecily Devereux. Peterborough, ON: Broadview, 2004.

Nelson, Claudia. *Boys Will Be Girls: The Feminine Ethic and British Children's Fiction 1857– 1917*. New Brunswick, NJ: Rutgers UP, 1991.

Pike, E. Holly. "The Heroine Who Writes and Her Creator." *Harvesting Thistles: The Textual Garden of L. M. Montgomery*. Ed. Mary Henley Rubio. Guelph ON: Canadian Children's P, 1994: 50–57.

Ross, Catherine Sheldrick. "Calling Back the Ghost of the Old-Time Heroine: Duncan, Montgomery, Atwood, Laurence, and Munro." *Studies in Canadian Literature* 4 (Winter 1979): 43–58.

Sands-O'Connor, Karen. "Why Jo Didn't Marry Laurie: Louisa May Alcott and *The Heir of Redclyffe*." *ATQ* 15.1 (March 2001): 23–41.

Sardella-Ayres, Dawn. "Under the Umbrella: The Author-Heroine's Love Triangle." *Canadian Children's Literature* 105–06 (Spring/Summer 2002): 100–13.

Seelye, John. *Jane Eyre's American Daughters: From* The Wide, Wide World *to* Anne of Green Gables; *A Study of Marginalized Maidens and What They Mean*. Newark: U of Delaware P, 2005.

Showalter, Elaine. *Sister's Choice: Tradition and Change in American Women's Writing*. Oxford: Clarendon, 1991.

Sturrock, June. *"Heaven and Home": Charlotte M. Yonge's Domestic Fiction and the Victorian Debate over Women*. Victoria, BC: English Literary Studies, 1995.

———. "Sequels, Series, and Sensation Novels: Charlotte Yonge and the Popular Fiction Market of the 1850s and 1860s." *Part Two: Reflections on the Sequel*. Toronto: U Toronto P, 1998: 102–17.

Trillin, Calvin. "Our Far-Flung Correspondents: Anne of Red Hair (What Do the Japanese See in *Anne of Green Gables*?)." *The New Yorker* 5 August 1996: 56–61.

Wadsworth, Sarah A. "Louisa May Alcott, William T. Adams, and the Rise of Gender-Specific Series Books." *The Lion and the Unicorn* 25.1 (2001): 17–46.

Walters, Karla. "Seeking Home: Secularizing the Quest for the Celestial City in *Little Women* and *The Wonderful Wizard of Oz*." *Reform and Counterreform: Dialectics of the Word in Western Christianity since Luther*. Ed. John C. Hawley. Berlin: Monton de Gruyter, 1994. 153–71.

Winn, Harbour. "Echoes of Literary Sisterhood: Louisa May Alcott and Kate Chopin." *Studies in American Fiction* 20.2 (Autumn 1992): 205–08.

Yeast, Denyse. "Negotiating Friendships: The Reading and Writing of L. M. Montgomery." *Harvesting Thistles: The Textual Garden of L. M. Montgomery*. Ed. Mary Henley Rubio. Guelph, ON: Canadian Children's P, 1994. 113–25.

Yonge, Charlotte M. *The Daisy Chain, or Aspirations, a Family Chronicle*. 1856. London: Macmillan, 1880.

Zita, Jacquelyn. "Rev. of *Bodies That Matter: On the Discursive Limits of Sex*," by Judith Butler. *Signs* 21.3 (Spring 1996): 786–95.

NOTES

1 Butler has her detractors (see Kaplan, Zita). Butler does not deny the material reality of the body, as these critics suggest. Particularly throughout *Undoing Gender*, she poignantly argues for the tragic reality of some individuals' bodies that receive violence because of their cultural unintelligibility. Butler attempts to show that the body takes on cultural significance through its gendering process and not the other way around.

2 See Sarah Wadsworth's "Louisa May Alcott, William T. Adams, and the Rise of Gender-Specific Series Books" for an exploration of this new trend in publishing in the mid-nineteenth century. See also Claudia Nelson's *Boys Will Be Girls* for an examination of the complex messages of some of these boys' and girls' books, and Sherrie A. Inness's collection *Delinquents and Debutantes* for discussions about girl culture as it has materialized in the twentieth century.

3 See June Sturrock's *Heaven and Home* (21), for example. It is interesting, and worthy of greater exploration, if outside the scope of this article, to examine scholars' quickness to ascribe both Yonge's and Alcott's inspiration to intellectual men (Keble for Yonge, Emerson for Alcott).

4 I include Seelye's book because it would be a critical oversight if I did not, particularly as it treats the emerging tradition of girls' stories. I do have tremendous problems with his scholarship, however, and I would be remiss if I did not mention them. He includes *Anne* in his study of American novels, with a quick dismissive aside as to why a Canadian novel might be thrown in with the American ones (at least in this regard, he acknowledges the Canadianness of the novel, unlike Foster and Simons's *What Katy Read*). Most importantly, however, Seelye's book hardly makes one reference to the wealth of criticism on these various girls' books, particularly Alcott's and Montgomery's. Published in 2005,

Seelye's book overlooks the rich scholarship available, instead treating these texts as if his were one of the first scholarly examinations of them. Indeed, much of his book comprises tedious plot summaries because he assumes that his readers will be unfamiliar with the novels (11), an assumption that reveals some disdain for his topic.

5 See Temma Berg for a detailed comparison of Anne and Alcott's Jo. E. Holly Pike links Montgomery's Emily and Alcott's Jo, as does Dawn Sardella-Ayres.

6 For various perspectives on Montgomery's influence, see the essays in *Making Avonlea: L. M. Montgomery and Popular Culture*, edited by Irene Gammel.

7 I must acknowledge here that Yonge's *The Daisy Chain* is not technically a girls' story, but a family chronicle. I would argue, however, that the tomboy Ethel emerges as the central and most compelling character in the large cast of May siblings, in the same way that Jo does in Alcott's family chronicle, *Little Women*.

8 In creating Anne as an orphan, Montgomery is, of course, drawing on other literary traditions, such as that established by Charlotte Brontë's *Jane Eyre*.

9 Of course, as I mentioned in the introduction, this tradition of gesturing backward to other literature is by no means confined to the girls' story tradition. However, it does seem to be a consistent feature of the girls' story. Ann-Marie MacDonald's *Fall on Your Knees* (2002) carries this tradition along by showing the Piper girls acting out Alcott's *Little Women*, for example.

CHAPTER EIGHT

Anne of Green Gables as Intertext in Post-1960 Canadian Women's Fiction

Theodore Sheckels

Margaret Atwood once commented, *"Anne of Green Gables* is subcutaneous in us all" (qtd. in Rubio, "Subverting" 9). By "us all," she meant Canadian women writers; by "subcutaneous," she meant just below the surface – so that the influence of L. M. Montgomery's 1908 novel could be discerned but usually was overlooked. Nonetheless, if the influence is indeed beneath the skin, it's in the flesh and, therefore, part of these writers' being. Whether or not this influence is conscious is beside the point. *Anne of Green Gables* provides Canadian women writers, such as Margaret Atwood, Margaret Laurence, Marian Engel, and Alice Munro, with a series of motifs that recur over time, changing shape and tone. Sometimes the authors do seem conscious of inviting Montgomery's work into their fiction as an intertext, but more often Montgomery's formative novel just finds its way in because it is embedded in the literary environment they inhabit as Canadian authors and – more important – Canadian women authors. Atwood's sense that Montgomery's *Anne* is subcutaneous suggests that, in her view, the *Anne* story pervades the unconscious of women writing within Canadian culture. She notes that she "absorbed it so thoroughly" ("Afterword" 141) that she could no longer pinpoint precisely when she first read the novel. Canadian women writers absorbed the book, later saw Kevin Sullivan's 1985 miniseries, and perhaps read the book to their own daughters. A formative text, which children's literature tends to be, gets beneath the skin, even when the skin is an entirely different genre of contemporary realism, a genre that can stand in a tense relationship with the romance of Montgomery's novel.

I wish to examine how recurrent motifs of *Anne* are given new skin and thereby new, rich meaning by subsequent female writers. All of the novels I mention could, of course, be discussed at considerable length. What I wish to focus on, given this volume's purpose, is not all that these many novels undertake and accomplish but, rather, the tensions that surface when readers encounter motifs they have seen before. Readers hearing echoes of *Anne* in contemporary realistic fiction find themselves sharply aware of Montgomery's romanticism and their own longings for romantic resolutions to what are really irresolvable problems facing young heroines, problems unmasked by contemporary women writers. Eight noticeable motifs provide the structure for the exploration of these tensions. The motifs include the redemptive and possibly dangerous setting of the island, a journey to which gives female protagonists the potential of new selves; the literal and symbolic condition of being an orphan, abandoned by and yet longing for parents; the intense desire to come to terms with stern mother figures who cannot express feelings; the existence of male rivals who bring out the (often intellectual) potential of heroines; the convention of the female "bosom friend" as an alternative, supportive relation; the rejuvenating force of nature, a central concern of many Canadian women writers; the bildungsroman development of the writer; and the artist's delight in and concern for words. (The latter two motifs perhaps permit the authors to comment self-reflexively on the author's sense of her own story, as Laura Robinson suggests elsewhere in this volume.)

Many of these motifs are also common in other national traditions. For example, the island, as a New World, is a central and ideological empire-building imperative in British fiction, particularly for children; the orphan offered British and American novelists the possibility of demonstrating the theme of liberal self-making; the female bildungsroman can hardly be thought of apart from British works such as Charlotte Brontë's *Jane Eyre* or American works such as Louisa May Alcott's *Little Women*; and an appreciation for nature, as well its rejuvenating potential, can be found in some form or another in romantic literature as well as in wilderness stories common to Canada. However, Montgomery combined these motifs in a unique way, giving them force and bringing them to life with her creation of Anne, the imaginative presence who authors her own sense of an island's meaning, brings about the redemption of stern adults, and exhibits the developmental potential of the female bildungsroman in nature as well as in the domestic realm. Montgomery's unique contribution altered these motifs for Canadian women writers and left to them a formative vision of inter-connected literary conventions. These conventions, of course, are interconnected largely within the genre of juvenile fiction, a genre that functions in romantic, not realistic terms. The tensions between text and intertexts are partially a result of genre shifting and partially a result of the willingness of the more contemporary writers to deal bluntly with many of the very serious problems girls and women face.

These more recent writers' conscious awareness of Montgomery's use of these motifs begs the question because readers construct the meaning of texts with varying levels of intertextual awareness. Readers confronting contemporary plots far scarier than anything in Anne's Avonlea world construct meanings that are nevertheless coloured optimistically by the presence of *Anne of Green Gables* as intertext. They thereby feel the tension between an often bleak reality and a desired idyll. These readers, however, do not cease constructing meaning after they have read the newer fiction. Rather, they return, literally or in their minds, to Montgomery's work and they construct meanings that are darkened by the post-1960 fiction that evokes *Anne*, creating a further tension as they realize the sinister potential behind many *Anne* motifs, such as that of the abused and abandoned child. Readers read later fiction through the subcutaneous lens of *Anne* as intertext, just as readers reflect on *Anne* through the lens of this later fiction. Intertextuality informs this interpretive cycle.

Some understanding of literary theory can help us distinguish the concept of influence from the idea of intertextuality, the former more narrow than the latter. We detect influence when we witness the presence of one particular literary work in a later work. For example, one can hardly miss the influence of William Shakespeare's *A Midsummer Night's Dream* on Nigerian playwright Wole Soyinka's *A Dance of the Forests*. Written in 1960 to celebrate his nation's independence, Soyinka's play sent its major characters into the woods, where magical events occurred that then transformed them into men and women with a keen consciousness of both their African past and present. Soyinka makes no explicit reference to Shakespeare's play; however, no commentator has doubted the influence, as no playwright with Soyinka's academic training and theatrical inclinations could possibly be sending his characters into magical woods without alluding to Shakespeare's play. However, influence studies have fallen out of fashion with the literary-critical environment's more general turn toward postmodernism and postmodern theory, a perspective that altered the conceptualization of the writer from a conscious subject to a relatively passive confluence of his/her linguistic and cultural contexts.

Within this new conceptualization, the critical concept of intertextuality emerged. Through a sequence of commentaries on Julia Kristeva's work (1980, 1984), several critics, Roland Barthes and Jonathan Culler notable among them, defined the critical concept of intertextuality as a characteristic of an author's production that he or she was sometimes conscious of and sometimes not. Intertexts, then, stem from an author's linguistic and cultural context; the study of intertextuality is therefore remote from the more narrow tradition of the influence study, which posited direct relations between a work and a preceding work or author. At the conscious extreme, analyses in the communication discipline, by Thomas Rosteck and Martha Solomon Watson, have demonstrated how intertexts that are certainly known by the creators enter into Bill Clinton's 1992 campaign film, *The Man from Hope*, as well as the foundational texts of the nineteenth-century American abolitionists and women's rights movements. Although those in literary studies have resisted analyses as blatantly instrumental as these, because of their implicit assumption that the creator is an autonomous subject (Morgan), many critics have admitted, as Kristeva said in an interview, that the creator is "one who produces a text by placing himself or herself at the intersection of this plurality of texts on their different levels" (Waller 281). Kristeva interestingly neither denies nor affirms the creator's consciousness of "this plurality of texts." A similar position is presented in Mikhail Bakhtin's study of Dostoevsky as well as his several studies of the novel, anthologized in *The Dialogic Imagination* (1981), where the "voices" that find their way into the novel's polyphony are sometimes invited in by the creator and sometimes just intrude. Literary theory thus offers a way of richly perceiving how *Anne of Green Gables* enriches later Canadian women writers, as well as allowing us to understand what happens to the *Anne* motifs when contemporary genres, concerns, and realism intrude and speak back to *Anne*.

RECURRENT MOTIFS

The island motif, the first I wish to discuss, is the subject of my book *The Island Motif in the Fiction of L. M. Montgomery, Margaret Laurence, Margaret Atwood, and Other Canadian Women Novelists* (2003). Montgomery's early life on Prince Edward Island, combined with exposure to literary islands in the works of William Shakespeare and Alfred, Lord Tennyson, perhaps drew her to the motif of the island as a redemptive and magical New World. In Montgomery's novel, the island is unambiguously redemptive ground: no Shakespearean or Tennysonian ambiguity for Montgomery's debut in juvenile fiction! Anne, upon arrival on Prince Edward Island, is in many ways a psychologically battered child. The death of her parents, her lonely times at the orphanage in Halifax, and her previous situations have all scarred Anne. Gradually, through the agency of the place as much as its people, Anne is healed.

We find a similar but much more radical use of the motif in Marian Engel's *Bear* (1976). Lou, *Bear*'s central character, is psychologically battered – by her monotonous job, by an abortion a lover compelled her to have, by his desertion of her, by her weekly near-rape by her boss atop his desk, by – possibly – sexual abuse as a child – and by her body's deprivation of sun and air. She is described as a mole, labouring in a library basement. The library into which she burrows acquires the estate of an eccentric character named Colonel Cary, who lives in an octagonal house on a remote Ontario island. Lou goes there to catalogue Cary's eclectic library. Once there, she must come to terms with Cary's pet bear and whatever the beast symbolizes. Yes, Lou does attempt to have sexual intercourse with the bear, but, rather than a bizarre story of bestiality, the novel is an almost magical one of redemption on a very special island. As a result of her stay on the island, Lou is rejuvenated, in body and spirit; furthermore, she is empowered to reject the oppressive life she had been living in Toronto (Cameron 92; Hair 37, 41; and Osachoff 20).

Bear, given its erotic nature, is quite obviously a far cry from *Anne of Green Gables*; however, its use of the island motif is strikingly similar. Anne and Lou are similarly redeemed by islands that focus and gather their full human potential. Lou's situation is far more dire than Anne's, however. As an orphan, Anne has experienced loneliness at the orphanage and cruel treatment at a previous posting. She has not, however, been the victim of sexual abuse; she has not been compelled to have an abortion against her will; she has not seen her body weaken and pale. As readers construct their meaning of *Bear*, the presence of the intertext ameliorates the *Bear* plot, making Lou's plight less dire and suggesting that islands can indeed have a special power to redeem because Anne's special island most definitely did. Readers wait for Lou's island to work the magic of Anne's.

Another interesting use of the motif, which counterpoints Montgomery's, is Margaret Atwood's in *Bodily Harm* (1982). In this novel, another oppressed Toronto woman flees for an island. Rennie Wilford, a magazine writer, has faced a noose left on her bed by a mysterious intruder, her boyfriend's rape fantasies, the violent pornography exhibit her editor maliciously sent her to cover, her partial mastectomy, her resultant loss of self-esteem, and her sexual and psychological abuse by her surgeon. She leaves for the Caribbean and what she thinks will be the task of writing a "lite" travel piece. The trip is intended, like Anne's to Prince Edward Island and Lou's to Cary Island, to redeem her and replenish her spirit. After all, as Jones has noted (92), Rennie is short for Renata, a name that entails rebirth. Instead, she stumbles into the midst of political turmoil she does not grasp and ends up in a third-world prison where women barter sexual favours for humane treatment. Rennie's island is not Anne's or even Lou's; there is no redemption to be found on it, and there may or may not be redemption from it, depending on whether the reader interprets the rescue by a Canadian government official at the novel's end as dreamt or fact. Readers nonetheless read Anne's Prince Edward Island into the meaning that they construct, thereby making the rescue scenario emotionally desirable, even if Atwood's carefully used verb tenses make it seem more a fantasy than a reality. A striking tension exists between how the story may well end and how readers, influenced by romantic conventions embedded in *Anne*, want the story to end.

In her critical study *Survival* (1972), Atwood posits the idea that nations have dominant "symbols." Survival was the dominant symbol for Canada, the frontier for the United States, the island for England. If she was partially correct for Canada, perhaps she was partially incorrect for Britain. Perhaps the island is as much a Canadian motif as a British one, except, in a nation with a colonial past, coloured by the desperate need to survive, the island is sometimes Montgomery's idyll but just as often the dangerous place of isolation it is in *Bodily Harm*. (It is never the moat-protected, castle-like island Atwood finds in British writing.) Reading *Survival*, one is struck by how gruesome the Canadian plots appear. Reading *Anne of Green Gables* naïvely would, of course, lead one in a very different direction. For those who read the post-1960 novels such as *Bear* and *Bodily Harm* and then reread *Anne*, Montgomery's classic will never be the same. Montgomery's optimism notwithstanding, Anne is lucky to have survived on her island when many abuses await an isolated young heroine, as the stories of Lou and Rennie attest. Heightened attention to Anne's vulnerability qualifies Montgomery's optimism.

Anne is, of course, an orphan. Children, whether literally orphaned or simply estranged from their parents, provide another motif. Being an orphan is, of course, a literal situation; however, that situation frequently serves in literature to point to a deeply felt separation and loneliness that erode one's self-esteem. So it is with Anne Shirley, for she is emotionally starved upon her arrival in Avonlea and exhibits so little self-esteem that she wants to reinvent herself as "Cordelia" – or at least "Anne" with an "e." Although Montgomery is not overtly writing a political allegory, Canada's estrangement from its mother country, and burgeoning sense of itself, may well have made this motif particularly compelling to her. The popularity in juvenile literature of orphan characters, who can build and indeed must build New Worlds for themselves, may also have steered Montgomery to this motif. The orphan, perfectly poised to depart for an island, thematically and symbolically replicates the condition of the lonely island as well.

Atwood's *Surfacing* (1972) and Margaret Laurence's *The Diviners* (1974) exhibit this same basic motif. In Atwood's novel, the central character – the never-named narrator – has been estranged from her parents. Now, her mother is dead, and her father has mysteriously disappeared. She and three friends venture to an island in northern Quebec, ostensibly to solve the mystery. Instead, she deals with the unnatural demons that beset both the world and her life. It is a matter of considerable debate if the narrator ever regains her wholeness (Sheckels 76). If she does, the vision in which she is reconciled with her parents and accepts their symbolic gifts plays a major role in her rebirth (Fiamengo 146). She must, in a psychological sense, cease being an orphan and reconnect with her lost parents and with nature, something Anne intuitively values. In Laurence's novel, the central character, Morag Gunn, loses her parents to a polio outbreak. She is raised by the town's trash collector, Christy Logan, and his socially embarrassing wife, Prin. She rebels against them and begins a quest for self and voice that takes her all over Canada and across the Atlantic to England and Scotland as well. Morag ultimately finds that she must embrace her adopted parents, even though it is only upon their deaths. In that embrace, she finds her self, her voice as a writer, and her heritage (Carolan-Broszy and Hagemann; Greene 193–94; Thieme; Warwick, *River* 50–51).

The abandoned children thus have to come to terms with parents, whether lost or adopted, offering thereby a parable of national importance. Anne, despite bumps along the road, comes to terms with her adopted parents in scenes that are extremely melodramatic; the recurrent theme of alienation and reconciliation sets a model that resides beneath the surface as readers interact with the later novels depicting estrangement. Readers of *Surfacing* want the bizarre visionary ending with its slight suggestion of reconciliation to reflect something other than the narrator's insanity; readers of *The Diviners* want Morag to be reconciled with Prin and Christy so much that they ignore the fact that she returns to them too late. The "subcutaneous" narrative expectations engendered by the *Anne* melodrama ironically surface the most when readers find their absence glaring at them. Contemporary writers are making the point that reconciliation is rare, not common, in real life, and readers cannot help but feel both their own longing for, and the forcing of reconciliation in, *Anne*.

Marilla Cuthbert is the stern parent figure in *Anne*. This is a third motif. She, of course, is redeemed by Anne from her heartbreak at losing John Blythe and the empty life of duty she has chosen to live since. This redemption benefits both Marilla and Anne, as we see in two of *Anne of Green Gables*'s most moving scenes. The first occurs when Marilla, upon Matthew Cuthbert's death, embraces Anne and tells her that "I love you as dear as if you were my own flesh and blood and you've been my joy and comfort ever since you came to Green Gables" (322). The second is when Anne gives up her scholarship to Redmond and stays with Marilla at Green Gables. Marilla responds, "You blessed girl! ... I feel as if you'd given me new life" (328). Not only does the child redeem herself, but she also converts others with her spirit.

The mother of the unnamed narrator in Atwood's *Surfacing* is also distant. However, she seems more stoic than stern. She is not redeemed, but the narrator's memory of her mother is redeemed through the peaceful vision the narrator has of her toward the novel's end (Staels 66). Since we doubt the narrator's sanity at that point, we must doubt both the vision and the redemption, but her imaginative redemption points to a possible resolution. Thus, *Surfacing* ends with an ambiguity lacking in the more melodramatic *Anne of Green Gables*. And only ambiguity, not redemption, awaits the parent figures in Margaret Laurence's *A Jest of God* (1966) and Alice Munro's *Lives of Girls and Women* (1971). In Laurence's novel, daughter Rachel Cameron successfully overcomes her oppressing, manipulative mother and leaves Manawaka for Vancouver (Baum 157; Hartveit 348; Martin 62–63; Stein 88–90). But she does not leave her mother behind. Rachel reverses power positions and, then, virtually tells her mother that she is leaving Manawaka for Vancouver (Stovel, *Rachel's* 68). Rachel thereby sustains the daughter-mother bond but with few genuinely loving feelings apparent on either side. The mother seems weakened by Rachel's assertion of control and little more. In Munro's work, daughter Del Jordan, after having failed to live her mother's very asexual dream for her, leaves Jubilee for Toronto to pursue a career as a writer (Susan Thomas 116–17). The mother is abandoned. Even worse is the fate of the stern mother figure in Atwood's *Lady Oracle* (1976). She and the novel's central character, Joan Foster, become increasingly alienated as the novel progresses, with daughter Joan discovering the depression behind her mother's stern behaviour only after the mother's death (Fenwick 53).

Rachel's mother, Del's mother, and Joan's mother are not Marilla, but joyless shadows of her, without the benefit of the sentimental novel. Daughters leave in the more contemporary worlds of Laurence and Munro and Atwood, rather than sacrifice themselves for stern mothers, as Anne does. Yet Marilla – or, rather, the possibility of Marilla – qualifies the readers' understanding of Laurence's and Munro's maternal characters: they could so easily be Marilla, readers think, if they would just overcome their fear, thwarted ambition, and depression. Those, however, are life's realities. Their sternness is tied to them, just as Marilla's is tied to her failed romance with John Blythe and the somewhat empty life that followed in its wake. Having read Laurence and Atwood, the reader rereads Marilla's joyful transformation as an unlikely response to deeply rooted needs for parental affirmation.

Another motif, a male rival, brings us to Montgomery's Gilbert Blythe, who initially taunts Anne and then engages in a fierce competition for academic honours with her. Along the way, they, of course, fall in love. Although they do not speak words of love to each other, they are implicit in Gilbert's declaration at the novel's end that "We are going to be the best of friends…. We were born to be good friends, Anne" (332). Providing a heroine with a romantic interest is, of course, a staple in the novel form. That he is a rival, as well as a potential suitor, allows Montgomery to both posit the equality between genders that ought to be and suggest the barriers that exist. Gilbert, after all, despite tying with Anne for top honors in Avonlea, does slightly surpass her in college and then must benevolently give her the teaching position in Avonlea.

Similar is the rivalry between Del Jordan and Jerry Storey in Munro's *Lives of Girls and Women*. They are the academic elite in their Jubilee, Ontario, class – Del in English, Jerry in mathematics and science, with the latter slightly privileged over the former. As such, they are often set apart from their classmates, who are far less concerned with academic matters. Although there is no spark between them, they comically proceed as if there might be, a process that climaxes in a comic scene during which Jerry probes Del's naked body as if she were a scientific exhibit, not a young woman (Besner 140–41). Jerry, however, is quickly neither a possible lover for Del nor her rival when a sudden spark ignites a fire of desire between Del and Garnet French (Besner 141; Gold 6), thereby shifting the focus of Munro's plot. Somewhat similar is the rivalry between Morag Gunn and Jules Tonnerre in *The Diviners*. They are the young social outcasts and would-be rebels of Manawaka – she the scavenger's foster daughter, he an impoverished *Métis*. Their rivalry leads to a moment of sexual bravado on Morag's part, which ends anticlimactically with his premature ejaculation. Despite this failure, he is able because of his gender to be the "better" rebel: he hits the road to write and perform his music; she leaves for university and then marriage. Years later, they unite as lovers – not rivals – and then serve as the unmarried and rarely-together parents to their daughter, Pique.

The story of Anne and Gilbert is comic, in line with Canadian critic Northrop Frye's descriptions in *Anatomy of Criticism* (and much Shakespearean practice). The story of Del and Jerry is also comic, but more in the sense of being amusing, laughable. It's the version of Anne-and-Gilbert that might have been if they had indeed been the stereotypical strong-in-English girl and the stereotypical strong-in-math-and-science boy – mismatched literary dreamer and calculating "nerd." The story of Morag and Jules is more coarsely real. They have talents, and they possess passion, but, caught in the socioeconomic structure of Manawaka, they become rivals in rebellion and compatriots in desire before going separate ways, Morag striving upward through education and Jules falling downward in an acceptance of his *Métis* inferiority. In both cases, readers want the couples to be Anne and Gilbert, a desire that calls attention to the power of the comic archetype skilfully deployed by Montgomery. These failed love stories, however, do cast a shadow upon *Anne* when the novel is re-encountered, a shadow that alters Montgomery's idyllic plot.

Still another motif is the female "bosom friend," embodied in *Anne of Green Gables* by Diana Barry. But the motif is not as simple as it initially seems. The motif, as initiated by Anne and Diana, features a counterpoint between the two. They manifest female friendship, but they also represent different life paths. Thus, they not only signal that there are different paths for women but prove the enduring quality of such friendship despite very different life choices. Here, as in Montgomery's insistence on a still-constrained equality between female and male rivals, a proto-feminism emerges. Montgomery stresses solidarity among women despite their different life decisions.

There are other "bosom friends" in Canadian women's writing who exhibit the same bond despite differences. Rachel and Calla in Laurence's *A Jest of God* have a strong bond: they mirror each other; Calla may even represent Rachel's Jungian shadow (Bailey 63–65). The strength of the bond overcomes Calla's lesbian embrace of Rachel; it overcomes Rachel's subsequent rejection of Calla. It is strong enough for Calla to see Rachel through her pregnancy scare, and – more important – it is strong enough for Calla to push Rachel, like a caged bird, out of Manawaka even though doing so means that she will lose her (Stovel, "Sisters" 71). Del and Naomi in Munro's *Lives of Girls and Women* exhibit a similarly strong bond, even though Del seems headed for university and Naomi for an early wedding. Rennie and Lora in Atwood's *Bodily Harm* also exhibit a strong bond, although only at the novel's conclusion. Initially Rennie rejects Lora because of her un-Canadian flamboyance and lack of sexual discretion. Rennie also, at that point, misperceives Lora as unintelligent (Jones; Rubenstein 126, 131). Rennie comes to learn that Lora is, to the contrary, quite politically savvy, and, then, she finds herself locked in a squalid prison cell with her as chaos engulfs the island. There, Lora sacrifices herself to the guard's sexual appetites to save Rennie from rape. Finally, after the guards beat Lora to near-death, Rennie embraces her, pulling her battered head onto her lap. She thinks of cleaning the bloody, pulverized flesh with her tongue, the way maternal animals do with their newborn. Rennie and Lora have moved from acquaintances to friends to something more profound in very short order (Stovel, "Reflections" 64–65).

Lora is a far cry from Diana Barry, but in all of these later novels the core ideas behind the Anne and Diana friendship are still apparent. There is a bond that survives trouble, a bond that endures despite stark differences between the girls or women involved. Rachel and Calla are separated by both religious beliefs and sexual orientation, Del and Naomi by academic aptitude, Rennie and Lora by sexual decorum. These differences are far more profound than that between Anne's red and Diana's raven tresses. Still, *Anne* as intertext causes readers to see that female solidarity is fundamental. The differences, whether superficial or profound, do not matter. In this case, intertextuality, as it affects the construction of the meaning of the post-1960 fiction and as it affects a rereading of *Anne*, neither lightens nor darkens matters. Female community transcends cultural change.

Anne delighted in the natural beauty of her beloved Prince Edward Island. Nature figures heavily in Montgomery's later works as well, such as in the other *Anne* novels, the two "Pat" novels, and the late *Jane of Lantern Hill* (1937). Although Anne's delight in the place's beauty, upon her arrival in Avonlea, is fanciful, it endures with less gushing as she matures. Nonetheless, it is never just delight in the scenery. Rather, it is premised on the belief that there is something almost immutable – and, therefore, beyond being threatened – in the beauty.

Thus, it is important to save the place Green Gables. That which withstands the threats of the world must be preserved – no matter what the sacrifice.

Natural beauty functions in similar ways in Audrey Thomas's *Intertidal Life* and Marian Engel's *Bear*. Thomas's central character, Alice Hoyle, looks to nature for life lessons as her personal world collapses. She finds sea creatures' ability to handle times of transition instructive as she faces similar moments. Engel's Lou eventually looks to nature as a source of bodily and spiritual renewal (Cameron). However, at first, paled by the city and battered by its life, she finds nature foreign. She grows to appreciate and delight in it as her tenure on Cary Island continues. She becomes one with nature. The moment she seeks to become one with nature's embodiment, the bear, she crosses the line between figure and ground, signifying that she is ready to return from nature rejuvenated. The stories of Alice and Lou seem consonant with that of Anne Shirley. Nature offers needed solace and potential joy, whether the problems are the adult ones of Alice and Lou or the more adolescent ones of Anne. Again, intertextuality reinforces, not qualifies.

But nature is not always present to offer solace; it can also be threatened – if not in Anne's world (except when Marilla announces that she must sell Green Gables), then in that of Montgomery's later heroines, such as Pat Garner, who witnesses the destruction of her "Silver Bush" paradise. The threat is even more vivid in other Canadian works. In Atwood's *Surfacing*, nature is threatened by humankind, who dam the lake, causing the water to rise and the lakeside flora to die, and who kill the fauna for sport or, in some cases, sick fun. In Atwood's more recent *Oryx and Crake* (2003), nature is further threatened, this time by gene-splicing scientists who can modify nature, for good or for ill, at their will or at their whim. The ultimate new Eden Crake creates and Oryx tends proves not a paradise-found but humanity's – perhaps life's – last gasp. As readers read these other stories – especially as they read Montgomery's own later stories, they construct a meaning that reflects what nature might be, as idealized in *Anne*. No matter how endangered nature might be, *Anne* echoes and reverberates its positive force – its need to be preserved for the dignity of the human soul. Unfortunately, these dire later stories also mark Montgomery's classic as fanciful when readers return to it with Montgomery's bleak later books, let alone the apocalyptic *Oryx and Crake*, in mind.

Anne Shirley was, of course, a fledgling writer, as are a large number of other characters created by Canadian women writers, as well as other characters created by Montgomery. The motif, as announced in Montgomery's novel, features the struggle to find one's own voice in a world that seems intent upon pigeon-holing one based on gender. The motif, then, follows the contours of the bildungsroman as that genre might be reinscribed by a woman. Although Montgomery's reading in the decade prior to writing *Anne of Green Gables* seems to have included little of this kind, she does refer to her earlier reading of Alcott, and, not long after seeing *Anne* into print, Montgomery becomes fascinated with the struggles of "that woman genius" Charlotte Brontë, especially as her story was told in Elizabeth Gaskell's biography (Rubio and Waterston 36). So, although Montgomery could probably not articulate the plight of a woman writer in mid-late twentieth-century feminist terms, the raw materials of a proto-feminist depiction were clearly available as she constructed the story of Anne as writer.

The "story club" Anne and her female friends found in their early teens has the girls writing what seem to be several different types of fiction, most inspired by Anne's ideas, for, she says, she has a million of them. The different types, however, are all variations on popular romance, the presumed "female" genre. Anne's case as a fledgling writer was, in one way, fortunate insofar as she had a strong female mentor in the person of Miss Stacy. Thus, she did not have to struggle too much on her own, and she did not find her voice suppressed by patriarchy. The constraints are present, for it is 1908 and women writers are not free to roam the possible genres and the possible plots; however, the constraints are weakened by the mentor's presence. Montgomery herself, without the help and the buffer of a female mentor, knew the constraints quite well.

More complex if not worse fates do await other would-be writers who come in Anne's wake. Some, such as Del Jordan in Munro's *Lives of Girls and Women* and Morag Gunn in Laurence's *The Diviners*, struggle to find their voice. Others, such as Atwood's Joan Foster in *Lady Oracle* (1976), resist the way their voice is seized from them. Del lacks good role models, since neither the dry historical recording of her uncle nor the hyper-emotional gushing of Jubilee's women's stories answers Del's need to talk about "the real world" in tones that communicate the intensity of the everyday (Besner 136; Godard, "Heirs"; Harris; Meindl 21; Warwick, "Growing" 204, 206; York, "Lives"; York, "The Rival"). Del, in the novel's last chapter, learns what she must be as a writer. Morag lacks models but also acquires in her older professor husband, Brooke Skelton, a mentor who increasingly stifles her creativity. Threatened by her success, he demeans her achievements. In critiquing her writing, as in all other phases of her life, he treats her as a child. Morag also has a difficult time finding her voice because the options before her as a female writer strike her as not being genuine (Boutelle; Carolan-Brozy and Hagemann; Godard, "Caliban's"; Godard, *The Diviners*; Howells 157; Sparrow). Atwood's Joan Foster, replete with Anne-like flaming red hair, finds her voice sooner (Fenwick). The world, however, will not let her have her voice: the world insists on interpreting it, whether it be the voice within Joan's gothic romances or the voice within the "automatic writing" with which she experiments. The world wants to label and thereby control her. Thus, she continually reinvents herself, often using her art as the means by which she executes these transformations (Maclean). Thus, in the end, she tries to fabricate her own death to escape such control – of her art and her life.

And, finally, Anne Shirley is fascinated with words – their beauty and their power. She evokes that power both as she writes and as she recites, but the fascination shows up most clearly in her fulsome descriptions of her emotional states, such as in her words to Diana. She tells Diana that "I will always love thee" and that "In the years to come thy memory will shine like a star over my lonely life." She asks if she could have "a lock of thy jet-black tresses in parting to treasure forevermore" (174). Her fascination with words also shows in her naming of places surrounding the Cuthbert farm in Avonlea such as "the White Way of Delight" and "the Lake of Shining Waters." As Rubio has argued, through Anne's naming, Montgomery may be satirizing romance without the satire diminishing either her charm or her stature, as a new Adam, bestowing names on the elements of her paradise ("Satire" 32–33).

This fascination with words is seen also in the quizzical playing of both Laurence's Morag in *The Diviners* and Audrey Thomas's Alice in *Intertidal Life*. Morag is always asking questions such as "What means *Law*" (25), "What means *Scavenger*" (26), and "What means *Leave the Room*" (27). She refuses to accept words as merely functional. She must unpack them, discovering their various peculiarities. Alice plays similar word games, reflecting her long-term struggle with words as woman and writer (Hales 78–79; Wachtel 39). For example, she frequently interpolates into her narration dictionary-like meditations on words such as "adore," "mother," "mummy," "deliver," "pudendum," and "cock." She also inserts rhymes, riddles, and word games, such as the "Una" one, which gives rise to the character's poet, "Una Verse," sexy lady, "Una Form," and bad-joke-telling "Una Corn." More profoundly, Alice implicitly recognizes that the world is built of words. As her world disintegrates, she forces the words to do the same. Both Morag and Alice ultimately wish to reinscribe the world along non-patriarchal lines (Hales). Morag, at middle age, seems successful; Alice's story is left unfinished by Thomas (Hutcheon 224–25). The power of words is unquestioned, though the effect differs.

The writing women in the later books then reflect attitudes toward both writing and words that are more sophisticated than those exhibited by Anne Shirley. These later women are much more aware of how they are constrained as writing women; they also possess a rather sophisticated if not postmodern appreciation of the arbitrary quality of language. They even, at times, hint at an awareness of language's rootedness in patriarchy and their – as women – existence outside language. These latter notes are faint, suggesting that feminism among contemporary Canadian women writers – at least the Anglophone ones – is surprisingly muted. Anne, as saluted as she might be by some feminist critics, lacks an awareness of her constraints as a would-be writer and of the language's arbitrariness. She accepts all the gendered givens and writes; she delights in language as she unwittingly demonstrates its arbitrariness by renaming. Her naïvete and her joy qualify how readers construct their meanings of the later women's stories. Morag succeeds; Del might, for she is yet young; Alice might, for her story ends in ambiguity; and Joan might, now that she is once more among the living. *Anne* as intertext lends these later stories hope, just as these women's stories as intertexts to *Anne* make us all too aware of how the struggle of a woman writer is far more complex than discerned or exhibited by Anne.

Conclusion: Dissonant Motifs

The motifs influenced by *Anne of Green Gables* are interesting in themselves, but they become even more interesting when we regard them as creating, for the most part, tensions against which contemporary Canadian writers are simultaneously struggling. More often than not, the *Anne* intertext sets the idyllic against more recent echoes that complicate if not threaten it. The post-1960 world of more recent women writers is simply not, and cannot even pretend to be, the largely idyllic situation depicted in an orphan's resurrection of herself and community through linguistic and imaginative power. *Anne* creates a dissonant polyphony as much as it creates harmonious recurrent motifs.

Anne's island is redemptive, but, sometimes, as these more contemporary women know, the literal or figurative island one chooses to retreat to may be ambiguous or, worse, dangerous. In Anne's world, orphans find parents and overcome the scars of their ragged upbringing. Beyond the idyll of Prince Edward Island, the story may not always end quite so positively: the damage may be too great. Similarly, not all stern parental figures experience wonderful transformation. Rather than find love in a life that had become nothing but duty, as in Marilla's case, some find loneliness or emptiness or bitterness. Rivalries with males do not always take a positive or romantic turn, and supposed "bosom friends" do not stay close or loyal. Some may even betray each other. Natural beauty, a staple in Anne's world, may be devastated; and the beauty of words may be lost or never discovered.

Post-1960 Canadian women writers have chosen, for the most part, formal realism. Thus, we enter into fictive worlds that we are urged to accept as representative of how life is. It is sometimes good, but more often than not troubled. Consider the life experiences of the heroines discussed in this essay: Lou, Rennie Wilford, *Surfacing*'s unnamed narrator, Morag Gunn, Rachel Cameron, Del Jordan, Alice Hoyle, Oryx, Joan Foster. What is their collective world like? Compulsory sex on one's boss's desk (Lou); a rape-fantasizing boyfriend (Rennie); unnecessary disfiguring surgery (Rennie); violent pornography (Rennie); a compulsory abortion (Lou and *Surfacing*'s narrator); a psychologically abusing husband (Morag); a controlling, passive-aggressive mother (Rachel and Joan); a claustrophobic small town (Rachel and Del); a husband's sexual betrayal (Alice); childhood prostitution (Oryx); critics and commentators who want to label one as a certain kind of writer (Joan). This collective world is not the world of Anne Shirley in Montgomery's novel, which may become through the lens of these later novels a powerful synecdoche for the stifling world of childhood and its false optimism.

But if Anne's world is entailed as intertext within this much scarier world, what does the resulting tension accomplish? Rather than call into question Anne's world, the tension may actually restore hope to the world inhabited by Anne's literary "sisters." What is "subcutaneous" in post-1960 Canadian women writers may then be the potential to triumph and delight despite the difficulties of places far more complex and sinister than Montgomery's fictive Avonlea. What is in the flesh of these writers may then be a furtive optimism despite the problems and horrors their realistic fiction presents before their readers. Although this look at Canadian women writers suggests changes in what fiction is for, the redemptive model of *Anne* may not be so far beneath the skin after all.

That redemptive model, of course, dates from 1908. It has often been reconstructed as generations of readers have first encountered Anne Shirley. From early on, however, *Anne* was not a book read once. If *Anne of Green Gables* serves as intertext as readers construct meanings of novels such as Laurence's *The Diviners*, Atwood's *Surfacing*, and Engel's *Bear*, these novels and others serve as intertexts as readers return to *Anne*. Just as *Anne* offers an optimistic qualification, these novels offer a pessimistic one. If *Anne of Green Gables* is happily not far beneath the skin when contemporary Canadian women writers write, their work then may toughen that skin so that readers one hundred years later appreciate all of the joy that is Anne Shirley while realizing, as Montgomery did in her personal life, that the joy must be tempered by a jolt of reality if one is to make the joy a reality.

WORKS CITED

Anne of Green Gables. Dir. Kevin Sullivan. Sullivan Films, 1985.

Atwood, Margaret. "Afterword: *Anne of Green Gables* by Lucy Maud Montgomery." *Moving Targets: Writing with Intent, 1982–2004*. Toronto: Anansi, 2004. 141–46.

Atwood, Margaret. *Bodily Harm*. Toronto: McClelland and Stewart, 1981.

———. *Lady Oracle*. Toronto: McClelland and Stewart, 1976.

———. *Oryx and Crake*. Toronto: McClelland and Stewart, 2003.

———. *Surfacing*. Toronto: McClelland and Stewart, 1972.

———. *Survival: A Thematic Guide to Canadian Literature*. Toronto: Anansi, 1972.

Bailey, Nancy. "Margaret Laurence and the Psychology of Re-Birth in *A Jest of God*." *Journal of Popular Culture* 15.3 (1981): 62–69.

Bakhtin, Mikhail. *The Dialogic Imagination: Four Essays*. Ed. Michael Holquist. Austin: U of Texas P, 1981.

———. *Problems of Dostoevsky's Poetics*. 1963. Rpt. Minneapolis: U of Minnesota P, 1984.

Barthes, Roland. "Theory of the Text." *Untying the Text: A Post-Structuralist Reader*. Ed. R. Young. London: Routledge and Kegan Paul, 1981. 31–47.

Baum, Rosalie Murphy. "Self-alienation of the Elderly in Margaret Laurence's Fiction." *New Perspectives on Margaret Laurence: Poetic Narrative, Multiculturalism and Feminism*. Ed. Greta M. K. McCormick-Coger. Westport, CT: Greenwood, 1996. 153–60.

Besner, Neil. "The Bodies in the Texts in *Lives of Girls and Women*: Del Jordan's Reading." *Multiple Voices: Recent Canadian Fiction*. Ed. Jeanne Delbaere. Sydney: Dangaroo, 1990. 131–44.

Boutelle, Ann Edwards. "Margaret Atwood, Margaret Laurence, and Their Nineteenth-Century Forerunners." *Faith of a (Woman) Writer.* Ed. Alice Kessler-Harris and William McBrien. Westport, CT: Greenwood, 1988. 41–47.

Cameron, Elspeth. "Midsummer Madness: Marian Engel's *Bear.*" *Journal of Canadian Fiction* 21 (1977–78): 83–94.

Carolan-Brozy, Sandra, and Susanne Hagemann. "'There is such a place' – Is There? Scotland in Margaret Laurence's *The Diviners.*" *Studies in Scottish Fiction: 1945 to the Present.* Ed. Susanne Hagemann. Frankfurt: Peter Lang, 1993. 145–58.

Culler, Jonathan. *The Pursuit of Signs: Semiotics, Literature, Deconstruction.* Ithaca, NY: Cornell UP, 1981.

Engel, Marian. *Bear.* Toronto: McClelland and Stewart, 1976.

Fenwick, Julie. "The Silence of the Mermaid." *Essays on Canadian Writing* 47 (1992): 51–64.

Fiamengo, Janice. "'A Last Time for This Also': Margaret Atwood's Texts of Mourning." *Canadian Literature* 166 (2000): 145–64.

Frye, Northrop. *Anatomy of Criticism: Four Essays.* Princeton, NJ: Princeton UP, 1957.

Gold, Joseph. "Our Feeling Exactly: The Writing of Alice Munro." *The Art of Alice Munro: Saying the Unsayable.* Ed. Judith Miller. Waterloo, ON: University of Waterloo P, 1984. 1–13.

Godard. Barbara. "Caliban's Revolt: The Discourse of the (M)other." *Critical Approaches to the Fiction of Margaret Laurence.* Ed. Colin Nicholson. Vancouver: U of British Columbia P, 1990. 208–27.

———. "'Heirs of the Living Body': Alice Munro and the Question of a Female Aesthetic." *The Art of Alice Munro: Saying the Unsayable.* Ed. Judith Miller. Waterloo, ON: U of Waterloo P, 1984. 43–69.

———. "*The Diviners* as Supplement: (M)othering the Text." *Open Letter* 7.7 (1990): 26–73.

Greene, Gayle. "Margaret Laurence's *The Diviners*: The Uses of the Past." *Critical Approaches to the Fiction of Margaret Laurence.* Ed. Colin Nicholson. Vancouver: U of British Columbia P, 1983. 177–207.

Hair, Donald S. "Marian Engel's *Bear.*" *Canadian Literature* 92 (1982): 34–45.

Hales, Leslie-Ann. "Meddling with the Medium: Language and Identity in Audrey Thomas' *Intertidal Life.*" *Canadian Women's Studies* 8.3 (1987): 77–79.

Harris, Margaret. "Authors and Authority in *Lives of Girls and Women.*" *Sydney Studies in English* 12 (1986–87): 101–13.

Hartveit, Lars. "The Jester Mask in Margaret Laurence's *A Jest of God* and *The Fire-Dwellers*." *English Studies* 78 (1997): 342–54.

Howells, Coral Ann. "Inheritance and Instability: Audrey Thomas' *Real Mothers*." *Recherches anglaises et nord-americaines* 20 (1987): 157–62.

Hutcheon, Linda. "'Shape Shifters': Canadian Women Novelists and the Challenge to Tradition." *Amazing Space: Writing Canadian Women Writing*. Eds. Shirley Neuman and Smaro Kamboureli. Edmonton, AB: Longspoon, 1986. 219–27.

Jones, Dorothy. "'Waiting for the Rescue': A Discussion of Margaret Atwood's *Bodily Harm*." *Kunapipi* 6.3 (1984): 86–100.

Kristeva, Julia. "Word, Dialogue, and Novel." *Desire in Language: A Semiotic Approach to Literature and Art*. Ed. L. S. Roudiez. New York: Columbia UP, 1980.

———. *Revolution in Poetic Language*. New York: Columbia UP, 1984.

Laurence, Margaret. *The Diviners*. 1974. Rpt. Chicago: U of Chicago P, 1993.

———. *A Jest of God*. Toronto: McClelland and Stewart, 1966.

Maclean, Susan. "*Lady Oracle*: The Art of Reality and the Reality of Art." *Journal of Canadian Fiction* 28–29 (1980): 179–97.

Martin, Mathew. "Dramas of Desire in Margaret Laurence's *A Jest of God*, *The Fire-Dwellers*, and *The Diviners*." *Studies in Canadian Literature* 19.1 (1994): 58–71.

Meindl, Dieter. "Modernism and the English Canadian Short Story Cycle." *Recherches Anglaises et Americaines* 20 (1987): 17–22.

Montgomery, L. M. *Anne of Green Gables*. Ed. Cecily Devereux. Peterborough, ON: Broadview, 2004.

Morgan, T. "The Space of Intertextuality." *Intertextuality and Contemporary American Fiction*. Ed. P. O'Donnell and R. C. Davis. Baltimore, MD: Johns Hopkins UP, 1989.

Munro, Alice. *Lives of Girls and Women*. Scarborough, ON: McGraw-Hill Ryerson, 1971.

O'Donnell, P., and R. C. Davis, ed. *Intertextuality and Contemporary American Fiction*. Baltimore, MD: Johns Hopkins UP, 1989.

Osachoff, Margaret Gail. "The Bearness of *Bear*." *The University of Windsor Review* 15 (1979–80): 13–21.

Rosteck, T. "The Intertextuality of 'The Man from Hope.'" *Bill Clinton on Stump, State, and Stage: The Rhetorical Road to the White House*. Ed. S. A. Smith. Fayetteville: U of Arkansas P, 1995.

Rubenstein, Roberta. "Pandora's Box and Female Survival: Margaret Atwood's *Bodily Harm*." *Journal of Canadian Studies* 20.1 (1985): 120–35.

Rubio, Mary. "Satire, Realism, and Imagination in *Anne of Green Gables*." *Canadian Children's Literature* 3 (1975): 27–36.

———. "Subverting the Trite: L. M. Montgomery's 'Room of Her Own.'" *Canadian Children's Literature* 65 (1992): 6–39.

Rubio, Mary, and Elizabeth Waterston, ed. *The Selected Journals of L. M. Montgomery*. Vol. 2. Toronto: Oxford UP, 1987.

Sheckels, Theodore F. *The Island Motif in the Fiction of L. M. Montgomery, Margaret Laurence, Margaret Atwood, and Other Canadian Women Novelists*. New York: Peter Lang, 2003.

Soyinka, Wole. *A Dance of the Forests*. New York: Oxford UP, 1963.

Sparrow, Fiona. "'This place is some kind of garden': Clearings in the Bush in the Works of Susanna Moodie, Catharine Parr Traill, Margaret Atwood and Margaret Laurence." *Journal of Commonwealth Literature* 25.1 (1990): 24–41.

Staels, Hilda. *Margaret Atwood's Novels: A Study of Narrative Discourse*. Tubingen: Francke, 1999.

Stein, Karen F. "Speaking in Tongues: Margaret Laurence's *A Jest of God* as Gothic Narrative." *Studies in Canadian Literature* 20.2 (1995): 74–95.

Stovel, Nora Foster. *Rachel's Children: Margaret Laurence's A Jest of God*. Toronto: ECW, 1992.

———. "Reflections on Mirror Images: Doubles and Identity in the Novels of Margaret Atwood." *Essays on Canadian Writing* 33 (1986): 60–67.

———. "'Sisters Under Their Skins': *A Jest of God* and *The Fire-Dwellers*." *New Perspectives on Margaret Laurence: Poetic Narrative, Multiculturalism, and Feminism*. Ed. Greta M. K. McCormick Coger. Westport, CT: Greenwood, 1996. 63–79.

Thieme, John. "Acknowledging Myths: The Image of Europe in Margaret Laurence's *The Diviners* and Jack Hodgins's *The Invention of the World*." *Critical Approaches to the Fiction of Margaret Laurence*. Ed. Colin Nicholson. Vancouver: U of British Columbia P, 1983. 152–61.

Thomas, Audrey. *Intertidal Life*. Toronto: General, 1984.

Thomas, Susan. "Reading Female Sexual Desire in Alice Munro's *Lives of Girls and Women*." *Critique* 36.2 (1995): 107–20.

Wachtel, Eleanor. "An Interview with Audrey Thomas." *Room of One's Own* 10.3–4 (1986): 7–61.

Waller, Margaret. "Interview with Julia Kristeva." *Intertextuality and Contemporary American Fiction*. Ed. P. O'Donnell and R. C. Davis. Baltimore, MD: Johns Hopkins UP, 1989. 280–93.

Warwick, Susan. "Growing Up: The Novels of Alice Munro." *Essays on Canadian Writing* 29 (1984): 204–25.

———. *River of Now and Then: Margaret Laurence's* The Diviners. Toronto: ECW, 1993.

Watson, Martha Solomon. "The Dynamics of Intertextuality: Re-Reading the Declaration of Independence." *Rhetorical and Political Culture in Nineteenth-Century America*. East Lansing: Michigan State UP, 1997. 91–112.

York, Lorraine M. "Lives of Joan and Del: Separate Paths to Transformation in *Lives of Girls and Women* and *Lady Oracle*." *The University of Windsor Review* 19.2 (1986): 1–10.

———. "The Rival Bards: Alice Munro's *Lives of Girls and Women* and Victorian Poetry." *Canadian Literature* 112 (1987): 211–16.

CHAPTER NINE

Interactions with Poetry: Metapoetic Games with *Anne* in Astrid Lindgren's *Madicken*

Cornelia Rémi

Although deeply rooted in Canadian literary memory, *Anne of Green Gables* has found friends in many parts of the world. One extraordinary instance of reception can be tracked in the writings of Swedish author Astrid Lindgren (1907–2002), world-renowned for her children's books, which document her particularly vivacious, durable, and productive individual occupation with *Anne*. In her autobiographical reminiscences, Lindgren stressed the novel's importance in developing her own childhood games; she described herself playing "Anne and Diana" with her best friend and vividly recalled how they metamorphosized their familiar surroundings into Anne Shirley's world of romance and fantasy. Such an active relation to literature recurs in Lindgren's published writings, which often deal with the mutually inspiring ties between fiction and reality. While every single encounter with *Anne* remains unique, a case study of Astrid Lindgren's dealings with the novel may help to determine some essentials of the beloved book, qualities that stimulated its transcendence of national and cultural boundaries.

Like a poetic magnifying glass, Lindgren's transforming reception uncovers fundamental elements of Montgomery's creation. Her reflections on playing "Anne" address a theme similar to the character Anne's own relationship to fiction; the Swedish author delineates an intense imaginative engagement with Anne's world and speaks of lifting Anne's play into her own childhood milieu. What turns out to be the heart of the novel's texture, then, is not the specific detail of its setting, but rather the theme of border-crossing between the two realms of real and fictional space. For Lindgren, Anne modelled a means of transforming a mundane environment into one of romance, independence, and freedom. Lindgren negotiated this tension not only in her own life, but also through her literary characters: she fed Anne's characteristics, enriched by her own experiences, back into the spiralling torrent of creativity emanating from Montgomery's novel.

Anne's outward appearance and her constant flow of ideas have been linked to Pippi Longstocking, one of Lindgren's most beloved characters. Madicken, an even closer relative of Anne's, has barely been noticed. The similarities between Madicken and Anne are not easy to spot at first sight, however. Since Madicken is only between six and eight years old in Lindgren's stories, her adventures address a much younger audience than Anne's, and consequently both the narrative style and the contents of *Madicken* are adjusted to children at the elementary school level. Nevertheless, the two characters have some distinctive features in common, among them first and foremost their tireless poetic creativity.

Both Anne and Madicken invent stories and incorporate themselves and their surroundings into them. Anne's re-enactment of Tennyson's "Elaine" is echoed in Madicken's biblically inspired games. Yet in all their attempts to recreate scenes from their favourite texts, the girls must discover that the dangers of reality tend to leak out into their assumedly secure fictional space: only their friends' intervention saves them both from drowning. When Anne balances along the ridge-pole of the Barrys' kitchen roof and Madicken undergoes a similar trial of courage on the roof of her school, these audacious walks along rooftops become a central image for both the vital importance and the risks of playing. Moreover, they signify the girls' choices in the process of growing up. Anne's transition from her fictional refuge to the actual world in which she must find her place corresponds to her passage from childhood and adolescence to adulthood. *Madicken* similarly reflects upon crossing into a new stage of life, but Lindgren and Montgomery sketch rather different options of handling the precarious tensions of such a liminal space. While Montgomery lets Anne grow up, mature, and submit her imagination to the demands of real life, Lindgren's approach is not quite so linear and univocal. Her major theme is not the transition from child to adult, but the savouring of childhood and of playing as its essence and centre. Madicken's and Anne's literal balancing acts and play-acting games provide summative indices of how the girls hover and oscillate between the worlds of fiction and reality, childlike playfulness and grown-up gravity. For

Lindgren, Anne represented the power of the imaginative mind and the spirit of childhood that must not be lost on any account, with all the attendant risks and wonders involved in literally balancing on rooftops and entrusting one's life to the currents of ponds and rivers.

Anne's integration into the context of native Swedish literature was prepared by a translation that transcended not only linguistic, but also cultural, borders and bridged the corresponding differences. By minimizing and adjusting unfamiliar elements of setting, it shifted Anne's story into Swedish reality. From an external point of view, this shows the indispensable hub of Anne's story. Her character emerges not from a certain landscape, but from her playful relation to it and the way she brings it to life, which a girl from any land can do.

FROM CANADA TO SWEDEN

Anne of Green Gables has been kept in continuous high regard in Sweden ever since it first appeared on the Swedish book market.[1] Its first translation, *Anne på Grönkulla*, was published as early as 1909, just one year after the English original. When the Swedish scientist and writer Bengt Lidforss visited New York in 1908, he happened to become aware of the book and sent a copy to his sister Karin Jensen, who fell in love with *Anne* as well and translated it for Gleerups publishing house. The book's immediate success in Sweden can be deduced from the rhythm of its three sequels' translations. Even the Swedish versions of *Anne in Avonlea* (1909), *Anne of the Island* (1915) and *Anne's House of Dreams* (1917) appeared in regular one-year-intervals after the publication of the originals.[2]

Some inconsistencies in the translation might indicate that Jensen either worked in several separate phases or that she lacked the time for a final, thorough proofreading. Certain key terms and phrases, like Anne's plea to have some "scope for imagination," are not allocated any consistent equivalents and therefore lose their formulaic effect.[3] The text presented to the Swedish audience naturally differed from the 1908 L. C. Page edition even in many other aspects.[4] Among the most conspicuous changes are the countless minor and major abridgments, ranging from single words to whole paragraphs,[5] which probably were caused by the publisher's demands.

Since most of the more substantial abridgments occur in the later chapters, which present an increasingly mature and grown-up Anne, there is a certain tendency to emphasize her childlike traits and to let her appear more girlish than she is in the original.[6] Instead of admitting that she plans to compete for the gold medal at Queen's, for example, she embarrassedly evades the question.[7] Other modifications support this impression. When the Swedish Anne tries to explain why she forgot to take a pie out of the oven, she does not relate a romantic daydream, but refers to a fairy tale. Instead of pretending to be "an enchanted princess shut up in a lonely tower," she re-enacts a scene from "Hansel and Gretel" and imagines herself pushing the wicked witch into her fiery death. Consequently, she treats her pie just as Gretel treats the witch: she leaves it in the oven (*Green Gables* 134, *Grönkulla* 185). Her reading habits have been adjusted as well to let her appear more feminine. Miss Stacy does not catch her absorbed by the chariot race in *Ben-Hur*, but by one of the Topsy scenes in *Uncle Tom's Cabin* (*Green Gables* 193, *Grönkulla* 260).

Most of Montgomery's numerous literary allusions and quotations have undergone similarly radical changes and are not recognizable as such any more. They have been dropped completely or translated literally and thus melted into the surrounding text.[8] As the literary canon of the Swedish target culture at the time of Jensen's translation differed considerably from the North American one, such changes probably could not be avoided. Therefore it remains a rare exception that at least the outlines of a poetic reference are preserved, although Jensen substituted a more familiar quotation for the original. When Anne recites the battle canto from Walter Scott's "Marmion," the quoted verses are essential for the atmosphere of the scene, since their sublime tone forms a comic contrast to Anne's mundane occupation of driving home the cows. Jensen replaces Scott's verses with some lines from Shakespeare's *Macbeth* (5.5.44–46), a text that Swedish readers were more likely to be acquainted with (*Green Gables* 184–85, *Grönkulla* 248).

Altogether, Jensen's translation aims at adapting *Anne* to the cultural context of her contemporary Swedish audience. Whenever there is an opportunity to do so, any features that might appear outlandish or exotic to a Swede are softened or changed, so that the reader is reminded as little as possible of the story's actual setting in the Canadian Maritimes. For instance, the translator avoids large accumulations of English names[9] and adapts both botanical and food terms to the Swedish flora and cuisine.[10] For a Swedish child not yet familiar with the habits and customs of other parts of the world, Jensen's translation provided ideal conditions to feel as close to Anne as if she were living on a nearby farm.

CORNELIA RÉMI

Anne and Astrid

An early reader of Montgomery's, Astrid Ericsson was a farmer's daughter from the Swedish province of Småland. Many years later – then the world-famous author, Astrid Lindgren – she often would name *Anne of Green Gables* as one of her favourite childhood books.[11] Not only did she read the novel, however, but she merged the text even deeper into her own reality by enacting it in her play (Edström, *Vildtoring* 82; Lindgren, "Anne" 245). Lindgren remembered that she had first read *Anne* when she was eleven years old; she had borrowed the copy of her friend Anne-Marie Ingeström. Together they brought the beloved book to life (Åhmansson, "Mayflowers" 17–18):

> And then, of course, *Anne of Green Gables*, my most unforgettable, for ever you will ride in the buggy with Matthew Cuthbert beneath the blossoming apple trees of Avonlea. How I lived with that girl! One whole summer we played Anne, me and my sisters, around the big pile of sawdust up by the mill. I was Diana Barry and the dung puddle behind the barn was The Lake of Shining Waters.[12]

Elsewhere Lindgren emphasized that she experienced reading *Anne* as some kind of release. The fictional character provided her with "an escape from … the restricted sphere" of her environment (Åhmansson, "Mayflowers" 18). Several factors supported her intense reaction. While the familiar setting in a rural community mirrored her own living conditions, Anne's deep love of nature and power of imagination, which overstepped the bounds of daily routines, reflected Astrid's desire to transform her reality and periodically escape it. Montgomery's fictional cosmos bore clear traces of an author addicted to language and literature (Karr 22–29). Likewise, Lindgren was a book addict, who would repeatedly express her love of literature, and consequently shape her novel *Madicken* as a story about stories and poetry and as an homage to their vivifying influence.

For a girl like Astrid, who was desperately hungry for reading and had only recently discovered the blessings of her school's library (Lindgren, *Samuel* 72–73), Montgomery's novel was just the book she had wished for. She cast herself into Anne's world just as Anne loses herself in literary texts, and just as Montgomery herself literally used to "live" in her favourite stories and become completely absorbed by them (Karr 23–24, 27–28; Drain 8). Anne's ability to sense some "scope for imagination"[13] almost anywhere pools the inventive momentum which results from this fascination with fiction. Her readers are driven to evolve their own poetic potential in games of all sorts. While Anne explores the world around herself with open eyes and an inquisitive mind,[14] she encourages her audience to watch their surroundings from entirely new perspectives as well,[15] to detect secrets and uncover hidden meanings.

Young Astrid perceived this creative impulse more than well. Her dealings with *Anne* anticipate and confirm the ideal of reading that she later would sum up in several magazine articles, as described by Helene Ehriander. In them, Lindgren outlines her conviction that good children's books must possess the power of stimulating their readers to interact with their story, because it is through this interactive dynamic that a book and its audience's imagination come alive (Ehriander 47–49). In Astrid Lindgren's case this effect turned out to be so durable that *Anne* left visible traces in her œuvre,[16] although more than twenty years would pass before she began publishing her own books. Many traits of Pippi Longstocking – redheaded, loquacious, vivacious, and inventive – bear resemblance to Anne Shirley, so that the two characters, despite all their equally obvious differences, might be interpreted as intertextual relatives.[17] Their undeniable parallels give evidence that Montgomery's stories merged into the pool of childhood experiences feeding Lindgren's inspiration (Åhmansson, "Mayflowers" 20). Even other books of hers feature similarities to *Anne*, however; the most striking parallels probably are to be found in *Madicken* (1960) and *Madicken och Junibackens Pims* (1976), the two volumes about Margareta "Madicken" Engström and her little sister Lisabet.[18]

So while on one hand *Anne* influenced Lindgren's childhood, another track leads from this childhood back into books. These tight bonds between autobiographical and intertextual influences are tied even more closely through the girl who became the model for Madicken's character. Astrid Lindgren based Madicken not only on herself,[19] but also on her lifelong friend Anne-Marie, who was responsible for Astrid's very first contact with *Anne* (Fries-Gedin; Strömstedt 169; Edström, *Vildtoring* 69). Not only did Anne-Marie's nickname provide the name for Lindgren's title character, but also many of the games depicted in *Madicken* were based on the friends' often wild and tomboyish play.[20] This connection documents the intertwined nature of personal and literary influences on Lindgren's writing. Her early, intense reading adventures (*Samuel August* 74) shaped her actions, her relationship with Anne-Marie, and her perception of the world. Much later, she characterized these experiences with fiction as "more real than reality, but nevertheless so unreal" ("Anne" 245). This tension could inspire attempts to change reality by means of one's own imagination, an incitement which Lindgren passed on to the characters in her books as well.

IMAGINATION: POISED BETWEEN TERROR AND WONDER

Both *Anne of Green Gables* and the two *Madicken* books stress the importance of imagination, of language and playing, of storytelling and reading. Poetic traditions that can stimulate one's imagination and trigger the creation of new texts and stories have a key function in both Montgomery's and Lindgren's fictional world. This suggests deep-rooted connections between their books and justifies a more detailed comparison of *Madicken* and *Anne*. A closer examination of their parallels and distinctive differences will elucidate the special quality of such fiction-related elements.

Madicken and Lisabet grow up in a spacious house just outside a small town, somewhere in the Swedish countryside, during the time of World War I. Although the two sisters appear to be playing all the time, the text also addresses more serious issues. Their father, an editor for the local newspaper, is committed to a humanist world view and encourages his children to perceive social injustices and the problems of the poor and needy, while their mother's philosophy is a little more conservative. She tries to protect her children against bad influences and is especially worried about Madicken's contact with the neighbouring family, the Nilssons, since Mr. Nilsson spends his days drinking and daydreaming; but she cannot stop Madicken from running over to meet her secret love, fifteen-year-old Abbe Nilsson. As his father puts next to no effort into earning money, Abbe is forced to earn his living by baking sugar pretzels. To entertain himself, he develops grand schemes for his future career as an explorer and adventurer and loves teasing his little admirer with fanciful stories,[21] although he is basically a kind and nice boy. Like the shabby red-haired sisters Mia and Mattis, who constantly seem to get into fights with Madicken and Lisabet, Abbe serves as a counter-image to Madicken's otherwise idyllic world and reminds the reader of the grim alternatives of life, which even Montgomery has included in Anne's history. Finally, there are Linus-Ida, an old widow who regularly helps with the laundry, and Alva, the kind house maid, who is always there to take care of the girls.

Both Madicken and Anne are very inventive – Madicken "gets ideas as fast as a pig blinks" (*Madicken* 2/8) – both repeatedly express their joy of life,[22] and both are virtually bursting with activity and curiosity about "all the things there are to find out about" (*Green Gables* 19). Not surprisingly, therefore, school is very important for them, both as a place of learning and of social contacts. Their curiosity extends even and especially to dangerous situations in which they experience a characteristic mixture of fear and fascination. Such a paradoxical response illustrates their sense of adventure and their courage in accepting certain risks and dealing with them, whether the threat of the bridge collapsing while Anne is driving over it or the thunderstorm that surprises Madicken's family during an outing:

I'm always afraid going over bridges. I can't help imagining that perhaps, just as we get to the middle, they'll crumple up like a jack-knife and nip us. So I shut my eyes. But I always have to open them for all when I think we're getting near the middle. Because, you see, if the bridge *did* crumple up I'd want to *see* it crumple. (*Green Gables* 23)

[Madicken] was frightened too, of course she was frightened, but underneath the frightened [Madicken] there was another [Madicken] who was shivering with secret joy because something could be so terrible and so beautiful, so dangerous and so splendid.[23]

For Anne, these feelings culminate in the Haunted Wood chapter (131–36). In this episode, her phantasies gain a liveliness that makes her lose the ability to separate them from reality, so that she finally repents the licence she has given to her imagination (136, 184). Madicken has a similar experience when she and Lisabet one winter morning decide to walk along the frozen river and pay a visit to a nearby farm – all on their own. Since the way is much longer than they expected, the girls begin to grow hungry and tired. Madicken starts to imagine that witches have put them under a spell:

'This is very strange,' she said. 'If we don't see Appletree Hill when we get round that corner we must be under a spell, and that'll be our bad luck.'

The idea began to nag at [Madicken]. It was all witch's work. The trees, so beautiful and dead in their wonderful, white-frosted branches ... trees like that could only grow in enchanted woods. The dark, smooth ice which sent children crazy and enticed them away, was a witch's pathway which had no end. Horrible little winter witches slid up and down there at night when it was too cold to fly on their broomsticks. Yes, the whole thing was witch's work. (*Madicken* 108/128)

Although this bewitched winter world appears to be closely related to Anne's Haunted Wood, the circumstances of its nascence are characteristic of Lindgren's very own approach to fantasy. Madicken does not end up being driven into repentance or substantial changes of behaviour by her icy ramble, nor is she anywhere near panicking like Anne; it is only Lisabet who finally starts crying in protest against her sister's teasing. While Anne experiences the superabundance of her own imagination as a "great shortcoming" (184), Madicken simply enjoys enhancing the thrill of the situation. Instead of "imagining ghosts into places" from a safe distance to begin with, as Anne does (*Green Gables* 136), she conceives the whole witch idea while she is right in the middle of a magic landscape. She finds pleasure in evolving an idea which fascinates her, heightens her sense of adventure, and intensifies her experience of the winter scene.

These parallel episodes indicate that Anne's and Madicken's ability to feel the sublime might be connected to another common trait of theirs – their love of nature, which gains a unique profile through their inclination to transform the world around them. Anne shapes her surroundings at Green Gables by giving names to trees, lakes, and flowers, thus sharing her spirit with them,[24] while Madicken animates her mother's birthday picnic by telling Lisabet about a stone inhabited by trolls (*Pims* 52/67). Like Anne, Madicken is also vain to a certain degree, although she is less worried about the colour of her hair than about her new sandals or the dress for her examination (*Pims* 12, 77/16, 99–100). This is not to be mistaken for a merely negative sign, however, but mainly indicates their fondness for all things fair and beautiful.

The girls also share a love of language and words. Arguing against Shakespeare's *Romeo and Juliet* (2.2, 43–44), Anne is convinced that roses would not be "as nice" if they were called an ugly name (38). Madicken thinks along the same lines when she scribbles "a pink rose for my hair" on her list of Christmas wishes. Asked by her little sister whether she is serious about this, she replies: "Not at all … I just wrote it because it sounds so beautiful" (*Madicken* 101–2/120). Lisabet's fascination for swear words, on the other hand, constitutes a comic counterpart to Madicken's aesthetic intuition and Anne's fondness of "big words."[25] As "a collector of words" (*Pims* 129/167), Lisabet loves questioning the meaning of terms, is overjoyed when she learns new swear words, and even starts business-like negotiations with her mother about using them: "Words were something [Lisabet] thought about a great deal" (*Pims* 85/111). But then, just like Anne, she also speaks her mind plainly and clearly. When her mother reprimands her for licking her plate after supper, she replies (85/111): "Then why did they go and invent a word *called* lick, if you're never allowed to do it?" Her fancy for nasty terms and phrases contributes to this frank openness (*Madicken* 110/131), a trait corresponding to Anne's naïve and honest criticism of the minister's tedious sermons and other circumstances (72), which a well-behaved girl is expected to accept quietly and without further comment.

Most importantly, however, Anne and Madicken love stories and poems, which they gather from different sources. They live in a world that appears saturated with poetry, from simple songs to the sophisticated presentations Anne witnesses at different concerts, or Madicken at the autumn ball.[26] Anne collects most of her poetic treasures from school readers (39–40, 71–72), but devours even sentimental and adventurous stories: her speech is interspersed with phrases from such texts. She likes to imagine herself "in the depths of despair" (28), sees her life as "a perfect graveyard of buried hopes" (37), and longs for "a kindred spirit" (34). Even the narrator of *Anne of Green Gables* becomes infected with her poetic fever, for embedded quotations and literary allusions tend to pop up even in unfocalized narrative passages or in chapter titles.[27] By evoking their original contexts, they nuance the story and point to the poetic qualities of Anne's own life, beyond all her romantic exaggeration.

Madicken, on the other hand, relies chiefly on oral sources for her poetic knowledge, since she has only just started school and is about to cross the border from merely oral perception to literacy.[28] Like Anne, she absorbs all kinds of poetry and tales,[29] from her mother's romantic songs to Linus-Ida's repertoire of pious ballads or biblical stories,[30] and turns them into songs and stories of her own.[31] She also passes some of this lore on to Lisabet. When her little sister begs her for thrilling tales about "ghosts and murderers and war" as they are going to bed in the evening (*Madicken* 45, 156/57, 180), she is served with the scary stories Madicken has heard from Abbe (79/95). Just like Anne, who loves inventing, narrating, and writing stories, Madicken thus exhibits a talent for storytelling, for advancing and passing on the poetic influences she experiences. Her stories may not be as ambitious as Anne's tale about the loss of Marilla's amethyst brooch or her composition "The Jealous Rival," which finally leads to the foundation of the story club (84, 168–69). But even though Madicken is only a first-grader, she can read and write well enough to design a newspaper of her own when she is sick at home and only has a copy of her father's paper and a drawing pad to entertain herself (*Madicken* 54–57/67–71). Stories and songs, be they self-invented or drawn from poetical tradition, heighten the girls' actual experiences and compensate for restriction and deprivation, just as their rich interior landscapes alter the actual world surrounding them. Both Madicken and Anne indulge in these gaps between ideals and reality.

TRANSITIONS AND BALANCING ACTS

Despite their similarities, the books are far from telling identical stories. The Swedish sisters are introduced in a completely different social context than Anne. Although social criticism is an important underlying theme, especially in the second *Madicken* book (Edström, *Vildtoring* 69–74), which frequently draws the readers' attention to the needs of those living under less fortunate circumstances, Madicken and Lisabet themselves have never been neglected or maltreated as the Canadian orphan girl has. They grow up in an intact, loving, and rather prosperous family and almost always have each other to play with. Unlike Anne, who needs her imagination to cope with the otherwise intolerable living conditions in her foster families and at the asylum,[32] Madicken can play just for playing's sake and imagine things just to increase the intensity of her experiences.[33] She may enjoy her fancies without Anne's painful realization that they alone never can completely compensate for deprivation and poverty: "But the worst of imagining things is that the time comes when you have to stop and that hurts" (33). When

Mrs. Barry forbids her to see Diana after the currant wine disaster, Anne indeed cannot find comfort with her former imaginary friends anymore. They fade away in the light of her real-life friendship with Diana (53, 111).

Neither are Madicken and Lisabet burdened with the same amount of house- and homework as their Canadian counterpart. But then, Anne is already eleven years old to start with, and the Engström girls are just six and five. By making Madicken so much younger than Anne, Lindgren preserved a key notion of her character that is already stressed in Jensen's translation. The manifestation of Anne that has etched itself into literary memory is first and foremost the little girl freshly arrived at Green Gables, neither the established teacher nor the mature woman portrayed in Montgomery's later books. Madicken is a counter-Anne insofar as she has all the opportunities and resources inaccessible to Anne at her age; but then, she is also a mirror-Anne, allowing Lindgren to imagine an alternative development of an essentially similar character. Symbolically, Madicken embodies the potential to keep the imaginative mind young.

For Anne's is a coming-of-age story, which accompanies its heroine through more than half a decade of her life, while each of the *Madicken* books covers only one year. Thanks to this much briefer time slot, Madicken does not change as significantly as Anne during the course of her story, although major alterations may lie ahead even for her. Her transition from a life at home to that of a schoolgirl leaves her less time for playing and fooling about with her sister than before.[34] Even the farewell to her fictitious alter egos, "Sebastian Nigge" and "Rickard," might indicate certain changes in her attitude; but then, Rickard is kept alive, since Lisabet incorporates him into *her* imagination. Her fancy school, where children have nits and only one nostril, serves as an eulenspieglish counterworld that mirrors Madicken's phantasies and confronts her with her own lies and tempers.[35] Lisabet continues the free life of a child, since the narration never reaches the point when she is sent to a real school as well.

While Madicken's and Lisabet's general relation to their imagination remains fairly unaltered, Anne must find a balance between fancy and reality in her new life at Green Gables, which does not require the full compensative power of her imagination anymore.[36] Although she continues treasuring her imagination as a vital ingredient of her existence (141, 218–19), she must be "cure[d]" from an excess of it (136, 184), "sober down" (78), and learn to "control" it (44) before she truly can settle down in her new life: "But of course I'd rather be Anne of Green Gables sewing patchwork than Anne of any other place with nothing to do but play" (79). Therefore she grows up even in her literary taste: she loses most

CORNELIA RÉMI

of her interest in "big words" and exotic stories when Miss Stacy makes her realize that she can express much more by writing about her familiar environment in a plain and simple style (205). Besides, she must promise Miss Stacy not to read books such as *The Lurid Mystery of the Haunted Hall* anymore (194), while Madicken may enjoy *The Secret of Phantom Castle* without being reprimanded (*Pims* 178/231). Their situation and development differ, although they apparently are dealing with nearly identical books: the original title of Madicken's reading corresponds almost exactly to that of Anne's in the Swedish translation.[37]

Despite these contrasts there is an underlying theme common to both stories, the passage to a new phase of life which the main characters undergo. Despite their age difference, starting school is a crucial experience that substantially changes Anne's and Madicken's life. Their transition to school proves a decisive turning point in their lives since it also comprehends a challenge to their imaginative habits. But while Madicken succeeds in maintaining the power of her poetic mind, Anne's is compromised and finally submitted to the demands of reality.

Behind the different outcomes of Anne's and Madicken's school experiences is the realization that imagination, despite its indispensable importance, never can completely replace reality. Everyone must find a personal balance between one's fancy and the actual world one must live in. Anne's and Madicken's developmental parallels and their differences resulting from this conflict are underlined in key episodes that summarize in a memorable and gripping picture the precarious equilibrium they must achieve. Real, daredevil balancing acts try their courage and character.[38] Anne's disastrous walk along the ridge-pole of the Barrys' kitchen roof marks a milestone in her educational process, for ultimately she is punished for an imprudent and impulsive decision (148–52). When the girls of Avonlea start challenging each other to increasingly difficult tasks, Anne, intending to defy and humble Josie Pye, manoeuvres herself into a quandary. She tries to outdo Josie's triumphant walk along the top of the board fence by telling her about an even greater heroic act. Since Josie questions her story about a girl able to walk the ridge-pole of a roof, Anne feels obliged to climb the roof herself and prove the truth of her assertion. But although she tries to stylize herself as a romantic heroine threatened by a tragic death, the outcome is not that glorious. After just a few dizzy steps, she falls off and breaks her ankle.

Lindgren tells an outwardly similar episode quite differently by shifting some of its substantial conditions and doubling the climactic scene.[39] When Madicken walks along the top of the schoolhouse roof, she does not pity herself or intend to stage a heroic scene – her suffering arises from sheer sympathy with her opponent. For it is not she who brings up the idea of climbing the roof, but her classmate Mia, whose suggestion is motivated by a pride differing from Anne's. While Anne chiefly intends to teach Josie a lesson, Mia fights for fundamental principles of her social status, such as acceptance and respect. By claiming that she is the only one who dares to undertake the risky balancing adventure, she hopes to obliterate her reputation as the needy pauper. Although she thinks hard in order to find a task incredible enough to leave the others awestricken by its mere mention, her self-confident statement provokes Madicken's competitive spirit: "'But I'm the only one who dares to walk along the top of the schoolhouse roof.' 'Huh, as if I didn't dare that too!'" (*Pims* 71/92). Madicken immediately accepts the hidden challenge, but regrets it at the same moment. Similar to Anne, neither she nor Mia are really keen on the hazardous experience: "Actually neither [Madicken] nor Mia wanted to climb any roofs that day, but the thing was said now and they would have to do it."[40] Thus Lindgren, unlike Montgomery, does not initiate a solitary and unique test of courage, but shows two girls in direct competition. Both Madicken and Mia walk along the roof, which gives their creator the opportunity to explore the feelings of her protagonist in great detail. Despite her initial fear, Madicken enjoys the act of balancing and her success, until Mia climbs up and tries to keep up with her. Unlike Anne, Madicken feels deep compassion for her rival and experiences Mia's attempt to walk the roof almost more intensely than her own. Consequently, the episode serves to document her empathy,[41] to tie a closer bond between her and Mia, and to prepare the ensuing events. For on their way up the fire escape ladder, both girls must climb past their head teacher's open window. While Madicken is content to take one anxious yet curious peep into his room, Mia secretly snatches his purse that is lying by the window. She spends the money on chocolates and bookmarks, which she generously starts distributing to all the other children at school – all except Madicken. When her guilt is finally proven, however, and the head teacher starts beating her in front of a horrified class, it is Madicken who interrupts the brutal punishment with an anguished cry. This action finally secures Mia's sympathy and friendship.

Thus, the balancing episode in *Madicken* is embedded into a wider story arc, which finally leads to a friendship between the two girls. Moreover, it does not end with a literal fall, albeit Mia's failure and her following behaviour might be interpreted as a symbolic one. Indeed, a literal fall from a roof has already taken place in the previous *Madicken* book, in which Madicken jumps from the woodshed in an attempt to fly, inspired by the sight of a bird hovering over her, by Abbe's song about being "as free as a bird" (*Madicken* 17/25), and by his stories about parachutes (36/47–48). Although this episode underlines the dangers linked to playing, it does not domesticate Madicken's activities: she continues climbing even higher roofs after this accident.[42] As a whole, therefore, Madicken's walk along the roof bundles up a more complex tissue of narrative threads than Anne's.

Nevertheless, the central image of a girl balancing on the narrow ridge of the roof, between imagination and reality, fear and resolution, both confirms the close relationship of the two stories and helps to emphasize their characteristic profiles. It summarizes the different outcome of the girls' transitional experiences: while Madicken succeeds in keeping her balance on the roof, just as she does in the liminal space between pure childhood and school life, Anne falls off. She cannot perpetuate an open, indeterminate rooftop identity, but must sacrifice parts of her childlike self while growing up. The complex relations involved in this process are condensed even more dramatically in a number of other scenes centred around a very special sort of games: games which deal with the problem of distinguishing and mediating between fiction and reality.

POETIC GAMES

The episodes that most strongly suggest a connection between *Madicken* and *Anne*, and that point to the very centre of Montgomery's and Lindgren's work, are those involving poetic games – games stimulated by stories and poems,[43] just like Lindgren's own childhood re-enactment of *Anne*. Madicken's idea to choose the woodshed for her outing with Lisabet, for example, is spurred by a story their mother has read to them (*Madicken* 30/40–41). Most of their poetic games, however, are inspired by the Linus-Ida's biblical stories. So when their father describes the destination of their family excursion, the cowslip meadow, as "a bit of the Garden of Eden" (*Pims* 53/69), Madicken decides to play "Adam and Eve" there. Elements of this fiction are kept upright although the game itself is interrupted by Petrus Karlsson's bulls. That the "Tree of Knowledge"[44] serves as a refuge for the girls adds a humorous touch to the whole scene, but also stresses the close relation between Madicken's creativity and her clever crisis management.

Such disturbances, underlining the fragile balance between imagination and reality, are characteristic of poetic games in both *Madicken* and *Anne*. The central game episodes in both books constantly deal with the borders between fiction and the actual world, between pleasure and fear, safety and danger. When Anne suggests to her friends a dramatization of Tennyson's "Lancelot and Elaine," a poem they have studied at school, she carefully prepares the necessary arrangements for the unfortunate lily maid's voyage (177–84). She organizes the central props, hands out the roles, and makes a great effort to create a convincing, thoroughly romantic atmosphere. That ambience is quickly broken, though, when the "death-barque" starts leaking and sinks, forcing a humiliated Anne to abandon her role and cling to a bridge pile until she is saved by Gilbert Blythe.

Catherine Sheldrick Ross has examined the tension between reality and imagination in this episode and demonstrated how in it Montgomery manages to strengthen the profile of Anne's character by contrasting several levels of fiction and reception of literature (46–48).[45] While on the one hand Anne fails to create a romantic setting because reality sabotages her plans, her own character and story gain a high verisimilitude, despite the paradoxical fact that her development is based on romantic formula itself. By learning to distinguish between romance and reality, she gains the freedom and accepts the responsibility to shape her life herself: "I have come to the conclusion that it is no use trying to be romantic in Avonlea" (184). Nevertheless, it is her enthusiasm for romance that continues to strike a chord with the reader.

Lindgren opens *Madicken* with quite a similar episode. Madicken and Lisabet are playing "Moses in the bulrushes," the biblical scene of baby Moses being saved from the Nile river by the Pharaoh's daughter (*Madicken* 8–16/16–24.). Their watery adventure actually resembles Anne's solemn staging of "Elaine" so much that it might be read as a travesty of the lily maid chapter. Although Madicken does not prepare her game as far in advance as Anne, she does her best to obtain some essential props such as her mother's dressing-gown for herself and the washtub as a basket for Lisabet, who is to play Moses. But just as in Anne's case, the dramatic scene is disturbed: first by a hole in the tub, then by Lisabet and Madicken themselves, who fall out of character at different stages of their game. Lisabet, who at the beginning still betrays her true identity by some unfitting remarks, quickly grows so deep into her role that she insists on maintaining it even when her sister calls the game off. Instead of posing as Pharaoh's daughter, Madicken rather wants to make a good impression on Abbe, who is watching from the Nilssons' jetty. The girls start fighting over whether the game

CORNELIA RÉMI

is still on or not, and are so busy discussing this border between game and reality that they end up plunging into "the Abyss," a deep hole in the river bed. Just as Gilbert frees Anne from her uncomfortable situation, Abbe pulls Madicken and Lisabet out of the river.[46]

Almost the same pattern applies to their game of "Joseph in the well" (*Madicken* 144–54/167–78). Again the game is disturbed, only this time the atmosphere is not broken, but sharpened and assimilated even more closely to the biblical model, when Madicken suddenly is overcome by her feelings and wants to take revenge on Lisabet. Her little sister has eaten a chocolate boy that Madicken had been given for Easter, and refuses to apologizes for this. Remembering the offence, Madicken abruptly abandons her role and playful behaviour. Because of her anger, however, she now resembles Joseph's brothers even more than when she was just playing them. She leaves a howling yet stubborn Lisabet alone in the empty well, along with a scrap of paper fixed on a stick next to it, on which she scribbles the announcement "BUTERFUL LITEL SLAVE FOR SALE" (*Madicken* 146/169). When she ruefully returns a while later, the border between fiction and reality has been transcended again – but without her intention. For Lisabet has vanished, and someone has added some lines to Madicken's note: "I BORT THIS SLAVE FOR 5p. ISIDOR TURKISH DOG AND SLAVE-TRADER" (149/172). Madicken, taking this message seriously, is desperate and already considers the life of an outlaw, when it turns out that again Abbe has interfered, saved Lisabet from her prison, and supplied her with sugar pretzels.

In all these cases, poetic games include a certain degree of unpredictability and danger. They tend to slip out of their players' control, and what seems thrilling and fascinating in Madicken's and Anne's fancies suddenly turns into real, immediate threats and perils.[47] When the children imitate their favourite literary scenes, they experience how incalculable life indeed is; they discover the cracks and tensions between their games and reality. Such unexpected outbursts of danger mirror the contingencies of a world that is too complex to be reduced to simple formulas.

But although these dangers limit the freedom that imagination grants, their challenge also contributes to strengthen the children's creativity and to prepare them for the further risks of life. While Montgomery moulds the lily maid adventure as the climactic culmination of a series of disciplining episodes, at the end of which Anne finally learns how to subdue her imagination (Ross 47–48), Lindgren encourages a lively use of imagination despite the nearly disastrous outcome of some of her protagonist's games. This encouragement becomes manifest in the final episode of *Madicken och Junibackens Pims* (*Pims* 178–82/231–36). When Madicken is faced with a real danger surpassing all horror scenes from her books, she manages to come up with a solution to ease the situation. One day she is home alone, sitting on the stairs outside the house, reading *The Secret of Phantom Castle* and keeping an eye on her baby sister Kajsa in her pram, when suddenly Lindkvist appears, a mentally deranged old man from the poorhouse. Since he is eager to possess something "which lives and moves" after the loss of his own wife and child, he tries to steal the baby. But Madicken offers him a kitten instead, following the example of her mother, who, in an earlier encounter with Lindkvist, filled his hands with sweets, thus tricking him into letting go of Lisabet (*Pims* 49–51/63–66). Kajsa is saved thanks to her sister's quick thinking, trained by reading and play-acting. Even Anne is not forced to discharge her imagination completely, although she, unlike Madicken, must learn to restrain most of it; she rather realizes that she can use it not only as a short-term escape from and defence against reality, but also as a powerful tool for shaping her further future.[48]

Because Lindgren depicts playing as the essence of life,[49] she also must include risks in her stories, as these are an indispensable element of both living and playing. Her texts insist on this message: games both sharpen children's sensitivity for the richness of opportunities around them and further their competence to cope with critical situations arising from these chances (Edström, *Kvällsdoppet* 93). The discovery of such existentially liberating skills can be read as an allegory of artistic creativity itself.[50] Therefore poetic games, which uncover more of these symbolic layers than other types of play, gain a special status. They offer an opportunity to catch a glimpse of the fictional process itself.

CONCLUSION: TRANSTEXTUALITY

Anne's and Madicken's poetic games reflect the intertextual relations into which they are woven, but they also parallel the games of Lindgren's own childhood and sketch some possible reactions of *her* readers. More than that, they reach back into Montgomery's life and draw inspiration from her experiences both within and outside texts. For, also in her case, life and stories appear intricately interwoven. Not only did she describe herself as "living" in stories; in a complex pattern of interaction between fact and fiction she also constructed her autobiographical accounts as stories, thus interpreting her life by means of texts and again reworking that life story into other texts (Drain 12–15, Karr 28). The creative chain resulting from this process connects Montgomery herself, her creature Anne Shirley, Astrid Lindgren, and Lindgren's poetic creations; it demonstrates that a reader is living her life by "rehearsing roles and becoming characters, identifying and imitating, internalizing and eventually improvising upon the structures" (Drain 8).

Lindgren indicates the particular relevance of poetic games in this process by having the Moses and the Joseph episode open and end her first *Madicken* book. It seems unlikely that she chose just these complementary biblical stories and reversed their chronological order by coincidence. Their inverted order suggests that Madicken's phantasies are by no means to be compared to an Egyptian enslavement that requires her final rescue and salvation from it. They rather epitomize the child's liberty of turning its imagination in any direction – as long as a protected space for these adventures is guaranteed. By positioning the Moses episode at the very beginning of the book, Lindgren introduces her readers to such issues of poetic interaction and to interactions with poetry. The Moses chapter fulfills this task on several levels: firstly, it may be read as an intertextual echo of the lily maid episode in *Anne*. Secondly, it transfers Anne's experiences to a rural Sweden at roughly the time of Lindgren's own childhood and thus echoes her own poetic games, games which on their part inspired and moulded her writing. And thirdly, the Moses episode addresses the imagination of Lindgren's audience and suggests a reader's reaction to *her* stories: active readers can translate them back into real-life games again and incorporate them into their own activities.

This tendency toward a transgression of narrative boundaries accounts for the literary function of Lindgren's and Montgomery's poetic games. The game episodes illustrate the origin of fiction, as they show how stories and poems emerge from lives and merge back into them, when their recipients transform their reading into actual experiences and actions. Thus, the interactions of texts and life both triggered by and depicted in *Anne* and *Madicken* document true transtextuality:[51] modes of handling texts that transcend the space of the text itself and reach out into life. Through this process poetic games gain metapoetic qualities, since they represent the generative and inspiring potential of fiction.

When Lindgren converts the games inspired by her own childhood reading back into literature, the next step consequently requires her readers to bring the stories back to life (Sundström 71). Again and again, she invites them to play and points out that opportunities for new games can be discovered almost anywhere,[52] just as Montgomery has Anne insist on a "scope for imagination" in any given situation. Lindgren's poetic transformation of *Anne* and of her own playing thus anticipates the reception she hopes to inspire, and refuels the creative circle of reading, playing, and telling that keeps our imagination alive.

WORKS CITED

Åhmansson, Gabriella. *A Life and Its Mirrors: A Feminist Reading of L. M. Montgomery's Fiction*. Vol. 1. Studia Anglistica Upsaliensia 74. Uppsala, Stockholm: Almqvist & Wiksell, 1991.

———. "Mayflowers Grow in Sweden, too: L. M. Montgomery, Astrid Lindgren and the Swedish Literary Consciousness." *Harvesting Thistles: The Textual Garden of L. M. Montgomery. Essays on Her Novels and Journals*. Ed. Mary Henley Rubio. Guelph, ON: Canadian Children's P, 1994. 14–22.

Death, Sarah. "Pippi Långstrump and Anne of Green Gables: Tribute and Subversion." *Proceedings of the 10th Biennial Conference of the British Association of Scandinavian Studies, held at the University of Surrey, Department of Linguistics and International Studies*. Ed. Gunilla Anderman and Christine Banér. Guildford: University of Surrey, 1995. 212–21.

Doody, Margaret Anne, and Wendy E. Barry. "Literary Allusion and Quotation in *Anne of Green Gables*." *The Annotated Anne of Green Gables, by Lucy Maud Montgomery*. Ed. Wendy E. Barry, Margaret Anne Doody, and Mary E. Doody Jones. New York, Oxford: Oxford UP, 1997. 457–62.

Doody Jones, Mary E. "Breaking the Silence: Music and Elocution." Lucy Maud Montgomery. *The Annotated Anne of Green Gables, by Lucy Maud Montgomery*. Ed. Wendy E. Barry, Margaret Anne Doody, and Mary E. Doody Jones. New York, Oxford: Oxford UP, 1997. 452–57.

Drain, Susan. "Telling and Retelling: L. M. Montgomery's Storied Lives and Living Stories." *Canadian Children's Literature* 81 (1996): 7–18.

Edström, Vivi. *Astrid Lindgren – Vildtoring och lägereld*. Stockholm: Rabén & Sjögren, 1992.

———. *Astrid Lindgren och sagans makt*. Skrifter utgivna av Svenska Barnboksinstitutet 62. Stockholm: Rabén & Sjögren 1997.

———. *Kvällsdoppet i Katthult: Essäer om Astrid Lindgren diktaren*. Skrifter utgivna av Svenska Barnboksinstitutet 83. Stockholm: Natur och Kultur, 2003.

Ehriander, Helene. "Astrid Lindgren och Rabén & Sjögren." *De Nio: Litterär Kalender 2006.* Stockholm: Norstedts, 2006. 42–56.

Fransson, Birgitta. "Boken om Pippi – en hommage till Anne på Grönkulla?" *Opsis Kalopsis* 3 (2005): 56–60.

Fries-Gedin, Lena. "Snabba Hjorten och Starka Armen." *Allrakäraste Astrid. En vänbok till Astrid Lindgren.* Ed. Susanna Hellsing, Birgitta Westin, and Suzanne Öhman-Sundén. Stockholm: Rabén & Sjögren, 2001. 12–28.

Genette, Gérard. *Palimpsestes: La littérature au second degré.* Paris: Éditions du Seuil, 1982.

Gustafsson, Magnus. "I himmelen där är en stor glädje: Folklig vistradition i Astrid Lindgrens författarskap." *Astrid Lindgren och folkdikten.* Ed. Per Gustavsson. Stockholm: Carlssons, 1996. 111–41.

Karr, Clarence. "Addicted to Reading: L. M. Montgomery and the Value of Reading." *Canadian Children's Literature* 113–14 (2004): 17–33.

Kvint, Kerstin. *Astrid i vida världen: Sannsagan om Astrid Lindgrens internationella succé. En kommenterad bibliografi.* Stockholm: Kvints, 1997.

Lindgren, Astrid. "Anne på Grönkulla och Mannen med stålnävarna." *Bokvännen* 10.11 (1955): 244–45.

———. "Det var bredd över min läsning vill jag påstå." *Barndomens Böcker. Barnboksförfattarnas Litteraturhistoria.* Eds. Annika Holm and Siv Widerberg. Stockholm: Gidlunds, 1984. 9–12.

———. *Kajsa Kavat.* 1950. Stockholm: Rabén & Sjögren, 2003.

———. *Madicken.* 1960. Stockholm: Rabén & Sjögren, 2007.

———. *Madicken och Junibackens Pims.* 1976. Stockholm: Rabén & Sjögren, 2004.

———. *Mardie.* Trans. Patricia Crampton. London: Methuen Children's Books, 1979.

———. *Mardie to the Rescue.* 1981. Trans. Patricia Crampton. London: Mammoth, 1993.

———. *Samuel August från Sevedstorp och Hanna i Hult.* 1975. Stockholm: Rabén & Sjögren, 2007.

———. *Sunnanäng.* 1959. Stockholm: Rabén & Sjögren, 2003.

Lindqvist, Karl. "Om konsten att ta kontakt: Muntligheten in Astrid Lindgrens författarskap." *Astrid Lindgren och folkdikten.* Ed. Per Gustavsson. Stockholm: Carlssons, 1996. 69–88.

Lundqvist, Ulla. *Århundradets barn: Fenomenet Pippi Långstrump och dess förutsettningar.* Stockholm: Rabén & Sjögren, 1979.

———. "Grönkulla och Villekulla (två så olika flickor har faktiskt likheter)." *Dagens Nyheter* 27 December 1975: 12.

Montgomery, Lucy Maud. *Anne of Green Gables: Authoritative Text, Backgrounds, Criticism.* Ed. Mary Henley Rubio and Elizabeth Waterston. New York, London: W.W. Norton, 2007.

———. *Anne på Grönkulla.* 1909. Trans. Karin Jensen. C. W. K. Gleerups ungdomsböcker 24. Lund: Gleerups, 1929.

Nikolowski-Bogomoloff, Angelika. "Out of Mind, Out of Sight? Ideological Dimensions in the American, British and German Translations of Astrid Lindgren's *Madicken*." The Astrid Lindgren Centennial Conference, "The Liberated Child – Childhood in the Works of Astrid Lindgren." Svenska Barnboksinstitutet, Stockholm. 31 May 2007.

Ross, Catherine Sheldrick. "Calling Back the Ghost of the Old-Time Heroine: Duncan, Montgomery, Atwood, Laurence, and Munro." *Studies in Canadian Literature* 4.1 (1979): 43–58.

Rubio, Mary. "Satire, Realism, and Imagination in *Anne of Green Gables*." *Canadian Children's Literature* 3 (1975): 27–36.

Ruhnström, Leif. "Ene unn'lie unge: Ett samtal med tre systrar." *Astrid Lindgren och folkdikten.* Ed. Per Gustavsson. Stockholm: Carlssons, 1996. 11–25.

von Schönborn, Felizitas. *Astrid Lindgren – Das Paradies der Kinder.* Freiburg/Br., Basel, Wien: Herder, 1995.

Soares, Paul. "Förnyelse av liv: Studie i en facettering av det astrid-lindgrenska hoppet. Med utgångspunkt i den tematiska kritiken och Jean-Pierre Richards temabegrepp." *Barnboken* 18.1 (1995): 22–28.

Strömstedt, Margareta. *Astrid Lindgren. En levnadsteckning.* 5th ed. Stockholm: Rabén & Sjögren 2003.

Sundström, Gun-Britt. "Barndomens glada, oskyldiga lekar." *De Nio: Litterär Kalender 2006.* Stockholm: Norstedts, 2006. 71–79.

Thomas, Gillian. "The Decline of Anne: Matron vs. Child." *Such a Simple Little Tale: Critical Responses to L. M. Montgomery's* Anne of Green Gables. Ed. Mavis Reimer. Metuchen, NJ, and London: Children's Literature Association and Scarecrow, 1992. 23–28.

Törnqvist, Lena. "Leka på allvar." *Allrakäraste Astrid. En vänbok till Astrid Lindgren.* Ed. Susanna Hellsing, Birgitta Westin, and Suzanne Öhman-Sundén. Stockholm: Rabén & Sjögren, 2001. 247–264, 297–98.

Wilmshurst, Rea. "L. M. Montgomery's Use of Quotations and Allusions in the 'Anne' books." *Canadian Children's Literature* 56 (1989): 15–45.

NOTES

1   See Åhmansson, "Mayflowers" 14, 18–19. References are to the Norton Critical Edition of *Anne of Green Gables* or the 1929 Gleerups edition of *Anne på Grönkulla*. For *Madicken* and *Madicken och Junibackens Pims*, respectively, I refer to the latest edition in the collection *Astrid Lindgrens samlingsbibliotek* and to Patricia Crampton's British translations *Mardie* and *Mardie to the Rescue*. For all references to *Pims* and *Madicken*, I will use the Swedish book titles, but cite the page numbers of the out-of-print English text first, followed by a forward slash and the corresponding Swedish page numbers.

2   *Vår vän Anne.* Lund: Gleerups, 1910; *Drömmens uppfyllelse.* Lund: Gleerups, 1916. *Anne i eget hem.* Lund: Gleerups, 1918.

3   This concerns even Marilla's "fiddlesticks," Matthew's "Well, I dunno," and some of Anne's fancy names: "the Dryad's bubble" is first rendered as "Dryadens springbrunn" (*Grönkulla* 99), then as "Skogsnymfens källa" (149, 182); "Willowmere" is introduced as "Klaröga" (104) but later turns into "Pil, pil, susa!" (117). When Anne mourns her failed attempt of dyeing her hair, the reference to a former statement of hers is lost. Instead of describing herself as being "in the depths of despair" (*Green Gables* 28, 173), which first has been translated literally (*Grönkulla* 30), she calls out "I am so desperate" (*Grönkulla* 232).

4   See even Åhmansson, "Mayflowers" 18–19, 22. I didn't have access to a 1909 first edition, but since, according to the Swedish Royal Library's catalogue, the number of pages has remained unchanged in the 1929 edition I used, I assume that no major changes occurred between these two.

5   Chapter 26, for example, "The Story Club is Formed," has been shortened almost by half; the beginning of chapter 21 is skipped completely, and Matthew's attempt to buy a dress for Anne at Samuel Lawson's store has been deleted.

6   Even the narrator's praise of Miss Stacy's method of educating independent minds (*Green Gables* 203) has vanished from the translated text.

7   See *Green Gables* 224 compared to *Grönkulla* 303 (my re-translation): "'It's much too early to raise this question,' said Anne and blushed."

8   Neither the Lowell quotation opening Chapter 2 nor the book's closing line from Browning's "Pippa Passes" can be recognized as poetry anymore (*Green Gables* 14, 245/*Grönkulla* 11, 332). The comparison of Marilla to the Duchess from Carroll's *Alice* is skipped (52/66), and so are the Longfellow reference in the heading of Chapter 31 (201/270), the Pope (203/273) and the Barrett Browning quotations (214/288), and the lines from Byron's *Childe Harold's Pilgrimage*, which have been replaced with a simple proverbial phrase (113/153).

9   Like in the description of the concert at the White Sands Hotel (*Green Gables* 212–13, *Grönkulla* 286).

10   Most notable in the description of the Barry family's garden (*Green Gables* 74–75, *Grönkulla* 97). Even the menu for Mrs. Barry's tea in Anne's honour is changed almost completely (*Green Gables* 121–22, *Grönkulla* 167) to include some more substantial dishes than "fruitcake and pound-cake": pickled sprats and hardboiled eggs.

11   Even though she had to rely on Jensen's Swedish translation in her first encounter with *Anne*, she probably read the original text later on; her English language skills were reportedly excellent. Besides, she probably became aware of Montgomery's original texts at the latest when her own sister Stina Hergin translated some of them into Swedish – among them *Anne of Windy Poplars* and *Emily of New Moon* (see Ruhnström 12).

12 Translation by Åhmansson, "Mayflowers" 14–15. See also Lindgren, "Det var bredd" 10; Lindgren, *Samuel August* 73–74.

13 *Green Gables* 15, 19, 31, 33, 53, 65, 67, 79, 104, 114, 188.

14 See *Green Gables* 55–56, 74, 79, 201.

15 See *Green Gables* 41, 53, 67: Anne imagines being a bee, a seagull, or the wind.

16 Just as many other children's classics: the red bird leading the orphans Mattias and Anna to the mythical paradise of "Sunnanäng" in the collection of the same title, for example, has a predecessor in the robin leading Frances Hodgson Burnett's Mary to the Secret Garden.

17 See Lundqvist, "Grönkulla"; Lundqvist, *Århundradets barn* 129; Death; Fransson 57–58; Edström, *Vildtoring* 82; Åhmansson, "Mayflowers" 19. I am indebted to Sarah Death for sending me a copy of her article.

18 For clarity's sake I will use the Swedish titles and characters' names, since they differ in the U.K. and U.S. editions. A first British translation by Marianne Turner, keeping the original title, was published in 1963 by Oxford UP. Later, Patricia Crampton translated both books for Methuen as *Mardie* (1979) and *Mardie to the Rescue* (1981), while Viking Press in the U.S. only published the first volume, *Mischievous Meg* (1962); see also Kvint 66. This U.S. translation by Gerry Bothmer differs considerably from the original, as Angelika Nikolowski-Bogomoloff pointed out in her presentation at the Astrid Lindgren Centennial Conference 2007. *Mischievous Meg* even omits a whole chapter ("Lisabet sticks a pea up her nose"), probably since its contents were regarded as unsuitable for an American audience. For the publication dates see Kvint 149–50.

19 See Strömstedt 170–77; von Schönborn 35. Edström (*Vildtoring* 22–23) and Soares have discussed the centrality of key actions in Lindgren's works, such as climbing, balancing, and jumping from heights.

20 See Fries-Gedin 15–18 and *Madicken* 4–5, 20, 31/11, 28, 42. According to Törnqvist 252–53, the *Madicken* books are among those works of Lindgren in which the vital activity of playing is especially prominent.

21 See *Madicken* 82-84/98–100 and *Pims* 30, 147–48/40–41, 192–93.

22 *Green Gables* 19, 88, 185, 243; *Pims* 5/7–8.

23 *Pims* 61/79–80. See also *Madicken* 86/103. Even Lisabet experiences this mixture of feelings (*Madicken* 31/42). Madicken's thoughts appear livelier in the original Swedish text than in the English translation, since the whole book is originally told in the present tense. The translator's choice of shifting the narration to the past tense has substantially changed Lindgren's characteristic "oral" narrative style.

24 See "the White Way of Delight" and "the Lake of Shining Waters" (*Green Gables* 22); "Bonny" and the "Snow Queen" (35); "the Dryad's Bubble" (76); "Idlewild" and "Willowmere" (78–79); "Lovers' Lane" and "Violet Vale" (89); "Victoria Island" (134) and "the Haunted Wood" (134–135). Anne's love for the trees at Green Gables, as contrasted to the miserable "weeny-teeny things" growing at the asylum (19), also might have contributed to inspire Lindgren's tale "Spelar min lind, sjunger min näktergal?" in *Sunnanäng*.

25 See *Green Gables* 19, *Madicken* 66/80, and *Pims* 129–30/167–69.

26 See *Green Gables* 76, 78; *Madicken* 20–21/28–29, opposed to *Green Gables* 126–27, 155–56, 189, 215–18 and *Pims* 137–38/178–80.

27 See *Green Gables* 14, 113, 142, 145, 165, 201, 203, 228, 233. Wilmshurst offers a comprehensive list of such quotations and allusions for all the *Anne* books. For a brief overview of the function of literary works quoted from or mentioned in *Anne of Green Gables*, see Doody and Barry.

28 Lindgren's works owe a debt to oral poetic traditions (see Lindqvist, Gustafs-

son). Listening to stories is an inspiration irresolvably intertwined with the creative process in her œuvre (Edström, *Kvällsdoppet* 94–96, and Edström, *AL och sagans makt* 47–49).

29 Certain elements of this poetic potpourri serve as a sort of counter-language to the idyllic atmosphere of her home (Edström, *Kvällsdoppet* 230–233). Regarding Lindgren's relation to language, see Edström, *Kvällsdoppet* 98–100, 196–214.

30 See *Madicken* 2–3, 15, 20, 30, 56, 70, 78–79, 85–86, 98–100/8–10, 23, 28, 40–41, 69–70, 85–86, 95, 102–103, 117–18; *Pims* 34, 55, 66–67, 95/45, 71, 86–87, 123–24. Linus-Ida's Christian convictions might even mirror the Presbyterian piety displayed by Marilla Cuthbert and Rachel Lynde to a certain degree, even though she does not express such a strict disdain ˙of fiction as these characters (*Green Gables* 170, 179).

31 See *Madicken* 2–3, 100/8, 118; *Pims* 63, 100/82, 129.

32 *Green Gables* 38–40. If there is any character in *Madicken* using imagination for similar purposes, it would be Abbe, whose plans of becoming an explorer and adventurer contrast sharply with his daily work in the kitchen.

33 This can be observed especially in the Christmas episodes: Madicken and Lisabet imagine baby Jesus lying in a manger at nearby Appletree Hill farm (*Madicken* 115/134–36), and Madicken treasures the experience of Christmas by asking Lisabet to imagine that the next day might turn out not to be Christmas Eve (126/145).

34 See *Madicken* 138/159–60. Soares (25–26) describes this tension between retaining a pastoral Arcadia and an orientation toward leaving it as the central principle of organization for *Madicken*.

35 See *Madicken* 21–25, 27, 44, 46, 57, 76/29–35, 37–38, 55–56, 58, 71, 92.

36 In Montgomery's later books, the changes of Anne's character compared to her first appearance seem even more radical; see Thomas.

37 Anne is reading "Spökslottets dystra hemlighet" (*Grönkulla* 261), while Madicken's book is entitled "Spökslottets hemlighet" – Lindgren has only omitted the adjective "dyster" (dark, grim).

38 This parallel "climbing motif" has been noted by Death 215, and Fransson 58.

39 See *Pims* 70–76/91–99. A different outcome of a similar bet is depicted in Lindgren's story "Hoppa högst" (in the collection *Kajsa Kavat*), which ends with the two competitors Albin and Stig both breaking their legs.

40 *Pims* 71/93. Strömstedt (173–74) points out that the school roof scene plays with an inversion of a traditional role scheme. It is not boys challenging and driving each other into a dangerous situation, but two girls, while their male classmates remain passive bystanders.

41 A poetic game mentioned later in the book proves that such games offer valuable training for the fluent transition of one point of view to another. Together with Mia and Mattis, Madicken and Lisabet start playing "The Good Samaritan," but finally end up playing robbers altogether (*Pims* 102–03/132–33).

42 Besides, at least for Abbe, the wish to fly is indeed fulfilled later on (*Pims* 152–54/198–201).

43 Edström, *Kvällsdoppet* 95, uses the expression "the literary game" to describe this active relation to texts; I prefer the term "poetic," which signals that both literary and oral traditions may be involved.

44 *Pims* 54/70; see even 56–58/72–75.

45 See even Åhmansson, *A Life* 101–14.

46 The fact that Abbe almost dies, just as Gilbert in *Anne of the Island*, is another parallel, although Madicken, unlike Anne, is sure that she wants to marry Abbe already before he falls ill (*Pims* 11/15).

47 The games depicted in *Madicken* are indeed more dangerous than those described in Lindgren's *Bullerby* ("Noisy Village") books; see Edström, *Vildtoring* 73.

48 See *Green Gables* 218–19; Rubio 64; Åhmansson, *A Life* 101–14.

49 See Edström, *Kvällsdoppet* 87–103, especially 88; Törnqvist 264.

50 See Edström, *Kvällsdoppet* 101 (my translation): "The important thing in her tales
   is the creative moment itself, when one's
   existence is changed. . . . The greatest
   intensity in her poetic world develops just
   when a child is released from its shackled
   condition and reaches the creative phase
   of imagination. It is quite unambiguous
   that this liberation also can be read as a
   metadescription of the poet's inspiration
   and of creative joy."

51 While Genette uses "transtextuality" as a
   general term for relations between texts, I
   suggest – based on its spatial implications
   – applying it to phenomena transcending
   the borders between the textual realm
   and its recipients' reality.

52 See Madicken's description of her home
   as a house with a seemingly universal
   aptitude to play in and around (*Madicken*
   4–5/11).

IV

MATURING ANNE:
GENDER AND EMPIRE

A Ministry of Plum Puffs: Cooking as a Path to Spiritual Maturity in L. M. Montgomery's *Anne* Books

Christiana R. Salah

In the preface to her 1859 bestselling *Book of Household Management*, Isabella Beeton declares that "there is no more fruitful source of family discomfort than a housewife's badly-cooked dinners and untidy ways" (iii). If the women of her time were to win their husbands' attention from the attractions of clubs and taverns, then wives "must be thoroughly acquainted with the theory and practice of cookery ... and all the other arts of making and keeping a comfortable home" (iii). For the modern reader, these statements may conjure up amusing images of TV housewives vacuuming in floral-print dresses and high heels, but the ideal of the domestic goddess was no laughing matter in the Victorian era. It was, in fact, nothing less than a religious imperative. Popular conviction held that homemaking was woman's sacred mission (Flanders 13). In her book of lectures on *The Duties of Women*, Victorian activist Frances Power Cobbe gives her female contemporaries the injunction that "if home be our kingdom, it must be our joy and privilege to convert that domain.... into a little province of the kingdom of God" (140). Manuals such as these were written to aid women of all walks of life in achieving the model of feminine perfection known (without irony) as the Angel in the House.[1]

Fifty years after Mrs. Beeton told her readers how to cultivate the perfect home, L. M. Montgomery spun the story of a girl in desperate need of that knowledge. Anne Shirley, the young heroine of *Anne of Green Gables*, is an orphan whose whole future security depends on her ability to please the middle-aged brother and sister who have taken her in. Published only a few years after Queen Victoria's death and set during her reign, *Anne of Green Gables* enters into the spirit of the Victorian quest for good Christian womanhood, with one important complication. No matter how hard Anne tries, she is incapable of conforming to her era's feminine ideal – and, far more unusually, the narrative likes her that way. By subtly undermining the conventions of the domestic coming-of-age story, Montgomery challenges established conceptions of what it means to be a good homemaker, a good Christian, and a good woman.

The domestic girl's novel, sometimes called "the female bildungsroman," was invented in the Victorian era expressly to praise and promulgate the period's ideal of femininity (Jackson and Kornfield 139). Louisa May Alcott's *Little Women* and the less-enduring "Pansy" (by Isabella Macdonald Alden) and "Elsie" books (by Martha Finley) are classic examples of this genre. Though popular and read for pleasure,[2] these novels had a twofold didactic agenda: they offered fictional examples of budding Angels in the House for girl readers to model themselves on, and they told cautionary tales of the harm done by girls who strayed from the righteous path by neglecting their chores, for example, or refusing to sacrifice their own pleasures to gratify their families. Although some heroines, like Jo March, do struggle against femininity, the stories still tended to conform to a single plot arc: what Judith Rowbotham, in her book *Good Girls Make Good Wives*, calls "a feminine odyssey to near perfection" (24). Heroines might rise or fall, but the magic combination of virtues constituting "near perfection" was rarely called into question. The perfect woman "was always modest, indicative of unselfish submission to those in due authority over her … educated as fitting for her station and abilities … able to make a contribution to household affairs [and] to add materially in a variety of ways to the comfort of the males in her life." And of course, she always found "inspiration and justification for her actions and her thoughts in sound, orthodox Christian doctrine" (Rowbotham 23).

It was vital for girls to acquire the skills of Christian homemaking, because when they became women the spiritual well-being of their households would (it was believed) lie in their hands. A dirty or disorganized home corrupted the minds and spirits of its inhabitants. Like the priest of a one-family parish, a woman set the moral tone for her entire household. Tending to her family's needs was her form of ministry; cooking and cleaning were acts of Christian service. The mature didactic heroine was indeed a "ministering angel," but the left hand was never to know what the right was doing. As *The Young Wife's Book* of 1836 counselled women, "A man by marrying places his domestic comforts in the power of his wife, and ... he must reap the benefit of labours which he *must never witness* in their progress" (209, emphasis mine). The wife's ministry was, perforce, a silent one; her perfect domestic productions were to speak for her. When a novel's young heroine proved her mastery of these self-effacing virtues, the plot was complete.

When Montgomery wrote *Anne of Green Gables*, she created a character who was everything the advice manuals said a young woman should be: domestic, obedient, loving, and not so highly educated as to put anyone else to shame. But that character, Diana Barry, was not the heroine of her novel. Montgomery's heroine, Anne, begins the book with everything to learn about domesticity except how to care for children. She walks into Green Gables and immediately throws her guardians' clean and tidy world into disarray. Yet in the process of disrupting domestic life, Anne becomes a minister in her own right, widening the spiritual and intellectual boundaries of the community around her, not through her productions, but through the charm of her character and her unconventional ideas.

When Anne first arrives in the Prince Edward Island village of Avonlea, she does seem poised to undertake one of Rowbotham's odysseys toward feminine perfection. After a life of "drudgery and poverty and neglect" (*Green Gables* 92), Anne is anything but "the Avonlea type of a well-bred girl" (67); she has no notion of how to behave amongst the critical denizens of her new community and resolves to immediately mould herself into a model girl. "I'll try to do and be anything you want me, if you'll only keep me," she tells her new guardian Marilla Cuthbert (97). But the reader who expects the pages ahead to transform Anne into this kind of girl will be astonished to see how her attempts to "contribute to household affairs" and to "ground her thoughts in Christian doctrine" become catastrophes so brilliant that neither household affairs nor doctrine remain the same when she's done with them. Most shockingly of all, the author deconstructs the established pattern of heroine maturation by rewarding Anne's domestic and social failures instead of punishing them! Not that Montgomery ever derides domestic or social excellence; she simply rejects their ascendancy over other values. A perfectly run household, she seems to say, is not necessarily the panacea the Victorians considered it; comfort food is a good thing, but not the only food a soul needs. Or, as Anne puts it, "plum puffs won't minister to a mind diseased" (*Avonlea* 101). The novel refuses to privilege traditional goodness over intelligence or aesthetics, just as Anne cannot choose whether she would rather be "divinely beautiful or dazzlingly clever or angelically good" (*Green Gables* 69). Montgomery does not subvert the didactic form to reject the values with which she was raised, but as a critique of the insular and inflexible mindset that presumes those values to be the only valid ones.

Some scholars have argued that since Anne enacts some of the behaviours of a proper Victorian woman by the end of the novel, her story is, after all, a validation of the didactic ideal.[3] But this reading neglects to take into account the way Anne changes the ideal even as she struggles to attain it. Rather than write a character who is transformed by outside conceptions of what she should become, Montgomery creates a heroine with the power to influence the thinking of those around her. What's particularly effective and disarming is that Anne has influence unknowingly, all the time believing she is hard on the heels of perfect girlhood. The chapter significantly titled "A New Departure in Flavourings" demonstrates how Anne's first public display of the skills every middle-class girl was expected to acquire quickly deteriorates into a spectacle. She bakes a cake in honour of the new minister and his wife's first visit to Green Gables, but flavours it with anodyne liniment (a topical pain-relieving fluid) instead of vanilla. Mortified, Anne flees the dinner table in tears. Mrs. Allen, the minister's wife, attempts to comfort her, remarking that "it's all just a funny mistake that anybody might make." "Oh no," replies Anne, "it takes me to make such a mistake" (214). She is right. Any young Victorian heroine might make an error in cookery, but it takes Anne Shirley to transform a social blunder into a "new departure."[4] When Mrs. Allen validates the girl's earnest intentions instead of condemning the imperfect performance, failure becomes victory. Anne's worth is affirmed, based on inner qualities rather than outward trappings.

Contrast this incident with another scene of ill-starred serving, appearing forty years earlier in Alcott's *Little Women.* Jo March, a heroine similar to Anne in her spunkiness and habit of getting into mischief, is given a week off from work. Her sisters decide to take a vacation as well. At the end of the week, their mother goes out for the day, leaving them to take care of the house. With a misplaced confidence in her own abilities, Jo offers to cook dinner for the family and two guests. Every single item is an unpalatable disaster. Though the dinner ends well enough, with "bread and butter, olives and fun" (Alcott 98), Jo is not allowed to live down the incident, which becomes "a standing joke" (97).

Her failures remain failures. Nor is the domestic ideal ever called into question; Jo and the other girls bitterly repent their week's vacation, and willingly swallow the lesson that "lounging and larking don't pay" (99). Despite her vivacious heroine, Alcott never really steps outside the strictures of the didactic form. The unquestioned importance of self-repression and sacrifice forms a through-line for the novel, and although Jo is a fictionalized version of Alcott herself, the author never fully endorses her heroine's life philosophy. Jo's strengths are shown to lie outside the domestic sphere, but her lapses in housekeeping and etiquette are never excused on those grounds, and rewards that readers desire for her are often given to her better-behaved sisters. Montgomery, on the other hand, showers Anne with narrative approval. Other characters may frown on Anne's quirky behaviour, but the novel clearly loves her just as she is. Anne does eventually acquire the prescribed heroic virtues (piety, housekeeping ability), but only after she has rearranged the priorities of her world.

It is in the progress of Anne's attempts to learn to cook that we most often see her reacting against her community's values. Culinary expertise becomes a metaphor for Anne's transcendence, and consequent widening of societal expectations. Montgomery spends the first part of the novel describing Avonlea's traditions, and the central portion showing how Anne upsets them one by one. The town of Avonlea is a force to be reckoned with; it may well be one of the most vibrantly realized communities in literature, and the village could be called a major character in its own right. The kitchen is a frequent staging area for Anne's clashes with this powerful collective, because Avonlea is an intensely domestic community. In this fictionalized vision of late-Victorian Prince Edward Island, the important members of society are all female. To these small town ladies, excellence in cooking, quilting, and other "women's work" is as important a status symbol as carriages and servants were to their London counterparts. Avonlea is also a strictly Presbyterian village. During Montgomery's childhood, "religion was still the strongest organizing force within local communities," and in her novel she heightens that sense of an intense communal force by excluding any mention of what religious diversity may have existed in Avonlea (Rubio 97). No one in *Anne of Green Gables* is ever identified as belonging to any other religion or denomination, forming a united front of Presbyterianism that Anne, "next door to a perfect heathen" (101), comes up against. In this town of Christian women, the kitchen is a sanctuary, and the primary ministry is to feed God's flock.

In the first chapter of the novel we receive a description of eminent citizen Rachel Lynde, who wields all the Avonlea female virtues: she is "a notable housewife" who "helped run the Sunday School, and was the strongest prop of the Church Aid Society and Foreign Missions Auxiliary" (53). Montgomery also brings Rachel's nosiness and lack of tact to our notice, but makes it clear that as a demonstrative Christian and a superior housekeeper, Rachel is guaranteed the respect of her community. The same is assured of Marilla Cuthbert, who is called a "famous cook" (167). Anne, on the other hand, is portrayed from her first appearance as unorthodox and seemingly powerless to command society's respect. Her experiences up to this point have taken place in a setting totally unlike Avonlea, a world with glass doors smashed by intoxicated men and preserves kept in the bookcase "when [there were] any preserves to keep" (107). When Matthew Cuthbert finds her at the train station, her clothes are barely decent and her manners highly irregular. Compared to Avonlea girls, she is a "freckled witch" (67).

Once Matthew and Marilla adopt her, Anne sets out to become a respected citizen and a "famous cook" herself. But her romantic perspective on cooking, characteristic of her perspective on life, conflicts sharply with the stolid attitudes of the town. At first her ideas are seen as nothing short of heresy. Avonlea women devote a great deal of time to making objects which are both practical and sensuous – delicious baked goods, gorgeous quilts, and so on – but are never shown to derive any aesthetic pleasure from them. This was not an attitude Montgomery approved of; she worried that among the good Christians of her acquaintance, the spiritual was too often divorced from and privileged over the physical. She remarked in her private journal that, after all, "mind and soul can express themselves only through the body" (White 85). On this subject, Anne's beliefs parallel her creator's. To her way of thinking, aesthetics and practicalities are not separable. Tea would taste sweeter from the rosebud spray tea set, boiled pork and greens are "a food unsuited to crises of feeling" (145), and no one should be expected to eat at all when "in the depths of despair" (78). Even in the sequel novels Anne maintains this distinctive viewpoint toward the productions of domesticity, writing a baking scene into her florid, melodramatic short story "Averil's Atonement."

As a narrative device, Anne's romanticism heightens the contrast between her and the town, but also functions as a test of other characters' capacity for reform. Anyone who shows an appreciation of Anne's effusive nature is immediately tagged as a "kindred spirit." Those characters who condemn her are implicated as figures of closed-minded extremism. This dynamic is illustrated in the chapter when Anne gets Marilla's permission to invite her best friend, Diana

Barry, to tea. She delights in the opportunity to play hostess for the first time, and glories in particular over the pleasing appearance of the raspberry cordial Marilla has suggested she serve: "I love bright red drinks, don't you?" she gushes to Diana. "They taste twice as good as any other color" (166). Of course, she has chosen the wrong bright red drink, and Diana goes home drunk on currant wine. But while the author appears to be punishing Anne's aestheticism and lack of domestic responsibility when Diana's mother forbids the girls to speak to each other, it is really Mrs. Barry, Diana's mother, who is being critiqued. The novel condemns her refusal to acknowledge that the incident was accidental, describing her as "a woman of strong prejudices" (172). Mrs. Barry is soon cosmically punished by her younger daughter's dangerous illness, and Anne rewarded with the opportunity to humble Mrs. Barry by saving the child's life. Though Diana and the "hired girl" are more proper and accomplished than Anne, both are helpless during Minnie May's illness, unable to do anything more useful than boil water. Anne's practicality and intuition win the day. The message is clear: to an *un*prejudiced mind, the Victorian ideal of femininity leaves a lot to be desired, because it neglects essentials in favour of appearances. A household run by Anne might not be a sanctum of domestic harmony, but the deepest needs of its members will be ministered to.

Two baking disasters bracket the currant wine incident, confirming the same message. First, Anne forgets to cover a pitcher of plum pudding sauce, and after discovering a mouse has drowned in it, forgets to tell Marilla before the sauce is brought out in front of respectable guests – including a "perfect housekeeper" whom Anne would like to impress. "I tried to be as polite and dignified as I could be," Anne tells Diana, "for I wanted Mrs. Chester Ross to think I was a ladylike little girl even if I wasn't pretty" (168). But Mrs. Ross reacts scornfully when the drowned-mouse mishap is revealed. This incident, though briefly mortifying for Anne, can chiefly be understood in light of the later, mirroring incident with the liniment cake. Again, Anne makes an error in the kitchen; again, it comes to light at the dinner table. But in this second anecdote, Mrs. Allen proves herself a kindred spirit by laughing rather than disapproving – and, unlike Mrs. Chester Ross, remains a prominent character for the rest of the novel. As Pike also argues (this volume), Anne's failures give others the opportunity to overcome their preconceptions, by recognizing the loving intention instead of the faulty result. Desserts, we find, can minister to diseased or circumscribed minds after all; the secret is in the spirit of the baking.

Mrs. Allen's ability to see Anne's value without being put off by her short-comings makes her a somewhat unusual character for this genre. Both Mrs. Allen and Miss Stacy, Anne's teacher, belong to a character type common to didactic novels: the righteous woman mentor. Particularly when there is no mother on the scene, "it was essential for apprentice good girls to have an image constantly before them on which to model themselves" (Rowbotham 25). But Montgomery undermines this cliché by depicting both women as drawn not to Anne's budding angelic qualities, but to her difference. Mrs. Allen could choose a more conventional little girl to mentor; there is even one provided: Lauretta Bradley, the "nice little girl" who receives the same invitation to tea at the manse as Anne (218). And Miss Stacy could lavish praise on Minnie Andrews, the "model pupil" whom the inept former teacher, Mr. Phillips, often lauded (175). But Lauretta goes home from the manse early, and Minnie never even rates a mention once the innovative "lady teacher" takes over Avonlea school. Both women single out Anne with their attention even though she is not the type to be moulded into anyone's image; as she tells Marilla, "Some people are naturally good, you know, and others are not. I'm one of the others" (217). Rather than remaking Anne, these influential women serve a different function: to provide her with a mature means of articulating her own ideas. Validated by their example, Anne feels confident in asserting that students should ask questions, that as much can be learned in nature as in a classroom, and that religion should not be a sorrowful thing, but a joyful one.

This last lesson, that religion can be aesthetic and pleasurable as well as straightforward and traditional, is perhaps the most important in Anne's quest for spiritual maturity. Her religious development exactly parallels her approach to cooking and housework. At the start of the novel Anne has barely had any religious training (as she tells Marilla, she never could care much for God after learning that he "made [her] hair red *on purpose*"), and as she grows, she revises her community's ideal of Protestant womanhood as significantly as she has their ideal of domestic womanhood (99). After a rocky start, during which she signs a prayer "Yours respectfully, Anne Shirley," wreathes her lacklustre church hat with wildflowers, and asks her Sunday school teacher's permission to recite "The Dog at His Master's Grave" instead of a Bible verse, Anne does learn to outwardly conform to Avonlea's Presbyterian practices. But from the first, she is aligned with a sort of natural inner spirituality quite different from the village's grim brand of religious feeling.

Like her notions about food, Anne's theology is aligned with the Romantic movement. Montgomery reinforces this connection by continually quoting or alluding to major Romantic and Romantic-influenced writers, including John Keats, Lord Byron, Sir Walter Scott, and Robert Browning. Unlike the traditional Presbyterian view, which divorced God from his creation and placed him at a distance accessible to humans only through the power of grace, the Romantics located God in nature and in the individual's emotional experiences. Anne's sentimental attachment to place and her religious codification of landscape are particularly reminiscent of Wordsworth. Perry Nodelman makes this connection when, using Wordsworth's phrase, he calls her a "seer blest," describing how, for Anne, "spontaneous feelings are prayer, and nature is God's cathedral" (Nodelman 35). White, describing Montgomery's nature-based take on Christianity, makes an almost identical comment: "Churches and forests were interchangeable" (White 86). Clearly this was another instance of the author's view finding expression through her creation (see Hilder, this volume, for more on this issue).

Also like the Romantics, Anne connects art with spirituality. Avonlea sees religion as a solemn duty and art as a potentially dangerous frivolity, but for Anne the two are inextricable. Given the Lord's Prayer to learn, she tells Marilla, "This isn't poetry, but it makes me feel just the same way poetry does" (106). A rapturous appreciation of beauty, whether natural or human made, is the heart of Anne's religion. Marilla at first feels "nervous" and "uncomfortable" when witnessing this unabashed joy (84). In one instance, after perceiving that "while this odd child's body might be there at the table her spirit was far away in some remote airy cloudland," Marilla asks herself: "Who would want such a child about the place?" (84). Yet, though it disturbs her, Marilla finds herself captivated by Anne's fervour, as Matthew immediately is. Having seen religion only through its outward trappings their whole lives, they are both disconcerted and enthralled to witness the substance of it, pure and unencumbered.

The novel's narrator plainly takes Anne's side on spiritual matters, whatever the other characters might say. The word "spiritual," in fact, is frequently used to describe Anne's face or expression, often when she is taking in something beautiful such as a sunset or poem. In dialogue, on the other hand, Anne is more than once referred to as a "witch," and the word "wicked" is applied to her with remarkable frequency. At one point, when Anne is looking at a picture of "Christ Blessing Little Children" and imagining herself into the scene, the narrator describes her as a "rapt little figure with a half-unearthly radiance"

(105). Marilla, in contrast, calls her "positively irreverent." The local dialect is peppered with religiously-coded language, generally of a forbidding nature: "a moral dread" (96), "devout relief" (110), "holy horror" (329), "unholy tendency to laughter" (173). This language heightens our perception of the gulf between Anne's spirituality and Avonlea's religious practice.

Anne senses this gulf, but though she longs to fit in, she plainly finds it difficult to reconcile the two viewpoints. When Marilla tells her to kneel to pray on her second night at Green Gables, Anne immediately begins by questioning the ritual:

> "Why must people kneel down to pray? If I really wanted to pray I'll tell you what I'd do. I'd go out into a great big field all alone or into the deep, deep woods, and I'd look up into the sky – up – up – up…. And then I'd just feel a prayer." (100)

Marilla is "embarrassed" by this speech, suggesting that somewhere within her repressed personality a chord has been struck. For some time, however, Anne and Avonlea religion continue to clash. Bored by the Sunday School Superintendent's long-winded prayer, Anne "gazed [out the window] and imagined all sorts of splendid things" (128). When rebuked by Marilla for inattention, Anne defends herself by describing the beautiful scene and her personal prayer of thanks to God for it. Again Montgomery hints, not so subtly, that the girl's stance is the more truly spiritual one. As happens so frequently throughout the novel, Marilla's thoughts interpret Anne's narrative power for the reader:

> Some of the things Anne had said … were what she [Marilla] had really thought deep down in her heart for years, but had never given expression to. It almost seemed to her that those secret, unuttered, critical thoughts had suddenly taken visible and accusing shape and form in the person of this outspoken morsel of neglected humanity. (130)

Marilla would like to reprove Anne for not respecting the religious forms she has herself been schooled to accept as sacred, but feels "helpless," recognizing that to do so would be to hypocritically deny part of her own nature. Anne, by personifying the repressed thoughts of the community, shows Avonlea the hypocrisy they have been guilty of for years.

Anne is totally unaware that her unorthodox spirituality might be shared by anyone in Avonlea. In fact, she quickly learns to compartmentalize "Sunday thoughts" from everyday thoughts. To her mind, at least for the first half of the novel, *religious* and *sad* are synonyms, as is demonstrated by amusing statements like "It isn't a really truly religious piece of poetry, but it's so sad and melancholy that it might as well be" (129), and "the choir are going to sing four lovely pathetic songs that are pretty near as good as hymns" (190). Eventually, though, Anne masters the outward forms of religion just as she masters cooking and keeping house – *after* having demonstrated to the community that inner qualities are more important than these accomplishments. She becomes a devout Presbyterian only after it is clear that Avonlea is shifting toward a more joyful, natural spirituality. The arrival of the Allens, chosen by the community to replace the old minister, "whom Anne had found lacking in imagination," is proof of this transformation (207). It is Mrs. Allen who finally "teaches" Anne the doctrine to which she subscribed all along: that religion is "a cheerful thing. I always thought it was kind of melancholy, but Mrs. Allen's isn't, and I'd like to be a Christian if I could be one like her" (209). And not only does Avonlea select the Allens as its spiritual leaders, but we are also told that the town "open[s] its heart to them from the start. Old and young liked the frank, cheerful young man with his high ideals, and the bright, gentle little lady" (208). The marriage of adjectives used to describe the Allens – frank *and* cheerful, ladylike *and* bright – indicates a significant widening in Avonlea's ideas; they are no longer satisfied with a ministry that is exclusively traditionalist.

Marilla serves as a barometer of this spiritual change. Though she may not walk through the natural world "with reverent steps and worshipping eyes, as if she trod on holy ground," as Anne does, Marilla's spirituality does become more expansive and romantic (200). Late in the novel, she responds to the arrival of springtime with a "deep, primal gladness" (247). And at one notable point, she actually concedes to Anne's idea that "it is ever so much easier to be good if your clothes are fashionable" (264), sewing a flounce into the girl's newest dress because Anne says it gives her "such a comfortable feeling deep down in [her] mind" (283). Romance is creeping into Avonlea. By the end of the novel, even

Rachel Lynde has started to unbend. For example, Mrs. Lynde once declared that she could never respect a minister after hearing him confess to stealing a tart as a small boy (246). Her subsequent remark that Anne makes the other Avonlea girls look "kind of common and overdone" (281) shows a radical change in her standards for what makes a good person, since she can recognize Anne's true worth in spite of her imperfect behaviour. Still more remarkable is the fact that plain-speaking Mrs. Lynde uses a flowery metaphor ("like them white June lilies she calls narcissus alongside of the big, red peonies") to express the distinction! No other character ever reaches Anne's heights of romantic vision, but as she shows her community that the stern Christianity of their prior practice did not reflect their private beliefs, some illumination is allowed in and some repressed enthusiasm finally let out.

Montgomery's quiet critique of leaden, uninspired faith is directly tied to her stance on domesticity in a scene in *Anne of Avonlea*, in which Anne and Diana prepare an elaborate meal for one of their favourite authors. In Charlotte E. Morgan, Montgomery creates a fictional foil for herself, an author who follows all the didactic conventions: "Mrs. Morgan's heroines never get into scrapes or are taken at a disadvantage, and they are always so self-possessed and such good housekeepers," an aggrieved Anne informs Marilla (*Avonlea* 137). In honour of the visit, Anne and Diana are determined to make themselves over into little Morgan heroines; they don white muslin dresses like those the girls in the books always wear, clean Green Gables so thoroughly that even Marilla looks sceptical, and whip up a meal a model housekeeper might envy. But they are not Mrs. Morgan's protagonists – they are Montgomery's, and she does not allow their personalities to remain subjugated for long.

Charlotte E. Morgan never shows, and the resultant dinner is a dismal experience for everyone present. Once Montgomery has successfully employed satire to undermine the message of standard didactic fiction, she goes a step further, providing a message of her own. Mrs. Morgan arrives unannounced on a day when Anne and the house are in disarray, but the unexpected party turns out to be a wild success in spite of several failures on a domestic level. Excellent company and conversation are shown to be the true ingredients in a successful gathering, "a feast of reason and a flow of soul" (180). With the failure of the original "ideal" party and the success of the idiosyncratic, spontaneous one, Montgomery ventures into unfamiliar territory for a girl's book. She shows that material perfectionism detracts from spiritual connection and intellectual exchange. Anne absorbs the lesson, declaring it to have been a "nicer time" than

CHRISTIANA R. SALAH

if she and Diana had been "cumbered with much serving," as originally planned (180). The latter quotation is a reference to the biblical story of Mary and Martha, and is indicative of a larger theme Montgomery explores throughout the series. The Bible praises Mary, who knows how to be still and keep an ear open for spiritual enlightenment, whereas the Victorians mistakenly idealized the perfect, bustling hostess, as typified by Martha.

When the growing-up process of the first novel is complete, Anne's cooking mishaps come to an end, but food retains its association with spiritual maturity (or the lack thereof) throughout the *Anne* series. Montgomery often employs an incident of cooking or eating when a new character is introduced, to show whether or not the new person is capable of a broadened, balanced spiritual viewpoint – in other words, whether or not he or she is a kindred spirit. Characters are essentially tested against the new standard Anne has created. An example of one who passes this test is Lavendar Lewis, an important new character in *Anne of Avonlea*. When Anne first meets the self-described "independent old maid," Miss Lavendar is having a tea party for imaginary guests (*Avonlea* 189). Miss Lavendar's attitude toward food is hearty and unconventional; she "live[s] in defiance of every known law of diet" (244). During another visit, she asks Anne what they should have for tea: "Do think of something nice and indigestible" (201). Feasting on candy, she remarks, "I've eaten far more than is good for me already but I'm going to keep recklessly on" (204). This eccentric dietary style instantly stamps Miss Lavendar as divergent from the regular run of kindly but constrained local ladies, aligning her with Anne as thoroughly as the fact that she "imagine[s] things too" (188). Miss Lavendar's culinary habits are placed in direct contrast with those of Mrs. Irving, grandmother of Anne's prize pupil, Paul Irving, who restricts Paul to a diet of simple, unpalatable foods. When Paul's father marries Miss Lavendar, we know that the boy's soul will thrive under her care as surely as we know that his taste buds will extol the change.

Other characters measured against Anne's domestic standard do not fare so well. In *Anne of the Island*, Anne and three friends set up house in "Patty's Place," where their lifestyle is quite independent. When her beau, Roy Gardner, tells Anne to expect a call from his mother and sisters, she immediately begins planning how to make a good impression. But her hopes of appearing prim and proper are foiled as usual; the Gardners arrive on the wrong day, while Anne and her housemates are indulging in a quiet evening in, pursuing various scholarly and domestic projects. To complete the comfortable scene, we are told that "a warm plummy odor filled the whole house, for Priscilla was cooking in the kitchen" (*Island* 213). The picture is reduced to chaos by the Gardners' knock. Priscilla, in a panic, thrusts her chocolate cake under a cushion, on which Roy's frosty sister Aline unknowingly sits. The inference is plain: as people from whose eyes cake must be shrouded – whose arrival inhibits the unconventional blend of domestic and intellectual pleasures practiced in Patty's Place – these women (and by implication, Roy) have no place in Anne's life.[5] Anne's true worth, like a rich chocolate cake, will always be hidden from the superficial, unspiritual Gardners.

Miss Lavendar's scenes and the milieu of Patty's Place have a thread in common: both highlight the pleasure offered by food and household life, if approached with the right attitude. Pleasure is a highly potent tool in Montgomery's series. In the original arc of her journey toward maturity, Anne employs pleasure as a method of claiming those elements of domesticity and religion most foreign to her impulsive, irrepressible personality. Scholars have already identified Anne's habit of renaming places as an act of authorship that gives her power over her surroundings.[6] Anne's imaginative approach to her mundane duties is also an act of authorship, setting her apart once again from the less empowered girl heroines who came before her.

What makes Anne Shirley such a beloved character, what makes her memorable, what makes her unique? Of many possible answers, her imagination is perhaps the most obvious. In her imaginative life, Anne rewrites the mundane elements of her daily life as Romance. When faced with didacticism, she "wave[s] the moral inconsequently aside and seize[s] only on the delightful possibilities" (*Green Gables* 107). She claims authorship of social rules and expectations by imagining them out to their most extreme conclusions, and then enjoying them. She turns respect for elders into a pleasure when she imagines the most debasing possible apology to offer Mrs. Lynde; Marilla feels "her scheme of punishment … going askew" when Anne begins to look a bit too "rapt and radiant" (120). In the same way, Anne revels in religious conformity by imagining herself as a cloistered nun with a tragic past, and enjoys the supposed female duty of self-sacrifice when she imagines nursing Diana through smallpox and then dying herself. These imagined scenes (the latter of which, interestingly, take place when Anne is supposed to be cooking) show us how Anne is able to deconstruct the model of feminine perfection and rebuild it to her own liking. She finds romance in the most solemn duties of the ideal woman, thereby negating the confining, individuality-threatening aspects of the model. From imagining pleasure into hypothetical scenes of duty, Anne focuses this transformative process outward

CHRISTIANA R. SALAH

onto her daily life, until Avonlea is deliberately converted, through her agency, into a space where she can be *both* a correct woman *and* a free one. By the time Anne is given the choice of selfishly pursuing her own ambitions or temporarily sacrificing them to support Marilla, Anne is powerful enough to rewrite this sacrifice (the ultimate Christian virtue) as a romantic source of pleasure. "There is no sacrifice," she tells Marilla, "don't you go pitying me ... there is no need for it. I'm heart-glad at the very thought of staying at dear Green Gables" (328).

Toward the end of *Anne of Green Gables*, Anne asks Marilla why women can't be ministers. "I think women would make splendid ministers," Anne announces, after stating that she would like to be one herself (282). What readers have by now perceived is that Anne is already a minister, preaching her creed of broad-mindedness, nature-based spirituality, and romance to everyone she meets, and converting most of them. In fact, Matthew's language, in describing the providential nature of Anne's arrival in Avonlea ("the Almighty saw we needed her"), evokes the idea of God assigning a prophet to convert a particular town (305). Anne tends to the spiritual needs of those with whom she interacts, and she does so through the medium of household life. Women, in Anne's view, would make splendid ministers, because they can pray, preach, *and* "turn to and do the work" (282). In other words, those who have power in the domestic sphere have the power to perceive the spirituality of the everyday, the seeming commonplaces that Anne's vision converts into sites of wonderment.

WORKS CITED

Alcott, Louisa May. *Little Women*. Ed. Anne K. Phillips and Gregory Eiselein. New York: W. W. Norton, 2004.

Beeton, Isabella. *The Book of Household Management*. London: S. O. Beeton, 1861.

Berg, Temma F. "*Anne of Green Gables*: A Girl's Reading." *Such a Simple Little Tale: Critical Responses to* Anne of Green Gables. Ed. Mavis Reimer. Metuchen, NJ: Scarecrow, 1992. 153–64.

Cobbe, Frances Power. *The Duties of Women: A Course of Lectures*. Boston: Geo. H. Ellis, 1884.

Devereux, Cecily. Introduction. *Anne of Green Gables*. By L. M. Montgomery. Peterborough, ON: Broadview, 2004. 12–38.

Flanders, Judith. *Inside the Victorian Home: A Portrait of Domestic Life in Victorian England.* New York: W. W. Norton, 2003.

Gaskell, Elizabeth. *Cranford.* New York: Penguin, 2006.

Jackson, Susan and Eve Kornfield. "The Female *Bildungsroman* in Nineteenth-Century America: Parameters of a Vision." *Such a Simple Little Tale: Critical Responses to Anne of Green Gables.* Ed. Mavis Reimer. Metuchen, NJ: Scarecrow, 1992. 139–52.

Mitchell, Sally. *The New Girl: Girl's Culture in England 1880–1915.* New York: Columbia UP, 1995.

Montgomery, L. M. *Anne of Green Gables.* Ed. Cecily Devereux. Peterborough, ON: Broadview, 2004.

———. *Anne of Avonlea.* Toronto: Bantam, 1981.

———. *Anne of the Island.* New York: Bantam, 1987.

Nodelman, Perry. "Progressive Utopia: Or, How to Grow Up Without Growing Up." *Such a Simple Little Tale: Critical Responses to* Anne of Green Gables. Ed. Mavis Reimer. Metuchen, NJ: Scarecrow, 1992. 29–38.

Rowbotham, Judith. *Good Girls Make Good Wives: Guidance for Girls in Victorian Fiction.* New York: Basil Blackwell, 1989.

Rubio, Mary Henley. "L. M. Montgomery: Scottish-Presbyterian Agency in Canadian Culture." *L.M. Montgomery and Canadian Culture.* Ed. Irene Gammel and Elizabeth Epperly. Toronto: U of Toronto P, 1999. 89–105.

The Young Wife's Book: A Manual of Moral Religious and Domestic Duties. Philadelphia: Carey, Lea, & Blanchard, 1836.

White, Gavin. "The Religious Thought of L. M. Montgomery." *Harvesting Thistles: The Textual Garden of L. M. Montgomery: Essays on Her Novels and Journals.* Ed. Mary Henley Rubio. Guelph, ON: Canadian Children's P, 1994. 84–87.

NOTES

1   This phrase, the title of an 1854 poem
     by Coventry Patmore, was used widely
     throughout the Victorian period and en-
     capsulates the literally inhuman expecta-
     tions placed on women of this era.

2   In *The New Girl*, Sally Mitchell points out
     that while didactic fiction was popular in
     the middle of the nineteenth century,
     by the end of Victoria's reign the divide
     between what girls wanted to read and
     what their elders preferred for them had
     widened somewhat (4). Still, such novels
     were well-liked by girls in the time period
     of Anne's youth, and she is cited as read-
     ing them (see Montgomery, *Green Gables*
     160).

3   In her introduction to the Broadview edi-
     tion, in the section on "Gender and the
     'Feminism' of Anne," Cecily Devereux
     writes that Montgomery's structuring of
     the novel stresses "a growth towards the
     'right' performance of femininity" (21).
     See this section for a summary of critics
     who agree with this assessment.

4   As E. Holly Pike points out in this vol-
     ume, Montgomery used a similar lini-
     ment cake anecdote in one of her early,
     strongly didactic stories. The conspicu-
     ous absence of a heavy-handed moral in
     the later text underscores Montgomery's
     effort to distinguish Anne from heroines
     gone before.

5   Anne does develop some degree of
     friendship with Dorothy Gardner, but
     despite their agreement to stay friends
     after Anne has rejected Roy, Dorothy
     never appears again in the series.

6   For more depth on this topic, see Temma
     F. Berg's discussion of naming and female
     empowerment in "Anne of Green Gables:
     A Girl's Reading" (157) and Melissa
     Mullins's portrayal of Anne as a poet re-
     envisioning her world, in this volume.

CHAPTER ELEVEN

The Ethos of Nurture: Revisiting Domesticity in L. M. Montgomery's *Anne of Green Gables*

Monika Hilder

Often applauded or disparaged, the subject of domesticity in L. M. Montgomery's *Anne of Green Gables* bears revisiting. On the one hand, *Anne* articulates woman's "rightful sphere" as mistress of the hearth, maternal keeper of kith and kin within the "narrow" parameters of the home. Anne is socialized into appropriately feminine housekeeping skills and, in the end, she chooses to postpone her education to care for Marilla at Green Gables. Later in the series, she even exchanges her academic and literary ambitions for the role of wife and mother. On the other hand, Anne's socialization occurs alongside strong encouragement for her ambitious academic and literary goals, which concern most of the first novel. The trajectory of Anne's coming-of-age raises the question, perhaps a rhetorical one, as to what extent L. M. Montgomery is beholden to the "colonization" of females as domestic servants of lesser value. Is Anne diminished by domesticity or is she not? Is Montgomery complicit with sexist patriarchy or does she offer a frequently overlooked view of domesticity as the humane heroic? In light of the achievements of recent feminist and other post-colonial criticism, these questions demand reconsideration.

For some critics, Anne's life path is yet another example of denigrated women who subject themselves, or are subjected, to patriarchal power through marriage. T. D. MacLulich criticizes Montgomery's "acquiescence to the secondary and largely domestic role her society traditionally assigned to women," arguing that the author's "thoroughly domestic imagination" made her prefer "traditional women's roles." Montgomery, like her heroines, "repeatedly ... minister[ed] to others rather than str[iving] after her own personal fulfillment" (464). He regards Anne's later choice to define herself primarily in terms of marriage and motherhood rather than literary creativity as "disappointing," "a failure ... of both the literary and the social imagination" (466). Similarly, Gillian Thomas speaks of the "decline" of Anne from the "spirited individualist" in the first book to a "dreary conformist" (24), "the willing victim of social convention" (25) in marriage and family. To her, the original Anne would not find in her later self a "kindred spirit" (28).[1]

Alternatively, some critics read Anne's life path as Montgomery's affirmation of an important, even powerful, femininity. Temma F. Berg speaks of Avonlea as "a town of Amazons" and the *Anne* books as "convey[ing] a subtle but revolutionary feminism which has empowered generations of young girls" (163). Shirley Foster and Judy Simons regard *Anne* as "revisionist" fiction that "deconstructs essentialist notions of gender . . . from a feminized perspective" (153, 161–62). Carole Gerson speaks of Montgomery's "message of responsible self-empowerment" (32); Patricia Kelly Santelmann notes the "community value of good housekeeping" and the overall power of female speech (65, 69); and Susan Drain regards Anne's choice to stay home with Marilla, as well as pursue her education and writing, as a construction of her own unconventional female identity (46–47). Similarly, Janet Weiss-Townsend rejects the reading of *Anne of Green Gables* as sexist and emphasizes Anne's unconventional traits, such as the aggression with which she pursues her dreams, independence, practicality, and imagination (110–11). Cecily Devereux makes the compelling argument that Anne's story celebrates a maternal feminism along the lines of the contemporary ideological vision of "imperial motherhood," a site of political power.

Since these two oppositional responses to female domesticity as either patriarchal repression or female liberation may bring us to a kind of impasse, I think it is worthwhile to revisit Montgomery's achievement in the spirit of post-colonial discourse that seeks to liberate silenced voices. Genuine feminist methodology, as Gillian Beer and Annette Kolodny have cautioned, does not colonize a text with our meanings but serves to free readers from prejudice and blindness (qtd. in Foster and Simons xii, 31). Similarly, as Julia McQuillan and Julie Pfeiffer remind us, "One of the central projects of feminist criticism has been

MONIKA HILDER

to rediscover and reinterpret works of fiction lost in patriarchal assumptions of female inadequacies" (17). Whereas some gender critics view female domesticity in marriage as imprisonment and a kind of death (see Carolyn Heilbrun qtd. in Campbell 142), L. M. Montgomery herself spoke of wifehood and motherhood as the highest of divine and natural callings ("Famous Author" 379–80).

Notably, nineteenth-century readers did not necessarily gender "feminine" traits and spheres as we now tend to, or assume that people have in the past. For instance, many men read girls' fiction (Foster and Simons 3–9), and in *Uncle Tom's Cabin*, for example, Harriet Beecher Stowe depicts the very masculine Tom as having "to the full, the gentle, domestic heart" (144), evidence of his spiritual maturity. As Elizabeth Rollins Epperly observes, Montgomery "[f]ollow[s] the best of nineteenth-century tradition" in "enshrin[ing] home as a sacred centre for family and the developing self" (211). In Epperly's view, Montgomery regards heroism for both genders in terms of "the (female) principles of cooperation and interconnection [that] best sustain the individual and the community" (248). Because we wrestle with a more fragmented view of domesticity and gender informed by an either/or mentality, a framework that limits women, some critics rigidly value domesticity as a lesser form of labour. But nineteenth-century female writers such as Montgomery and Stowe held a more holistic view, a both/ and perspective that honoured and considered domesticity as an ethos apart from gender and therefore a site for human empowerment. This discussion has important implications for how we read the past and the present, as well as how we choose to design the possible future.

In the spirit, then, of reassessing our values and assumptions, in this chapter I will consider domesticity as an ethos of nurture that transcends gender and therefore may subvert and transform sexism. I will argue that Montgomery's celebration of *domesticity*, best characterized as *an ethos of personal nurture for others*, helps twenty-first-century readers reconsider what values we tend to privilege, the traditionally viewed "masculine" values of reason, autonomy, activity, aggression, and egotistical power of classical heroism, and which values we tend to disparage, the traditionally viewed "feminine" values of imagination, interdependence, passivity, care, and humility of Christian heroism. In particular, I will argue that, unlike commerce, domesticity in *Anne of Green Gables* and other *Anne* books celebrates this transcendent ethos of nurture or care as the genuinely heroic way to live. In addition to the various female figures who exhibit this heroism (Marilla, Rachel Lynde, Miss Stacy, Mrs. Allan, Anne, and Diana), it is especially noteworthy that male figures, of whom Matthew Cuthbert is the best example, illustrate features ordinarily linked with the "feminine" and the "domestic" – gentleness, shyness, attentiveness to the importance of aesthetics, emotional nurture, selflessness, and commitment to family. This linkage is crucial to consider because Montgomery celebrates a domesticity that is, in some important ways, essentially non-gendered. Her vision of domesticity embraces all of humanity.

The tension between "masculine" classical heroism and "feminine" Christian heroism cannot be over-emphasized. Whereas classical heroism espouses conquest, Christian heroism espouses nurture. Whereas the classical hero wins through physical and/or intellectual power, the spiritual hero wins through humility and love. To illustrate archetypal heroes with biblical value systems: the teenager David slays the giant, and the apparent criminal Jesus dies and saves the world. Montgomery's subversion of the boundary between female domesticity and male commerce is rooted in this Judeo-Christian meta-narrative, in which humility is the central virtue. In doing so, she asks us to move beyond the view that "female" domesticity is inferior to "active masculinity," of primacy in the outside world of commerce and politics. Humility, then, becomes a kind of "agency,"[2] which challenges the familiar dichotomy of passivity/activity. While the classical "male" world of commerce tends to commodify and so devalue human life (e.g., relationships and emotion), the Christian "female" world of domesticity affirms it. Certainly Matthew's central role as a nurturer problematizes a feminist reading of *Anne of Green Gables* in interesting ways, returning us to the deep concerns of how we silence through "patriarchal" assumptions, as well as liberate through strategic re-readings.

L. M. Montgomery addresses the notion of domesticity as an inferior female state throughout the *Anne* books. The young Anne of Green Gables enthusiastically dreams of fame and adventure beyond conventional domesticity: "Oh, I would dearly love to be remarkable" (*Green Gables* 228). When she ultimately chooses the "narrow path" (332) of nurturing Marilla in Avonlea instead of continuing formal education at college, and later exchanges a career in writing for motherhood – "I'm writing living epistles now" (*Anne of Ingleside* 268) – the author invites her readers to consider the ethos of care. Does domesticity diminish women? The author points to this question with gentle irony when Anne as matron reflects on maternal emotion: "We mothers are a foolish race" (*Anne of Ingleside* 160). Similarly, her daughter Rilla observes that in a world of male heroics, "It's a little hard to remember all the heroines" (*Rilla of Ingleside* 148). Clearly, if the virtues associated with the "feminine" are heroic, they often go "unsung" in the "masculine" world of fame and glory. But beyond ironic recognition, Montgomery extols "feminine" virtues in no uncertain terms. In *Anne of Green Gables*, Anne declares that the choice to nurture Marilla at Green Gables is "no sacrifice" (328). Notably, this ethos is not gendered; Gilbert Blythe similarly sacrifices his own interests for Anne and Marilla's sake.[3]

In contradistinction to the laurels that self-interest may bestow, the narrator emphasizes the peace and joy that are rooted in the moral vigour of the choice to nurture others: "[Anne] had looked her duty courageously in the face and found it a friend – as duty ever is when we meet it frankly" (326). In *Anne of Ingleside*, "the joyful mother of five" (2), "the chatelaine" (14), prays for the help that mothers need to guide, love, and understand their children (34). She laughingly dismisses the suggestion that domestic life might be dull (56) as she considers how she "hold[s] all the threads of the Ingleside life in her hands ... to weave into a tapestry of beauty" (55)[4] – the ultimate calling. As Devereux argues, Anne's "path is to be understood as progressive, her taking up of motherhood as a professional decision" ("Writing" 17). Indeed the domestic ideal of "the holy passion of motherhood" (*Anne's House of Dreams* 116) is the realization of a successful quest (Devereux, "not one" 121), never a diminished existence. Anne's life path undoubtedly bears comparison with that of her son, Walter, in *Rilla of Ingleside*. This gifted poet, who has a premonition of dying on the battlefield, believes that he will never write the great poems he once dreamed of writing. Instead he speaks of having won true freedom of spirit, whether he lives or dies, because he has "helped make Canada safe for the poets of the future ... the workers ... the dreamers" (191). As Owen Dudley Edwards comments, Walter's courage has "a feminine quality superior to unthinking masculinity" (129). Self-sacrifice, not self-aggrandizement, constitutes greatness.

In a society defined by the "community value of good housekeeping" (Santelmann 65), one in which Rachel Lynde presides as the paragon of virtue and expertise, Montgomery regards domesticity as a transcendent concept of nurturing human beings first and foremost. For example, when we glimpse Matthew in a domestic act of service, so unobtrusively that one hardly notices him "ha[ving] the fire on and ... the breakfast ready when Marilla came down" (265), we understand that Matthew's nurturance involves quiet, ongoing care for his family. Matthew and Marilla's lifetime habit of care for each other, now extended to Anne, elevates the girl from an orphan – adopted for domestic service – to beloved family member. In other words, she moves from a point of value in a capitalist economy to a new framework of childhood and Christian duty. As

Foster and Simons say, "Green Gables becomes her true home in both an earthly and a spiritual sense" (156). While there may be admittedly "so little scope for imagination in cookery," as Anne observes (167), there is infinite value in the particularity of home and place amongst loved ones. The transitory importance of political power, which attracts Marilla and Rachel briefly, wanes beside the lasting intimacy of "Anne and Matthew [who] had the cheerful kitchen at Green Gables all to themselves" (179–80). Home takes centre stage. What indeed can matter more than the loving family circle at the heartbeat of life? Clearly, for Montgomery, true heroes exchange "patriarchal" values of fame and self-fulfillment for the transcendent need to nurture and, in turn, be nurtured by others.

In *Anne of Green Gables*, many female characters exhibit this heroism of nurture, and the women who do not merely heighten the heroism of the women who do. Rachel Lynde, though at first "properly horrified" (Ch. 9 title) by Anne and regarded as "a meddlesome old gossip" (117) by Matthew, is a key matriarch who understands that "flesh and blood don't come under the head of arithmetic" (235). She shows increasing care for Anne. Miss Stacy and Mrs. Allan are central mentors in Anne's life. Diana is a soulmate. The story is a chronicle of Marilla's journey from a stern rationalism to a widening experience of emotional depth. The unaccustomed "throb of maternity she had missed, perhaps" (123) intensifies until she at last verbalizes her love for Anne after Matthew's passing:

"Oh, Anne, I know I've been kind of strict and harsh with you maybe – but you mustn't think I didn't love you as well as Matthew did, for all that.... It's never been easy for me to say things out of my heart, but, at times like this it's easier. I love you as dear as if you were my own flesh and blood and you've been my joy and comfort every since you came to Green Gables." (322)

The bad mother figures like Mrs. Peter Blewett, as Devereux notes, are foils to the good ones ("Writing" 17–18). Certainly lesser or non-nurturing women, like prejudiced and "cold, sullen" Mrs. Barry (172), "selfish old" Miss Barry (269), and the earlier Marilla – all redeemed by the impact of Anne's spirit – serve as warnings on how not to live in the quest for wholeness. In addition to the various nurturing female figures in the story, Matthew Cuthbert is the living embodiment of domesticity. I turn now to how his exemplification of the ethos of nurture impacts our reading of the novel as a whole.

Matthew Cuthbert, "the shyest man alive [who] hated to have to go among strangers or to any place where he might have to talk" (54), "an odd-looking personage" (61) who "had looked at twenty very much as he looked at sixty" (62), is the prototype for unobtrusive male figures in a seemingly matriarchal Avonlea. Along with Gilbert Blythe, who is also emotionally astute and quiet, Matthew exhibits many qualities associated with the "feminine."[5] He is a listener, whereas the women are talkers; he is sympathetic, whereas they are decidedly pragmatic; he is apparently submissive, whereas they are assertive; and he is, on the whole, gentle, whereas they are aggressive. As "shy and silent" (55) as his father before him, similar to Thomas Lynde, who is referred to as "a meek little man whom Avonlea people called 'Rachel Lynde's husband'" (54), Matthew is "ludicrously afraid" of Anne at first (64). He "dreaded all women except Marilla and Mrs. Rachel [because of] an uncomfortable feeling that the mysterious creatures were secretly laughing at him" (61). He manifests the self-consciousness that we associate with femininity today. Matthew is truly a person set apart from the socially engaged and dominantly verbal world of prominent women like Marilla and Rachel Lynde. Whereas the women speak and pride themselves on airing competent opinions, he is typically modest and unassuming in his relationship with Anne. When asked of what the wild plum tree in bloom makes him think, he answers simply, "Well now, I dunno" (65). Matthew is the epitome of the unassuming "lesser" being, who on the surface defers all decisions to Marilla. His apparently weaker position is illustrated in the low visibility he chooses to have at Green Gables:

> As a general thing Matthew gravitated between the kitchen and the little bedroom off the hall where he slept; once in a while he ventured uncomfortably into the parlor or sitting-room when the minister came to tea. But he had never been up-stairs in his own house since the spring he helped Marilla paper the spare bedroom ... four years ago. (118)

He is the archetype of the domestic servant whose low profile invites thoughtful consideration in light of recent feminist and other post-colonial criticism. Is he "colonized" by his matriarchal society, Marilla in particular? To what extent does he successfully subvert this hegemony, and liberate himself and others in the process?

As some have commented, Matthew may be regarded as "a victim of gender ideology" (Foster and Simon 163), associated with "'the masculine tyranny' of Calvinism" (Gay 105). "Just like a woman," Matthew is a gentle listener who is emotionally attuned to Anne. And Marilla, "just like a patriarch," sometimes disparages his emotional connection with Anne as "most ridiculous" (*Green Gables* 84) and "queer" (85); "he's listening to her like a perfect ninny. I never saw such an infatuated man," Marilla declares (136). But Anne affirms Matthew's sensitivity, praising him as "a kindred spirit" (84), and explains to Marilla the depth of communication or communion that such kindred spirits have. "Matthew and I," Anne says, "are such kindred spirits I can read his thoughts without words at all" (183). She continues, "You didn't know just how I felt about it, but you see Matthew did. Matthew understands me, and it's so nice to be understood, Marilla" (191).[6]

Significantly, Matthew exercises the role of unconditional love and grace in Anne's life. Just as he cannot bear to tell Anne about the "mistake" of her adoption (64), because he feels that to do so would be akin to murdering an innocent creature (73), so he continues to mediate on her behalf. He urges Marilla to adopt her and consistently counters her rigid approach to punitive childrearing with his emphasis on compassion. While he agrees that Marilla should be in charge of her discipline, he cautions, "Only be as good and kind to her as you can be without spoiling her. I kind of think she's one of the sort you can do anything with if you only get her to love you" (98). This radical emphasis on loving compassion as the highest and only truly effective mode of child care is echoed in the incident of Anne's apology to Mrs. Lynde. He counsels compassion: "Don't be too hard on her, Marilla. Recollect she hasn't ever had any one to teach her right" (117). When Anne looks "small and unhappy" in her room, "Matthew's heart smote him" (118), and he gently asks her, "Anne, how are you making it, Anne?" (118). With the incident of the missing amethyst brooch, "he could not so quickly lose faith in [her]" (142), and again points to mercy: "Well now, she's such a little thing. And there should be allowances made, Marilla. You know she's never had any bringing up" (146). He is the embodiment of love at the heartbeat of life.

Instead of scolding, he puts down his tea and takes time to listen to Anne's fairy story (164). As he was from the start, declaring her to be "a real interesting

MONIKA HILDER

thing" (80), Matthew remains fascinated by Anne's effervescent imagination. He cherishes thinking about how he will provide for Anne (239). He esteems her virtuous character as being of utmost importance: "She's smart and pretty, and loving too, which is better than all the rest" (305). He has unfailing loving pride in Anne and is unafraid to voice it, even if it is the softest suggestion: "'Reckon you're glad we kept her, Marilla?' whispered Matthew" (315). As he declares on his last night, and in the same breath repairs gender inequity,

> "Well now, I'd rather have you than a dozen boys, Anne. Just mind you that – rather than a dozen boys. Well now, I guess it wasn't a boy that took the Avery scholarship, was it? It was a girl – my girl – my girl that I'm proud of." (318)

Anne's memory of this, like that of his last "shy smile" (318), is her legacy, her inheritance of love and identity. As the narrator says in *Anne of Avonlea*, while others may have "forgotten quiet, shy, unimportant Matthew Cuthbert," Anne "could never forget the kind old man who had been the first to give her the love and sympathy her starved childhood had craved" (125).[7]

Importantly, Matthew's unassuming "feminine" ways, practiced with remarkable tenacity, subvert and ultimately transform the bold confrontational "masculine" modes of behaviour. His whispers and silences carry tremendous weight in the novel, suggesting perhaps a different idea of patriarchal power. Unlike the patriarch who imposes his will with verbal confidence, much in the style of Marilla, Matthew clings to his ideas "with the most amazing silent persistency – a persistency ten times more potent and effectual in its very silence than if he had talked it out" (84). As Marilla's complaint about his subversive weapon of silence suggests, it works. In her words, "I wish he was like other men and would talk things out. A body could answer back then and argue him into reason. But what's to be done with a man who just *looks*?" (86). Verbally expressed reason, or rationalism, then proves an inferior weapon in Montgomery's world; love alone, as embodied in Matthew's looks and silences, and sometimes soft words, all the more powerful for their rarity, is what overcomes evil and heals the world. Whereas Marilla's attempts at bold matriarchy in imposing her will on Anne often fail, Matthew's subversive gentleness ("with the air of a burglar [he] crept up-stairs" (118)) wins the girl's heart.

Anne returns Matthew's nurture in countless ways. When he counsels her to apologize to Mrs. Lynde, she responds, "I'd do anything for you – if you really want me to" (119). She resolves to match her political affiliation with his (181). When Anne learns the happy news about her tie for first place in final examinations at Queen's, her first thought is to run to tell Matthew (293), showing that she views her achievements as partially *his*. She overcomes her stage fright at the hotel recital with the resolve to not disappoint him (301). As she declares to Marilla, "I shall always be your little Anne, who will love you and Matthew and dear Green Gables more and better every day of her life" (304). Gay suggests that the women in the story have overcome the patriarchal Calvinistic qualities of "harshness and rigidity" with female qualities of "networking" (106), but I would argue that the women at times mirror patriarchal harshness and rigidity, and that Matthew, rather, offers a model of gentle leadership from which Marilla and others learn. Notably, Matthew's sacrifice shows Anne her Christian duty; she remains at Green Gables to minister to Marilla. Matthew is a meek patriarch, whom they all respect, who disconnects notions of aggression and colonization from patriarchy, replacing them with gentleness and emotional responsiveness.

Matthew's domesticity is kindred to Anne's sentiments because he values aesthetics and imagination. Whereas Marilla begins as "a woman of narrow experience and rigid conscience" (57), who is "always slightly distrustful of sunshine, which seemed to her too dancing and irresponsible a thing for a world which was meant to be taken seriously" (56), Matthew finds Anne "real interesting" (80), and does not dismiss female aesthetics. When, like Sleeping Beauty, the bewitched Matthew awakens to the beauty of female dress and endeavours to satisfy Anne's dreams of the same, Rachel Lynde enthusiastically muses, "I'm sure the child must feel the difference between her clothes and the other girls'. But to think of Matthew taking notice of it! That man is waking up after being asleep for over sixty years" (235).[8] The beautiful dress that he gives Anne for Christmas echoes the morning glory of the created world in which Anne exalts, mirroring the novel's Christian understanding of nature as a manifestation of divine glory. Also, Matthew awakens to and affirms what the narrator describes as Anne's "birthright of fancy" (334), correcting Marilla's hope that she be cured of imagination. He cautions Anne, "Don't give up all your romance, Anne, a little of it is a good thing – not too much, of course – but keep a little of it, Anne, keep a little of it" (262).

Significantly, the very setting of Green Gables is emblematic of Matthew's aesthetic sensibilities. The "orchard-embowered house," set as far away from society as Matthew Cuthbert's father could arrange (54), suggests a gender reversal. The homestead is now a "male" retreat of domesticity, the security of hearth and home, away from the active "female" bustle of matriarchal (or "patriarchal," as it may be alternatively read) society. Unlike Carol Gilligan, who expresses a gendered view of psychosexual traits, Montgomery, as Berg has pointed out, conflates traits because "[m]en and women alike have to wrestle with contrary impulses" (Berg 162). Furthermore, the "sweet old-fashioned flowers which his mother had planted in the homestead garden in her bridal days and for which Matthew had always had a secret, wordless love" (320) are emblematic of his association with "feminine" qualities. Like these white Scotch roses "so small and sweet on their thorny stems" (323), so Matthew's shy, unassuming life of service and deep feeling is a legacy of love that is far-reaching, nourishing Anne and so, in turn, generations to come. Anne's musing that in heaven "[p]erhaps the souls of all those little white roses that he has loved so many summers were all there to meet him" (323) underscores the deep care that Matthew has exhibited all his days. If this deep care is also dark, it is arguably the darkness of self-sacrifice that enables love to thrive.

Always "a good, kind brother" (321) who never shirked from his "masculine" role as provider and caregiver, as Marilla attests, Matthew embodies the selfless commitment that Anne then chooses to show Marilla at the end of the story. And just as the flower metaphor links Matthew with Anne, who is often compared to white narcissus (281), so this practice of care is depicted as a "narrow" path along which bloom "flowers of quiet happiness" (332). Devereux has noted that this is an allusion to a line in John Greenleaf Whittier's "Among the Hills" ("Flowers spring to blossom where she walks / The careful ways of duty"), an American settler poem in which "the woman softens the rough life of the 'homestead'" (Green Gables 332). But Montgomery's use of it here underscores the fact that she celebrates domesticity in ways that transcend cultural constructions of gender, a domesticity that is not so much restriction as Christian empowerment, a Christianity informed by Romanticism. Matthew's quiet life of care points to the countercultural principle of interdependence: as the narrator notes, "All things great are wound up with all things little" (179). And it is no coincidence that Anne's peace over Matthew's earthly life well-lived – one that extends into eternity and points to the connectedness between generations – is followed by her exuberant view of this world as sublime: "'Dear old world,' she murmured, 'you are lovely, and I am glad to be alive in you'"(331). This view is what prepares her to seek Gilbert's love at last (331). Love for others, not self-aggrandizement, is the heroic vision of Montgomery's world.

Moreover, Matthew's ethos of nurture undoes the hegemony of the outside world of commerce and politics. As mentioned above and elsewhere (Hilder 51, Kornfeld and Jackson 150, McQuillan and Pfeiffer 19), domesticity of this kind is deeply antithetical to capitalism. Unlike the utilitarian world at the turn of the century, in which orphans were regarded as commercial property and females had a decidedly lower economic value in a rural community like Prince Edward Island, Matthew from the start regards Anne with an unconditional caring attitude, as a human being whom he ought to nurture. When Marilla asks the utilitarian question, "What good would she be to us?" (80), and insists that Anne, like any commercial product that fails to satisfy, has "got to be despatched straight-way back to where she came from" (81), Matthew opposes this rationalistic ethos with the moral challenge, "We might be some good to her" (80). Significantly, he later identifies Anne's presence in their lives as coming from the heart of God: "She's been a blessing to us, and there never was a luckier mistake... if it *was* luck. I don't believe it was any such thing. It was Providence, because the Almighty saw we needed her, I reckon" (305). With his strong commitment to family as an immeasurable blessing characteristic of divine design, also articulated by Marilla in her declaration of love for Anne, Matthew helps form Anne's character and destiny as a whole person rooted in love. After the hotel concert she easily rejects the lure of materialism:

"I don't want to be any one but myself, even if I go uncomforted by diamonds all my life. I'm quite content to be Anne of Green Gables with my string of pearl beads. I know Matthew gave me as much love with them as ever went with Madame the Pink Lady's jewels." (302–03)

And after lingering at his grave she affirms the beauty of the world, her joy at being alive (331), and faith in ultimate wellness: "God's in his heaven, all's right with the world" (334). Arguably, Matthew is not so much "a victim of gender ideology" after all, but a hero who successfully subverts capitalism and liberates Anne and others in the process.

So the sweet (or not so sweet?) story of *Anne of Green Gables*, regarded by some as female diminishment, may be alternatively read as a story of female and, moreover, *human* empowerment. The story could be summed up as a daughter replacing the Christian patriarch who sacrifices for her. She, in turn, passes on this same torch of genuine love. Regardless of our conclusions over this contentious question, certainly revisiting Montgomery's one-hundred-year-old classic invites us to consider that the dismissal of domesticity as inferior is "a form of 'cultural loss of memory'" (Suzanne Clark qtd. in Rubio 167). As McQuillan and Pfeiffer point out, "Feminism does not necessarily condemn conventionally 'female' choices" (29). Similarly, in the words of feminist writer Barbara Risman, traditionally female values construct communities:

> The most important lesson I have learned, and from my mother, is that our post-gender families must elevate the traditionally female values of nurturing and homemaking above all else – for it is this work, what women have always done, that turns isolated individuals into families and communities, brick and mortar in[to] hearth and home, and gives meaning to our lives. (qtd. in McQuillan and Pfeiffer 29)

Alternatively, considering domesticity as a subversive celebration of the non-gendered ethos of nurture invites us to not only recover cultural memory, but raise consciousness of the ways in which we may either silence or give voice to the ethos of personal nurture for others. In L. M. Montgomery's world, heroism has a humble and loving, paradoxically quieter and more powerful, face.

WORKS CITED

Berg, Temma F. "*Anne of Green Gables*: A Girl's Reading." *Such a Simple Little Tale: Critical Responses to L. M. Montgomery's Anne of Green Gables*. Ed. Mavis Reimer. Metuchen, N.J., and London: Children's Literature Association and Scarecrow, 1992. 153–64.

Campbell, Marie. "Wedding Bells and Death Knells: The Writer as Bride in the *Emily Trilogy*." *Harvesting Thistles: The Textual Garden of L. M. Montgomery*. Ed. Mary Henley Rubio. Guelph, ON: Canadian Children's P, 1994. 137–45.

Devereux, Cecily. "Introduction." *Anne of Green Gables*. By L. M. Montgomery. Peterborough, ON: Broadview, 2004. 12–38.

———. "'Not one of those dreadful new women': Anne Shirley and the culture of imperial motherhood." *Windows and Words: A Look at Canadian Children's Literature in English*. Ed. Aïda Hudson and Susan-Ann Cooper. Ottawa: U of Ottawa P, 2003. 119–30.

———. "Writing with a 'Definite Purpose': L. M. Montgomery, Nellie L. McClung and the Politics of Imperial Motherhood in Fiction for Children." *Canadian Children's Literature* 99 (2000): 6–22.

Drain, Susan. "Feminine Convention and Female Identity: The Persistent Challenge of *Anne of Green Gables*." *Canadian Children's Literature* 65 (1992): 40–47.

Edwards, Owen Dudley. "L. M. Montgomery's *Rilla of Ingleside*: Intention, Inclusion, Implosion." *Harvesting Thistles: The Textual Garden of L. M. Montgomery*. Ed. Mary Henley Rubio. Guelph, ON: Canadian Children's P, 1994. 126–36.

Epperly, Elizabeth Rollins. *The Fragrance of Sweet-Grass: L. M. Montgomery's Heroines and the Pursuit of Romance*. Toronto: U of Toronto P, 1992.

Foster, Shirley and Judy Simons. *What Katy Read: Feminist Re-Readings of 'Classic' Stories for Girls*. Iowa City: U of Iowa P, 1995.

Gay, Carole. "'Kindred Spirits' All: Green Gables Revisited." *Such a Simple Little Tale: Critical Responses to L. M. Montgomery's Anne of Green Gables*. Ed. Mavis Reimer. Metuchen, N.J., and London: Children's Literature Association and Scarecrow, 1992. 101–8.

Gerson, Carole. "'Fitted to Earn Her Own Living': Figures of The New Woman in the Writing of L. M. Montgomery." *Children's Voices in Atlantic Literature and Culture: Essays on Childhood*. Ed. Hilary Thompson. Guelph, ON: Canadian Children's P, 1995. 24–34.

Gilligan, Carol. *In a Different Voice: Psychological Theory and Women's Development*. Cambridge: Harvard UP, 1982.

Hilder, Monika B. "'That Unholy Tendency to Laughter': L. M. Montgomery's Iconoclastic Affirmation of Faith in *Anne of Green Gables*." *Canadian Children's Literature* 113–14 (Spring/Summer 2004): 34–55.

Kornfeld, Eve, and Susan Jackson. "The Female Bildungsroman in Nineteenth-Century America: Parameters of a Vision." *Such a Simple Little Tale: Critical Responses to L. M. Montgomery's* Anne of Green Gables. Ed. Mavis Reimer. Metuchen, NJ, and London: Children's Literature Association and the Scarecrow, 1992. 139–52.

MacLulich, T. D. "L.M. Montgomery's Portraits of the Artist: Realism, Idealism, and the Domestic Imagination." *English Studies in Canada* 11.4 (1985): 459–73.

McQuillan, Julia and Julie Pfeiffer. "Why Anne Makes us Dizzy: Reading *Anne of Green Gables* from a Gender Perspective." *Mosaic* 34.2 (2001): 17–32.

Montgomery, L. M. *Anne of Avonlea.* 1909. Toronto: Seal, 1984.

———. *Anne of Green Gables.* 1908. Ed. Cecily Devereux. Peterborough, ON: Broadview, 2004.

———. *Anne's House of Dreams. 1922. Toronto: Seal, 1983.*

———. *Anne of Ingleside.* 1939. Toronto: Seal, 1983.

———. "Famous Author and Simple Mother." 1925. *Anne of Green Gables.* Ed. Cecily Devereux. Peterborough, ON: Broadview, 2004. 379–84.

———. *Rilla of Ingleside.* 1920. Toronto: Seal, 1987.

Robinson, Laura M. "'Pruned down and branched out': Embracing Contradiction in *Anne of Green Gables.*" *Children's Voices in Atlantic Literature and Culture: Essays on Childhood.* Ed. Hilary Thompson. Guelph, ON: Canadian Children's P, 1995. 35–43.

Rubio, Jennie. "'Strewn with Dead Bodies': Women and Gossip in *Anne of Ingleside.*" *Harvesting Thistles: The Textual Garden of L. M. Montgomery.* Ed. Mary Henley Rubio. Guelph, ON: Canadian Children's P, 1994. 167–77.

Santelmann, Patricia Kelly. "Written as Women Write: *Anne of Green Gables* within the Female Literary Tradition." *Harvesting Thistles: The Textual Garden of L. M. Montgomery.* Ed. Mary Henley Rubio. Guelph, ON: Canadian Children's P, 1994. 64–73.

Stowe, Harriet Beecher. 1852. *Uncle Tom's Cabin.* New York: Simon & Schuster, 2002.

Thomas, Gillian. "The Decline of Anne: Matron vs. Child." *Such a Simple Little Tale: Critical Responses to L. M. Montgomery's* Anne of Green Gables. Ed. Mavis Reimer. Metuchen, NJ, and London: Children's Literature Association and Scarecrow, 1992. 23–28.

Weiss-Townsend, Janet. "Sexism Down on the Farm? *Anne of Green Gables.*" *Such a Simple Little Tale: Critical Responses to L. M. Montgomery's* Anne of Green Gables. Ed. Mavis Reimer. Metuchen, NJ, and London: Children's Literature Association and Scarecrow, 1992. 109–17.

NOTES

1　Commenting on Gillian Thomas's view of the subsequent *Anne* novels as "progressively unsatisfactory" because Anne exchanges writing ambitions for motherhood, Cecily Devereux points out that this is indeed the path Anne has chosen by the end of *Anne of Green Gables* ("Introduction" 22). This choice reinforces the position articulated in this chapter that the values associated with domesticity are pervasive in Montgomery's work and not suggestive of a subsequent "decline."

2　Laura M. Robinson has also argued that Anne's choice to tend to Marilla in her old age may be read as her agency in character construction, rather than conformity to passive victimization.

3　Whereas Drain describes Gilbert as "too good to be true" (45), Berg regards his choice to sacrifice his ambition in order to support others, first his father, and then Anne, in the terms of the qualities often associated with the feminine but in fact better seen as humane (161–62).

4　This is a powerful metaphor that challenges the contemporary view that parents, and mothers in particular, ought not to "micro-manage" their children's lives – that this is debilitating and unnecessary for both generations. In contrast to the current business metaphor of efficiency, Montgomery affirms the artistry of engaged parenthood as healthy and vital. This view is worth comparing to the narrator's claim that "Mothers were the same all through the centuries ... a great sisterhood of love and service ... the remembered and the unremembered alike" (*Anne of Ingleside* 157).

5　Eve Kornfeld and Susan Jackson speak of Montgomery's "'good' (feminized) men" (144) and Carole Gay regards Matthew and Gilbert as "'kindred spirits' who share traditionally women's values ... without becoming emasculated" (104).

6　In consideration of the fact that Marilla declares Anne has "bewitched" Matthew (80), and thinks that she will also be sub-ject to Anne's "spell" (86), it is reasonable to ask to what extent Matthew (as well as Marilla, and others) is "under Anne's influence." And is there a dark side to the girl's influence? Stated most starkly, does Matthew's nurturance of Anne kill him? Since Matthew seems to die in response to his shock over the loss of their life's savings when Abbey Bank fails, it is arguable that intense anguish for one's loved ones can cause death. At the very least, Matthew and Marilla's mutual regard for each other as well as their choice to nurture Anne require self-denial. While this is not "dark" in a moral sense, it may be considered dark in terms of its difficulty.

7　The language of emotional starvation raises the question, does Anne eat Matthew up? As noted above, does Matthew's nurturance of Anne result in his death? While the thought of Anne's craving for love and Matthew's willingness to offer his love can suggest psychological carnivorousness, it can also suggest Christ's sacrificial death. The difference is important. While carnivorousness implies trapping unwilling victims for one's own survival, Christ's sacrifice proposes liberation for the otherwise doomed. Similarly, the sacrament of communion invites the believer to draw strength from the fact of Christ's victorious sacrifice. And unlike the self-contained consumption of carnivorousness, Christ's sacrifice inspires growing circles of selfless love. In the Christian world of L. M. Montgomery, Matthew's nurture of Anne's hunger and Anne's responsiveness in love for him and others suggest this life-giving sacrifice.

8　Matthew's awakening here, together with the description that he "looked at twenty very much as he looked at sixty"(62), suggests sexual connotations when approached from the viewpoint of a Freudian reading. But is subliminal pedophilia a reasonable reading of Matthew's psychology? Another reading, close to the heart of Montgomery's Romanticism, is

that Matthew's latent childlike wonder
is at last aroused. Under Anne's influence, Matthew breaks free from the rigid
interpretation of Calvinism and overall
utilitarianism of his upbringing to enjoy
aesthetics and offer nurture to a child.

CHAPTER TWELVE

Constructing a "New Girl": Gender and National Identity in *Anne of Green Gables* and *Seven Little Australians*

Sharyn Pearce

In an important article entitled "Cultural Studies, New Historicism and Children's Literature," Tony Watkins argues that myths of national identity are woven into children's literature. According to him, L. Frank Baum's *The Wonderful Wizard of Oz* is a quintessentially American text in that it represents a vision of a utopian society that is progressive and oriented to the future, and that encompasses the progress of ordinary self-reliant people. On the other hand, Kenneth Grahame's *The Wind in the Willows* represents a backward-looking myth of English national identity because of its nostalgia for a pre-industrial Arcadia made up entirely of men. Using Watkins' work as a reference point, I should like to examine two quite different texts – L. M. Montgomery's *Anne of Green Gables* (1908) and Ethel Turner's *Seven Little Australians* (1894) – which, like *The Wonderful Wizard of Oz* and *The Wind in the Willows*, were produced around a century ago. My intention here is to examine how these particular texts construct national identity and, more particularly, how gender plays a key role in the mythologizing process.

Certainly the national agenda of a children's novel becomes most visible when distinct national traditions are compared. Without doubt, extra-literary cultural formations shape literary discourse, especially in the realm of children's literature, which is imbued with the notion that children and young adults can be "moulded" into adults of desired ideological orientation or social conditioning. From the beginning of children's literature onward, children's novels have been heavily pedagogical and riddled with the moralism, enthusiasms, and values of their times. Clearly, novels can operate as powerful shapers of children's imaginations and can transmit, consciously or otherwise, myth-like messages about national identity. As Richard Slotkin has observed, "Through myths the psychology and worldview of our cultural ancestors are transmitted to modern descendants, in such a way and with such power that our perception of contemporary reality and our ability to function are directly ... affected" (qtd. in Watkins 185). *Anne of Green Gables* and *Seven Little Australians* are easily the most popular and certainly the most enduring of the early children's novels in Canada and Australia, respectively. *Seven Little Australians*, Ethel Turner's first and most successful novel, is a watershed in Australian children's books because it is urban, nationalistic, and full of memorable characters. Captain Woolcot, his second wife, Esther, his children, Meg, Judy, Pip, Nell, Bunty, Baby, and the General, live in a house on the Parramatta River, near Sydney. This story revolves around the escapades of the children, particularly the strong-minded and rebellious Judy, as well as her older sister, Meg, and her adolescent love affairs. I think we can consider Judy, the hero of Turner's novel, to be like Anne: a New Girl. Both *Seven Little Australians* and *Anne of Green Gables* respond to similar colonial contexts, and they reinforce nationalistic parables by using New Girls to symbolize the future hopes of their respective nations. Parent-child dynamics in both texts establish generational difference and the distinct values of the New Girls as national heroes, both located on the margins of the empire. While Anne and Judy are undoubtedly constrained by a narrow and parochial world, these spirited and assertive girls nonetheless represent a distinctive movement away from the imperial centre to the development of an independent cultural identity. Anne and Judy diverge from the imperial "ideal" girl by refusing to conform to prescribed gender roles. And so both novels vividly inform readers about what it means to be a girl in two of the most rapidly developing nations of the British Empire, at a time when emerging national pride and often aggressive literary nationalism created the need for youthful, independent cultural heroes.

THE COMMONWEALTH CONNECTION

The choice of these seminal texts is, I trust, an apposite one. While *Anne of ·Green Gables* is most usually thought of as an iconic Canadian text, it has often been compared with other seminal North American works. It has been bracketed most frequently with Louisa May Alcott's *Little Women*, but comparisons have also been made with other American versions of the nineteenth-century female bildungsroman, such as Kate Wiggin's *Rebecca of Sunnybrook Farm* (see, for example, Kornfeld and Jackson). A different comparative approach is just as intriguing and potentially even more insightful, but it has, until now, received scant scholarly attention. Both Canada and Australia have broadly similar historical narratives, both far-flung British colonies that later became members of the British Commonwealth of Nations. Both countries contained settler communities from the British Isles struggling to cope with harsh new conditions and to contain the indigenous "Other." Over time, both Canada and Australia began to evolve substantially different national identities from that of the Mother Country. Both countries consisted of immigrants searching for a new sense of "Home," and in so doing, both countries happened to produce iconic texts centring upon female protagonists for whom home has a poignant value.

Surely *Anne of Green Gables* and *Seven Little Australians* are emblematic of the countries that produced them. When these texts were first published, both Canada and Australia were culturally and politically dependent upon Britain: the British Commonwealth then spanned one-quarter of the globe, and accounted for one-quarter of the world's inhabitants (see Lee). Then, as now, these two colonial nations shared – for the most part – a common language and history through the experience of British rule. Moreover, at a time when most children's literature emanated from England, and when British literature was the dominant "norm" against which "local" Commonwealth literature was measured, both these texts were immediate bestsellers in their countries of origin. For example, when Ethel Turner's *Seven Little Australians* was first published in 1894, it created a literary sensation. The Australian edition was sold out in seven weeks, and it was reprinted every year for the next twenty years (Pearce 11). The novel has never been out of print, and it has spawned radio plays, a film, an award-winning television series, and even a musical. Similarly, *Anne of Green Gables* reached an exceedingly broad Canadian readership, selling over nineteen thousand copies in its first five months of publication (Gammel and Epperly 10), and being reprinted sixteen times in its first two years (Devereux 11). Its unbroken multiple print history, together with its numerous spin-offs, is unprecedented for a Canadian children's story. Both novels thus instantly resonated with local audiences, with *Anne of Green Gables* reaching a huge international audience as well (*Seven Little Australians* experienced moderate success overseas, but its fame mostly resides in Australia).

Both *Seven Little Australians* and *Anne of Green Gables* are the products of a specific time and place, and a recognizable discourse of national self-representation, together with contemporary politics concerning nation and race, is embedded in each. Ethel Turner was only twenty-one when she wrote Australia's best-known and best-loved children's story about the adventures of a family of seven children living on the outskirts of Sydney. Turner was a strong patriot; this young writer was mentored by A. G. Stephens, literary editor of the Sydney *Bulletin*, a weekly magazine that espoused an aggressive literary nationalism and an equally vehement republicanism. The *Bulletin*, and Stephens himself, had a broad impact upon the production of Australian literature, and in dictating the tastes of the Australian literary public. It is generally agreed that the *Bulletin* was responsible for the birth of genuinely "Australian" writing, including the careers of iconic Australian writers like Henry Lawson and "Banjo" Paterson, whose tales of the Australian bush responded to the magazine's drive for native-born-and-bred cultural heroes (Pearce 11). Furthermore, A. G. Stephens placed Turner as one of the leading figures in Australia's literary flowering, and remarked that few other writers had created "such moving emotional art" (qtd. in White 53).

Numerous critics have linked Montgomery with nationalistic fervour. Mavis Reimer has noted that within twenty years of the publication of *Anne of Green Gables*, critics regarded Montgomery as a member of "the first authentically Canadian, self-conscious school of national literature," corresponding to a growing sentiment among Canadian authors "that life around them was as interesting as that in England or the United States" (qtd. in Reimer 176). More recently, Thomas MacLulich has argued that Montgomery was part of the early-twentieth-century Canadian writers who "start[ed] to free themselves from a highly class-conscious or European view of literature, and beg[an] to create a body of fiction that [was] thoroughly North American in spirit" (9). Laura Robinson has decided that Montgomery's novels, by "their setting, their references to domestic politics, and their focus on national identity [are] distinctly Canadian," helping to construct and shape Canadian cultural identity for readers at home and abroad (19). Indeed, Robinson's essay is part of Irene Gammel and Elizabeth Epperly's

1999 collection, which explicitly addresses Montgomery's nationalism and her role in promoting a particular construction of the nation. The editors argue that popular culture has played a significant part in constructing Canadian culture by creating its own cultural genealogies on a grassroots level rather than through the school curriculum. By this means, "Montgomery powerfully intervened in the shaping of Canadian culture, carving out spaces of pleasure" (6), intruding into the space of the national and the political, and ultimately "reconfiguring the official signifiers of Canada" (5–6).

Both novels construct the quintessential identity of the nation by mythologizing an Anglo-Saxon background. Cecily Devereux has argued that *Anne of Green Gables* is "a crucial part of the nation's literary history" (11), and a text that is "firmly embedded in the discourse of Canadianness" (11), that is, the "shared values that underpin nationalism" (11). While Anne's image has become "an identifiable and identificatory motif" of the country (12), more particularly still the text is "part of the iconography of twentieth-century English-Canadian nationalism" (17). As Devereux has noted, further, *Anne of Green Gables* "reproduces a particular vision of the English-Canadian nation as a racially constituted community, a branch of the imperial racial organisation of 'Saxondom'" (23), and Canadians are implicitly presented as "an ethnic grouping that … is located within an Anglo-Celtic settler culture" (23). It is a striking fact that the construction of national culture in both texts is quite narrowly defined, as a particularly Anglo-Saxon racial configuration of "Australianness" is also to be found in Turner's novel. Irish-Australians, like Montgomery's French-Canadians, are largely absent, and when they do appear, they are caricatured as incompetent, untrustworthy, and slatternly servants. Moreover, in both texts, indigenous characters are erased from this peculiarly monocultural view of the nation.

It is clear that both these novels exist within "a specifically ideological framework of emergent nationhood defined ethnically and represented in an imagined community," dominated by Anglo-colonial politics of race and nation (Devereux 23). And in creating this precise ideology of nation, both writers reveal a similar upbringing and outlook. Firstly, they were white, middle-class, and Protestant. And while they were both socially conservative, they were nonetheless keenly aware of the limitations of women's roles in the patriarchal order of the time. Both were to become respectable wives and mothers, and while they strongly adhered to the values of traditional domestic femininity, each yearned, after a fashion, for a less constrained order for women and, in particular, women writers like themselves who were restricted by the patriarchal attitudes of the times.

For both women were also marginalized as children's writers, and while both were eager to move on from that gendered literary ghetto, they received little support from their mentors and publishers. When Turner dared to turn her pen to adult novels, for instance, A. G. Stephens was far from effusive in his praise, declaring that he preferred Turner to "prattle pleasantly" in her charmingly girlish manner within her correct womanly sphere of children's writing (qtd. in White 53). Stephens savaged Turner's work whenever she strayed from her circumscribed area, forcing her to remain writing children's stories, even though she privately declared them worthless: "Never think that fragrant pile of rubbish books lying about the continent is in the least my 'something'; they have just been my bread and butter," she once declared at a particularly jaundiced moment (qtd. in White 51). According to *Anne* scholars, Montgomery's situation was uncannily similar to this; Reimer says that at times Montgomery saw her writing as "an empty achievement" (169), and she was pressured by her publishers to keep up the *Anne* treadmill long after she felt that the lode was exhausted (166). And Carol Gay goes further, arguing that although Montgomery created in her fiction a landscape dominated by "woman's culture," she herself lived in a man's world:

It was a world that brought her pain, confusion, and ultimately, like many other women writers, tragedy. In order to accommodate it, she lived an almost schizophrenic life as a minister's dutiful, full-time wife, while maintaining at the same time an active, full-time career as a professional writer in which she consciously and unconsciously gave free rein to the intellectual and imaginative world she was afraid to reveal as a wife and mother. (107)

Both women were actively engaged with notions of nationalism and identity construction in their literary works, but they were also well aware of the problems that their gender created for them on both a personal and a professional level.

Constructing the "Imperial" Girl

Like the comparisons between Australian and Canadian children's fiction, the adolescent girl in imperial literature has been little investigated to date (the most helpful analysis is Judith Rowbotham's *Good Girls Make Good Wives* [1989]). One of the main reasons for this relative dearth of scholarly attention lies in the fact that this girl did not ever have a high profile in imperialistic children's literature, and she rarely appeared in the highly popular boys' adventure stories that romanticized and valorized the exploits of juvenile male empire builders. For the stereotype of the colonial boy as a courageous and gallant lad is very well-developed indeed. In the colonial children's literature manufactured for British audiences in the late Victorian and Edwardian eras in particular, the typical male adolescent comes from good, solid, Anglo-Saxon stock. He is no intellectual, but he is honest, practical, and self-reliant, and proves to be brave and gallant in the face of pressure. Physical prowess and moral integrity combine to ensure that he is able to rule his social inferiors at "Home" (that is, England) and the lesser races abroad, and he will later put these sterling qualities to the service of the nation. He is a thoroughly responsible lad, conscious of his imperial destiny to colonize another England in a far-flung part of the Empire, and he holds an unchallenged belief in the moral and ethical correctness of this Western imperial expansion. E. L. Haverfield's *Queensland Cousins*, which was published in London in 1908, offers a typical example of this imperial boy. Its hero, Eustace, earns his badge of manhood through a series of potentially life-threatening adventures involving devious and barbaric savages in the Australian Outback. He nonetheless behaves like a gentleman at all times, and is always protective of his mother and sisters.

By comparison, the imperial girl is a colourless, two-dimensional figure, hovering only in the margins of that other staple of the colonial literature diet, the family story. These girls are denied access to the boys' life-threatening but sinew-enhancing dramas, and have a very low profile generally. The typical girl is no quester, and there is no thorny path to womanhood commensurate with the boys' journey to manly self-definition. She remains indoors in almost purdah-like confinement, kept there by her male kin, who are fearful of her defilement by her racial inferiors: "Home," then, is a secure place where young girls avoid contamination by the monstrous "Other." Her destiny lies in her biology, as a future receptacle for further generations of sturdy Anglo-Saxon stock, while her husband carves a future out of the wilderness. As a consequence, for the most part imperial girls stay within the confines of the domestic world, patiently sewing, reading useful works, and being virtuous. While their male equivalents are required to demonstrate that they possess the fierce pluck and dogged tenacity of an imperial male icon, and to reveal unquestioning heroism, chivalry, and a sense of duty at all times, the girl is merely required to give unquestioning support for, and admiration to, all the males in her life. Her role is a traditional "waiting" one, and she appears as a colourless backdrop in the otherwise stirringly colourful panorama of British imperialism at work. In a nutshell, she reveals only too clearly that to be born female is to be born into a world that demands submission, passivity, and dependency – a world, in fact, where girls customarily get the short straw. Once more, *Queensland Cousins* offers a pertinent example of the difference in gender roles in the imperial novel, as Eustace's twin sister, Netta, is a sketchily drawn, largely ornamental creature who loves pretty things, and whose thoughts rarely go beyond an idle interest in clothes and chattering with other girls. Incarcerated within the family home, her future realm, she passively and vapidly awaits her destiny as wife and mother.

The colonial family novel was written for the most part by English writers like E. L. Haverfield who had never visited the colonies but imagined them as a fascinating source of exotic colour. As Rowbotham has noted, these novels were designed for a particular female audience, and were "orientated around a desire to ensure the continuation of a series of values, for the ultimate goal of national and imperial preservation" (210). Girls in these novels rarely deviate from the narrow limits prescribed for English girls who were destined to become English mothers and, hence, the mainstays of the English family. These texts are informed, to a marked extent, by nineteenth-century arguments about the position and role of women in England and the Empire, arguments expressed most fully in John Ruskin's sentimentalizing address "Of Queen's Gardens," in which he disingenuously expounds the notion of the "separate spheres," in order to restrain potentially insurgent women:

> The man's power is active, progressive, defensive. He is eminently the doer, the creator, the discoverer, the defender. His intellect is for speculation and invention, his energy for adventure, for war and for conquest.... But the woman's power is for rule, not for battle, and her intellect is not for invention or recreation, but sweet ordering, arrangement and decision. (71)

This peculiarly nineteenth-century doctrine of the polar differences between the sexes is reinforced by writers like Coventry Patmore, who first coined the term "the Angel in the House," and saw the home as a sanctuary, a haven of spirituality presided over by an ethereal "angel-wife" (321), and the Poet Laureate Alfred Tennyson, who argued against a university education for women and felt that it was in the nation's interests to contain women within their proper domestic sphere:

> Man for the field and woman for the hearth:
>
> Man for the sword and the needle she:
>
> Man with the head and woman with the heart;
>
> Man to command and woman to obey;
>
> All else confusion. (814–15)

According to this worldview, women's moral superiority, coupled with their unique natural and nurturing qualities, ensured their sovereignty in the household realm, but rendered them powerless in any wider spheres. Its influence in children's literature was pervasive, for the ideal Victorian lady, with her characteristic air of gentle, otherworldly and self-sacrificing resignation, was at once an ideal and impressionable Victorian girl. It is entirely logical, then, that in the colonial family story, girls do little more than wait patiently at home for the boys to come home from adventuring, to listen to their tales of derring-do. Put succinctly, the stories are persuasive tools of socialization whereby girl readers are prepared for their later married lives.

CONSTRUCTING THE "NEW" GIRL

The strongly gender-differentiated destinies implicit in the imperial worldview of Victorian and Edwardian times are not, however, simply reflected in *Anne of Green Gables* or *Seven Little Australians*. In these novels New World girls – because they were created by a native-born Canadian and an Australian writer, respectively, rather than by British authors – are demonstrably more self-sufficient, active, and adventurous than their British cousins. Both Montgomery and Turner stress the healthy outdoor environments where their protagonists are completely at home, and in doing so present Canadian and Australian girls as vigorous, wholesome, happy, and close to nature, enjoying idyllic childhoods spent largely out of doors. In fact, both Anne Shirley and Judy Woolcot are figuratively as well as literally worlds removed from their imperial counterparts. For a start, neither girl is picturesquely or ethereally beautiful. The red-haired "born Canadian" (14) of Montgomery's text does not initially seem like a beauty in the making: "Her face was small, white and thin, also very much freckled; her mouth was large and so were her eyes, that looked green in some lights and moods and grey in others" (19). Native-born Australian Judy is equally freckled and scrawny in appearance: "She was very thin, as people generally are who have quicksilver instead of blood in their veins, she had a small, eager face, with very bright eyes, a small determined mouth, and a mane of untidy, curly dark hair that was the trial of her life" (11). Both girls seem to be impoverished and untidy offspring of British beauty, reminiscent of changeling creatures.

More importantly still, their personalities are completely different from the insipid imperial norm. These girls are passionate, imaginative, feisty, yet sensitive; they are candid, impetuous, and above all else, unconventionally high-spirited. Their inventive, inquiring, creative minds are far removed from the "sweet orderliness" of Ruskin's description, and indeed, Turner actually notes that "Judy's brilliant inventive powers plunged them all into endless scrapes" (12) and that "she was the worst of the seven, probably because she was the cleverest" (12). Like Judy, Anne is a natural ringleader, and her active imagination leads her into a host of schemes that go spectacularly wrong. Unlike their imperial counterparts, they, no less than the boys, can take part in escapades. Their gender has not stood in the way of their intellects or their imaginations. They are the embodiments of New World enthusiasm and Commonwealth hopes for the future, the less powerful sex offering the fertile potential of the land.

Moreover, these two colonial girls are worlds removed not only from their imperial cousins, but from their parents as well. *Seven Little Australians* seems to be diametrically opposed to the colonial novels that preceded and paralleled it. Turner was inspired by the *Bulletin*'s ethos of ardent Australianness. Her identically aggressive patriotism is apparent in the famous disclaimer on the first page of the novel, in which the author notes that children born in Australia, unlike those born in England, are never perfect:

It may be that the miasmas of naughtiness develop best in the sunny brilliancy of our atmosphere. It may be that the land and the people are young-hearted together, and the children's spirits not crushed and saddened by the shadow of long years' sorrowful history. There is a lurking spectacle of joyousness and rebellion and mischief in nature here, and therefore in children ... the spirited, single-hearted, loyal ones who alone can "advance Australia." (7–8)

Turner's coupling of the land and the people is in keeping with the nationalistic discourse of the time. Australia was regularly presented as a "young" country, immature but vital, eagerly awaiting a future without the strictures enforced by the "mother" country. For example, in *Seven Little Australians* there is more than a generation gap dividing Captain Woolcot, English-born and educated at Rugby school, and his unruly Australian offspring. Captain Woolcot personifies the rigid world of the English middle class: he endorses the values of correct etiquette, children who are preferably neither seen nor heard, and the imposition of plenty of discipline.

His cultural outlook is completely different from that of his children, those merry inhabitants of the lawless house known as "Misrule," who are emblematic of the exuberant, informal country of their birth. While the New World children bond affectionately with one another, they have a distant but dutiful relationship with their Old World father, who is remote, unsympathetic, and preoccupied with his own interests and pleasures. When he sends the children off to their stepmother's property in the Bush, for instance, he suddenly assumes a "jaunty air as if the prospect of two months' bachelordom was not without its redeeming points" (136). Turner makes it clear that these seven little Australians bring themselves up; their father intrudes upon their freedom only intermittently to reprimand, chastise, or beat them, while their sweetly ineffectual stepmother, Esther, the mother of the youngest of the seven, is barely older than they are. These children are indomitable, and it takes more than one hapless parent to fence them in.

Montgomery similarly celebrates imperfect children (for how else could you describe Josie Pye?) and in doing so strategically inscribes and signifies Canadian distinctiveness. And Anne, too, inhabits a radically different world from that of her elders. An orphan who lost her parents at an early age, she has endured a number of unpleasant surrogate parents before coming to live with Marilla and Matthew Cuthbert. The elderly brother and sister are more sympathetically drawn than Captain Woolcot (after all, they are Canadians, too, rather than unwilling transplants from England, and Marilla herself emphatically rejects adopting a British Barnardo boy, declaring "no London street Arabs for me," and deliberately choosing a "native-born Canadian" [14]). Nevertheless the Cuthberts are also staid and emotionally repressed people, dour and set in their ways, and Anne's presence and youthful zest bring them to life. Early on, Marilla remarks: "It isn't as if we were getting [an orphan boy] from England or the States. He can't be much different from ourselves" (15). Yet, as the narrative indicates, this statement could not, in fact, be farther from the truth. According to Robinson, Marilla is a "petrified conception of Canadian identity" (29); her harsh and rigid upbringing prevents her from expressing her feelings, and she is unable to articulate her love for Anne until the end of the novel. Robinson argues that "[r]igid identities formed in generations of family and clan life, in danger of merging into rigid nationalism" (29) are opened up in the presence of this more youthful and vibrant representation of the nation, whose orphan condition represents a fantasy of no parentage or mother country, even a condition of abandonment or abuse. Frank Davey also views Anne as a regenerative force, as a catalyst for Marilla's redemption and regeneration (171), for, as Rachel Lynde confirms, Marilla "mellows" through Anne's influence, and her own inability to drill Anne into a tranquil uniformity.

Finally, it is noteworthy that while so many of the imperial texts of the time reinforce parental morals to often tearful, penitent children, in these two texts the parental lectures fall on deaf ears. Instead, both older generations learn wisdom, often belatedly, from the girls themselves. Marilla is overly fond of rather Waspish moralizing, but she is repeatedly revealed as mistaken in her pronouncements and punishments. Similarly, Rachel Lynde and Josephine Barry are proven wrong in their judgments about Anne and her conduct, and they become better and happier people because of Anne's humanizing influence. In *Seven Little Australians* the message is even more insistent: Captain Woolcot uses harsh disciplinary measures in an attempt to bend his children to his way of thinking, but his draconian methods never work, and ultimately he is the one to learn a lesson from his offspring. The colonies, it seems, are "writing back," and the native-born-and-bred children are colonizing the national space for themselves.

MAIDENS NO MORE

The worlds of *Anne of Green Gables* and *Seven Little Australians* are not, however, made up only of sunny, New World paradises. Both novelists stress that tragedy might strike their special female protagonists:

> That restless fire of hers that shone out of her dancing eyes, and glowed scarlet on her cheeks in excitement, and lent amazing energy and activity to her young, lithe body, would either make a nobler, daring, brilliant woman of her, or else she would be shipwrecked on rocks the others would never come to, and it would flame up higher and higher and consume her. (Turner 28)

> For Anne to take things calmly would have been to change her nature. All 'spirit and fire and dew', as she was, the pleasures and pains of life came to her with trebled intensity. Marilla felt this and was vaguely troubled over it, realizing that the ups and downs of existence would probably bear hardly on her impulsive soul. (181)

Both girls are viewed as volatile and at sea, literally a liminal space between landed nations and rigid traditions. And indeed, the worst does come to pass, and both *Anne of Green Gables* and *Seven Little Australians* end with a death. There is risk inherent in losing or cutting off parent figures. In Montgomery's text Matthew's heart attack and Marilla's threatened blindness mean that the stage is set for Anne, newly reconciled with Gilbert Blythe, to sacrifice herself for the call of the family hearth and to remain in Avonlea. And so "old Canada" in part passes on, while romance – or what Gammel and Epperly describe as "the romantic plot of male desire and female delaying" (10) – lies tantalizingly in the air as the novel draws to a close. In Turner's text, however, the child predeceases the parent, and it is Judy, brimful of promise and life, who dies. Hers is also a self-sacrificing gesture: as a result of protecting her young stepbrother from a falling tree, she breaks her back and dies. In a complete contrast with the usual nineteenth-century child departing the world in a pious, self-effacing manner, Judy hogs the limelight, refusing to leave, and in her own characteristic way fights off the blandishments of death for as long as she can, bitterly asking her sister: "How would you like to die, Meg, when you're only thirteen?" (185). This is one colonial heroine, then, who is not eager to leave the national stage. Judy's death affects the rest of her New World family: "Her death made [her father's] six living children dearer to his heart, although he showed his affection very little more" (192). Meg, Judy's older sister, is purified by suffering and witnessing Judy's premature death. She is transformed from a scatterbrained flirt into a gentle and compassionate woman: "[S]he had grown older; she would never be quite so young again.... There was a deeper light in her eyes" (189). Like Anne, she is destined for marriage and motherhood, and her suitor also lingers in the wings at the novel's end. Both novels thus open the possibility for New Girls, only to fear the newness of what they have unleashed.

In both texts it appears evident that the carefree world of the Commonwealth girls cannot last forever. Eve Kornfeld and Susan Jackson argue that female bildungsromans like *Anne of Green Gables* involve a framework of a feminine utopia through which the problems of adolescence are solved. Heroines are given the freedom of development they have not found in a male world. The critics make the point, however, that girls in the end are still precluded from entering the male world fully and finally:

> The boundaries of the feminine utopia can become oppressive
> after the girl heroine has passed through adolescence. Although she
> can dream as much as she wants, duty to family must be her first
> concern, even if it gets in the way of her own plans. Anne's ambition
> leads her to desire entrance into the traditionally male world of the
> university. This desire cannot be realised until she has done her duty
> in the matriarchal world. And even then, Anne cannot leave home.
> (150–51)

And so, as Anne approaches puberty, her personality changes as she learns "to conform to the social and behavioural expectations of Avonlea" (Rubio 70). She becomes "a tall, serious-eyed girl" who is "pruned down and branched out" (274), and the loss of this "little girl" gives Marilla a "queer, sorrowful sense of loss" (253). This metamorphosis into more conventional womanliness is denied to prepubescent Judy. The site of her death, at her stepmother's parental property in the heart of the Australian Bush, is highly significant. Here her younger brother Pip is allowed to participate in masculine enjoyments such as camp-drafting, but as she is soon to become a young woman these experiences are denied to her. Pip's generous but condescending offer to make her his future aide-de-camp surely amounts to a symbolic death knell. In both texts it seems evident that the special childhood freedoms of colonial children, regardless of their gender, stand in heightened and ironic contrast to the restrictions that inhibited Canadian and Australian women like Montgomery and Turner.

Because of their gender, girls have only a limited time to share the national space with their brothers. Both authors imply that with womanhood comes a softening, a gentleness, that links all women. For girls, childhood is a period of freedom followed by an abrupt change as puberty nears, and marriage and motherhood loom (unless they are killed off first). The nationalist priorities and the associated myth making of the time meant the eventual glorification of male cultural heroes. While both authors were reconciled to women's domestic role in the patriarchal world of which they were a part, they nonetheless managed to create texts where girls could, for a brief time, flower as unique cultural heroes of their time and place, as emblems of the brave new world of the Commonwealth. It was these children – and not what they become – that captured the imagination of their nations.

If Watkins is right, and children's texts do work as indicators of national identity, then these two authors construct images of femininity distinctly at odds with what went before. Both offer a development or life cycle arc for the rise and eventual succumbing of colonial spirit. Neither forward-looking like *The Wonderful Wizard of Oz* nor backward-looking like *The Wind in the Willows*, *Anne of Green Gables* and *Seven Little Australians* contain an essentially "Commonwealth" form of subversive myth making, for the myth remains even after the girls move on. And yet although these two texts seem at first sight to be very different from those imperial novels that they supplanted, at the very end the message concerning gender seems to be depressingly similar. Girl protagonists, like their creators, are then put back firmly into their place.

WORKS CITED

Alcott, Louisa May. *Little Women*. 1868–69. New York: Penguin, 1989.

Baum, L. Frank. *The Wonderful Wizard of Oz*. New York: Harper Trophy, 2001.

Davey, Frank. "The Hard-Won Power of Canadian Womanhood: Reading *Anne of Green Gables* Today." *L. M. Montgomery and Canadian Culture*. Ed. Irene Gammel and Elizabeth Epperly. Toronto: U of Toronto P, 1999. 163–82.

Devereux, Cecily. "'Canadian Classic' and 'Commodity Export': The Nationalism of 'Our' *Anne of Green Gables*." *Journal of Canadian Studies* 36.1 (2001): 11–30.

Gammel, Irene, and Elizabeth Epperly. "L. M. Montgomery and the Shaping of Canadian Culture." *L. M. Montgomery and Canadian Culture*. Ed. Irene Gammel and Elizabeth Epperly. Toronto: U of Toronto P, 1999. 3–13.

Gay, Carol. "Kindred Spirits All: *Anne of Green Gables* Revisited." *Such a Simple Little Tale: Critical Responses to* Anne of Green Gables. Ed. Mavis Reimer. Metuchen, NJ: Scarecrow, 1992. 101–08.

Grahame, Kenneth. *The Wind in the Willows*. New York: Aladdin, 1989.

Haverfield, E. L. *Queensland Cousins*. London: Nelson, 1908.

Kornfeld, Eve, and Susan Jackson. "The Female *Bildungsroman* in Nineteenth-Century America: Parameters of a Vision." *Such a Simple Little Tale: Critical Responses to* Anne of Green Gables. Ed. Mavis Reimer. Metuchen, N.J.: Scarecrow, 1992. 139–52.

Lee, Christopher. *This Sceptred Isle: The British Empire*. BBC World Americas, 2005.

MacLulich, Thomas. *Between Europe and America: The Canadian Tradition in Fiction*. Toronto: ECW, 1988.

Montgomery, L. M. *Anne of Green Gables*. Sydney: Angus and Robertson, 1987.

Patmore, Coventry. "The Angel in the House." *New Oxford Book of Victorian Love*. Oxford: Oxford UP, 1987. 321.

Pearce, Sharyn. "Literature, Mythmaking and National Identity: The Case for *Seven Little Australians*." *Papers: Explorations into Children's Literature* 7.3 (1997): 10–16.

Reimer, Mavis. "Suggestions for Further Reading: A Guide to the Research and Criticism on *Anne of Green Gables*." *Such a Simple Little Tale: Critical Responses to* Anne of Green Gables. Ed. Mavis Reimer. Metuchen, NJ: Scarecrow, 1992. 165–90.

Robinson, Laura M. "A Born Canadian": The Bonds of Communal Identity in *Anne of Green Gables* and *A Tangled Web*. *L. M. Montgomery and Canadian Culture*. Ed. Irene Gammel and Elizabeth Epperly. Toronto: U of Toronto P, 1999. 19–30.

Rowbotham, Judith. *Good Girls Make Good Wives: Guidance for Girls in Victorian Fiction.* Oxford: Blackwell, 1989.

Rubio, Mary. "Anne of Green Gables: The Architect of Adolescence." *Such a Simple Little Tale: Critical Responses to* Anne of Green Gables. Ed. Mavis Reimer. Metuchen, N.J.: Scarecrow, 1992. 65–82.

Ruskin, John. *Sesame and Lilies: Two Lectures.* London, Oxford UP, 1912.

Tennyson, Alfred Lord. "The Princess." *The Poems of Tennyson.* Ed. Christopher Ricks. Oxford: Oxford UP, 1987. 814–15.

Turner, Ethel. *Seven Little Australians.* London: Ward Lock, 1894.

Watkins, Tony. "Cultural Studies, New Historicism and Children's Literature." *Literature for Children: Contemporary Criticism.* Ed. Peter Hunt. London: Routledge, 1992. 173–95.

White, Kerry. "Blooming with Childhood's Fragrance: Sweet Words and Tough Times for Women Writers in the 1980s." *Australian Feminist Studies* 7–8 (1988): 49–63.

Wiggin, Kate Douglas. *Rebecca of Sunnybrook Farm.* London: Adam and Charles Black, 1950.

CHRONOLOGY OF IMPORTANT EVENTS IN THE LIFE AND CAREER OF *ANNE'S* CREATOR, LUCY MAUD MONTGOMERY*

1873   Prince Edward Island entered the Confederation of Canada; the federal government assumed the colony's debt for building a railway, begun in 1871

1874   Lucy Maud Montgomery was born 30 November in Clifton, Prince Edward Island, Canada

1876   L. M. Montgomery's mother, Clara Woolner Macneill Montgomery, died of tuberculosis; during her mother's illness, Maud had moved in with her maternal grandparents, Alexander Marquis Macneill and Lucy Woolner Macneill

1881   L. M. Montgomery's father, Hugh John Montgomery, moved to Prince Albert, Saskatchewan

1889   L. M. Montgomery began keeping a journal, a practice she would continue her entire life; the ten handwritten volumes that she left to her son were edited by Mary Rubio and Elizabeth Waterston and selections were published by Oxford University Press in five volumes (1985, 1987, 1992, 1998, and 2004)

1890   L. M. Montgomery lived with her father and his new wife for a year before returning to live with her maternal grandparents; she also published her first poem, "On Cape Leforce," in the Charlottetown *Patriot*

1893   L. M. Montgomery attended Prince of Wales College in Charlottetown, completing her teacher's licence in 1894

1894   L. M. Montgomery taught school in Bideford, Prince Edward Island

1895   L. M. Montgomery studied literature at Dalhousie University in Halifax, Nova Scotia, for a year; while there, she began receiving compensation for her published poems and stories

1896   L. M. Montgomery taught school in Belmont and Lower Bedeque, Prince Edward Island, for two years; she became engaged to Edwin Simpson but would break the engagement the following year after falling in love with Herman Leard, who died in 1899

1898   L. M. Montgomery's grandfather died and she moved back to her maternal grandmother's house, helping run the Cavendish post office in their home

1900   L. M. Montgomery's father died; Montgomery recorded making $96.88 from her writing the prior year, but in December recorded that she is beginning to make a "liveable income for myself by my pen"

1901   L. M. Montgomery worked as proofreader and writer in Halifax for the newspapers *Chronicle* and *Echo*

1902   Montgomery became close friends with Frede Campbell, whose death from pneumonia in 1919 deeply affected her. She also began a lifelong correspondence with Ephraim Weber; their letters were published in *The Green Gables Letters* (1960), edited by Wilfrid Eggleston, and *L. M. Montgomery's Ephraim Weber: Letters, 1916–1941* (2000), edited by Hildi Froese Tiessen and Paul Gerard Tiessen

1903   L. M. Montgomery began a lifelong correspondence with George Boyd Macmillan; their letters were published in *My Dear Mr. M.* (1980), edited by Francis W. P. Bolger and Elizabeth R. Epperly; Montgomery recorded earning $500 from writing that year, and told Macmillan that she had a list of about 70 periodicals to which she regularly sent work. Montgomery recorded making nearly $600 from her writing in 1904

1905   L. M. Montgomery began writing *Anne of Green Gables* in secret; its intricate composition history is retraced in *Looking for Anne of Green Gables: The Story of L.M. Montgomery and Her Literary Classic* published by Key Porter Books and St. Martin's Press (2008)

1906   Montgomery became engaged to Ewan Macdonald; in this year, Montgomery published at least 44 stories in 27 magazines, demonstrating her literary reputation

1908   *Anne of Green Gables* was published by L. C. Page and Company in Boston, after at least four rejections; illustrations were done by M. A. and W. A. J. Claus and George Gibbs. By December, *Anne* was in its seventh printing, and Pitman published the novel in England.

1909   *Anne of Avonlea*, sequel to *Anne of Green Gables*, was published by L. C. Page and Company

1910   *Kilmeny of the Orchard* was published by L. C. Page and Company; Montgomery received $7,000 in royalties from her writing

1911   L. M. Montgomery married Ewan Macdonald, following her grandmother's death, and moved to Ontario, where he ministered St. Paul's Presbyterian Church in Leaskdale

        The Story Girl was published by L. C. Page and Company; May, Grosset, and Dunlap published a popular edition of *Anne of Green Gables*

1912   *Chronicles of Avonlea* was published by L. C. Page and Company, and L. M. Montgomery's son, Chester Cameron Macdonald, was born

1913   *The Golden Road*, sequel to *The Story Girl*, was published by L. C. Page and Company

1914   L. M. Montgomery's son, Hugh Alexander, was born and died at birth; WWI began

1915   L. M Montgomery's son, Ewan Stuart Macdonald, was born; *Anne of the Island*, sequel to *Anne of Avonlea*, was published by L. C. Page and Company

1916   L. M. Montgomery published *The Watchman and Other Poems* with Toronto-based McClelland, Goodchild and Stewart

1917   *Anne's House of Dreams*, sequel to *Anne of Windy Poplars*, was published by McClelland and Stewart; Montgomery published her serialized autobiography, *The Alpine Path: The Story of My Career* in the Toronto magazine *Everywoman's World*, and voted for the first time

1918   L. M. Montgomery sued L. C. Page for selling the rights to May, Grosset, and Dunlap without her consent and royalties; WWI ended

1919   L. M. Montgomery's suit against L. C. Page succeeded and she sold all rights to her first seven *Anne* books to Page for $18,000; L. C. Page licensed rights for a silent film of *Anne*. The film was directed by William Desmond and starred Mary Miles Minter

    Rainbow Valley, sequel to *Anne of Ingleside*, was published by McClelland and Stewart

1920   The unauthorized *Further Chronicles of Avonlea* was published by L. C. Page; Montgomery began what would be an 8-year lawsuit against Page

    A new edition of *Anne of Green Gables*, with scenes from the film, was published, and *Anne of Green Gables* entered its 50th impression

1921   *Rilla of Ingleside*, sequel to *Rainbow Valley*, was published by McClelland and Stewart

1923   *Emily of New Moon* was published by McClelland and Stewart; Montgomery was the first Canadian woman to become Fellow of the Royal Society of Arts in Britain

1925   *Emily Climbs*, sequel to *Emily of New Moon*, was published by McClelland and Stewart; L. C. Page issued a new edition of *Anne of Green Gables* with illustrations by Elizabeth Withington, and Harrap published a new edition in Great Britain

1926   *The Blue Castle* was published by McClelland and Stewart

1927   *Emily's Quest*, sequel to *Emily Climbs*, was published by McClelland and Stewart

1929   *Magic for Marigold* was published by McClelland and Stewart; stock market crash

1931   *A Tangled Web* was published by McClelland and Stewart

1933   *Pat of Silver Bush* was published by McClelland and Stewart; Page issued a "Silver Anniversary" edition of *Anne of Green Gables* with illustrations by Sybil Tawse

1934   *Anne of Green Gables* entered its 71st impression, and RKO produced
a talking picture starring Dawn O'Day, who assumed the stage name
of Anne Shirley for the rest of her career; Montgomery published
Courageous Women with McClelland and Stewart

1935   *Mistress Pat*, sequel to *Pat of Silver Bush*, was published by McClelland
and Stewart, and Grosset and Dunlap produced a cloth edition of
Anne of Green Gables. The original copyright was renewed in the U.S.,
Montgomery was elected to the Literary and Artistic Institute of
France, and she moved to Toronto

1936   *Anne of Windy Poplars*, sequel to *Anne of the Island*, was published by
McClelland and Stewart; Cavendish was selected as the site for a
National Park on Prince Edward Island

1937   *Jane of Lantern Hill* was published by McClelland and Stewart

1939   *Anne of Ingleside*, sequel to *Anne's House of Dreams*, was published by
McClelland and Stewart

1942   L. M. Montgomery died and was buried at the Cavendish Community
Cemetery; the first Canadian edition of *Anne of Green Gables* was also
published by the Ryerson Press

* I have compiled this chronology from many sources, listed below:

Andronik, Catherine M. *Kindred Spirit: A Biography of L. M. Montgomery, Creator of* Anne of
Green Gables. New York: Atheneum, 1993.

"Chronology" and "Life." L. M. Montgomery Institute, University of Prince Edward Island.
23 May 2008. <http://www.lmmontgomery.ca>

Devereux, Cecily. "Introduction" and "Lucy Maud Montgomery: A Brief Chronology." *Anne
of Green Gables*. Peterborough, ON: Broadview, 2004. 12–41.

Gammel, Irene, ed. *The Intimate Life of L. M. Montgomery*. Toronto: U of Toronto P, 2005.

Lefebvre, Benjamin. "Books by L. M. Montgomery." L. M. Montgomery Research Group,
University of Toronto. 23 May 2008. <http://lmmresearch.org>

Pike, E. Holly. "L. M. Montgomery and Literary Professionalism." *100 Years of Anne with an
'e': The Centennial Study of* Anne of Green Gables. Calgary: U of Calgary P, 2009
(this volume).

About the Contributors

JOY ALEXANDER was a secondary school English teacher for twenty years before taking up her present position in 1995 as a lecturer in education in the School of Education at Queen's University, Belfast, N. Ireland, where she has responsibility for the training of prospective English teachers. She has published a number of articles on matters relating to English teaching. Joy's interest in L. M. Montgomery's stories began in childhood, and she is proud of her collection of early Harrap (UK) editions of almost all of L.M. Montgomery's books. She retains an interest in children's literature, especially in Belfast-born C. S. Lewis, who, like L. M. Montgomery, lost his mother in childhood and transferred the landscape he grew up in into the fictional world he created.

HOLLY BLACKFORD is associate professor of English at Rutgers University–Camden. She teaches and publishes literary criticism on American, children's, and adolescent literature, as well as literatures in English. She has published articles on Louisa May Alcott, Emily Brontë, J. M. Barrie, Carlo Collodi, Anita Diamont, Julia Alvarez, Shirley Jackson, Margaret Atwood, Lewis Carroll, L. M. Montgomery, Henry James, and Mark Twain. Her book *Out of this World: Why Literature Matters to Girls* (Teachers College Press, education division of Columbia, 2004) analyzes the empirical reader-responses of girls to literature. From 2004 to 2006 she held an International Reading Association research award ($9400) for the study of teen responses to *Adventures of Huckleberry Finn* and *To Kill a Mockingbird*. She currently chairs the article award committee of the International Children's Literature Association.

HILARY EMMETT is a lecturer in English at the University of Queensland in Australia. In her recently completed doctoral dissertation at Cornell University, "'Passion more than fraternal': Towards a Poetics and Politics of Sisterhood in the American Novel," she explored the representation of sisterhood in the fiction of a nation that imagined itself as a "brotherhood of man." The essay in this volume brings together her research interest in the repression of women's voices (and their melancholic resurfacing), with her experiences of teaching children's literature at Cornell University. She is currently working on a new project, provisionally entitled *The Discipline of Girls: 1870–1920*, which brings together texts from Australia and North America in order to investigate the imbrication of discourses of imperialism, citizenship, true or ideal womanhood, and education in texts written for girls in this period.

IRENE GAMMEL is professor of English and Canada Research Chair in Modern Literature and Culture at Ryerson University in Toronto, where she also directs the Modern Literature and Culture Research Centre dedicated to the preservation and study of early-twentieth-century texts, photos, and artefacts. She is the author of several books, including *Looking for Anne of Green Gables: The Story of L.M. Montgomery and Her Literary Classic* (Key Porter Books [CND], St. Martin's Press [US], 2008) and *Baroness Elsa: Gender, Dada, and Everyday Modernity: A Cultural Biography* (MIT Press, 2002). Her edited books include *The Intimate Life of L. M. Montgomery* (2005), *Making Avonlea: L. M. Montgomery and Popular Culture* (2002), and *L. M. Montgomery and Canadian Culture* (1999), all with the University of Toronto Press. She is also the curator of the exhibition *Anne of Green Gables: A Literary Icon at 100, April 17, 2008 – March 1, 2009*, in Toronto, Ottawa, Vancouver, Winnipeg, and Prince Edward Island.

MONIKA B. HILDER is associate professor of English at Trinity Western University. She specializes in children's literature and fantasy literature, and has published on C. S. Lewis, George MacDonald, L. M. Montgomery, and literature as ethical imagination. Her recent articles have appeared in *Seven: An Anglo-American Literary Review*, *Canadian Children's Literature*, *Journal of Curriculum & Supervision*, and *Teaching Education*. Her chapter on George MacDonald appeared in *Sublimer Aspects: Interfaces between Literature, Aesthetics, and Theology* (Cambridge Scholars Publishing), and her chapter on L. M. Montgomery is published in *Feminist Theology with a Canadian Accent: Canadian Perspectives on Contextual Feminist Theology* (Novalis).

MELISSA MULLINS is a doctoral candidate at the University of Connecticut. Working under Margaret Higonnet, she has published and presented on a variety of subjects, including the work of Philip Pullman, the colonization of the reader in Disney adaptations, nineteenth-century burlesque adaptations of fairy tales, and the rhetoric of Orientalism in nineteenth-century fashion writing.

ELEANOR HERSEY NICKEL is an English professor at Fresno Pacific University in California, where her teaching load includes children's and young adult literature, and literature and film. She has published articles on Hollywood romantic comedy, television series such as *The X-Files* and *Seinfeld*, and television adaptations of novels by Edith Wharton and Willa Cather. Her work on the roles of reading and writing in Kevin Sullivan's first two *Anne of Green Gables* miniseries has been published in *Canadian Children's Literature* and *Making Avonlea: L. M. Montgomery and Popular Culture.*

SHARYN PEARCE teaches in the Faculty of Creative Industries at Queensland University of Technology in Brisbane, Australia, where she is Faculty Teaching Fellow as well as Deputy Head of Creative Writing and Cultural Studies. She has published extensively in the field of children's/young adult literature and cultural texts, with over fifty articles and book chapters to date. Her co-edited collection of scholarly essays, *Youth Cultures: Texts, Images and Identities* (Praeger, 2003), was an International Research Society for Children's Literature (IRSCL) Honor Book.

E. HOLLY PIKE (PhD, SUNY Buffalo) is associate professor of English and Acting Principal at the Sir Wilfred Grenfell College of Memorial University of Newfoundland, Corner Brook, NL. She is the author of *Family and Society in the Works of Elizabeth Gaskell* (Peter Lang, 1995) and has previously published on L. M. Montgomery in *Harvesting Thistles: The Textual Garden of L. M. Montgomery*, *L. M. Montgomery and Canadian Culture*, *Making Avonlea: L. M. Montgomery and Popular Culture*, *Storm and Dissonance: L. M. Montgomery and Conflict*, and the online philosophy journal *Animus*. She is currently working on a book-length study of Montgomery's career.

CORNELIA RÉMI is assistant professor of German literature at Ludwig-Maximilians-Universität, Munich. Her research focuses on interferences of poetry and different forms of spirituality, intermedial relations, erudite communication in the Early Modern era, and strategies of poetic self-reflection. She has published book-length studies on Friedrich Spee and Clemens Brentano, as well as essays about the emblematic handling of political aggressions, organizational principles of devotional texts, poetic models of love, and King Solomon as an ambiguous literary authority. Apart from her academic teaching, she has also given workshops in creative writing at the Bücherpiraten Festival for Children's and Young Adult Literature in Lübeck.

LAURA ROBINSON is associate professor of English literature at the Royal Military College in Kingston, Ontario. She has published articles on L. M. Montgomery in *Storm and Dissonance, Canadian Studies: An Introductory Reader, Canadian Literature, L. M. Montgomery and Canadian Culture*, and *Children's Voices in Atlantic Literature Culture*, as well as articles on Ann-Marie MacDonald in *Canadian Literature* and on Margaret Atwood in *English Studies in Canada*. Her short fiction has appeared in *Wascana Review, torquere, Frontiers, Her Circle*, and *EnterText*.

CHRISTIANA ROSE SALAH is a fiction writer and a graduate student at the University of Connecticut. Her academic interests include fairy tale studies, children's and young adult literature, and the Victorian novel, focusing particularly on themes of feminism, landscape, and the home. She has studied Irish mythology and literature at University College Cork in Ireland, and received a Masters of Fine Arts in Creative Writing from Emerson College in Boston. She has presented on the idea of space and mapping in the *Harry Potter* novels at a conference in Salem, Massachusetts, and a version of her "Plum Puffs" essay at the 2008 L.M. Montgomery Institute conference. She is currently at work on a historical novel.

THEODORE F. SHECKELS (PhD, Penn State) is professor of English and Communication at Randolph-Macon College, Ashland, Virginia. He is the author of six books: three on political communication topics; three on literary. The latter are *The Lion on the Freeway: A Thematic Introduction to Contemporary South African Literature* (1996), *Celluloid Heroes Down Under: Australian Cinema, 1970–2000* (2002), and *The Island Motif in the Fiction of L. M. Montgomery, Margaret Laurence, Margaret Atwood, and Other Canadian Women Novelists* (2003). He has published on L. M. Montgomery in *The American Review of Canadian Studies* and in Irene Gammel and Elizabeth Epperly's *L. M. Montgomery and Canadian Culture*. He is President of the American Association of Australian Literary Studies and the editor of *Margaret Atwood Studies* (formerly, *The Margaret Atwood Society Newsletter*).

Index

Claus, W. A. J., 46, 119
Clinton, Bill, 146
Coates, Donna, 96
Cobbe, Frances Power, 193
Coleridge, Samuel Taylor, xxxi, 66, 69–70
colonial literature, xxxiii–xxxv, 229–45
Compayre, Gabriel M., xxviii
composition of *Anne*, xi–xiii, xxx, 1–39,
    83–84, 100, 234
The Congregationalist (publication), 27
Converse, Frank H., 29
cooking, xxxiv, 193–227
Craig, Patricia, 128
creativity, in *Anne*, 46, 49, 57–58
Crockett, Beverly, xx
Crompton, Patricia, 188n18
Culler, Jonathan, 146
Cummins, Maria, 14
Cuthbert, Marilla, xiv–xv, 10, 70–71, 150–51,
    220, 240
Cuthbert, Matthew, xiv–xv,xxxiv, 47–49,
    86–88, 103n5, 213–14, 217–23, 240

D

Daddy-Long-Legs (Webster), 14
Daily Echo (publication), xviii, 29
The Daisy Chain (Yonge), xxxii–xxxiii, 125–38
Dalhousie University, 25
A Dance of the Forests (Soyinka), 145
Darwin, Charles, xxv, xxviii
Davey, Frank, 240
David Copperfield, 14, 70
Dawson, Janis, 21n14
Dayre, Sydney, 29
Days of Youth (publication), 35
death, xxxii, 81–104, 241–43
Death, Sarah, 17, 189n38
The Delineator (publication), 29
Delinquents and Debutants (Inness), 142n2
Denby, David, 103n3
Dennis, Barbara, 128
development
    of Anne, 52–53, 63–80, 193–245
    of Anne and Astrid Lindgren's Madicken,
        165–90

developmental psychology, history of,
    xv–xxviii
Devereux, Cecily, xii, 209n3, 212, 215, 221,
    226n1, 233
The Dialogic Imagination (Bakhtin), 146
Dickens, Charles, 14
The Diviners (Laurence), 149, 152, 155–56,
    158–59
domestic abuse, 82, 89–90, 157–59
domesticity, xxxiii–xxxv, 193–227
Doody, Margaret Anne, 56, 188n27
Dora (Freud), 83
Dostoevsky, Fyodor,146
Doyle report on emigration, 1875, xxvi
Drain, Susan, 58, 65, 80n1, 212, 226n3
Drummond, W. B., xvi
The Duties of Women (Cobbe),193

E

East and West (publication), 28
Eaton, Anne Thaxter, 128
Eban Holden (Bachellor), 37
ecology, as theme in *Anne*, 41–60, 165–90,
    201
Edström, Vivi, 188n19, 188n28, 188n29,
    189n43, 189n47, 189n49, 190n50
Edwards, Owen Dudley, 215
Ehriander, Helene, 170
Eliot, T. S., xxxi, xxxii, 63, 73–75, 80n4
    "Tradition and the Individual Talent,"
        xxxii, 63, 73–75
    "The Waste Land," 80n4
Elsie Dinsmore (Finley), 65, 194
Emerson, Ralph Waldo, 7, 21n14, 129, 142n3
emigration of British orphans, xxiii–xxvii
Emily of New Moon (Montgomery), 13, 103n4,
    142n5, 187n11
emotion, in *Anne*, 66–70, 214–23
Empire literature, xxxiii–xxxv, 235–37
Engel, Marian, xxxiii, 143–63
    Bear, 147–48, 158–59
Epperly, Elizabeth, 21n14, 55, 73, 134, 213,
    232, 241
Evening World (publication), 40n4

F

Fall on Your Knees (Ann-Marie MacDonald), 142n9
family chronicle, 125–42, 229–45
Family Herald (publication), 28
Farm and Fireside (publication), 27
feeling, in *Anne*, 66–70
femininity, 193–227, 229–43
feminism, xxxiii–xxxv, 106–8, 211–14
films, of *Anne*, xxxii, 74, 105–21
Finley, Martha, 65, 194
formula fiction, 1–21
Foster, Shirley, 128, 212, 216
Fransson, Birgitta, 189n38
Fraser, Dan and Simon, 91
"The Fraser Scholarship" (Montgomery), 20n11
Freud, Sigmund, xiv, xxviii, 83, 103n1
friendship, female, 106–8,153, 178
Fries-Gedin, Lena, 188n20
Froebel, Friedrich, xx, xxvii
Frye, Northrop, 152
"The Function of Criticism at the Present Time" (Arnold), 63, 74–75

G

games, with language, 126–27 , 131, 156–57, 165–90, 189n41, 189n47
Gammel, Irene, xii, xiii, xxx, xxxi, 92, 100, 103n10, 106, 107, 113, 142n5, 232, 241
Garvin, Harry, 68
Gaskell, Elizabeth, 155
Gay, Carole, 226n5, 234
gender, 125–38, 193–206 , 211–23, 229–43
Genette, Gérard, 190n51
geography, as theme in *Anne*, 41–60
Gerson, Carole, 212
Gilligan, Carol, 221
girlhood, xxxii–xxxv, 125–38, 165–90, 193–245
girls' fiction, 125–38, 194
"The Girls' Impromptu Party" (Montgomery), 28

global literature, *Anne* as, 1–37, 125–38, 165–90, 229–50
Godey's Lady's Book (publication), xxx, 6–9
Goethe, Johann Wolfgang von, 129
"The Gold-Link Bracelet" (Montgomery), 35
Golden Days Club, 28
Golden Days for Boys and Girls (publication), 28, 33–34
Goldsby, Jacqueline, 103n8
Good Girls Make Good Wives (Rowbotham), 194, 235–36
Goody Two-Shoes, 14
Grahame, Kenneth, 229
Gray, Harold, 20n13
Green Gables, 46–51, 221
grief, xxxii, 81–104
Griffin, Farah Jasmine, 103n8
Gubar, Marah, 106

H

Hall, G. Stanley, xxviii
"Hansel and Gretel," 168
"Harbor Sunset," (Montgomery), 29
Harbour, J. L., xxx, 10–14, 20n10
Harper, Marjory, xvii
Haverfield, E. L., 235–36
Heath, Shirley Brice, xviii
Heaven and Home (Sturrock), 142n3
Hegel, G. W. F., 104n12
The Heir of Redclyffe (Yonge), 129
Henry Holt Company, 37
Hergin, Stina, 187n11
Herman, Judith, 103n6
heroism, of Matthew, 217–23
"Her Own People" (Montgomery), 20n11
heterosexuality, 105–21
Heywood, F. H., xxiv
home, 193–227
"A Home-Sick Heart" (Montgomery), 28
homosexuality, 106–8
Hope, Anthony, 37
housekeeping, 193–207
Howells, W. D., 32, 37, 40n6
Huckleberry Finn, 14
Hulme, 73
Hynes, Samuel, 103n11

"Truth and Falsity in an Ultramoral Sense"
(Nietzsche), 63, 76–77
Turner, Ethel, xxxiv, 229–45
Turner, Marianne, 188n18
Twain, Mark, xvi, xxxv, 14

U

"Uncle Chatterton's Gingerbread"
(Montgomery), 30
Uncle Tom's Cabin (Stowe), 84, 129, 168
unconscious, in Anne, xiv–xvii, xxxv
in Anne and Rilla, 81–101
Undoing Gender (Butler), 142n1

V

Vance, Mary (of Rainbow Valley), 87–90,
103n7
Vance, Michael E., xvii
Victorian literary criticism, xxxi, 64, 70–76,
80n2
Viguers, Ruth Hill, 128
violence, 91–92
Von Schönborn, Felizitas, 188n19

W

Wadsworth, Sarah A., 128, 142n2
Warner, Susan, 14, 65, 103n4, 129
"The Waste Land," 80n4
The Water Babies (Kingsley), xxii
Waterston, Elizabeth, xii
Watkins, Tony, 229
Watson, Martha Solomon, 146
Weber, Brenda R., 106
Weber, Ephraim, xvi, xxix, 3, 7, 25, 27, 28, 30
Webster, Jean, 14
Weiss-Townsend, Janet, 212
What Katy Read (Foster and Simons), 128
What Maisie Knew (James), xv, xxix
Whittier, John, xviii, 221
"Why Not Ask Miss Price" (Montgomery),
20n11

The Wide Wide World (Warner), 14, 65, 103n4,
129
Wiesenfeld, Joe, 119
Wiggin, Kate, xiii, 12–13, 20n4, 20n5, 21n16,
130, 231
Wilmshurst, Rea, 40n2, 188n27
Wilson, Christopher P., 23, 24
The Wind in the Willows (Grahame), 229
Winn, Harbour, 129
Wolf, Shelby, xviii
womanhood, xxxiii–xxxv, 193–245
The Wonderful Wizard of Oz (Baum), 229
Wordsworth, William, xvii, xxv, xxix, xxxi,
53, 63, 67, 69, 201
World War I, 82, 91–101, 171
writing
as trope in girls' fiction, 125–38
as trope in Canadian women's fiction, 144,
154–57

Y

Yonge, Charlotte, xxxii–xxxiii, 65, 125–38
The Young Wife's Book, 195
You're a Brick, Angela! (Cadogan and Craig),
128
The Youth's Companion (publication), 27

Z

Zelizer, Viviana, xx